7-17

Radical Ideas
and the Schools

Edited by:

Jack L. Nelson
Rutgers University

Kenneth Carlson
Rutgers University

Thomas E. Linton
*University of Illinois
Chicago Circle*

HOLT, RINEHART AND WINSTON, INC.
New York   Chicago   San Francisco   Atlanta
Dallas   Montreal   Toronto

901.9
N 427 r

Preface

Where is education in the Age of Aquarius? Can it be true that the cultural revolution, the counter-cultural revolution, and the counter-counter-cultural revolution have met their match in the chalk-dusty passageways of Our Miss Brooks and Room 222? Or are the battles of school reform and social revolution being fought on the playing fields of Summerhill and the Teacher Drop-out Center? Will Dick and Jane be replaced by Eldridge Cleaver and the Urban Guerillas or the McGuffey Readers?

Consider recent evidence of the intertwining of society and the schools:

A schoolteacher writes an especially popular book titled *How to Survive in Your Native Land*. Two professors of education produce the best-selling treatise, *Teaching as a Subversive Activity*. A vagabond former student pens *Steal this Book*, a handbook for ripping off society and education. A Catholic monsignor with a doctorate in history, and a program in Mexico to teach language, authors *Deschooling Society*. A self-proclaimed anarchist writes of schools and society in *Growing Up Absurd*. And an English professor, describing teaching as "The Absurd Calling," in the September, 1971, AAUP Bulletin—a normally safe and staid magazine for professors—says, "To some degree, classrooms are irrelevant today; life itself is a highly charged lesson plan."

Meanwhile, back in life, attacks against sex education—like those supported by the John Birch Society—cause New Jersey to declare a moratorium on sex instruction in schools. The California state superintendent of schools produces a report on moral education

8|8|6

that brands humanism as an evil influence. CBS television surveys discover, as H. H. Remmers had shown a decade earlier, that the Bill of Rights is so poorly respected in test situations that it would probably not pass if voted on today. Legislatures consider bills to pay public tax money directly to church-related schools, and politicians run on platforms which support prayers in public schools.

Student riots and student rights move town and gown to bitter fights, protective ordinances, and 18-year-old voting power conflicts. Kent State and Jackson State bear tragic testimony to the community's involvement in academe. A local school board president in New York City suggests that astrology may hold some answers for educators. Kenneth Clark, the distinguished educator, in his presidential address to the American Psychological Association, proposes consideration of periodic drug injections for world leaders to help control international aggression. A male classroom teacher with fourteen years experience undergoes sex change surgery and the school board suspends her charging that her state teaching license is invalid.

Can anyone argue that schools are vacuum-packed? Indeed, the evidence shows dramatic interrelations between schools and their societies, including the vast domain of radical social ideas. This collection of readings was designed to illustrate radical ideas in a variety of social settings and to indicate their implications for the schools. A society electrified by radical ideas for reform produces currents and cross-currents that directly affect social institutions. Alternatives for educational reform likewise have an impact on the nature of society. Radicalism is a social and an educational force that needs open debate.

As in any such work, we wanted to include much more, but the possibilities are endless. We hope this book offers a mosaic of dissent that assists in the thoughtful determination of change in schools and in society.

We want to acknowledge our intellectual debts to colleagues, professors, students, wives, children, and friends who passed on bits of information, overwhelming concepts, and underground sheets.

J. L. N.
K. C.
T. E. L.

Table of Contents

81816

viii   Contents

introduction

Radicalism in Perspective

Radicalism, like beauty, is in the eye of the beholder. What is considered radical in one context is seen as popular in another. From the viewpoint of monarchies in Europe and Tories in North America near the end of the 18th century, America represented a radical departure from accepted standards of government. Current Communist literature describes America as a prime example of reactionary imperialism. Social reform policies proposed by Norman Thomas in the 1920s and 30s in the United States were deemed radical then but are commonplace now. Abolitionists were radicals in the 19th century but are a majority at this time. Free public education was an extreme view in most nations but is now the dominant form of schooling in the most powerful countries. A student labeled radical at a cloistered, quiet religious college may be simply another member of a large number of dissenting students at a turbulent, massive state university.

Radical ideas have perplexed, annoyed, and changed societies since groups of men have existed. Radicalism is neither an American nor a contemporary trademark. In virtually every society and in each era, men take positions which differ dramatically and extensively from the common view. Sometimes these minority views gain favor and become more generally accepted; at other times the holders of minority views are castigated and persecuted.

Ideas considered heretical in some societies are popular in others, and ideas whispered among advocates during one historical period are standard knowledge during another.

Current concern with radical ideas in society and in schools, and the social turmoil which may accompany such ideas, gives the misleading impression that radicalism is new and threatening. Radical ideas may threaten the precarious stability of societies, but they are not new. Howard Mumford Jones, the distinguished historian, documents the radicalism of early America and points out that the definition of radicalism differs in time, place, and perspective. He cites example after example of radical men and ideas from the exploratory period through the radical American Revolution to what he terms the possible twilight of America's radical reputation, the "New Deal" of F. D. R.[1] The revitalization of radicalism in America as both a social and an art form in recent years shows that, although the international reputation for radicalism may have passed from the United States, the roots of radicalism run deep and the branches extend broadly throughout the country.

THE RADICAL IMPACT

It is on these grounds that the study of radical men and ideas is pertinent to an understanding of society and its institutions. No society remains static—all are in varying stages of change, and the dynamics of social change are partly the result of radical views from other times and places. As societies change, so do social institutions. Family, religion, crime, medicine, communications, organizations, and education have undergone evolutionary and revolutionary alteration in different societies at different times. Although the impact of a specific radical view on any social institution is difficult to measure, there are significant indications of institutional change related to radical ideas. Social club organization was modified by the prohibition movement. Family structure has been altered by the once radical idea of women's suffrage. Religion is being influenced by birth control, abortion reform, and the "God is Dead" viewpoint. Each of these would have been viewed as extreme heresy in earlier times. Income tax, social security, and federal aid to education were radical ideas at their inception.

This is not to say that all radical ideas work or have merit. Indeed, many radical views have been totally ignored, proven unworkable, or thoroughly discounted. Anarchy as a political form has never gained many adherents in modern society. After Washington's time, proposals to establish an American monarchy have been ignored or derided. Abolition of the monogamous family structure of man-wife-

[1] Howard Mumford Jones, O Strange New World, New York: The Viking Press, 1964.

children has been seriously questioned by many, but an effective alternative has so far not been developed. Sterilization of all criminals and physically defective individuals has been discussed by many but has never been popularly accepted. The return to elitist standards for education based on aristocratic values and traditions has not found favor in current society. There are many radical men and ideas whose contributions cannot even be recalled because they did not achieve notoriety in their own time. The premise of this book is that prominent radical social ideas are worthy of study, not because they are eminently valuable in themselves necessarily, but rather for their value in analyzing and understanding current issues in society and education.

DEFINING RADICALISM

Although radicalism may be merely a label applied to any idea that differs from one's own, a clearer statement of the dimensions of radicalism would include the idea of basic opposition to the popular mores, opinions, and values of a given society at a particular time. In these terms, a radical idea would be one that proposes a dramatic or extensive change in a major aspect of the life pattern of any culture.

Radicalism may be viewed as positive or negative depending upon the purposes of those who promote a particular radical doctrine. Negative radicalism preaches the abolition of a presumed major evil in society without offering any particular social alternative. Those who see capitalism as an evil and propose radical elimination of that economic system without proposing a better one to replace it may be seen as negative radicals. They may speak or act in a manner which is essentially destructive, such as that involved in the bombing of a bank, a business, or a university. A positive radicalism example would be utopian writers who propose idyllic situations for the good of all men without necessarily castigating the present condition of man. Monasteries, communes, gurus, and B. F. Skinner's *Walden* 2 typify this approach to social behavior. Most radical social theories combine the idea of exorcising evils and substituting utopias and involve, therefore, both negative and positive radicalism. The radical view fundamentally assumes that there are basic wrongs in the social system and its institutions and that these require drastic changes in order to produce the better society.

In essence, the radical's views are in direct opposition to the values and customs of his own culture. He desires to change specific conditions in the culture so that the alternative model corresponds to his idealization of a better society. Radicals may be found in many different occupational areas. The thrust of radical ideas may come from an informed student group, a worker's revolt, an organization, or an individual. The impact of a particular radical idea varies from no alteration to the initiation of major social changes.

Confusion created by ideas and individuals that do not fit the right-left or conservative-liberal polarity shows the weakness of labels. Dogma associated with collective societies and socialist economics has been challenged by the new left as insufficient for permitting each person to "do his own thing." The Youth International Party (YIPPIES) stresses a lack of social restraint and great personal freedom. Some labeled right wingers protest this individualistic notion as lacking in social responsibility. They strongly support devotion to the nation and emphasize law and order social restrictions. This apparent disparity between leftist support for individualism and rightist support for social control is further complicated by recent advocacy by both right and left radicals for a form of libertarianism. Lehr and Rossetto claim libertarianism for the right but note that "refugees from the Old Right, the Old Left and the New Left" are embracing individualism in the concept of liberty.[2] deRuggiero, in a classic work on European liberalism, sees both individual liberty and social liberty as dimensions of liberalism.[3]

Although the labels of right and left, conservative and liberal are shaggy and imprecise, they are commonly employed and can be a helpful shorthand when one considers the context in which they are used. This book uses the terms to avoid excessive explanation, but their limitations are recognized.

Clinton Rossiter recognized the difficulty in defining terms that have wide public usage but lack precision. He proposed a spectrum of seven "terms" running sequentially as follows: revolutionary radicalism, radicalism, liberalism, conservatism, standpattism, reaction and revolutionary reaction. The basic distinction among them, in Rossiter's view, is their attitude toward change and reform in areas like law, human relations, economics, customs, and education. Radicalism, including the revolutionary forms, is committed to thorough change. Liberalism, conservatism, and standpattism are varieties of attitudes which promote change over stability or stability over change but are relatively

[2] Stan Lehr and Louis Rossetto, Jr., "The New Right Credo—Libertarianism," *New York Times Magazine*, January 10, 1971. See also Jerome Tuccile, "A Split in the Right Wing," *New York Times*, January 28, 1971, p. 35.

[3] Guido de Ruggiero, *The History of European Liberalism*, tr. by R. G. Collingwood, New York: Oxford University Press, 1927; Beacon Press paperback, 1959.

content within the existing social system. Reaction and revolutionary reaction are attitudes which Rossiter defines as desiring to change toward the past, relishing earlier times, and willing to act "radically" to return the society to the ideals of a period perceived as superior to the present. The revolutionary aspects of radicalism and reaction exist in the willingness to use violence if necessary to obtain goals. Rossiter notes the close proximity of radicalism and reaction to each other in terms of specific beliefs and behaviors.[4]

Radical thought and action may be drawn from either end of a spectrum of social and political ideas. The common use of the terms right and left in regard to political, economic, and social thought is modified by adding the term radical. The radical right and radical left are positions of polarity that could be diagrammed as follows:

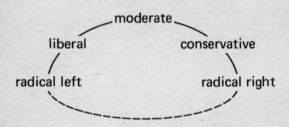

In political science literature, the term "reactionary" is used to signify the extreme right and "radical" is reserved for the far left. In this book, "radical" is used to refer to both ends of the spectrum. Both the far right and the far left are in agreement that basic changes are needed to reform existing social institutions. They differ not in their radicalism per se but in the particular goals or means they view as important for the society. The radical right is a term which may be legitimately used to describe men and ideas of the far right politically.[5]

Figure 1 indicates the spread of ideas and suggests that radical right and radical left are opposite. In many respects this is true. However, as the broken line implies, there are often areas of agreement between radicals of the right and left which are not shared by those in the middle of the spectrum. Drastic change in some social institutions

[4] Clinton Rossiter, *Conservatism in America: The Thankless Persuasion*, Second Edition, New York: Vintage Books, 1962.

[5] Daniel Bell, ed., *The Radical Right*, Garden City, New York: Anchor Books, 1963. See also John A. Hamilton, "Year of the Radical Reactionary," *New York Times*, November 2, 1970, p. 47; Benjamin R. Epstein and Arnold Forster, *The Radical Right*, New York: Random House, 1967.

is frequently a goal agreed to by both sets of radicals. Both may agree, for example, that the welfare system needs to be completely overhauled if not eliminated as it is presently maintained. Yet both the right and the left may hold quite different views on why reform should occur and on the best means of accomplishing the desired ends. They may agree on isolationist policies in international affairs but for different purposes.

In addition, individuals may agree to radical right or left ideas in one sphere of society but be moderates, conservatives, or liberals in regard to most aspects of the culture. Thus, one can agree to radical school reform while maintaining moderate views about the rest of society. This makes it difficult to label individuals as radicals, although it is a common practice. Since most people share cultural values of the society into which they were born, the concept of a totally radical individual is not easy to assume. A belief in the rationality of man, for example, may be shared by members of the establishment and those who are advocating revolution. They differ in interpretations and conclusions. Those labeled campus moderates and campus radicals agree on the protection of free speech but differ in what that protection means.

Radicalism contains the seeds of self-destruction. A radical view is necessarily one which is in opposition to a commonly held idea. If the radical view becomes popular or powerful—by persuasion or force —it is no longer radical. To the extent that a radical idea is accepted in a society, it changes from radical to moderate. As acceptability increases, radicalism decreases. Presumably, the goal of a radical group is to gain power in order to have its radical ideas adopted. The achievement of that goal produces the demise of the group as a radical faction.

This is not merely a semantic snag resulting from our definition of radicalism. It is important to an understanding of psycho-social dynamics in radicalism. It helps to explain why radicals of one period are moderates of another and vice versa. It also suggests that the professional radical has a difficult time when he begins to develop influence. He needs to choose among alternatives which include social respectability as a result of adoption of his ideas, compromises and modifications in putting the ideas into practice, co-optation to stifle him, or shifting ideas to retain his radical life style. If a group advocating the abolition of marriage and the substitution of free love without restriction is able to convince enough people or the right people to support them, the resulting change in society makes the free-love advocates the establishment while marriage supporters become the dissidents. An early member of the Free Love Society, who gained notoriety as a radical and who relished the distinction, must now choose to defend the new establishment, withdraw silently, or take up a new cause. Typically, social change is much more complex than the example given, but the concept of successful radicalism being self-destroying is a useful perspective.

Walter Weyl discusses aspects of this weakness in radical movements. He describes two groups of radicals: those by environment and those by temperament. He argues that a radical by environment is slower but more sure, while a radical by temperament is faster, more violent, and less realistic. It is the latter, contends Weyl, who fades quickest when his emotions are deflected into war or social upheaval. The radical ideas are forsaken for the emotional behavior. An environmental radical, however, draws from the conditions of life to which he has been subjected and has more staying power. Weyl also writes of the relation of age to radicalism, proposing that the period of adolescence "is the true day for revolt," while age brings pleasant spouses, self-indulgence, and expertise in why "every thing is impossible."[6]

Radicalism, then, has several dimensions. It is conditioned by time and space. Radical ideas are those that fundamentally conflict with popular ideas. Radicalism can incorporate destructive, utopian, or combination positions. Radicals may be those who support a radical idea in one or more spheres of life but needn't be totally opposed to all aspects. Not all radical ideas gain supporters. For the few that develop public notoriety, many fail to attract general attention. And the radical idea that becomes popularly accepted is no longer a radical idea.

RADICAL THOUGHTS AND RADICAL ACTS

There is a current tendency to equate radicals with violence. Although physical violence is a radical act in a society which formally outlaws such behavior, it does not follow that violence is the only form of radicalism. Some might note that violence is a general social condition and, therefore, not radical. Regardless of whether violence is seen as radical or non-radical, there are other acts which are radical but not violent. Passive resistance and peaceful civil disobedience as advocated by Gandhi, Thoreau, and Martin Luther King represent radical behavior which is non-violent. Living in communes, existing without modern technology, or engaging in satan worship are other examples of radical behavior that needn't be violent.

[6] Walter Weyl, *Tired Radicals and Other Papers*, New York: B. W. Huebsch, Inc., 1921.

Recent reports have documented the extent and tradition of violence in American life, most notably the report of Hugh Davis Graham and Ted Robert Gurr[7] and the task force report directed by Jerome H. Skolnick.[8] Both documents were submitted to the National Commission on the Causes and Prevention of Violence and posit that violence has long been one form of American protest behavior. This does not make it more or less radical than peaceful acts of protest or the espousal of radical ideas. Violence is dramatic and public, leading to a common assumption that radicalism and violence are virtually synonymous. It is true that some radicals advocate violence and that violence may result from belief in certain radical values, but there is no necessary correlation between physical destruction and radical thought.

In addition, it might be useful to delineate radical behavior from radical thought. In practice, the two may coincide, but it is possible to consider radical ideas outside of individual radical behavior. A person may advocate the abolition of government while personally accepting the rewards and penalties of a government. Marshall McLuhan proposes a radically different way of viewing environment which suggests that printing is outmoded, but he does it in printed books.[9] There is also adequate evidence of people who engage in radical behavior without obvious radical thought. A sexual deviate may not have considered a rationale for his behavior, but seeks gratification merely as a physical act. An eccentric who carries a bag of leaves around town may have no thoughtful radical purpose or design. A sniper shooting at students on a campus may be emotionally disturbed but not a follower of some radical ideology.

INTELLECTUAL TRADITIONS

Radical ideas are usually expressed to stimulate action and change behavior. Solid and consistent logic, emotional barrages of fiery rhetoric, and persuasive examples of goodness or evil are utilized to convince people to become believers, advocates, and practitioners. Regardless of the immediate behavioral consequences of radical viewpoints, the ideas themselves can be considered. This intellectual tradition of radicalism has been the subject of many writers.

Staughton Lynd traces American radicalism from ideas of Rous-

[7] Hugh Davis Graham and Ted Robert Gurr, *The History of Violence in America*, New York: Bantam Books, 1969.

[8] Jerome H. Skolnick, *The Politics of Protest*, New York: Simon and Schuster, 1969.

[9] Marshall McLuhan, *Understanding Media*, New York: McGraw-Hill, 1964.

seau and Marx through Thomas Paine, Thorstein Veblen, and W. E. B. DuBois. His is a political analysis, centering on concepts of government. The tradition of radical thought that Lynd describes lies in the relation of man to state. It presumes an intuitive sense of rightness in man, individual freedom, social responsibility to fulfill human needs and not the protection of property, citizen rights to disobey oppressive laws and to overthrow "incurably oppressive governments," and primary allegiance to mankind not nations. This radical tradition in America, says Lynd, derives from both English and American ideas.[10]

The "Radical Republic" of eighteenth-century America described by Howard Mumford Jones incorporated aspects of both right- and left-wing thinking. He identifies the British philosopher Edmund Burke and the American pamphleteer Thomas Paine as representatives of the radical right and radical left respectively.[11]

Jones' depiction of the raucous and unstable nation shows the influence of multiple radical ideas:

> . . . What a country! A menace, the product of harebrained theory, a stirrer of dissension, the conqueror of the Barbary pirates, wily in diplomacy, a country that invited the discontented to come to its shores and live while in the same breath it passed the odious Alien and Sedition Acts! A country boiling with odd, revolutionary notions about law, language, loyalty oaths, landholding, the rights of man, representative government and the disestablishment of religion![12]

T. B. Bottomore glances briefly at social criticism in classical Rome and Greece and settles on the Age of Enlightenment as the beginning of Western radical thought. Bottomore notes the different course of dissent in Europe and in America, exemplified by Herbert Spencer's social theories seen as radical in England but standard in the United States in the nineteenth century.[13] Spencer, supporter of individualism, representative democracy, industrial technology, and natural social evolution, is portrayed by Richard Hofstadter as a dominant figure in American intellectual thought, while he was virtually ignored in Europe.[14] Bottomore's essays treat contemporary radical thought in the United States and Canada as well as their European counterparts.

[10] Staughton Lynd, *Intellectual Origins of American Radicalism*, New York: Pantheon Books, 1968.

[11] Jones, *op. cit.*, p. 279.

[12] *Ibid.*, p. 275.

[13] T. B. Bottomore, *Critics of Society: Radical Thought in North America*, New York: Pantheon Books, 1968.

[14] Richard Hofstadter, *Social Darwinism in American Thought*, Boston: Beacon Press, 1955.

Arthur Schlesinger suggests that the speed of reform in America is the result of two factors: Early settlers were not overburdened by national traditions, and the immigrants tended to be those who had rebelled at conditions in their homelands. Schlesinger writes of the "revolt against revolt," in which reactions to ideas considered radical produced opposing radical ideas and actions.[15]

This radical reaction in recent times is what Peter Schrag calls the "Other Radicals." Schrag writes of such groups as the John Birch Society, Liberty Lobby, Twentieth Century Reformation Hour, the Manion Forum, the Life Line Foundation, and others which, he states, have differences of view but share certain concerns about a Communist Conspiracy; government programs in civil rights, poverty, and foreign aid; the peace movement; sex education; and black and student militancy. As Schrag points out, the radical right is difficult to define because it stretches from the edges of conservatism to hard-line racist groups like the Ku Klux Klan and the American Nazis.[16] The same is, of course, true of the radical left which encompasses the fringes of liberalism as well as revolutionary groups like the Weatherman faction of Students for a Democratic Society.

A special meaning for the term radical as it relates to the contemporary student movement is suggested by Harold Taylor. His concept is that a radical is one who makes judgments about qualities of life in terms of experience and consequences rather than by reference to authority or ideology. This, Taylor maintains, is in the radical tradition of pragmatism as developed by William James and John Dewey.[17]

Ideological considerations in politics, religion, and economics, however, have provided impetus to the radical right in America. David H. Bennett analyzes four "radicals of the right" and their movement during the depression. His treatment of Father Charles Coughlin, Rev. Gerald L. K. Smith, Dr. Francis E. Townsend, and Representative William Lemke and the Union Party shows the use of fundamentalist religious doctrine, anti-Communism, and economic utopias in forging an intense political campaign.[18] The causes of Senator Joseph

[15] Arthur M. Schlesinger, *The American as Reformer*, Cambridge, Massachusetts: Harvard University Press, 1950.

[16] Peter Schrag, "America's Other Radicals," *Harper's Magazine*, August 1970, pp. 35–46.

[17] Harold Taylor, *Students Without Teachers: The Crisis in the University*, New York: McGraw-Hill, 1969.

[18] David H. Bennett, *Demagogues in the Depression: American Radicals and the Union Party, 1932–1936*, New Brunswick, New Jersey: Rutgers University Press, 1969.

McCarthy in the 1950s, the Know-Nothings, the Birch Society, the Klan, and others of the right are also related to ideological considerations according to Seymour M. Lipset's analysis. Lipset, however, states that there is no single unifying ideology of the right but that there are some common grounds in Americanism and anti-Communism.[19]

Although the radical left has held and continues to hold views with ideological components, there are new developments in radical thought that appear to transcend traditional ideologies. The historic economic, political, and social positions which permeated western leftist thought and caused men like Robert Owen, R. H. Tawney, Eugene V. Debs, William D. Haywood, and C. Wright Mills to be labeled radical,[20] are now seen as moderate by some factions of the new left. Socialism, worker's democracy, and internationalism are no longer the primary pursuits of all those who pose radical ideas on the left. A form of humanism and a sense of community and self-identity are counterposed against technology, individualism, and alienation as the new battleground. This is the anti-technology counter-culture described by Theodore Roszak,[21] the anti-alienation alternative society defined by Kenneth Rexroth,[22] the anti-individualism expressed by Philip Slater,[23] and the anti-establishment movements outlined by Arthur Waskow.[24]

Radical ideas have long and colorful histories. The dynamics of social change provide constant opportunities for expressions of unor-

[19] Seymour Martin Lipset, "The Sources of the 'Radical Right' (1955)" and "Three Decades of the Radical Right: Coughlinites, McCarthyites, and Birchers (1962)" as found in Bell, *The Radical Right, op. cit.*, pp. 307–446.

[20] See such works as: Robert Owen, *A New View of Society*, London, 1817, Facsimile reproduction by The Free Press of Glencoe, Illinois; R. H. Tawney, *The Radical Tradition*, London: George Allen & Unwin, Ltd., 1964; Joseph R. Conlin, *Big Bill Haywood and the Radical Union Movement*, Syracuse: Syracuse University Press, 1969; Priscilla Long, ed., *The New Left*, Boston: Porter Sargent Publisher, 1969; Irving Howe, ed., *The Radical Imagination*, New York: The New American Library, 1967; Howe, *The Radical Papers*, Garden City, New York: Doubleday & Co., 1966; Paul Jacobs and Saul Landau, *The New Radicals*, New York: Random House, 1966; Christopher Lasch, *The New Radicalism in America*, New York: Alfred Knopf, 1965.

[21] Theodore Roszak, *The Making of a Counter Culture*, Garden City, New York: Doubleday & Co., 1969.

[22] Kenneth Rexroth, *The Alternative Society*, New York: Herder & Herder, 1970.

[23] Philip Slater, *The Pursuit of Loneliness*, Boston: Beacon Press, 1970.

[24] Arthur I. Waskow, *Running Riot*, New York: Herder & Herder, 1970.

thodox views. Periods of crisis offer more compelling environments for movements, demagogues, rash behavior, and rapid communication of radical thoughts, but the intellectual roots of radicalism reside in the considered judgments of those who reflect on the human condition.

Social Institutions and Radical Social Ideas

One of the dominant characteristics of any social institution is that it shares in the society of which it is a part. That is, institutions do not exist outside of or unrelated to societies.[25]

Prisons, developed to separate individual deviates from their society, do not operate in a vacuum. They are established to fulfill social functions. Laws discriminate criminal acts from acceptable behavior, provide processes for whatever the society feels justice is, prescribe punishments according to social norms, determine who judges and who is judged, specify the manner of operation for prisons and similar containment facilities, and offer remedies for prison practices which society feels are unacceptable. Laws are made and changed by social process, and prisons are somewhat different now from what once were. And prisons are different in America from those in other areas.

Hospitals as social institutions also reflect society. They are modified as societies place new demands, and they modify society as they change. Health insurance developed from social needs, medical provisions, and public acceptability. Medical doctors now require extensive education and strict licensing. This results from notions of public protection and professionalization. It has also produced a shortage of doctors and considerably improved the economic and social status of practitioners.

Formal religion exists as a social institution, tempered by and influencing social changes. Churches and temples operate on a tax-free basis in America. The U. S. Constitution calls for the separation of church and state. Religions are expected to be responsive to demands for stability by invoking traditional doctrine and for change by social activism.

Prisons, hospitals, and religions serve to illustrate the transactional relationship among institutions and society. Neither these formal institutions nor informal ones like mass media, athletics, and mothers-in-law are separate from society. The relationship among them is not unilateral—where society demands and institutions respond. Nor is it merely interactional—where both society and institutions act on each

[25] Jack L. Nelson and Frank P. Besag, *Sociological Perspectives in Education: Models for Analysis*, New York: Pitman Publishing Co., 1970.

other. Rather, the relationship is transactional—where continuing change occurs in institutions and society along several dimensions and in complex ways. Prison reform is not a singular, separate occurrence. It is part of a network of developments among institutions, individuals, and society at large. There are multiple causes and effects.

Because radical social ideas have the potential for influencing socially accepted thought and behavior, they are appropriate subjects of study for those interested in social change. The transactional concept of social processes, which assumes that change in one segment or institution of society results from and effects change in other segments, makes a broad study of social ideas—radical and moderate—necessary. The presumably radical idea of a guaranteed annual wage does not result simply from welfare bureaus, nor will it only affect present welfare recipients. The old debtor's prisons, free medical clinic facilities, religious charities and preachings, social concepts of equality and hard work, competition-based economics, free schooling, and mass-media advertising each contribute to and will be affected by changes inherent in the radical idea. Even if a specific radical idea is not successful, it may stimulate social institutions or individuals to non-radical change. To the extent that a radical idea has public notoriety, it presents an environment for social and institutional modification.

This does not, once again, mean that any notorious radical idea will produce a change in its favor. In fact, radical ideas also produce alterations in opposition to the idea. A radical proposal to permit the sale of hard drugs in schools as a convenience to students would cause reconsideration of drug-abuse problems in schools and might change school regulations to be more strict in surveillance, searches, and reporting of drug use. The point is that radical ideas, if adequately disseminated, assist in the determination of policies and practices of institutions and their societies.

RADICALISM AND EDUCATION

Education, both formal as in schooling and informal as in life experience, is a social institution sharing in society and participating in the transactional process. Radical ideas in society, in other social institutions, and in regard to education itself have the potential of great or modest change in the way we think about schools, students, teachers, curriculum, and learning. Mass free public education was a radical idea in earlier times. It did not develop spontaneously from schoolmasters or professors, and its effects have certainly not been limited to what goes on during school hours. Major social ideas about equality, participatory citizenship, labor and economics, industrial development, child welfare, class struggles, and human nature contributed to and have been influenced by mass education.

Schools have emerged as major social institutions involving virtually every person for sustained periods of time in generally prescribed activities. The basic purpose is to transmit the accumulation of cultural fact and fancy deemed appropriate by those in educational power. Schools incorporate the dominant norms and values of their societies and engage in the socialization process to produce citizens with similar beliefs.

This social stability function of schools is highly consistent with their roles as reflectors of society and maintainers of the culture. Oftentimes schools are even more conservative in their patterns of change than the general society because they are perceived as the protectors of the past. Hair-length regulations have changed more slowly, and frequently with greater institutional reluctance, in schools than in many other areas of society. Citizen rights to free expression, assembly, and due process are continually challenged in schools because of social questions about the citizenship of students. This is clearly indicated in the vagueness surrounding underground newspapers, school speaker policies, and rights of teachers to deal with controversy in the classroom.

Despite the Supreme Court ruling in the Tinker Case that protected free expression of unpopular beliefs by secondary-school students, some school districts still have restrictive regulations, censorship, and covert means to prevent student expression of opinion in sensitive areas.[26] Teachers are still being fired or reassigned for raising questions about the norms and values of the society. No one in recent times has met the fate of Socrates, who challenged the popular ideas of his time and was condemned to die for corrupting the morals of youth, but many have felt a similar wrath from the society. As an educator he raised serious questions about man and society. This radical education was met by a radical response and Socrates' resulting death.[27]

The reflective, protective, status quo education system is consistent with aspects of socialization that call for noncritical assimilation of the traditions and mores of a society but is inconsistent with the dynamics of an open society based on enlightened citizens and persistent change. If decisions in a democracy are to be based on consideration of all available evidence and ideas, and students in schools are

[26] *Tinker et al.* v. *Des Moines Independent Community School District et al.*, 393 US 503, Decided February 24, 1969.

[27] B. Jowett, *The Dialogues of Plato*, Vol. I, New York: Random House, 1937.

expected to develop skills in critical analysis as a prelude to those decisions, the literature of dissent must be open to inquiry. Radical ideas, as this chapter has proposed, are worthy of consideration, not because they are good ideas, but because they are ideas—and ideas are the means for vitality in a dynamic society. The intellectual energy required to reject a radical idea is more important to this social vitality than the passive acceptance of the status quo. Schools exist not only to pass on the historic wisdom and folly of the society but to provide the means for new directions, different mistakes, and alternative truths.

Since a democracy rests on both majority rule and minority rights, the protections afforded to insurgent groups to advocate positions, gather together in coalitions, and attempt to persuade members of the society must be guaranteed. The Bill of Rights provides this protection although at times these constitutional rights are infringed by censorship, illegal search and seizure, and political harassment by the majority-controlled legal and police systems. Indeed, surveys conducted by H. H. Remmers, the Gallup Poll, and CBS-TV over the past two decades indicate that the Bill of Rights would have great difficulty in gaining public support if it were placed on a ballot today.[28] The unpopularity of some Supreme Court decisions reflects this position. Simple majority rule would likely restrict rights of free expression and assembly. Protection of minority rights insures the vitality of an open society. The improvement of civilization depends upon the opportunity for insurgents to become the majority by persuasion.

Schools have an obligation to cause students to explore divergent ideas as a means for continuing open dialogue and to provide students with the necessary skills in critical analysis in order to diminish susceptibility to demagogues and propaganda. One must confront demagoguery and propaganda from experience and knowledge rather than naïveté and ignorance. This experience and knowledge is not gained by limiting access to ideas and restricting students' viewpoints to those deemed safe by the authorities.

Higher educational institutions have been remiss in providing opportunities for those going into teaching to grapple with radical social ideas and to see educational implications. Seldom are these students, who will become educational decision-makers in public and private schools, asked to consider dissident viewpoints in their own education. It would be unlikely that teachers who are unaware of

[28] H. H. Remmers, ed., *Anti-Democratic Attitudes in American Schools*, Evanston, Illinois: Northwestern University Press, 1963. See also John C. Pock, "Attitudes Toward Civil Liberties Among High School Seniors," in D. Sobul, ed., *The Bill of Rights: A Handbook*, New York: Benziger Bros., 1969.

radical positions would be able to introduce their students to new ideas. While it is true that many colleges expect their teacher-education students to examine radical school ideas, it is unusual for them to undertake study of the interrelationships between radical social thought and the schools.

The intent of this book is to stimulate consideration of radical ideas about social systems, aspects of morality, concepts of knowledge, and schools. These are obviously areas which overlap and intertwine, but they have been separated in the organization of the book for convenience of study and to provide emphasis. Section One on social systems includes two areas of dominance in social life—power and wealth. In the vernacular of academic disciplines they are represented by politics and economics, though they incorporate philosophy, sociology, and geography. Power and wealth are systemic in the sense that they pervade the entire society. Drastic changes in these areas are directly related to all parts of the system. Although that is also more or less true of radical change in areas covered by other chapters, e. g., religion, it appears more dramatically in power and wealth.

Section Two includes some key aspects of morality where radical change has been proposed. The underlying theme here is the notion of distinctions between good and evil and how those distinctions should be made. Since schools convey moral values to the young, divergent views of morality should be examined. We teach children not to fight in school, but teach them how to fight in the military. We formally teach the evils of drugs, racism, religious intolerance, and anti-social sexual deviance while informally providing means for drug distribution, racial discrimination, religious bigotry, and sexual repression.

Section Three presents views on knowledge and its relation to society and education. Schools are considered a knowledge industry, yet the definition of knowledge is often culturally limited. What we know, how we know, and why we know are crucial questions for educators and may demand radical answers.

Finally, Section Four deals directly with schools, offering diverse ideas on rationales for changing schools, strategies to effect long-term or extensive change, and tactics for quicker change. Mid-century criticism of schools was exemplified by the Council for Basic Education, James Koerner, Arthur Bestor, Mortimer Lynd, and others who protested the movement to progressive education and permissiveness.[29]

[29] Arthur E. Bestor, *The Educational Waste Lands*, Urbana, Illinois: University of Illinois Press, 1953; Hyman G. Rickover, *Education and Freedom*, New York: Dutton, 1959; James D. Koerner, ed., *The Case for Basic Education*, Boston: Little, Brown, 1959; Mortimer Smith, *And Madly Teach*, Chicago: Regnery, 1949.

Current critics condemn schools for dehumanization, conformity, indoctrination, and too little progressive education.[30]

Jean François Revel, French philosopher and social critic, wrote a best-selling book in France that was later published in America and in which he presents a case for the new American revolution.[31] He argues that the United States is the only place that the revolution can develop, and that there is evidence for stating that it has already begun. His evidence includes the civil rights movement, women's liberation, black power, anti-Viet Nam War activities, the hippies, and student revolts. Part of Revel's rationale for this provocative position is that the United States is the best informed society in history, and that this knowledge assists in the perception of social problems and reform solutions. Clearly, the schools bear some credit—or disdain, if you wish— for this knowledge acquisition. Schools may be holding back the revolution by backward education, or assisting in its development.

Because education is an intellectual as well as physical and emotional endeavor, ideas are important. Highly divergent ideas deserve the consideration of thoughtful educators, not merely because of some possible impact on schools, but also because intelligent decisions presume awareness of alternatives, and educators are rightly expected to make intelligent judgments. All possible alternatives are never known, but there is a need to weigh options that do not typically appear in popular forums. Radical ideas exist, and this book presents a sampling of the literature of dissent.

[30] See such works as: Paul Goodman, *Compulsory Miseducation*, New York: Horizon Press, 1964; Edgar Z. Friedenberg, *Coming of Age in America*, New York: Random House, 1965; Jerry Avorn, *Up Against the Ivy Wall*, New York: Atheneum, 1969; Robert Theobald, *An Alternative Future for America*, Chicago: Swallow Press, 1968; Jonathan Kozol, *Death at an Early Age*, New York: Houghton Mifflin, 1967; John Holt, *How Children Fail*, Pitman Publishing Co., 1964.

[31] Jean François Revel, *Without Marx or Jesus*, Garden City, New York: Doubleday & Co., 1971.

section ONE

Radical Social Systems

"A nation without means of reform is without means of survival."
—Edmund Burke

"Every revolution was once a thought in one man's mind, and when the same thought occurs to another man, it is the key to that era."
—Ralph Waldo Emerson

chapter 1

Power and Social Control

Who controls? Who decides? Who acts? Who responds? Who succumbs?

These questions are measures of power. The ability to exert influence, cause behavior, and make binding decisions is an ambition that drives politicians, bullies, and parents. Those who have power typically dislike giving it up; those who don't have power experience difficulty getting access to it. Tensions between the powerful and the powerless have fueled slavery, revolution, annihilation, martyrdom, and warfare. Uses and abuses of power have occurred throughout human history. Concepts of power and the means of manipulation have changed over time and differed among societies.

In some societies control of individual and social behaviors is vested in religious leaders who interpret natural phenomena and their implications for human life. In some societies control is centralized in military or police organizations. In some societies control is divided among tribal political leaders in a form of feudalism. In some societies control rests in a network of affiliations among industrialists, politicians, and landed gentry.

Mass democracy, as envisioned by eighteenth-century political philosophies, assumed that power is distributed among the people. The "Social Contract" concept that government is based on will, not force, and justice, not might, draws from Aristotle, St. Thomas Aquinas, John Milton, Adam Smith, John Locke, Jean-Jacques Rousseau, and David Hume. Its American modifiers include Thomas Jefferson, Abraham Lincoln, and Louis Brandeis. The theory of community that presumes government by consent of the governed conveys power by agreement, individual liberty with social responsibility, and opportunities for expressions of dissent including the overthrow of those in power. It is this theory of shared and transferable power that underlies the United States Constitution and Bill of Rights.

Classic representative democracy embodies the ideas that individual citizens have ultimate control; that there is a community of interests that are shared by citizens; that rational and free discussion by enlightened citizens is imperative; and that social decisions made by representatives incorporate the public will. Laws, media, and schools are expected to express these ideals by protecting citizen rights, providing opportunities for open discussion, and educating citizens. Critics of American society challenge these and other social institutions. Some argue that the theory is inadequate; others raise serious questions about the practices.

Divergent minds such as C. Wright Mills and Dwight Eisenhower both spoke of the threat of power concentrated in the hands of a corporate few. Karl Marx saw class struggle rather than community interest as a power source. Abbie Hoffman and the Yippies challenge the concept of rationality as a base for decision-making. The John Birch Society condemns school practices as indoctrination, not enlightenment. And groups seeking shares in control through Black Power, Student Power, People Power, and the like have seen laws used as repressive agents to deny their concept of the public will.

Power politics using the schools as pawns has long been practiced in America. School budgets now consume a large proportion of tax money available at the local and state level. City councils, mayors, and boards of education fight power battles to gain and exercise control over these budgets. Taxpayer groups lobby effectively for turning down school budgets. In major metropolitan areas the schools are a rich stage for political wars. The movement toward decentralization of large school districts, as in New York City, is essentially a power struggle representing political interests in much the same way that earlier moves toward centralization and consolidation of districts were pushed by state legislatures.

The very structure of education removes it from being a purely professional enterprise. State constitutions provide for state legislatures to have virtually complete control over the organization, operation, staffing, curriculum, and economics of public schools. The U. S. Constitution does not mention education, and thus it is under state control. Much authority is delegated to local lay boards of education for operation of schools, but they still fall under state law. It is only in severely limited ways, as in the Supreme Court action in the Brown decision of 1954 declaring segregation in schools unconstitutional that the federal government becomes active. The aftermath of that decision clearly shows the power framework in which schools reside. Eighteen years after the decision we still have segregated schools North and South because of political manipulations at the community, state, and federal level.

Federal school aid is another area of power conflict. Until federal aid was tied to national defense in NDEA legislation and the G. I. Bill, and after years of having it blocked in Congress, there was almost no financial assistance for schools from other than local property taxes and state support. Now, although federal financing remains at an average of less than ten percent of local school budgets, it has become a national political issue. Public funds for private schools is another political football that involves dominant religions and constitutional questions. A long history of separation of church and state is threatened by power plays of religious leaders and politicians.

Developments in public employee power systems are paralleled in the schools. Teacher organizations have become negotiating agents with school boards over curriculum determination, teaching loads, and special school programs, as well as salary and fringe benefits. Teacher militancy has not arisen in a social vacuum. Militant groups seeking power in international affairs and domestic relations provided models for teacher power strategies, just as teacher militancy offers examples to police, clergy, and students.

Internal power politics also exist in schools. Any seasoned teacher, administrator, or student can cite startling examples of defeat or success for educationally sound ideas as a result of pressure politics rather than rational inquiry. Robert Hutchins once described faculty meetings at the University of Chicago, where he was president, in power politics terms. Making it in schools as a student, teacher, or administrator requires power considerations not unlike those of congressmen seeking legislation or favor. Who's Afraid of Virginia Wolf and Up the Down Staircase may have tarnished the great American dream of college and school life, but they present a part of the real world of schools. Concepts of regimes, dynasties, insurgents, conspiracies, establishments, and radicals are as available in school examples as in the political world.

Selections for this chapter do not deal directly with school situations for reasons described in the Introduction. They are presented to provide a spectrum of views on power and its exercise in the society at large. The obvious question for educators to consider in reading these selections is what implications does this position have for education in its external and internal power struggles.

The Politics of "the Movement"

Tom Hayden

The likelihood of a radical coalition continuing long enough to attract a sizable constituency of influential citizens is not great. Two major factors hinder such development: (1) the threat radical movements represent to the established order creates a reactive and usually repressive counter-movement that carries the force of laws designed to protect those already in power; and (2) the diverse natures, philosophies, and tactics of radical groups prevent them from unifying for common causes for extended periods. The first factor uses power to smash, exile, or co-opt a coalition, while the second spawns internal battles over goals, methods, and spoils. These conditions have continued to plague radical groups who plan mass movements.

This statement of the struggles between those in power and groups of insurgents collectively known as "the Movement" was written by one of the founders of Students for a Democratic Society. The history of SDS illustrates both political reprisal and internal dissension. The idea of radical coalitions has been proposed often, but positions, events, and strategies seem to militate against it. Hayden's comments about schools as agents of barbarism and the educational implications of a mass poor movement are important considerations of this article. Schools have traditionally neglected the poor and favored the rich.

My own disenchantment with American society was not caused by its racial bigotry, its warlike posturing, its supreme respect for money. All these might be understood as irrationalities which could be struck from the national character if only rational men were mobilized more effectively. But when events prove this assumption false, then disenchantment really begins—with the understanding that the most respected and enlightened Americans are among the most barbarous.

Take just two examples. There is a conventional notion that the Southern racial crisis is caused and prolonged by "white trash"—an isolated and declining remnant in our society. We are told that rational men are attempting, within the framework of due process, to educate these minority elements to a more progressive social outlook. But this picture is shattered every day by events in the Black Belt. There the murderers of civil rights workers again and again include men like Byron de la Beckwith, the respected downtown businessman who shot Medgar Evers in the back. They are middle class and enjoy the broad support of their local communities.

When this is pointed out, of course, we are told that respectable men are murderers only in places like Mississippi. By national standards the Black Belt killers are not respectable. But is Mississippi an isolated part of America? If not, who at the national level is responsible for the state of terror in Mississippi? Part of the answer, I am afraid, is that leading Northerners buttress the Southern status quo. Without dozens of companies owned from the North, plus the billions provided by defense contracts and agricultural subsidies, Mississippi could not have survived the postwar period as a racist state. Mississippi Power and Light, for example, many of whose personnel are connected with the White Citizens Council, is owned and controlled by the same men who play leading roles in another corporation known for its enlightenment, Harvard University.

A second example: we are told that the United States is on the side of the new nations and the exploited and impoverished peoples of the third world. But once again the facts have nothing to do with this happy picture—as the affairs of an American businessman like Charles Engelhard of New Jersey suggest. In his mid-forties, Engelhard is already renowned in business circles and has become an important political figure in the liberal wing of the Democratic Party. He was sent by the President to represent the U.S. at occasions as vital as the celebration of Algerian independence. He was a friend of John F. Kennedy; Lyndon Johnson praises him as a "great humanitarian." How did he become so famous? Presumably because he owns the controlling interest in the mines of the Republic of South Africa. But aren't those mines a blasphemy against the values of the free world? And is Engelhard an isolated and unrespectable member of that world?

This is civilized barbarism—pernicious, sophisticated, subtly concealed from the public view, massively protected from political attack. The barbaric America is invisible to the majority of its people, who are lodged in occupations and social positions which form a desensitizing trap. They are at the bottom, or in the middle, of organizations whose official purposes are justified in abstract terms. Their views, inherited from their families or implanted by the school system, and fed every day by the mass media, permit them to screen out threatening information or alternative ways of seeing the world.

The usual way to "escape" the trapped condition of ordinary Americans is to ascend to higher levels of influence and knowledge in some key institution. But while an overview of society is gained from these positions, a new trap is waiting. For entry into higher organizational circles depends upon accepting their general design and purpose. This means that people in "responsible" positions are most often blind to immoral consequences of their work. Their blindness is intensified by the belief that they are close to people's problems and that administrative remedies exist for whatever arises. This is the usual attitude among public servants, from police to administrators of the War on Poverty.

II

This national trance depends upon one crucial assumption: that American society is being improved domestically. The legitimacy gained by the industrial unions, the liberal welfare legislation which was passed in the thirties and forties, and now the civil rights and anti-poverty reforms of the sixties—these are seen as part of a long sweep toward a society of economic and social justice. But there is, in fact, little evidence to justify the view that the social reforms of the past thirty years actually improved the quality of American life in a lasting way. And there is much evidence which suggests that the reforms gained were illusory or token, serving chiefly to sharpen the capacity of the system for manipulation and oppression.

Look closely for a moment at the social legislation upon which the notion of domestic improvement is based. The Wagner Act was supposed to effect unionization of workers; but today the unionized labor force is shrinking with the automation of the mass-production industries, and millions of other workers, never organized, are without any protection. The Social Security laws were supposed to support people in distress, but today many are still not covered, and those with coverage can barely make ends meet. Unemployment compensation policies were supposed to aid men in need of jobs, but today many are still without coverage, while benefits represent a smaller and smaller share of the cost of living. The 1946 Full Employment Act was supposed to guarantee federal action to provide a job for every American who needed one, but today the official (understated) unemployment rate is close to 6 per cent. The 1949 Public Housing Act, sponsored by conservative Robert Taft, was to create 800,000 low-cost units by

1953, but today less than half that number are constructed, many of them beyond reach of the poor. The difficult struggle to enact even a token policy of public medical care, the hollow support for public education, the stagnation and starvation of broader programs for health, recreation, and simple city services—all this evidence for a simple truth: *the welfare state is a myth*.

Seen in the context of a history of unkept promises, the 1965 anti-poverty program should evoke no optimism. The amount of money allocated is a pittance; most of it is going to local politicians, school boards, welfare agencies, housing authorities, professional personnel, and even to the police; its main thrust is to shore up sagging organizational machinery, not to shift the distribution of income and influence in the direction of the poor. Some of the more sophisticated liberals understand that the "involvement of the poor" is essential to an effective program, but this is seen in capitalist-psychological terms, stressing the need to "repair" the defeatist self-image which supposedly excludes the poor from sharing in the enterprise system. A few people, including members of the Administration, see "involvement" in political terms as well. But this participation is frustrated by the poverty planners' undeviating allegiance to existing power centers. In reality, then, the poor only *flavor* the program. A few are co-opted into it, but only as atomized individuals. They do not have independent organizational strength, as do the machines and social agencies.

But the quality of the welfare state is best illustrated by the sluggish way in which it responds to pressure for civil rights reform. It required the slaughter of little girls, a near blood bath in Birmingham, violence toward Northern whites, students and ministers, an outbreak of riots across the North, and the organization of an independent political party in Mississippi before the Administration began to move on the civil rights front. And that motion gives little hope of real progress. Indeed, the 1965 Voting Rights Bill actually shrinks the existing powers of the federal government (as established in such codes as Section 242, Title 18, which provides for criminal prosecution of people acting under cover of law to violate others' constitutional rights). It leaves the decision to take action to the Attorney General; it involves complicated and time-consuming procedures for local Negroes; it provides no protection against intimidation for civil rights workers or local people.

In all these areas, from the Wagner Act to the newest civil rights legislation, my criticism has been narrowed to the question: did the legislation achieve, or does it offer some hope of achieving, its stated purposes? The tragedy, however, is not simply that these programs fall short of their goals. Rather, the goals themselves are far from desirable to anyone interested in greater democracy and a richer quality of social life. Welfare and public housing policies, for instance, are creating a new and public kind of authoritarianism. Public relief clients and tenants, lacking any protective organizations, are subject to the caprice and cruelty of supervisors, investigators, and local machine politicians. Similarly, labor and civil rights legislation creates tools for government intervention at moments of sharp social conflict, without really changing the tyrannical conditions in which millions of workers and Negroes live. The full employment and anti-poverty acts, along with the relief measures of the thirties, give the government power to cushion the economic situation just short of the point of mass unemployment. Programs such as urban renewal serve as the major domestic outlet for investment capital and, consciously or not, as a means of demoralizing and politically fragmenting the poor. The national government thus becomes the chief force for stabilizing the private economy and for managing social crisis. Its interests, institutions, and personnel have merged with those of high finance and industry.

The traditional left expectation of irreconcilable and clashing class interests has been defied. Still assuming such antagonisms, however, many leftists tend to view each piece of social legislation as a victory which strengthens the "progressive" forces. They see a step-by-step transformation of society as the result of pushing for one "politically acceptable" reform after another. But it appears that the American elite has discovered a long-term way to stabilize or cushion the contradictions of our society. It does this through numerous forms of state intervention, the use of our abundant capacity for material gratification, and the ability to condition nearly all the information which people receive. And if this is the case, then more changes of the New Deal variety will not be "progressive" at all. Except for temporarily boosting income for a few people, this entire reformist trend has weakened the poor under the pretense of helping them and strengthened elite rule under the slogan of curbing private enterprise. In fostering a "responsible" Negro and labor leadership and bringing it into the pseudo-pluralist system of bargaining and rewards, a way has been found to contain and paralyze the disadvantaged and voiceless people.

III

Why have liberal strategies failed to secure substantial reforms over the last three decades? The answer can only be grasped by looking at the general organizing concepts of American liberal and labor leaders. These begin with the view that the American masses are "apathetic" and can only be roused because of simple material needs or during short periods of great enthusiasm. The masses most likely to move, it is said, are those who have gained something already: the unionized workers, registered voters, property owners. Those less likely to move are the people on the absolute bottom with nothing to lose, for they are too damaged to be the real motor of change.

From this rough description of the masses, liberals go on to argue the need for certain sorts of organizations. The masses need skilled and responsible leaders, they insist. It is best if these leaders have rank-and-file experience and operate within a formally democratic system. But this grass-roots flavor must not obscure the necessity for leaders to lead, that is, put forward a program, a set of answers that guides The Movement. And because they monopolize leadership experience, it soon appears to these leaders that they alone are qualified to maintain the organization.

The perilous position of The Movement, owing to attacks from centralized business and political forces, adds a further incentive for a top-down system of command. The need for alliances with other groups, created in large part through the trust which sets of leaders develop for each other, also intensifies the trend toward vertical organization. Finally, the leaders see a need to screen out anyone with "communist-oriented" views, since such individuals are presumably too skilled to be allowed to operate freely within The Movement. Slowly an elite is formed, calling itself the liberal-labor community. It treats the rank and file as a mass to be molded; sometimes thrust forward into action, sometimes held back. A self-fulfilling pattern emerges: because the nature of the organization is elitist, many people react to it with disinterest or suspicion, giving the leadership the evidence it needs to call the masses apathetic.

The pressures which influence these leaders come, not primarily from below, but from the top, from the most powerful men in the country. Sometimes bluntly and sometimes subtly, the real elite grooms responsible trade union and civil rights leaders. The leaders' existence comes to depend upon the possibility of receiving attention from the President or some top aide, and they judge organizational issues with an eye on this possibility. There is usually no question about the leaders' primary loyalty to the "national interest" as defined by the Administration, even though they always believe their judgments are independently made. Thus most of the civil rights leadership in 1964, fearing the Goldwater movement and hoping for civil rights legislation from a victorious Johnson Administration, called for a "moratorium" on mass demonstrations. The labor leadership performed the same function for the same reasons during World War II; the irony is that their critics in that period included A. Philip Randolph and Bayard Rustin, two Negroes who pushed for the 1964 moratorium.

A recent incident clarified the political role of this leadership and pointed towards the possibility of an alternative strategy. This was the challenge posed by the Mississippi Freedom Democratic Party and the Student Nonviolent Coordinating Committee at the 1964 Democratic National Convention.

Members of the FDP trooped into Atlantic City to argue for their rightful control of the Mississippi Democratic seats. They found substantial support from rank-and-file members of Northern delegations who favored their modest demand for at least equal treatment with the racist party at the convention. Here was a chance, it was thought, to end Southern obstruction of the Johnson administration's program. But then the Democratic leadership let its position be known: the FDP was morally sound, but "illegal" and "not qualified." Support within the delegations wavered. The FDP's last chance for success depended on rallying national liberal-labor leaders to support its demand for a floor debate, in front of the television cameras. But some Negro leaders worked against the Mississippi party, others took a vacillating position, and no one would stand firmly with them. To do so, the leaders claimed, would jeopardize Humphrey's chance at the vice-presidency, strengthen Goldwater's hand, and split the FDP from its "allies" in the liberal-labor world. The FDP members decided that the fate of Humphrey and Goldwater depended, in fact, upon the same power structure that was determining their own fate. Not wanting the kind of "allies" and "victories" being offered, they went home. Their real allies were the poor people waiting in the Delta; and their real victory was in being able to maintain fidelity to those allies. This was a victory because it kept the movement alive and gave its members some real understanding of what was needed to change the national situation.

IV

The Mississippi challenge to the convention points toward a new kind of politics and a new kind of organizing, which has at least an outside chance of truly changing American society. This stirring we call The Movement.

The Movement tries to oppose American barbarism with new structures and opposing identities. These are created by people whose need to understand their society and govern their own existence has somehow not been canceled out by the psychological damage they have received. For different reasons such needs survive among the poor, among students and other young people, and finally among millions of other Americans not easily grouped except by their modest individual resistance to the system's inhumanity. It is from these ranks that The Movement is being created. What kind of people, more exactly, are they, and what kind of organizational strategy might they develop?

1. An Interracial Movement of the Poor

The Mississippi sharecroppers are the most visible and inspiring representatives of an awakening that is taking place among the poor in America. Their perspective centers on Negro freedom, of course, but they are committed deeply to the idea of a movement of all the powerless and exploited. In certain ways theirs is a radicalism unique because of Black Belt conditions. Their strength comes from a stable system of family life and work. Politics is new and fresh for them; they have not experienced the hollow promises of an opportunistic liberal-Negro machine. Their opposition's naked brutality keeps them constantly in a crisis framework. The broadening of their movement into Arkansas, Alabama, Louisiana, Georgia, the Carolinas, and Virginia, already under way, can be expected to challenge fundamentally the national coalition directing the Democratic Party. Already the Democrats are trying to groom moderate and liberal politicians to provide an "alternative" to the segregationists and the independent FDP. Probably this effort will succeed, in the sense that political moderates will begin to compete for electoral power and leadership of the civil rights forces, mostly basing their strength in the cities, among privileged Negroes. The FDP, as a structure, may be absorbed into the national party, if only because it has no other, more effective place to go. But since the new Southern power structure will not solve the problems of poverty and race which have plagued the North for generations, there is very little chance that this movement of poor people will be entirely co-opted or crushed.

In the black ghettos of the North, The Movement faces heavier obstacles. There work is often deadening, family life distorted; "proper" political channels are sewers; people are used to, and tired of, party organizers exploiting them. The civil rights movement does not touch these hundreds of ghettos in any significant way because of the middle-class nature of its program and leadership. However, the Harlem rent strikes and the activities of Malcolm X were clear evidence that there are in the ghettos people prepared to take action. Some of them are of Southern background; some are housewives with wasted talents; some are youth with no future for their energy; some are junkies and numbers men with little loyalty to their particular game. Different as the forms of their discontent may be, the discontent itself is general to the ghetto and can be the mainspring for action. Under present conditions political movements among these people are likely to be based on a race consciousness which is genuine and militant—and which is also vital because of the failure of whites to act in favor of equal rights. The ghetto race consciousness, however, is intertwined with the consciousness of being both poor and powerless. Almost of necessity, the demands that the ghetto poor put forward are also in the interest of the white poor, as well as of middle-class professionals who depend on the expansion of the public sectors of the economy.

But will white working-class and poor people take up these issues, which the "Negro problem" by its nature tends to raise? The negative evidence is plentiful. Poor whites, such as those in parts of the South who are truly irrelevant to the modern economy, tend to see their plight (sometimes with accuracy) as personal rather than social: a function of sickness, bad luck, or psychological disorder. Poverty is not seen clearly as the fate of a whole interracial class, but only as the fate of individuals, each shamed into self-blame by their Protestant ideology. Working-class whites, on the other hand, are more likely to be conscious of their problems as a group, but they tend to defend their scarce privileges—jobs, wages, education for their children—against what they see as the onslaught of Negro competition. While "backlash" did not split the alliance of white working people with the Democratic Party in 1964, it does serve as a barrier to an alliance with the Negro poor. But it is foolish to be rigid about these notions. Whites *are* being organized, on a mass basis, in areas of Appalachia where there exists a common culture and an industrial union tradition, and where the blame for misery can be laid to the coal operators, the conservative United Mine Workers, and the government. They also have been organized in Cleveland, where they face the "welfare situation" together.

But these organizing efforts were led by local people or independent organizers outside the structure of the labor movement. Today there are millions of workers trapped by the organizational framework of the AFL-CIO. Their unrest at times moves the international unions slightly, but the internationals are more dependent on government and business than on their own members, and, in addition, they seem to possess effective techniques for curbing shop revolts. It is not simply the "better objective conditions" which split the white from the Negro poor but the existence of trade unions which actively distort the better aspirations of their members. Economic and social conditions, of course, are not improving and workers' discontent is evidenced by the recent wave of rank-and-file revolts. But whether or not this discontent spurs a coalition of poor whites with Negroes depends, most of all, on whether a way can be found to organize workers independent of AFL-CIO routines. Concretely, that means democratic control by the workers of their union locals, and the entry of those locals into political activities and coalitions on the community level. It also means community action and organization among the millions of low-paid workers presently outside the labor movement.

The crucial importance of community work can be grasped only if one understands the sorts of ideas the American poor have about themselves. They operate with a kind of split consciousness. On the one hand, poor people know they are victimized from every direction. The facts of life always break through to expose the distance between American ideals and personal realities. This kind of knowledge, however, is kept undeveloped and unused because of another knowledge imposed on the poor, a keen sense of dependence on the oppressor. This is the source of that universal fear which leads poor people to act and even to think subserviently. Seeing themselves to blame for their situation, they rule out the possibility that they might be qualified to govern themselves and their own organizations. Besides fear, it is their sense of inadequacy and embarrassment which destroys the possibility of revolt. At the same time this set of contradictory feelings results in indirect forms of protest all the time: styles of dress and language, withdrawal from political life, defiance of the boss's or the welfare worker's rules and regulations.

There can be no poor people's movement in any form unless the poor can overcome their fear and embarrassment. I think the release comes from a certain kind of organizing which tries to make people understand their own worth and dignity. This work depends on the existence of "material issues" as a talking and organizing point—high rents, voting rights, unpaved roads, and so on—but it moves from there into the ways such issues are related to personal life. The organizer spends hours and hours in the community, listening to people, drawing out their own ideas, rejecting their tendency to depend on him for solutions. Meetings are organized at which people with no "connections" can be given a chance to talk and work out problems together—usually for the first time. All this means fostering in *everyone* that sense of decision-making power which American society works to destroy. Only in this way can a movement be built which the Establishment can neither buy off nor manage, a movement too vital ever to become a small clique of spokesmen.

An organizational form that suggests the style of such a movement is the "community union," involving working-class and poor people in local insurgency. Open and democratic, the community union offers a real alternative to the kind of participation permitted in civil rights groups, trade unions, and Democratic Party machines. It might take a variety of forms: block clubs, housing committees, youth groups, etc. The union's insistence on the relevance of "little people," as well as its position outside and against the normal channels, would create a rooted sense of independence among the members.

The problem of politics among the poor is severe. In the first place, their potential electoral power is low because of their location in gerrymandered political districts, their rapid movement from house to house, and the complicated and discriminatory electoral procedures in many cities. Beyond these problems lies the obvious and well-grounded cynicism of the poor about elections. Given all these conditions, it is barely conceivable that a poor person could be elected to an important political office. Even were this possible, it would be on a token basis, and the elected official would be under strong pressure to conform to the rules of the game. Thus the orthodox idea of politics is contradictory to building a movement. The Movement needs to discover a politics of its own. This might be done by electing people who will see their office as a community organizing tool, letting community people participate directly in decisions about how the office should be used. This experiment is being made in Atlanta where a SNCC field secretary, Julian Bond, was elected in June 1965 to the state legislature. What might be done is to contest the basic class and racial injustices of American politics, demanding that poverty areas be granted political representation, or running freedom elections to dramatize the lack of representation for the boxed-in poor. This sort of thing would probably mobilize more poor people than orthodox electoral activity. The mobilization would be "practical" from the standpoint of getting modest reforms; more importantly, it would point toward the need to rearrange American political institutions to fit the needs of excluded people.

2. A Student Movement

If poor people are in The Movement because they have nothing to gain in the status system, students are in it because, in a sense, they have gained too much. Most of the active student radicals today come from middle- to upper-middle-class professional homes. They were born with status and affluence as facts of life, not goals to be striven for. In their upbringing, their parents stressed the right of children to question and make judgments, producing perhaps the first generation of young people both affluent and independent of mind. And then these students so often encountered social institutions that denied them their independence and betrayed the democratic ideals they were taught.

They saw that men of learning were careerists; that school administrators and ministers almost never discussed the realities the students lived with; that even their parents were not true to the ideals they taught the young.

It was against this background of tension that young people became concerned in the early sixties about war, racism, and inequality. By now the empty nature of existing vocational alternatives has pushed several hundreds of these students into community organizing. Working in poor communities is a concrete task in which the split between job and values can be healed. It is also a position from which to expose the whole structure of pretense, status, and glitter that masks the country's real human problems. And, finally, it is a way to find people who want to change the country, and possibly can do so.

When a student comes into a community there are countless obstacles in his way. He is an outsider, he is overeducated, he has nothing concrete to offer people, and often he is white in a Negro ghetto. At the same time, however, he brings something with him: the very presence of students suggests to the poor that their more activist notions may be right after all. The student alone can say, "Look, I come from the world that says you are not qualified, and I know that is a lie. I come to you because you can teach me as much as I can teach you." Students can also make the poverty problem visible and threatening because they create resources previously unimaginable. Parents and universities become energized; money can be raised; contacts can be set up with other people's organizations around the country. Finally, students and poor people make each other feel real. What has flowed from this connection is most of the vitality of the civil rights and anti-poverty movements over the past five years.

Now it appears that students are finding ways to organize effectively around other problems too: university reform and peace. The Berkeley "uprising" and the April March of 20,000 against the war in Vietnam were major departures from the inconsequential student politics of the old days. On many campuses students are beginning to form unions of their own, as well as independent seminars pointed toward the eventual organization of a "free university." In addition, they are beginning to mobilize community action against the Vietnamese war—thereby encountering their friends already at work among the poor. These efforts may thread the several protest movements in the country into a grass-roots coalition.

3. Middle-Class Insurgents

A centralized and commercial society wastes the talents and energies of millions of individuals. Some of these are women who are excluded from male-dominated vocations. Some are people with human values who cannot assert them effectively within organizations attached to the Cold War consensus. Some were politically active in the thirties but faded away when popular movements declined. Some are part of the postwar generation that missed the experience of a radical movement altogether, and who are lodged uncomfortably in publishing houses, universities, and labor bureaucracies.

The new movements are opening great possibilities for participation by such middle-class people. Their activity often includes vital financial support, but it can and does go further. Insurgency within American institutions is spreading: professors fighting their administrations, lawyers against the bar association, welfare workers against the political machine, muckrakers against the press establishments. This insurgency is bound to increase as the new generation of student activists graduates into the professions. And it is an insurgency which needs a movement of poor people, insistently demanding new social purposes from the professionals.

To summarize: The Movement is a community of insurgents sharing the same radical values and identity, seeking an independent base of power wherever they are. It aims at a transformation of society led by the most excluded and "unqualified" people. Primarily, this means building institutions outside the established order which seek to become the genuine institutions of the total society. Community unions, freedom schools, experimental universities, community-formed police review boards, people's own anti-poverty organizations fighting for federal money, independent union locals—all can be "practical" pressure points from which to launch reform in the conventional institutions while at the same time maintaining a separate base and pointing toward a new system. Ultimately this Movement might lead to a Continental Congress called by all the people who feel excluded from the higher circles of decision making in the country. This Congress might even become a kind of second government, receiving taxes from its supporters, establishing contact with other nations, holding debates on American foreign and domestic policy, dramatizing the plight of all groups that suffer from the American system.

If it is hard to imagine this kind of revolutionary process in the United States, it might be because no previous model of revolution seems appropriate to this most bloated and flexible of the advanced societies. There may be no way to change this country. At least there is no way we can bank on. Both technological change and social reform seem to rationalize the power of the system to drain the heart of protest. The Movement at least suggests that we bank on our own consciousness, what there is of our own humanity, and begin to work.

Americanism versus Amorality

Robert Welch

The last reading condemned the immorality of America. Robert
Welch, founder of the John Birch Society, writes of the amorality
of those who support or condone communist ideas. Welch
proposes a positive Americanism based on individual freedom, less
government, and more personal responsibility. He analyzes the
battle against government power, collectivism, and loss of spiritual
faith.

Robert Welch, widely known as the founder and primary
intellect of the John Birch Society, has written and lectured on the
power seeking of communism. In renouncing the atheism of
communist ideology, Birch concedes some defects in Christianity
but proposes a broader faith in its place. He invokes humanitarianism
as a goal and argues that communist power practice has been
anti-humanitarian. The definitions Welch provides for ideologies
labeled as communist and americanist (sic) show the power
dimensions of each.

Education as a social institution is responsive to both
individual and collective pressures. If Welch's Americanism becomes
the dominant value in political and economic life, serious questions
are raised about compulsory schooling, required texts and courses,
and public taxation to support schools. These same questions,
interestingly, are raised by new left advocates and anarchists.
Perhaps labels are not meaningful devices for separating people,
yet Welch uses them in this article and teachers utilize them in
classroom activities.

Now, gentlemen, in looking thoroughly and realistically at the danger
to everything we have inherited, spiritual as well as material, and at
the cause of that danger, we come to the second of the fundamental
reasons for deep and basic anxiety. And putting that matter bluntly at
once, the reason is simply loss of faith. Not just loss of faith in God

Reprinted by permission of the publisher. *The Blue Book of the John
Birch Society*, Robert Welch, Belmont, Mass., 1961.

and all his works but loss of faith in man and his works too, in his reasons for existence, in his purposes, and in his hopes.

Now I know that there are still millions of devout Catholics, fundamentalist Protestants, and faithful Jews in this country who still believe unquestioningly in the divine truths and powers which their Bibles reveal to them, and whose conduct and relations with their fellow men are guided strictly by the precepts of their religious faith— or who at least feel that they have sinned whenever they have transgressed such precepts as understood by their consciences. I have hundreds of good friends in those categories, including some in this room.

Let us all thank whatever God we severally worship that there is so large a remnant of the really true believers still left. We honor them. We need their steadying adherence to the rock of reverence, and their aspiration of unwavering obedience to ancient and divine commandments. We desperately need their unshakable confidence in absolutes, in eternal principles and truths, in a world of increasing relativity and transitoriness in all things. We admire them. In fact, as will become more clear tomorrow, the young man I admire most of all of those America has produced was a fundamentalist Baptist missionary named John Birch. My own obsession with this fight against the increasing forces of evil in the world, which—as already explained—has caused me to give up business career and income and any prospect of ever having any peace or leisure again during my lifetime, is due in large part to my admiration for John Birch; to my feeling that I simply had to pick up and carry, to the utmost of my ability and energy, the torch of a humane righteousness which he was carrying so well and so faithfully when the Communists struck him down.

We must not only know the truth, but face the truth, if it is to set us free or to keep us so. And the fundamental truth of our times, gentlemen, as distinguished from the fundamentalist truth, is just this. Except for the diminishing number of fundamentalists of all religions, and the increasing but still comparatively small percentage of the human race which has fervently accepted Communism as a religion, all faith has been replaced, or is rapidly being replaced, by a pragmatic opportunism with hedonistic aims. And what a fall that is for a race which can boast of once having listened to a St. Augustine, a St. Francis of Assisi, a John Milton, or an Alfred Tennyson. The further and more specific manifestation of that fundamental truth is that *in Western Europe and America today we are living in a spiritual vacuum*, exactly as were the Romans after they had lost any real faith in their pagan gods and before the rise of Christianity.

In the middle of the nineteenth century Lord Tennyson, with one of the greatest and most rational minds, at the very apex of the enlightenment achieved by the Western European Civilization, could still write with complete conviction:

> Our little systems have their day;
>   They have their day and cease to be:
>   They are but broken lights of thee,
> And Thou, O Lord, art more than they.

Compare that with the acutely cynical flippancy of a current gem, which goes something as follows:

> A life force afflicted with doubt,
> As to what its own being was about,
>   Said: "The truth I can't find,
>   But I'm creating a mind,
> Which may be able to figure it out.

And in that comparison you can see the magnitude of our loss, as to a base for our morals, our purposes, and our aspirations.

For the next part of the truth we must face is that for the past several hundred years our morality, in Europe and America, was tied to a belief in the rewards and punishments delineated by Christian dogma; to the accepted commandments of a very real and very majestic deity; and to the desire of the true believer to become worthy of the love of an omniscient living God. The reality and earnestness of Christian faith was the foundation of our ethics, and the substance of our consciences. When Voltaire said that if God did not exist we should have to invent him, it was a very blasphemous remark but a very penetrating one, as to the dependence at that time of morals, humanitarianism, and purposes on what has since come to be called the anthropomorphic conception—that is, a God in whose image man himself was created.

Through many centuries Christianity, despite all of its splits and schisms, supplied the fabric of morality for the whole Western World—through its threats of punishments, promises of rewards, and the humanizing effect of its proffered love by and for a Divine Father. But despite all the billions of words that have been written to the contrary, that fabric is now pierced and torn and weakened beyond needed dependability. For a vast majority of those who proclaim themselves Christians today, and attend church services, do not really and literally believe in either the punishments, the rewards, or even in the physical and biological existence of a Divine Father with any interest in their personal lives and actions. The momentum of a former belief, and the customs which grew out of it, still have great value. But the fabric is worn too thin to have its old effectiveness.

Now please do not jump to any conclusions that I want to see Christianity denied, discarded, or even further weakened, in the slightest. Exactly the opposite is true, as I hope to make clear when we come back to this subject from the constructive side tomorrow. But I am not in favor of trying to reimpose all or any of the strands of a fundamentalist faith on those whose reason, whether right or wrong, has honestly told them that we cannot know such positive things about the Unknowable. For that would be like trying to tie the waves of the ocean together with ropes, or to confine them with fishing nets.

But I believe there is a broader and more encompassing faith to which we can all subscribe, without any of us doing the slightest violation to the more specific doctrines of his own creed or altars of his own devotion. And I believe it is an ennobling conception, equally acceptable to the most fundamentalist Christian or the most rationalistic idealist, because its whole purport is to strengthen and synthesize the ennobling characteristics of each man and the ennobling impulses of his own personal religion. It is a conception which the Baptist John Birch, the Catholic Hilaire Belloc, and the agnostic Thomas Jefferson would alike have welcomed. And in the short time we can give to so mighty a subject, in this particular program, I shall return to it tomorrow to the extent necessary for its place in my immediate proposals. What I am trying to do now is merely to make a realistic appraisal of our weaknesses, because without doing so we can only dissipate our remaining strength in trying to build fortifications and temples on sinking mud or shifting sand.

For not only is this loss of reinforcing faith in the cement of our morals a weakness in itself of immense significance, but like all of our weaknesses it has been pounced upon by the Communists, and used and made worse by them with great skill and determination for their own purposes. When an individual American, or any other human being, sees himself as no longer responsible to a Divine Being, but as merely a living accident, not connected in any way with cosmological purpose, it becomes far easier for him to make his decisions about his own life and actions entirely on the basis of his temporal comforts and the earthly desires of his own personality. If he is the kind of man that wants financial success for the ease, or leisure and travel, or the prestige which it supposedly brings (and sometimes does), he is not going to buck Communist pressures in any way that will endanger that success or handicap his progress. If he is imbued with ambition for power, he is more readily inclined to get on the Communist bandwagon, if that seems to be the surest *road* to power (as it certainly does to a great many Americans today). The Communists are able to use this lack of moral stamina among their enemies in a thousand ways to make their own progress easier and the conquest of those enemies more rapid.

The most terrible result of this collapse of the rock of faith on which our morality was built is the rise of the amoral man—of which the usual Communist himself is the most illustrative example. For an amoral man, like Stalin, is infinitely worse, from the point of view of a humanitarian civilization, than an immoral one like Hitler. An immoral man may lie, steal, and murder; the worst of them even without any seeming limit or hesitation. But it hurts his conscience. He is, at least potentially, susceptible to humanitarian or moral considerations, to some extent, and if they are presented cogently enough to him. There is even the possibility always that he may sometime, or in some ways, repent and make what amends he can for his crimes.

An amoral man, however, has simply wiped out his conscience, along with any reason for its existence. He is not immoral, even when performing coldblooded mass murders, because to him there is no such thing as either morality or immorality. There is only the pragmatic consideration of the advantages or disadvantages to himself, for his own personal desires or plans, in any action—whether it be the building of a monument or the murder of his wife. And these amoral men, the products of a materialistic and sophomoric disillusionment, who have not yet gone on in their thinking to deeper and more permanent truths, now stalk in our midst in greater numbers than ever before in history. Such men, among the Communists, and they are plentiful and highly placed, have no real dedication even to Communism. They regard it merely as an expedient means to satisfy their personal ambitions more nearly than would any other star to which they might hitch their wagons.

But on our own side of the fence, among the millions who either are, or pretend to be, non-Communists, the amoral man, who has no slightest inner concern with right or wrong, is one of the greatest causes of our constant retreat, and one of the greatest dangers to our survival. And he doesn't wear any label. He usually lives up to the appearance of excellent morals, because it is expedient for his purposes, and you will usually find him in church on Sunday morning, maybe even a Catholic church. But as a member of the United States Senate, running for the presidency, and smart enough to know the strong Communist support behind-the-scenes which he will have to get in order to have any chance of being nominated in 1960, such an amoral man can do a tremendous amount of ball-carrying on behalf of the Communist aims here in the United States; and he can do an almost equal amount of damage to anti-Communist morale in other parts of the world, by his well-publicized speeches against Chiang Kai-shek or in favor of the Algerian rebels. Or an amoral man, as the head of a great so-called Republic, may have no slightest scruples or concern about its fate or the fate of other nations, in the face of Communist conquest and of the cruel tyranny of their rule. And any similarity of characters in this story to any living persons is not coincidental.

. . . As important and absolutely vital as our stopping the Communists has become, and as much as our loss of moral fibre is now deliberately made more rapid and more damaging by the Communists for their present and future purposes, even throwing the Communists completely out of the picture would not stop the fatal deterioration in our sense of values which is now in process. Besides the short-term job of eliminating the Communist danger—and Herculean as that job may be, it has to be done in a short term or it can't be done at all—we have the equally important longer-range job of ending this mass psychological flight towards amorality; and of restoring convincing reasons for men once again to strive to live up to moral and humanitarian ideals. Otherwise, there is no chance of saving our Christian-style civilization from self-destruction; and it will merely go down to chaos, and the ultimate serfdom of the weak under the strong, more lingeringly than if it is destroyed and its once-free members are enslaved by the Communists.

But whereas stopping the disease of collectivism is a matter of honest diagnosis and drastic surgery, this equally gigantic problem is one of restoration rather than of removal. We have to find something to live for, gentlemen, that is greater than ourselves, or we surely fall back from the semi-civilized level of existence, which man has laboriously achieved, into a moral jungle and its inevitably concomitant intellectual darkness. I tried to put the picture of where we are heading in a sonnet to my good friend Alfred Noyes about a year ago—and fortunately a few months before he died. Because it summarizes, as concisely and as expressively as I know how, the outlook I have been trying to define, I am asking your leave to read it at this point.

To Alfred Noyes

As after Rome, now once again the drapes
  Of ignorance and bigotry and lust
  May close upon the scene. Insentient dust
Will bury the forgotten stage. And apes
Who know not man, his glory and his dreams,
  His wish to be more worthy of his God,
  Will stalk the earth and wield the brutal rod,

And stamp upon each tiny light that gleams.
Amid the dull collective monotone
  Of universal serfdom will be lost
The memory of song and singer. Prone
  And helpless, soon, upon the rubbish tossed,
Will die the Muse. Let us rejoice to own
  This one great poet more before the holocaust.

And it is not only the muse of poetry that will die of abuse and neglect, if man's loss of faith in there being anything in the universe worth while except his appetites is permitted to continue. But we do not have to let it continue. Before our very eyes lie all the incentives man needs to set him back on the road of striving towards moral perfection, true intellectual greatness, civilized relationships, and eternal hope for a still better and greater future, which seemed to him to be such natural goals a hundred years ago. Making those incentives understood, and giving contemporary man a renewed faith in himself, in his destiny, and in a still greater God than was recognized and worshipped by his ancestors, is a task for myriads of dedicated individuals over generations of time. We can only contribute all we are able to its proper beginning. But without such a goal and purpose all of our efforts simply to stop Communism, or to destroy an ephemeral conspiracy of gangsters, are not only doomed to failure. Even if successful they would but postpone the days of darkness for our children, for their children, and for a race of men that once knew the light.

We shall return to the constructive side of this need and this undertaking in the morning.

The greatest enemy of man is, and always has been, government. And the larger, the more extensive that government, the greater the enemy.

Now clearly the United States which, throughout its early centuries, was the greatest beneficiary from the scarcity of government that the world has ever known, should not only return to the right course for its own further growth in prosperity, freedom, and happiness, but should set an example again for the whole world. In fact, the world *americanist*, with a small *a*, should be made, and become understood, as the very antithesis of socialism, and communism with a little *c*. For the *communist*—using the word now with a little *c* to denote a theoretician rather than a member of the conspiracy—the communist believes that a collectivist society should swallow up all individuals, make their lives and their energies completely subservient to the needs and the purposes of the collectivist state; and that any means are permissible to achieve this end. The true *americanist* believes that the individual should retain the freedom to make his own bargain with life, and the responsibility for the results of that bargain; and that means are as important as ends in the civilized social order which he desires. The same two words, with initial capitals, Communists and Americanists, should merely denote the aggressive fighters for these two mutually exclusive philosophies.

But Americanism, as either a phrase or a force on the contemporary world scene, has been eroded into something negative and defeatist. It has come to represent merely a delaying action against the victorious march of its enemy, collectivism. The air is full of clarion calls to Americans to organize, in order better to fight against socialism, communism, or some vanguard of their forces.

Twice each day the mail brings to my desk pleas for me to contribute money, or effort, or moral support, or all three, to some group which is battling to hold back some particular advance of collectivist storm troops. Even those organizations or activities which bear a positive label are motivated by negative thinking. An association *for* the Bricker Amendment is, in reality, an association *against* the intervention of international socialist forces in the control of our domestic lives.

Americanism has become primarily a denial of something else, rather than an assertion of itself. And there are many of us who think that this should be true no longer. We think that Americanism should again come to mean, and to be, a positive, forward-looking philosophy; a design and example of social organization which boldly and confidently offers leadership along the one hard but sure road to a better world.

It is not just in the United States, of course, that all the aggressiveness is on the side of the socialist–communist allies. In the world-wide ideological struggle which divides mankind today, we conservatives fight always on the defensive. The very name by which we identify ourselves defines our objective. It is to conserve as much as we can, out of all we have inherited that is worth while, from the encroachments and destructiveness of this advancing collectivism. We build no more icons to freedom; we merely try to fend off the iconoclast.

Such has been the pattern during the whole first half of the twentieth century. From the bright plateaux of individual freedom and individual responsibility, which man had precariously attained, there has been a steady falling back toward the dark valleys of dependence and serfdom. But this ignominious retreat has been just as true of Americans, the heirs of a strong new society, as of the tired residual legatees of an old and enfeebled European civilization. During this long and forced retreat we have fought only a rearguard and sometimes delaying action. We have never been rallied to counterattack, to break through the enemy or rout him, and to climb again beyond our highest previous gains. And in the unending skirmishes, to hold as much as possible of the ground currently occupied, we have lost all sight of the higher tablelands of freedom which once were our recognized goals. I for one, and many others like me, are no longer willing to consider only when to retreat and how far. There is a braver and a wiser course.

If we heirs of all the ages are to find a turning point in this rapid and sometimes stampeding descent, in which we are abandoning instead of improving our inheritance; if the last half of the twentieth century is to see the curve that measures individual dignity turn upward; if the men who really wish to be free and self-reliant are to begin climbing back up the mountainside; then the goal must be known, and the purpose of aggressive offense must replace defensive defeatism as the banner under which we march. It is fatal to be merely against losing ground, for then there is no way to go but back. We have to be for something; we must know what that something is; and we must believe it is worth a fight to obtain. Reduced to its simplest and broadest terms, that something is less government and more responsibility. For both less government and more responsibility bring increasing opportunities for human happiness.

Due to the tremendous momentum given us by our hardworking, ambitious, and individualistic forefathers, our nation is still by far the most dynamic in the world in its productive processes, and in its influences on the whole world's standard of living. We must again become equally dynamic in our *spiritual* influence; in our positive leadership and example to provide a governmental environment in which individual man can make the most of his life in whatever way *he*—and not his government—wishes to use it.

There are many stages of welfarism, socialism, and collectivism in general, but communism is the ultimate state of them all, and they all lead inevitably in that direction. In this final stage, communism, you have a society in which class distinctions are greater than in any other, but where position in these classes is determined solely by demagogic political skill and ruthless cunning. You have a society in which all those traits which have helped to make man civilized, and which our multiple faiths have classified as virtues, are now discarded as vices—while exactly their opposites are glorified. And you have a society in which every *fault* of government that we have discussed above is held to be a *benefit* and a desirable part of the framework of life.

But there is an exactly opposite direction. It leads toward a society in which brotherhood and kindliness and tolerance and honesty and self-reliance and the integrity of the human personality are considered virtues; a society which venerates those traits exactly because they have helped the human animal to achieve some degree of humanitarian civilization, and are the common denominators of all our great religions. This direction leads toward a governmental environment for human life founded on the basis of long experience with government; on experience which shows government to be a necessary evil, but a continuous brake on all progress and the ultimate enemy of all freedom. It is the forward direction, the upward direction—and americanism, I hope, shall become its name.

The Declaration of Independence

Thomas Jefferson, et al.

As one of the most famous documents in American history, the Declaration of Independence was not only a radical statement of beliefs but also a striking position on the distribution of power. Notions of equality, consent of the governed, and rightness in revolution appear as contemporary issues despite the 1776 date of publication.

Adoption of the Declaration of Independence by delegates to the Second Continental Congress, July 4, 1776, followed a resolution stating that the colonies are "free and independent states, absolved from all allegiance to the British Crown. . . ." A committee, including Jefferson, John Adams, Benjamin Franklin, Roger Sherman, and Robert Livingston, was formed to draft a statement of reasons for the separation. Jefferson was the primary draftsman of this declaration, with modifications by others on the committee and a signature, at its adoption, by John Hancock, who added, "There, I guess King George will be able to read that." These founding fathers, now revered by the national establishment, were part of a radical movement that spanned years of ideas, numbers of unknown radical writers, and such now distinguished names as Thomas Gage, Patrick Henry, and Thomas Paine. Surely the British and the Tories in America viewed the group with alarm and suspicion at least as strong as contemporary radical groups are viewed.

Schooling throughout the world was elitistic and highly selective on socio-economic grounds during this revolutionary period. Although Jefferson advocated more open access to schooling, and Franklin developed the academy in the mid-1700s to provide opportunities for secondary education for poor but talented youth, there was little that could be called mass education and very limited public support. This was especially true in Europe where schools were utilized to ensure class and caste distinctions. The social and political rumblings that produced the Declaration of Independence and the American Revolution also provided new and radical ideas for education. The consistency between democracy and mass education seems self-evident now even though equality of opportunity in society and education has not yet been achieved. The quality of both democracy and mass education may be improved by reconsideration of their purposes and practices.

When in the Course of human events, it becomes necessary for one people to dissolve the political bands which have connected them with another, and to assume among the powers of the earth, the separate and equal station to which the Laws of Nature and of Nature's God entitle them, a decent respect to the opinions of mankind requires that they should declare the causes which impel them to the separation. We hold these truths to be self-evident, that all men are created equal, that they are endowed by their Creator with certain unalienable Rights, that among these are Life, Liberty and the pursuit of Happiness. That to secure these rights, Governments are instituted among Men, deriving their just powers from the consent of the governed, That whenever any Form of Government becomes destructive of these ends it is the Right of the People to alter or to abolish it, and to institute new Government, laying its foundation on such principles and organizing its powers in such form, as to them shall seem most likely to effect their Safety and Happiness. Prudence, indeed, will dictate that Governments long established should not be changed for light and transient causes; and accordingly all experience hath shewn, that mankind are more disposed to suffer, while evils are sufferable, than to right themselves by abolishing the forms to which they are accustomed. But when a long train of abuses and usurpations, pursuing invariably the same Object evinces a design to reduce them under absolute Despotism, it is their right, it is their duty, to throw off such Government, and to provide new Guards for their future security. Such has been the patient sufferance of these Colonies; and such is now the necessity which constrains them to alter their former Systems of Government. The history of the present King of Great Britain is a history of repeated injuries and usurpations, all having in direct object the establishment of an absolute Tyranny over these States. To prove this, let Facts be submitted to a candid world. He has refused his Assent to Laws, the most wholesome and necessary for the public good. He has forbidden his Governors to pass Laws of immediate and pressing importance, unless suspended in their operation till his Assent should be obtained; and when so suspended, he has utterly neglected to attend to them. He has refused to pass other Laws for the accommodation of large districts of people, unless those people would relinquish the right of Representation in the Legislature, a right inestimable to them and formidable to tyrants only. He has called together legislative bodies at places unusual, uncomfortable, and distant from the depository of their public Records, for the sole purpose of fatiguing them into compliance with his measures. He has dissolved Representative Houses repeatedly, for opposing with manly firmness his invasions on the rights of the people. He has refused for a long time, after such dissolutions, to cause others to be elected; whereby the Legislative powers, incapable of Annihilation, have returned to the People at large for their exercise; the State remaining in the mean time exposed to all the dangers of invasion from without, and convulsions within. He has endeavoured to prevent the population of these States; for that purpose obstructing the Laws for Naturalization of Foreigners; refusing to pass others to encourage their migrations hither, and raising the conditions of new Appropriations of Lands. He has obstructed the Administration of Justice, by refusing his Assent to Laws for establishing Judiciary powers. He has made Judges dependent on his Will alone, for the tenure of their offices, and the amount and payment of their salaries. He has erected a multitude of New Offices, and sent hither swarms of Officers to harrass our people, and eat out their substance. He has kept among us, in times of peace, standing Armies without the Consent of our legislatures. He has affected to render the Military independent of and superior to the Civil power. He has combined with others to subject us to a jurisdiction foreign to our constitution, and unacknowledged by our laws; giving his Assent to their Acts of pretended Legislation: For Quartering large bodies of armed troops among us: For protecting them, by a mock Trial, from punishment for any Murders which they should commit on the Inhabitants of these States: For cutting off our Trade with all parts of the world: For imposing Taxes on us without our Consent: For depriving us in many cases of the benefits of Trial by Jury: For transporting us beyond Seas to be tried for pretended offences: For abolishing the free System of English Laws in a neighbouring Province, establishing therein an Arbitrary government, and enlarging its Boundaries so as to render it at once an example and fit instrument for introducing the same absolute rule into these Colonies:

For taking away our Charters, abolishing our most valuable Laws, and altering fundamentally the Forms of our Governments: For suspending our own Legislatures, and declaring themselves invested with power to legislate for us in all cases whatsoever. He has abdicated Government here, by declaring us out of his Protection and waging War against us. He has plundered our seas, ravaged our Coasts, burnt our towns, and destroyed the Lives of our people. He is at this time transporting large Armies of foreign Mercenaries to compleat the works of death, desolation and tyranny, already begun with circumstances of Cruelty & perfidy scarcely paralleled in the most barbarous ages, and totally unworthy of the Head of a civilized nation. He has constrained our fellow Citizens taken Captive on the high Seas to bear Arms against their Country, to become the executioners of their friends and Brethren, or to fall themselves by their Hands. He has excited domestic insurrections amongst us, and has endeavoured to bring on the inhabitants of our frontiers, the merciless Indian Savages, whose known rule of warfare, is an undistinguished destruction of all ages, sexes and conditions. In every stage of these Oppressions We have Petitioned for Redress in the most humble terms: Our repeated Petitions have been answered only by repeated injury. A Prince, whose character is thus marked by every act which may define a Tyrant, is unfit to be the ruler of a free people. Nor have We been wanting in attentions to our Brittish brethren. We have warned them from time to time of attempts by their legislature to extend an unwarrantable jurisdiction over us. We have reminded them of the circumstances of our emigration and settlement here. We have appealed to their native justice and magnanimity, and we have conjured them by the ties of our common kindred to disavow these usurpations, which, would inevitably interrupt our connections and correspondence. They too have been deaf to the voice of justice and of consanguinity. We must, therefore, acquiesce in the necessity, which denounces our Separation, and hold them, as we hold the rest of mankind, Enemies in War, in Peace Friends.

We, therefore, the Representatives of the united States of America, in General Congress, Assembled, appealing to the Supreme Judge of the world for the rectitude of our intentions, do, in the Name, and by Authority of the good People of these Colonies, solemnly publish and declare, That these United Colonies are, and of Right ought to be Free and Independent States; that they are Absolved from all Allegiance to the British Crown, and that all political connection between them and the State of Great Britain, is and ought to be totally dissolved; and that as Free and Independent States, they have full Power to levy War, conclude Peace, contract Alliances, establish Commerce, and to do all other Acts and Things which Independent States may of right do. And for the support of this Declaration, with a firm reliance on the protection of divine Providence, we mutually pledge to each other our Lives, our Fortunes and our sacred Honor.

John Hancock

Button Gwinnett	Thos. Nelson jr.	Richd. Stockton
Lyman Hall	Francis Lightfoot Lee	Jno Witherspoon
Geo Walton.	Carter Braxton	Fras. Hopkinson
Wm. Hooper	Robt. Morris	John Hart
Joseph Hewes,	Benjamin Rush	Abra Clark
John Penn	Benja. Franklin	Josiah Bartlett
Edward Rutledge.	John Morton	Wm: Whipple
Thos. Heyward Junr.	Geo Clymer	Saml. Adams
Thomas Lynch Junr.	Jas. Smith.	John Adams
Arthur Middleton	Geo. Taylor	Robt. Treat Paine
Samuel Chase	James Wilson	Elbridge Gerry
Wm. Paca	Geo. Ross	Step. Hopkins
Thos. Stone	Cæsar Rodney	William Ellery
Charles Carroll of	Geo Read	Roger Sherman
Carrollton	Tho M:Kean	Saml. Huntington
George Wythe	Wm. Floyd	Wm. Williams
Richard Henry Lee	Phil. Livingston	Oliver Wolcott
Th: Jefferson	Frans. Lewis	Matthew Thornton
Benja. Harrison	Lewis Morris	

Anarchy

Rudolf Rocker

One of the systems of political thought which has historically been considered radical in America is anarchy. Often anarchy is mistakenly equated with bombings, and seldom is a thoughtful statement of rationale for anarchy presented. Rudolf Rocker, a

Reprinted by permission of the publisher. "Anarchism and Anarcho-Syndicalism" by Rudolf Rocker in *European Ideologies: A Survey of Twentieth Century Ideas*, edited by Feliks Gross, N.Y. Philosophical Library, 1961.

German bookbinder and author, lived in France, England, and the United States. He died in 1958 as one of the most prominent writers on the theory of anarchy. The following essay presents anarchy as an ideology opposed to all political and social institutions which are compulsory or nonvoluntary. The redistribution of social and economic power and its relationship to a fuller sense of human growth is strongly stated.

Robert Welch's propositions on individualism and collectivism appear earlier in this chapter. Anarchy represents an ultimate form of individualism, while the thesis of non-government which anarchy advocates is contained in the theories of communism. In all three—Welch's americanism, anarchy, and theoretical communism—the government is the culprit. Education systems are mainly governmental agencies in America. Public education is the dominant form for schooling in this society. The form of schooling in an entirely individualistic, anarchistic society is difficult to imagine.

Much of the current antagonism toward public education as presented by writers like Friedenberg, Illich, Goodman, Holt, Kozol, and others reflects the values of anarchism as an alternative to compulsory forms of education. Further, the Free School Movement and many of the highly critical articles on education in the underground press represent more direct expressions of the counter-culture's involvement with the values of an anarchistic model.

Anarchism is a definite intellectual current of social thought, whose adherents advocate the abolition of economic monopolies and of all political and social coercive institutions within society. In place of the capitalist economic order, anarchists would have a free association of all productive forces based upon co-operative labor, which would have for its sole purpose the satisfying of the necessary requirements of every member of society. In place of the present national states with their lifeless machinery of political and bureaucratic institutions, anarchists desire a federation of free communities that shall be bound to one another by their common economic and social interests and arrange their affairs by mutual agreement and free contract.

Anyone who studies profoundly the economic and political development of the present social system will recognize that these objectives do not spring from the utopian ideas of a few imaginative innovators, but that they are the logical outcome of a thorough examination of existing social maladjustments, which, with every new phase of the present social conditions, manifest themselves more plainly and more unwholesomely. Modern monopoly–capitalism and the totalitarian state are merely the last stages in a development which could culminate in no other end.

The portentous development of our present economic system, leading to a mighty accumulation of social wealth in the hands of privileged minorities and to a constant repression of the great masses of the people, prepared the way for the present political and social reaction and befriended it in every way. It sacrificed the general interests of human society to the private interests of individuals, and thus systematically undermined a true relationship between men. People forgot that industry is not an end in itself, but should be only a means to insure to man his material subsistence and to make accessible to him the blessings of a higher intellectual culture. Where industry is everything, where labor loses its ethical importance and man is nothing, there begins the realm of ruthless economic despotism, whose workings are no less disastrous than those of any political despotism. The two mutually augment one another; they are fed from the same source.

Our modern social system has internally split the social organism of every country into hostile classes, and externally it has broken up the common cultural circle into hostile nations; both classes and nations confront one another with open antagonism, and by their ceaseless warfare keep the communal social life in continual convulsions. Two world wars within half a century and their terrible after effects, and the constant danger of new wars, which today dominates all peoples, are only the logical consequences of this unendurable condition which can only lead to further universal catastrophes. The mere fact that most states are obliged today to spend the better part of their annual income for so-called national defense and the liquidation of old war debts is proof of the untenability of the present status; it should make clear to everybody that the alleged protection that the state affords the individual is certainly purchased too dearly.

The ever-growing power of a soulless political bureaucracy that supervises and safeguards the life of man from the cradle to the grave is putting ever-greater obstacles in the way of cooperation among human beings. A system that in every act of its life sacrifices the welfare of large sections of the people, of whole nations, to the selfish lust for power and the economic interests of small minorities must necessarily dissolve the social ties and lead to a constant war of each against all. This system has merely been the pacemaker for the great intellectual and social reaction that finds its expression today in modern fascism and the idea of the totalitarian State, far surpassing the obsession for power of the absolute monarchy of past centuries and seeking to bring every sphere of human activity under the control of the State. "All for the State; all through the State; nothing without the State!"

became the *leitmotif* of a new political theology. As in various systems of ecclesiastical theology God is everything and man nothing, so for this modern political creed the State is everything and the citizen nothing. And just as the words the *"will of God"* were used to justify the will of privileged castes, so today there hides behind the *will of the State* only the selfish interests of those who feel called upon to interpret this will in their own sense and to force it upon the people.

In modern anarchism we have the confluence of the two great currents that before and since the French Revolution have found such characteristic expression in the intellectual life of Europe: socialism and liberalism. Modern socialism developed when profound observers of social life came to see more and more clearly that political constitutions and changes in the form of government could never get to the root of the great problem that we call the "social question." Its supporters recognized that an equalizing of social and economic conditions for the benefit of all, despite the loveliest of theoretical assumptions, is not possible so long as people are separated into classes on the basis of their owning or not owning property, classes whose mere existence excludes in advance any thought of a genuine community. And so there developed the conviction that only by the elimination of economic monopolies and by common ownership of the means of production does a condition of social justice become feasible, a condition in which society shall become a real community, and human labor shall no longer serve the ends of exploitation but assure the well-being of everyone. But as soon as socialism began to assemble its forces and become a movement, there at once came to light certain differences of opinion due to the influence of the social environment in different countries. It is a fact that every political concept from theocracy to Caesarism and dictatorship have affected certain factions of the socialist movement.

Meanwhile, two other great currents in political thought had a decisive significance on the development of socialist ideas: liberalism, which had powerfully stimulated advanced minds in the Anglo-Saxon countries, Holland and Spain in particular, and Democracy in the sense, to which Rousseau gave expression in his *Social Contract*, and which found its most influential representatives in the leaders of French Jacobinism. While liberalism in its social theories started off from the individual and wished to limit the State's activities to a minimum, democracy took its stand on an abstract collective concept, Rousseau's *general will*, which it sought to fix in the national state. Liberalism and democracy were preeminently political concepts, and since most of the original adherents of both did scarcely consider the economic conditions of society, the further development of these conditions could not be practically reconciled with the original principles of democracy, and still less with those of liberalism. Democracy with its motto of *equality of all citizens before the law,* and liberalism with its *right of man over his own person,* both were wrecked on the realities of capitalist economy. As long as millions of human beings in every country have to sell their labor to a small minority of owners, and sink into the most wretched misery if they can find no buyers, the so-called equality before the law remains merely a pious fraud, since the laws are made by those who find themselves in possession of the social wealth. But in the same way there can be no talk of a right over one's own person, for that right ends when one is compelled to submit to the economic dictation of another if one does not want to starve.

In common with liberalism, anarchism represents the idea that the happiness and prosperity of the individual must be the standard in all social matters. And, in common with the great representatives of liberal thought, it has also the idea of limiting the functions of government to a minimum. Its adherents have followed this thought to its ultimate consequences, and wish to eliminate every institution of political power from the life of society. When Jefferson clothes the basic concept of liberalism in the words: "That government is best which governs least," then anarchists say with Thoreau: "That government is best which governs not at all."

In common with the founders of socialism, anarchists demand the abolition of economic monopoly in every form and shape and uphold common ownership of the soil and all other means of production, the use of which must be available to all without distinction; for personal and social freedom is conceivable only on the basis of equal economic conditions for everybody. Within the socialist movement itself the anarchists represent the viewpoint that the struggle against capitalism must be at the same time a struggle against all coercive institutions of political power, for in history economic exploitation has always gone hand in hand with political and social oppression. The exploitation of man by man and the domination of man over man are inseparable, and each is the condition of the other.

As long as a possessing and a nonpossessing group of human beings face one another in enmity within society, the State will be indispensible to the possessing minority for the protection of its privileges. When this condition of social injustice vanishes to give place to a higher order of things, which shall recognize no special rights and shall have as its basic assumption the community of social interests, government over men must yield the field to the administration of economic and social affairs, or, to speak with Saint-Simon: "The time will come when the art of governing men will disappear. A new art will take its place, the art of administering things." In this respect anarchism has to be regarded as a kind of voluntary socialism.

This disposes also of the theory maintained by Marx and his followers that the State, in the form of a proletarian dictatorship, is a necessary transitional stage to a classless society, in which the State, after the elimination of all class conflicts and then the classes themselves, will dissolve itself and vanish from the canvas. For this concept, which completely mistakes the real nature of the State and the significance in history of the factor of political power, is only the logical outcome of so-called economic materialism, which sees in all the phenomena of history merely the inevitable effects of the methods of production of the time. Under the influence of this theory people came to regard the different forms of the State and all other social institutions as a "juridical and political superstructure on the economic edifice" of society, and thought that they had found in it the key to every historic process. In reality every section of history affords us thousands of examples of the way in which the economic development of countries was set back for centuries by the State and its power policy.

Before the rise of the ecclesiastical monarchy, Spain, industrially, was the most advanced country in Europe and held the first place in economic production in almost every field. But a century after the triumph of the Christian monarchy most of its industries had disappeared; what was left of them survived only in the most wretched condition. In most industries they had reverted to the most primitive methods of production. Agriculture collapsed, canals and waterways fell into ruin, and vast stretches of the country were transformed into deserts. Princely absolutism in Europe, with its silly "economic ordinances" and "industrial legislation," which severely punished any deviation from the prescribed methods of production and permitted no new inventions, blocked industrial progress in European countries for centuries, and prevented its natural development. And even now after the horrible experiences of two world wars, the power policy of the larger national states proves to be the greatest obstacle to the reconstruction of European economy.

In Russia, however, where the so-called dictatorship of the proletariat has ripened into reality, the aspirations of a particular party for political power have prevented any truly socialistic reorganization of economic life and have forced the country into the slavery of a grinding State Capitalism. The proletarian dictatorship, which naïve souls believe is an inevitable transition stage to real socialism, has today grown into a frightful despotism and a new imperialism, which lags behind the tyranny of fascist states in nothing. The assertion that the State must continue to exist until society is no longer divided into hostile classes almost sounds, in the light of all historical experience, like a bad joke.

Every type of political power presupposes some particular form of human slavery, for the maintenance of which it is called into being. Just as outwardly, that is, in relation to other states, the State has to create certain artificial antagonisms in order to justify its existence, so also internally the cleavage of society into castes, ranks and classes is an essential condition of its continuance. The development of the Bolshevist bureaucracy in Russia under the alleged dictatorship of the proletariat—which has never been anything but the dictatorship of a small clique *over* the proletariat and the whole Russian people—is merely a new instance of an old historical experience that has repeated itself countless times. This new ruling class, which today is rapidly growing into a new aristocracy, is set apart from the great masses of the Russian peasants and workers just as clearly as are the privileged castes and classes in other countries from the mass of the people. And this situation becomes still more unbearable when a despotic State denies to the lower classes the right to complain of existing conditions, so that any protest is made at the risk of their lives.

But even a far greater degree of economic equality than that which exists in Russia would be no guarantee against political and social oppression. Economic equality alone is not social liberation. It is precisely this which all the schools of authoritarian socialism have never understood. In the prison, in the cloister, or in the barracks one finds a fairly high degree of economic equality, as all the inmates are provided with the same dwelling, the same food, the same uniform, and the same tasks. The ancient Inca state in Peru and the Jesuit state in Paraguay had brought equal economic provision for every inhabitant to a fixed system, but in spite of this the vilest despotism prevailed there, and the human being was merely the automation of a higher will on whose decisions he had not the slightest influence. It was not without reason that Proudhon saw in a "socialism" without freedom the worst form of slavery. The urge for social justice can only develop properly and be effective when it grows out of man's sense of freedom and responsibility, and is based upon it. In other words, *socialism will be free or it will not be at all*. In its recognition of this fact lies the genuine and profound justification of anarchism.

Institutions serve the same purpose in the life of society as physical organs do in plants and animals; they are the organs of the social body. Organs do not develop arbitrarily, but owe their origin to definite necessities of the physical and social environment. Changed conditions of life produce changed organs. But an organ always performs the function it was evolved to perform, or a related one. And it gradually disappears or becomes rudimentary as soon as its function is no longer necessary to the organism.

The same is true of social institutions. They, too, do not arise arbitrarily, but are called into being by special social needs to serve definite purposes. In this way the modern State was evolved, after economic privileges and class divisions associated with them had begun to make themselves more and more conspicuous in the framework of the old social order. The newly-arisen possessing classes had need of a political instrument of power to maintain their economic and social privileges over the masses of their own people, and to impose them from without on other groups of human beings. Thus arose the appropriate social conditions for the evolution of the modern State as the organ of political power for the forcible subjugation and oppression of the non-possessing classes. This task is the essential reason for its existence. Its external forms have altered in the course of its historical development, but its functions have always remained the same. They have even constantly broadened in just the measure in which its supporters have succeeded in making further fields of social activities subservient to their ends. And, just as the functions of a physical organ cannot be arbitrarily altered so that, for example, one cannot, at will, hear with one's eyes or see with one's ears, so also one cannot, at pleasure, transform an organ of social oppression into an instrument for the liberation of the oppressed.

Anarchism is no patent solution for all human problems, no Utopia of a perfect social order (as it has so often been called), since, on principle, it rejects all absolute schemes and concepts. It does not believe in any absolute truth, or in any definite final goals for human development, but in an unlimited perfectibility of social patterns and human living conditions, which are always straining after higher forms of expression, and to which, for this reason, one cannot assign any definite terminus nor set any fixed goal. The greatest evil of any form of power is just that it always tries to force the rich diversity of social life into definite forms and adjust it to particular norms. The stronger its supporters feel themselves, the more completely they succeed in bringing every field of social life into their service, the more crippling is their influence on the operation of all creative cultural forces, the more unwholesomely does it affect the intellectual and social development of power and a dire omen for our times, for it shows with frightful clarity to what a monstrosity Hobbes' *Leviathan* can be developed. It is the perfect triumph of the political machine over mind and body, the rationalization of human thought, feeling and behavior according to the established rules of the officials and, consequently, the end of all true intellectual culture.

Anarchism recognizes only the relative significance of ideas, institutions, and social conditions. It is, therefore not a fixed, self-enclosed social system, but rather a definite trend in the historical development of mankind, which, in contrast with the intellectual guardianship of all clerical and governmental institutions, strives for the free unhindered unfolding of all the individual and social forces in life. Even freedom is only a relative, not an absolute concept, since it tends constantly to broaden its scope and to affect wider circles in manifold ways. For the anarchist, freedom is not an abstract philosophical concept, but the vital concrete possibility for every human being to bring to full development all capacities and talents with which nature has endowed him, and turn them to social account. The less this natural development of man is interfered with by ecclesiastical or political guardianship, the more efficient and harmonious will human personality become, the more will it become the measure of the intellectual culture of the society in which it has grown. This is the reason that all great culture periods in history have been periods of political weakness, for political systems are always set upon the mechanizing and not the organic development of social forces. State and Culture are irreconcilable opposites. Nietzsche, who was not an anarchist, recognized this very clearly when he wrote:

> No one can finally spend more than he has. That holds good for individuals; it holds good for peoples. If one spends oneself for power, for higher politics, for husbandry, for commerce, parliamentarism, military interests—if one gives away that amount of reason, earnestness, will, self-mastery which constitutes one's real self for one thing—he will not have it for the other. Culture and the State—let no one be deceived about this—are antagonists: the *Culture State* is merely a modern idea. The one lives on the other, the one prospers at the expense of the other. All great periods of culture are periods of political decline. Whatever is great in a cultured sense is nonpolitical, is even antipolitical.

Where the influence of political power on the creative forces in society is reduced to a minimum, there culture thrives the best, for political rulership always strives for uniformity and tends to subject every aspect of social life to its guardianship. And, in this, it finds itself in inescapable contradiction to the creative aspirations of cultural development, which is always on the quest for new forms and fields of social activity, and for which freedom of expression, the many-sidedness and the continual changing of things, are just as vitally necessary as rigid forms, dead rules, and the forcible suppression of ideas are for the conservation of political power. Every successful piece of work stirs the desire for greater perfection and deeper inspiration; each new form becomes the herald of new possibilities of development. But power always tries to keep things as they are, safely anchored to stereotypes. That has been the reason for all revolutions in history. Power operates only destructively, bent always on forcing every manifestation of social life into the straitjacket of its rules. Its intellectual expression is dead dogma, its physical form brute force. And this unintelligence of its objectives sets its stamp on its representatives also, and renders them often stupid and brutal, even when they were originally endowed with the best talents. One who is constantly striving to force everything into a mechanical order at last becomes a machine himself and loses all human feelings.

It was from this understanding that modern anarchism was born and draws its moral force. Only freedom can inspire men to great things and bring about intellectual and social transformations. The art of ruling men has never been the art of educating and inspiring them to a new shaping of their lives. Dreary compulsion has at its command only lifeless drill, which smothers any vital initiative at its birth and brings forth only subjects, not free men. Freedom is the very essence of life, the impelling force in all intellectual and social development, the creator of every new outlook for the future of mankind. The liberation of man from economic exploitation and from intellectual, social, and political oppression, which finds its highest expression in the philosophy of anarchism, is the first prerequisite for the evolution of a higher social culture and a new humanity.

Postscript 1968 to "Repressive Tolerance"

Herbert Marcuse

This 1968 postscript to Marcuse's essay "Repressive Tolerance" presents a critique of presumptions underlying democratic protection of dissent. The concept of legitimacy is seen as a deterrent to radical groups who are frozen out of adequate opportunities to protest. The inequality of access to power is clearly shown. As a dominant intellectual source for the new left, Marcuse presents an interesting view of education and the establishment.

Education has been cited as an important means for extending tolerance. Numerous school districts have written statements of objectives which include the goal of developing tolerance in students. Teachers are expected to be models of toleration; children are taught to be tolerant of other's opinions and rights; and democratic decision-making in faculty meetings and classrooms assumes the pre-condition of tolerance. Marcuse argues that tolerance is a device used by the majority to extend their will over minorities. His point is that already existent inequalities in the society, and presumably in the schools, warp tolerance and permit those in power to continue, even in the guise of balanced presentations of views. Teachers are typically expected to present "both sides" of issues and to give equal time. Marcuse presents a moral framework that alters this concept and supports intolerance by minorities in the present system.

Under the conditions prevailing in this country, tolerance does not, and cannot, fulfill the civilizing function attributed to it by the liberal protagonists of democracy, namely, protection of dissent. The progressive historical force of tolerance lies in its extension to those modes and forms of dissent which are not committed to the status quo of society, and not confined to the institutional framework of the established society. Consequently, the idea of tolerance implies the necessity, for the dissenting group or individuals, to become illegitimate if and when the established legitimacy prevents and counteracts the development of dissent. This would be the case not only in a totalitarian society, under a dictatorship, in one-party states, but also in a democracy (representative, parliamentary, or "direct") where the majority does not result from the monopolistic or oligopolistic administration of public opinion, without terror and (normally) without censorship. In such cases, the majority is self-perpetuating while perpetuating the vested interests which *made* it a majority. In its very structure this majority is "closed," petrified; it repels "a priori" any change other than changes within the system. But this means that the majority is no longer justified in claiming the democratic title of the best guardian of the common interest. And such a majority is all but the opposite of Rousseau's "general will": it is composed, not of individuals who, in their political functions, have made effective "abstraction" from their private interests, but, on the contrary, of individuals who have effectively identified their private interests with their political functions. And the representatives of this majority, in ascertaining and executing its will, ascertain and execute the will of the vested interests which have formed the majority. The ideology of democracy hides its lack of substance.

In the United States, this tendency goes hand in hand with the monopolistic or oligopolistic concentration of capital in the formation of public opinion, i.e., of the majority. The chance of influencing, in any effective way, this majority is at a price, in dollars, totally out of reach of the radical opposition. Here too, free competition and exchange of ideas have become a farce. The Left has no equal voice, no equal access to the mass media and their public facilities—not because a conspiracy excludes it, but because, in good old capitalist fashion, it does not have the required purchasing power. And the Left does not have the purchasing power because it is the Left. These conditions impose upon the radical minorities a strategy which is in essence a refusal to allow the continuous functioning of allegedly indiscriminate but in fact discriminate tolerance, for example, a strategy of protesting against the alternate matching of a spokesman for the Right (or Center) with one for the Left. Not "equal" but *more* representation of the Left would be equalization of the prevailing inequality.

Within the solid framework of preestablished inequality and power, tolerance is practiced indeed. Even outrageous opinions are expressed, outrageous incidents are televised; and the critics of established policies are interrupted by the same number of commercials as the conservative advocates. Are these interludes supposed to counteract the sheer weight, magnitude, and continuity of system-publicity, indoctrination which operates playfully through the endless commercials as well as through the entertainment?

Given this situation, I suggested in "Repressive Tolerance" the practice of discriminating tolerance in an inverse direction, as a means of shifting the balance between Right and Left by restraining the liberty of the Right, thus counteracting the pervasive inequality of freedom (unequal opportunity of access to the means of democratic persuasion) and strengthening the oppressed against the oppressors. Tolerance would be restricted with respect to movements of a demonstrably aggressive or destructive character (destructive of the prospects for peace, justice, and freedom for all). Such discrimination would also be applied to movements opposing the extension of social legislation to the poor, weak, disabled. As against the virulent denunciations that such a policy would do away with the sacred liberalistic principle of equality for "the other side," I maintain that there are issues where either there is no "other side" in any more than a formalistic sense, or where "the other side" is demonstrably "regressive" and impedes possible improvement of the human condition. To tolerate propaganda for inhumanity vitiates the goals not only of liberalism but of every progressive political philosophy.

I presupposed the existence of demonstrable criteria for aggressive, regressive, destructive forces. If the final democratic criterion of the declared opinion of the majority no longer (or rather not yet) prevails, if vital ideas, values, and ends of human progress no longer (or rather not yet) enter, as competing equals, the formation of public opinion, if the people are no longer (or rather not yet) sovereign but "made" by the real sovereign powers—is there any alternative other than the dictatorship of an "elite" over the people? For the opinion of people (usually designated as The People) who are unfree in the very faculties in which liberalism saw the roots of freedom: independent thought and independent speech, can carry no overriding validity and authority—even if The People constitute the overwhelming majority.

If the choice were between genuine democracy and dictatorship, democracy would certainly be preferable. But democracy does not prevail. The radical critics of the existing political process are thus readily denounced as advocating an "elitism," a dictatorship of intellectuals as an alternative. What we have in fact is government, representative government by a non-intellectual minority of politicians, generals, and businessmen. The record of this "elite" is not very promising, and political prerogatives for the intelligentsia may not necessarily be worse for the society as a whole.

In any case, John Stuart Mill, not exactly an enemy of liberal and representative government, was not so allergic to the political leadership of the intelligentsia as the contemporary guardians of semi-democracy are. Mill believed that "individual mental superiority" justifies "reckoning one person's opinion as equivalent to more than one":

> Until there shall have been devised, and until opinion is willing to accept, some mode of plural voting which may assign to education as such the degree of superior influence due to it, and sufficient as a counterpoise to the numerical weight of the least educated class, for so long the benefits of completely universal suffrage cannot be obtained without bringing with them, as it appears to me, more than equivalent evils.[1]

"Distinction in favor of education, right in itself," was also supposed to preserve "the educated from the class legislation of the uneducated,"

[1] *Considerations on Representative Government* (Chicago: Gateway Edition, 1962), p. 183.

without enabling the former to practice a class legislation of their own.[2]

Today, these words have understandably an antidemocratic, "elitist" sound—understandably because of their dangerously radical implications. For if "education" is more and other than training, learning, preparing for the existing society, it means not only enabling man to know and understand the facts which make up reality but also to know and understand the factors that establish the facts so that he can change their inhuman reality. And such humanistic education would involve the "hard" sciences ("hard" as in the "hardware" bought by the Pentagon?), would free them from their destructive direction. In other words, such education would indeed badly serve the Establishment, and to give political prerogatives to the men and women thus educated would indeed be anti-democratic in the terms of the Establishment. But these are not the only terms.

However, the alternative to the established semi-democratic process is *not* a dictatorship or elite, no matter how intellectual and intelligent, but the struggle for a real democracy. Part of this struggle is the fight against an ideology of tolerance which, in reality, favors and fortifies the conservation of the status quo of inequality and discrimination. For this struggle, I proposed the practice of discriminating tolerance. To be sure, this practice already presupposes the radical goal which it seeks to achieve. I committed this *petitio principii* in order to combat the pernicious ideology that tolerance is already institutionalized in this society. The tolerance which is the life element, the token of a free society, will never be the gift of the powers that be; it can, under the prevailing conditions of tyranny by the majority, only be won in the sustained effort of radical minorities, willing to break this tyranny and to work for the emergence of a free and sovereign majority—minorities intolerant, militantly intolerant and disobedient to the rules of behavior which tolerate destruction and suppression.

[2] *Ibid.*, p. 181.

chapter 2

Wealth and Its Distribution

Who should control the means of production? Within the framework of capitalist theory it was obvious that it would be those who were aggressive and clever enough to gain control of the productive machinery and were therefore best able to profit from that control and to maximize their personal power and profit at the expense of the general society. It has been argued that these privately-owned corporate groups are more efficient as producers than if the State owned and managed the major manufacturing and service corporations. Private managers may be more concerned with maximizing their profit and eliminating waste so they can increase their profit margins.

In addition to the question of efficiency there is the problem of the different valuation placed on human priorities versus the value placed on maximizing individual power and economic gain. Essentially, the question of who owns the productive apparatus involves value and ethical choices about the kind of society one feels will benefit the greatest number of people in a particular social system. A value question precedes the question of the most efficient means of economic organization. The choice of an economic model involves basic assumptions about the nature of man, his inherent abilities, and the kinds of justice and socio-economic standards which are his due. Capitalist assumptions about the nature of man tend to argue for a production and a distribution system which primarily rewards those with the greatest manipulative capacities in the marketplace and generally assumes that those with lesser degrees of ability and talent should be relegated to lower places in the socio-economic scale.

The socialist approach to human society, on the other hand, holds the view that man is the result of environmental conditioning. The economic order should be one which provides a large number of economic options for the different types of ability levels present in all societies. It would deny the argument that a small group of individuals within particular societies are vastly more capable than others and should be rewarded in terms of their greater capacity. The socialist view holds that man is conditioned to behave in accordance with the socio-economic order in which he lives. Within a capitalist system a particular set of beliefs are accepted by the general population. While in a socialist system, another belief system is fostered and accepted by the members of that system. In a system which places a high priority on the maximization of individual power, competition, and self-aggrandizement, the average citizen assumes that the competitive struggle for economic survival is simply the nature of human life. A socialist system presumes that the greater good is to society and individual self-development can be stifled. The myths and rituals of every economic order are bolstered by a continuous forced feeding of propaganda through the mass media and the schools.

The basic philosophy of American capitalism has been that goods and services are produced primarily for a profit. An individual's worth has been judged traditionally in terms of his ability to save and produce on an ever increasing basis. The system is structured in such a way that a large proportion of the population, approximately three-fourths of the nation, are able to obtain continuous work and annually increase their share of the available goods and services in the society. These millions, who are effective within the system, benefit on a continuous basis from that system as consumers and are expected in turn to become efficient counter-exploiters within the economy as a routine part of their daily existence.

The present system assumes that the "good" individual is one who continuously seeks to increase his work load and produce more goods and services. Hard work and the desire to increase one's share of society's rewards is a sign of respectability, security, and good citizenship. In this view, the central purpose of human life is to maximize one's effectiveness as a competitor and to merge one's individuality with the system. Since the majority are well rewarded economically by this system, it rarely occurs to them that alternative life styles may be far more meaningful.

The consumer in this system is routinely subjected to various forms of exploitation in the market place. Within the present system the individual makes points and survives most effectively by, in turn, manipulating and exploiting other individuals in the larger market place. An individual's success is judged by his effectiveness as a manipulator of the system. It is assumed that the corruption of the system, as well as the destructive consumer aspects of the system, must be routinely accepted by the conforming member in order for him to maximize his own personal gain and power. Within the present system the individual is expected to present a facade of humanistic concern for the general society, while in reality practicing various kinds of acceptable deceit on his fellow citizen in order to enhance and increase his share of personal power and property. In sum, the system conditions the individual to a double set of human and social values.

It is also assumed that unemployment is a given and is fundamental to the established order within the framework of a freely competitive economic system. For example, a limited amount of labor may be a requisite for a particular phase of the yearly cycle, and manpower has to be dismissed from a particular company in order for the organization to remain competitive within the industry. Individuals within this system are regarded as producers for the system, and it is essential that they conform to the dictates and vagaries of this uncoordinated marketing system.

Another assumption is that large numbers of individuals within the society are not viewed as effective producers; hence, they are not well rewarded by the system. Within a highly competitive market-oriented system there are many groups within the population who are not able to compete for various reasons. Among these groups may be included the aging, the handicapped, those with little formal education, adolescents, and various ethnic and racial groups who serve an important scape-goating function within the capitalist ethic. This kind of economic machine can utilize only a limited number of producers and competitors within its factories and companies. It follows that large population groups have to be rejected in order for the corporate system to maintain its economic solvency and perpetuate its control of the larger society.

Socialist systems, in practice, have also shown a variety of lacks in humanitarianism. None has been able to fully equalize conditions or opportunities for its citizens. Bureaucratic nightmares, government domination, and human exploitation for national industrial goals have plagued socialist plans for the new order. Social class structures based on party position or administrative station have replaced those based on heredity and wealth. This is the new establishment. While general standards of life may have improved, a poverty class remains.

Rapid economic development has demanded immense personal and mass sacrifice from workers. Questions of individual interest in crafts-manship, quantity and quality of consumer goods, and alienation from a technological society occur in both capitalistic and socialistic societies.

New left radicals, as well as right-wing reactionaries, have attacked socialism as an inadequate economic system for providing for individuality. Libertarianism, a belief in high degrees of individual free-dom, can be seen as either right or left wing. Chapter 1 contained views on anarchic and collective power. This chapter looks at economic problems and potential solutions.

Social institutions, including schools, share in the production, consumption, and distribution of wealth in any society. Defects in any economic system are replicated to a greater or lesser degree in the schools of that society.

The economic system should be subordinated to the develop-ment of higher-level social values based on human needs and aspira-tions. The motives of greed and individual exploitation should not continue to dominate our social and economic planning but should rather give way to an alternative model which places primary emphasis on more humane social goals. Changes within our educational system would also be essential if we are to change our present priorities. Our schools have been notorious for presenting values and myths which perpetuate the dominant economic establishment. The schools have continuously presented a picture of a humanely oriented society work-ing toward democratic ends, even though this picture is essentially false and there is little evidence to support this mythology. The schools for a long time have been subordinate to the most hypocritical values of the socio-economic order. They have chosen at all educational levels to perpetuate the dishonesty and corruption of the system.

The radical activists and writers who have been criticizing the schools both from the left and the right have generally agreed that the central purpose of the schools has been lost. The present system does more to destroy human potential and develop social alienation than it does to honestly initiate true educational development. Our school system has essentially become a factory, a place in which children are processed and expected to learn to accept the most routine and barbaric values that our socio-economic system has created. They are taught to conform and accept the major failures of the society in which they live. They are rarely taught to understand or critically examine the basic pathology which is inherent in the United States system. It is time for the little red school house to renounce its policies of anti-intellectualism, conformity, and fear and to begin to move toward a more liberating and a more humane model for the educational process. Changes in our educational system are urgently needed if we are to develop a more effective human community and to liberate our children from the platitudes and deceptions which have been their daily fare for too long a period. We must develop new educational forms which will excite the children's desire for learning and help them to build a more civilized society than the one their parents have accepted and sanctioned.

A New View of Economics

Robert Theobald

Robert Theobald has written extensively on the problems of
modern technology and its impact on traditional social-economic
life. He states that there is a need for major revolutionary change
involving the adaptation of the new technology so that the
technical and the humanistic needs are adequately balanced. Our
highly developed modern technology needs to be utilized for the
development of a more equitable society than has previously
been the case. The author has been an advocate of the guaranteed
annual income concept as an effective device in raising the living
for millions of currently disadvantaged Americans. The guaranteed
annual income, it is argued, does not involve a negative social
stigma as does the more traditional welfare approach. It could
serve as the economic basis for a more effective and productive
means of reaching for all members of the society.

Theobald is British by citizenship and education but now
lives in America, where he thinks the cybernetic age will first
develop new life styles. He advocates a total restructuring of the
economic system based on a theory of abundance rather than
scarcity. Our present economic beliefs lead to pursuit of material
gain because we fear scarcity and undertake hoarding and
wide consumption to get "our share." Theobald contends that
scarcity-bred insecurity causes overconsumption, not conservation.
He argues that belief in the ability to produce enough to satisfy
our needs will alleviate the drive to keep up with or surpass the
Joneses in material accumulation and will enhance socio-economic
moves toward improved social interests such as education.

American schools have taught scarcity economics, free
enterprise, and material success as positive goals for generations.
It has taken years to move economic education from pure
Adam Smith free market-place ideas to consider Keynesian
government-intervention positions. Theobald represents different
ideas that deserve intellectual attention in schools and practical

Robert Theobald, from *An Alternative for America* (1st edition) ©
1968. Reprinted by permission of The Swallow Press, Inc.

consideration for what they might mean to the system of education in a society.

. . . Each man must be provided with the potential to control the conditions of his own life and that the failure to develop this potential leaves him with no choice but to fall into anomie and apathy on the one hand or violence on the other.

It is in this context that today's potential abundance takes on its full meaning: man now has the material ability to provide all human beings with the goods and services required to serve as the basis for full human development. Today, national and international poverty results from a failure of will rather than a failure of productive ability; those who are powerless sense or know this and naturally consider it intolerable.

We have no choice, therefore, but to create a new social order, one where powerlessness has been abolished. For only then will man's drive toward self-actualization be capable of fulfillment and his self-destructive tendencies, generated through failure to honor the fundamental necessity for self-actualization, be eliminated.

The new reality of today is a very simple one: man now has the power to do what he wants to do. This development is revolutionary because until just this moment of history man has been constrained by his environment. As a result of this novel power, man's present cultural system has become irrelevant, in the same way as man's cultural system became irrelevant when he moved from his hunting and gathering stage to his agricultural stage.

The reasons man has this power can be very briefly set out. First, he has power because he has energy, energy being derived today primarily from fossil fuels, but coming tomorrow from nuclear energy. Nuclear energy has the peculiar characteristic that it not only produces energy but in the very process of producing energy it can create more fuel to produce more energy. We are very rapidly getting to the energy potential for a perpetual motion machine. Energy can be used for anything that man wishes—to produce metals from low grade ores, to turn the desert into a garden or whatever it strikes his fancy to do.

The second reason for our power I like to call "alchemy." By that I mean the ability to manipulate the basic building blocks of nature to create materials with the types of properties that one desires. The word alchemy is appropriate for two reasons. It reminds us that some of the materials we have created are already considerably more valuable than gold, and it reminds us of what would happen to the economic system if we simply developed the ability to produce gold. In other worlds, the economic system is running on a mythology; and the mythology is extraordinarily vulnerable.

The third factor which gives us power is the educational possibilities of our culture. For the first time it is possible for a very substantial proportion of the population to learn for twenty-two years of their lives or more. The fact that we are still running colleges which are largely producing surrogate computers is not the fault of the situation but only the fault of the people within the system. By "producing surrogate computers" I mean that we are educating people who can give answers to questions which have already been posed, which is what a computer can do, rather than teaching them how to pose questions. This is disastrous because the computer will certainly learn to answer structured questions better than we can.

The fourth factor that we have going for us is the computer. The computer is a wonderful instrument. A computer is a wonderful way of solving problems. But you had better be careful because the computer will give you the "right" answer.

A war planner of a friendly power asked its computer, "What steps should I take to do the most harm to Russia?" The computer, after whirring a few times, came back with an answer, "Bomb the United States." The computer was strictly logical because if this friendly power bombed the United States "intelligently," the U.S. would assume that it had been bombed by Russia. It would then bomb Russia and it could certainly do much more harm to Russia than the friendly power could, because America has more bombs. Theoretically, the great advantage about human beings is that when they see that sort of chasm they stop and say, "No, that wasn't what I meant." But computers aren't that sensible.

Using a computer is a good way of getting away from responsibility. We use it in California as a justification for logging redwood groves. The way that this gets done is to instruct the computer to build the best road, and then to inform the computer that the best road is the cheapest road. Next one feeds into the computer the values for the various strips of land, and of course you put in a very low value for the redwoods because, after all, they are not doing any good, are they? The computer then designs a road which goes through the redwood system. Then one says, "It wasn't our fault. You know, logic compels us to build the road through the redwood groves. We regret this as much as anybody else."

The computer is a very good servant and a very bad master. There is rather distressing evidence that the computer is becoming a new god. When the computer has spoken, who shall question it? There is no doubt in my mind that the computer has been one of the factors that has led us into the present disastrous situation in Vietnam. I think that everybody now agrees that Vietnam is a disastrous mess. People may disagree about what should have been done or what ought to be done now, but the assumption that errors have been made is common to all of us. One of the factors that got fed into the computer is that the willingness of societies to surrender is a function of the number of bombs dropped on it. Being British I have some grave doubts about this!

Man's new power is not, despite the apparent realities, simply an American or a Western phenomenon. That it can be so limited is one of the great comforting myths. I am asked why I talk about the whole world in these terms. I am told to look at Asia, at Latin America, at Africa, all of whom do not have power. But everybody knows that mankind has power. We live, as McLuhan has put it, in a global village. And the fact that some continents do not yet have the power does not prevent them from knowing that they ought to have the power and that they can have the power if the rich are willing to develop it and share it with them.

It would appear at first sight as though a society in which man had power over the conditions of his life would be extremely desirable: indeed, at some level, it is. But this power doesn't mesh with out present social system, and as a result we fall into five very serious traps. The first of these traps is what I call the war trap, the fact that in our international system the ultimate sanction in international dispute is war. Each country must therefore be able to defend itself against any potential attacker, which means that it must install and indeed invent any weapon or defense system that it can. This results in a profoundly unstable world. We have to take the same leap in international affairs as we took in personal affairs sometime ago when we abolished dueling. I was taught when I was young that we abolished dueling because people became humane. I have reached the conclusion that this is not true, but that basically people discovered that dueling with modern weapons was too dangerous. Let me point out that we now have available approximately thirty tons of TNT per person, plus enormous destructive potential through biological and chemical weapons. The statement that "war will wipe us out or we will wipe out war" remains as true as it was when it was first stated, but we have numbed ourselves to its reality.

The second trap is the efficiency trap. We run a society in which if something can be done more efficiently, immensely strong forces come into action to ensure change. But the very fact that man has such power over his environment means that he may wish to preserve certain possibilities of human activity which are not efficient. He must therefore change the socioeconomic rules governing international trade and the relationship between income and work.

This can be seen most clearly in relationship to job patterns. In our society everybody must hold a job, unless he is independently wealthy or in a certain very limited group. Computers and machinery are becoming more efficient but men are not becoming more efficient nearly as fast. The efficiency of computers doubles at the present time about every three years, and the cost of computer work probably goes down to one-tenth of its previous cost. At the same time the cost of hiring a worker continues to rise. It is therefore not surprising that a very severe problem of unemployability is emerging. The data are now quite clear: there are more and more people at the bottom of the society who do not have jobs and who are not about to get jobs.

There are only two ways out of this trap. One of them is the idea that the government should become the employer of last resort. That sounds good until you analyze it. What happens when the government becomes the employer of last resort? Some 1,000,000 or more unemployables are placed under the control of federal bureaucrats. These people are unskilled, uneducated, untrained and uninterested in work. The program runs for six months and then Congress wants to know what's going on. It levels charges of inefficiency and lack of control, so the bureaucrats start to tighten up. They pass rules such as: anybody who is fifteen minutes late for work loses a day's pay. Another rule might be: in order to ensure efficient operation of the system, nobody may change his government-supported job more than once in six months. I would suggest a short word for the result of such rules— an old-fashioned word—slavery. If you think it is an unfair word, I would suggest that you look at some existing national and state welfare policies. The only other alternative is the guaranteed income which says that people are entitled to income as a right and that society has a responsibility to find meaningful work for people to do.

The next trap is the consumption trap, which is related to our productive capacity. If everybody has to have a job we must be willing to consume everything we can produce. We must therefore convince people they should buy. This is particularly visible in our patterns of advertising for children from 1 to 5, in an era where television is the prime parent. Television encourages frenetic consumership and permanent debt. "Daddy, Daddy, please buy me . . ."

I said this on TV recently, and somebody said to me, "Well it is really quite all right because children have understood by the age of ten that all advertising is false, anyway." And I said, "You know, if you are right—and you may be right—you have probably explained to me why it is that young people are thoroughly discontented with the society in which they find themselves."

The fifth trap is the education trap. If you have to bring up people so that they will accept the present traps—the war trap, the efficiency trap, the job trap, and the consumption trap—you dare not set people free to think and study. The educational system ceases to be an opportunity for people to find out for themselves what they believe and becomes a method of manipulating people into accepting what the society currently accepts. It serves as a method for inculcating a set of beliefs from the past which are not relevant to today's world.

Sin, Morality, and Poverty

William Stringfellow

A dominant theme in the American national character has been that of equating poverty with sin, immorality, and the lack of human respectability. A major deterrant in our inability to deal honestly with poverty in America is in large part a result of the residual American belief that poverty is a result of laziness and lack of ambition. Since the individual is lazy, irresponsible, and unproductive in the competitive high-achieving American sense, it therefore follows that poverty is his just reward. It is assumed that the poor must always be with us because inherently in the nature of human life, there are those who are lazy and incompetent and who deserve to be rejected by the social system. The system rewards those who fit the dictates of the social-economic apparatus and punishes those who are not able to meet the efficient machine's criterion for acceptance.

Essentially, the American case is based on a survival of the fittest rationale, or jungle-law concept, which argues that human life is an extension of man's evolutionary struggle for survival. Those who are most successful within the competitive scheme of nature are justly rewarded for their abilities and hard work. However, those who are not able to maximally compete in the system receive as their due either minimal rewards as in the case of the majority or basic rejection by the system as in the case

of many ethnic and racial groups in the United States. This
rationale has permitted a relatively small group of white
establishment leaders to build an economic system which
perpetuates the equation of poverty and incompetency and permits
the economic establishment to exploit this mythology in order to
continuously increase its economic and social power. In this
view, poverty is therefore deserved and its own reward. To liquidate
poverty is therefore to thwart nature and her natural forms of
justice.

Stringfellow suggests that the essential problem in the
United States is whether or not the rights of property shall continue
to have primacy over the rights of a more complete form of
human development for all citizens in the society. He indicates
that our fascination with materialism—the acquisition of money
and the accumulation of property—has relegated to a subservient
status all of those in our society who are not effective competitors
or consumers. The role of the respectable member of our society
is to insulate himself against the existence of the unwanted
and rejected people.

Historically, the competitive achiever has ignored those who
are brutalized and conditioned for failure by the system. Educational
institutions, as radical writers have noted, have engaged in this
brutalizing and failure conditioning. For many children the earliest
awareness of public failure is at the hands of a teacher. Surely
schools are the only socially sanctioned formal institution which can
methodically separate successful children from failures using
the school's own criteria. Families and peer groups may do it
informally, and state reformatories may act on children after
they have been separated, but schools have the official right, even
responsibility, to systematically produce failures. School failure
is correlated with poverty in our society, and as Stringfellow
indicates, this makes it equivalent to sinfulness.

In addition to being a respected author, William Stringfellow
is a lawyer. His published works include *Free in Obedience*,
My People Is the Enemy, and *A Private and Public Faith*.

The moral complacency of most citizens in regard to poverty is largely
due to the success this society has achieved in keeping the poor out of
sight: the mind is not appalled by conditions the eyes have not seen;
the conscience is not moved by what the nostrils have not inhaled.

Concealment, indeed, is one synonym for ghettoization. Whether
the concealment of poverty in urban society has been wickedly calcu-
lated I doubt, although the consistency and similarity of the patterns of
concealment throughout the country make that a fascinating hypothe-
sis. More likely, as far as most middle-class citizens are concerned, the

poor have been put out of sight almost inadvertently; very often this has been done in the name of renewal and for the sake of civic improvement. Thus the reconstruction of the central city in Minneapolis caused the relocation of the old downtown Negro ghetto to another part of the city. It seems as if in one stroke the blight of the downtown area has been removed and the Negroes have vanished. In Buffalo, the new thruway to handle the increased traffic from the white suburbs to the business district has been constructed right over the roofs of the tenements, quite effectively and very effectually hiding the ghetto and literally burying its residents. In principle, the same approach has been taken in almost every city.

The concealment of poverty by ghettoization of the poor means that both prosperous and poor live so separately and have so little human contact of any kind, are so accustomed to acting out a charade instead, that each regards the other in sterotypes which seldom contain much truth. The most popular stereotype of the poor is that in America a person is poor by choice and not because of circumstances beyond his own influence. Thus, if the poor were not so lazy, they would not be poor. If the poor were not so promiscuous, they would be able to support themselves. If the poor were not so profligate in drugs and drink and other dissipations, they would escape from their misery. These are the common variations of the same theme that accounts for poverty as proof of moral decadence. Driven to its ultimate logic, to be poor is a grave sin. Such a stereotype of the poor is credible and popular among the prosperous because it implies that to be prosperous is a sign of moral superiority.

Neither side of the stereotype is true, however, either empirically or theologically. Poverty, like wealth—in America as elsewhere—is more often a matter of inheritance and coincidence than of choice or initiative.

Apart from a few of those saints, I have yet to meet a man who elected to be poor, and I have never met an affluent man whose estate could be truthfully accounted for as his own individual accomplishment. If one is born an American Indian—for instance in Oklahoma, where most Indians subsist on governmental charity—the chances are about three to one that one will, like his forefathers, remain confined to a reservation, never have his intelligence or other capabilities recognized or utilized, be deprived of any education qualifying him to leave the reservation and secure and hold outside employment, or, in turn, be able to locate a habitable place to live off the reservation, enter a church, obtain a loan, be bonded, open a charge account, secure a license from public agencies, or even conveniently get a haircut. Much the same is the lot of the offspring of migrant crop workers in California, in New England, in Virginia, in upstate New York, and elsewhere in the country, or, to take another example, of the heirs of miners who have been unemployable for a generation in Appalachia. And, if one is an American Negro male and is born in the ghetto, it is probable that one will die in the ghetto.

This stereotype that the poor are morally deficient and that, therefore, their poverty is their own fault, is particularly asserted at the present time as a desperate rationalization for the denial of equal rights in society to Negro citizens in the Northern cities. The argument is that many ethnic groups have immigrated to this country—Jews and Poles and Hungarians and Italians and Portuguese and Irish and Germans—and while suffering some discrimination and conflicts, have gradually and successfully been absorbed and accepted in American society. Parts of Harlem used to be immigrant slums—those other groups escaped from the slums and have "made it" in this country; why haven't the Negroes done the same? The answer, unhappily, is ludicrously obvious; it is also very sad and terrible. The answer is that the pattern of assimilation in urban life of immigrants from other nations has not been applicable to Negro citizens because Negroes are *not* immigrants. Apart from the Indians, they are the earliest Americans, arriving as they did, however reluctantly, three centuries ago when the slave trade to the North American continent began. They have a venerable and utterly unique American ancestry that no others —of all the varieties of language, nationality, or race which have come to America—can claim or approximate. Moreover, the precedent of immigrant assimilation in the great Northern cities has not applied to Negro citizens because *white supremacy has been the dominant ethic in virtually every realm of society in America for the past three hundred years and remains entrenched even today*. In 1966, of course, it is often a *de facto*, patronizing racism, more subtle than in the days of chattel slavery or of militant segregation in the post-Civil War era, but it has remained effective enough to imprison and immobilize multitudes of Negroes for generations in the urban North. Immigrants from Europe surely had trials and travails on coming to these shores, but they never threatened by their presence or challenged by their conduct the ethic of white supremacy. Thus their eventual assimilation was not hindered, once language barriers had been muted, cultural distinctions diluted, and religious and nationalistic prejudices challenged. It is white supremacy—not moral inferiority, and not choice—that accounts for the black ghettos.

One of the ironies for those among the white and the prosperous who fondly preach free enterprise and individual initiative as the virtues which, no doubt they can be, is that racial supremacy is so manifestly inconsistent with these ideas. It is an extravagant hypocrisy for white people who are well off to scold Negroes who are not, for lack of enterprise after having kept them for so long in servitude, then in separation, and now locked up in the slums. Whites cannot really have it both ways: If they cherish freedom of initiative, they must forgo white supremacy; if they have more affection for the latter, let them at least forbear from denouncing those whom they oppress.

One corollary of the racial and class separation of society is the notion that whatever the legitimate needs of the poor, they can be met through private philanthropy. However, this assumes that—despite their radical separation from the poor—the prosperous are enlightened and compassionate enough to make need the measure of their charity. But the concealment of poverty from those who are not poor refutes such an assumption. Such reasoning also takes for granted that organized charity is seriously committed to the service of human need, a premise which is difficult to defend if one considers the diversion of charitable contributions to the financing of expensive promotions and self-serving bureaucracies. Institutionalized private charity is a monster, exploiting human suffering in appeals to the crudest motivations, with much of the money going to the professional fund-raisers rather than to heal the sick, comfort the afflicted, or accomplish much of any practical charity at all. The truth is that private institutionalized charity in America has now become so heavily oriented toward its own maintenance that it has little left over to meet the empirical needs of those whom it purports to help. All the while, a spirit of condescension is cultivated that corrupts the good intentions of the prosperous and nurtures a spirit of despair that demeans recipients of charity as human beings. To put it bluntly, private charity has simply become too fat, too introverted, too manipulative of both donors and named beneficiaries to commend it as a sensible way of resolving any of the substantive issues of American poverty.

Theologically, the dual stereotype of the poor as morally defective and the prosperous as morally excellent is objectionable as a crude doctrine of justification by works, which ignores the fact that there is an obvious interdependence between rich and poor. To use an ordinary example, most white people in this society are investors in life and property insurance. On the surface, this seems a prudent and morally innocent action in which a man takes some precautions against certain predictable risks for the benefit of his family or himself. At the same time, I suppose, most white folks—at least theoretically—disapprove of slums and would just as soon see them vanish from the cities. Yet the lives of men are so entangled in this world that there *is* a relationship between the purchase of insurance, on one hand, and the preservation of slums, on the other.

Insurance companies in many jurisdictions are restricted as to their permissible investments; real estate is one of those commonly allowed. In the great cities insurance companies have become substantial speculators in real estate, and the impact of their manipulations has contributed to the demolition of some blighted sections, the dispossession of tenants from the site, and the reconstruction of the site into commercial or residential properties that the dispossessed legally cannot afford or are not entitled to occupy. Thus the slum dweller is driven deeper into the ghetto, and the slums become fewer but worse. I am not advocating that all conscientious citizens divest themselves of insurance policies because their insurers may be involved in real estate speculations that aggravate the slums, but the beginning of conscience, in a Christian sense, is realizing that every action or omission, even those which seem routine and trivial, is consequentially related to the lives of all other human beings on the face of the earth. Even the typical prudent act of buying insurance is not morally innocuous but extremely ambiguous, and entangles one man in the existence of others in many ways unintended and, as yet, unknown. The same sort of thing can be said, in principle, of any form of investment or saving, not just insurance, which is something trustees of church and college endowments might keep more prominently in mind if they are not to continue to practice the blatant hypocrisy of investing in enterprises that contradict what the churches preach and the colleges teach. Conscience, in other words, is knowing that men are related to, and responsible for, each other in all things. That is why poverty cannot be accounted for by blaming it on the poor, since the prosperous are proximately involved in the institutionalization of poverty in society.

Poverty and Ideology

The moral stamina to utilize the resources and technology of this society to abolish poverty begins in the awakening of conscience and in the commitment of citizens to some fundamental idea of society.

No reference is made here to those ideological conflicts which preoccupy so much public attention but which have so little substantive significance for the nation. In other words, the conflict as to the form of society in America is not, as nearly as I can make out, capitalism *vs* communism. Few citizens, I suspect, could be intelligently articulate about the differences between them, in terms of economic theory, and the matter becomes truly theoretical because neither system exists in practice in the developed countries of the modern world.

Contemporary Soviet society bears about as little resemblance to classical Marxism as modern American society does to laissez-faire capitalism. Those in the Soviet Union and the United States who mourn such mutations of, and departures from, ideological doctrine are at least responding appropriately: both communism and capitalism *are* dead. Meanwhile, China, which, significantly, is increasingly considered both as the hobgoblin of American vested interests in Southeast Asia and the competitor of Soviet vested interests throughout the Eastern world, is more plausibly comprehended in terms of the traditional hegemony of an emerging great power.

Classically, of course, both capitalism and communism emerge as responses to the Industrial Revolution, which began in Europe two centuries ago and which quickly matured in the United States. Whatever the merits of either in their origination, both were addressed to conditions of primitive industrialization that no longer prevail in this nation or, one gathers, in Europe, the Soviet Union, and Japan. The realities which America in the middle of the twentieth century confronts are those of a mass, urbanized, automated, cybernated society. In regard to those realities, however they may be dealt with, both capitalism and communism are ideologically obsolete, and it is morally and intellectually dissipating to engage the attention and energies of society in an endless sham battle over ideas which have been superseded by advances in science and technology that were not even imagined at the inception of either capitalism or communism. For the present realities, both of these ideologies seem too old-fashioned and reactionary.

If the ideological conflict between capitalism and communism is ridiculous in the United States today, inasmuch as neither practically exists nor could be established, and if that struggle saps the moral strength of the nation by distracting citizens from urgent actual problems, that does not mean there are no serious ideological differences among us. On the contrary, the country still suffers from the same ideological split which divided the nation in the first place. The authentically American ideological controversy, still unresolved, is concerned over which is more suitable as the constitution of society—the rights of property or the rights of human beings.

That dispute, of course, was embodied in some of the pre-Revolutionary protests, and later in the squabbles between Jefferson and Hamilton. It emerged again in the debate over whether property was to be a condition of suffrage and elective office, in the abolitionist movement, somewhat belatedly in the campaign for woman suffrage, and eventually in the labor revolution. It is raised again nowadays, of course, in the civil rights movement and the war on poverty, but also in other realms, for example in the impact of technological change upon work, and in the universities, where money remains the principal qualification for entrance into higher education.

I had supposed—naïvely, as it turns out—that the American ideological struggle had been settled irrevocably a century ago by the Civil War. Even taking into consideration all the other skirmishes before and since, it was that momentous division of the nation that dramatized the issue of property *vs* persons most terribly and most bluntly. After all, *ideologically*, what was the Civil War about? It was about whether certain human beings are property or persons: if chattels, then society belongs to those who acquire, possess, or control property; if persons, then human rights, verified by nothing more than being a human being, have precedence in society over property.

Subsequent events demonstrate that the American ideological conflict was not decisively settled by the Civil War; at the very least, the struggle continues. The crises of poverty, race, and technology in contemporary America have provoked a strenuous resurgence in the advocacy of mere property rights as the basis of society. Some argue, of course, that the acquisition and possession of property itself represents a human right from which all other rights are appropriately derived. It is a self-serving argument—persuasive only to those already privileged with money and other forms of property, or to those who labor under the illusion that someday they will somehow accumulate property.

Whether this American ideological conflict will ever be resolved and, if so, whether property or persons will be subordinated, one to the other, remains in doubt. Whatever the outcome, I contend that insofar as the property ethic prevails, our idea of democracy will have been forfeited and the nation deprived of the moral authority to banish poverty.

PROPERTY, MONEY, AND THE ETHICS OF SOCIETY

The popular fascination with property as the fundamental institution of society is fixed in America upon the symbol of money.

A Christian who is also an American can hardly be unaware of the special irony involved in his attempt to analyze the meaning of money, both socially and theologically. A banker or money-changer might wish to disqualify me from having any views—just because I do not happen to have any money to boast of. But is it not the truth that those who do not have money know as much about its meaning as those who possess it? On the other hand, a pauper or beggar might complain that it is gratuitous to speak of money if one is, as I am, a young, white, Anglo-Saxon, Episcopalian, Harvard attorney, for whom obtaining a position, accumulating money, and acquiring whatever money can buy takes no remarkable effort. The subject is compelling for me precisely because in this society it is simple for some to make money if they choose to do so, while very difficult for others.

One is haunted by the impression that, for Christians, if not for other men, the issues of money and property of all sorts were long ago settled. Heed these examples:

Jesus admonished the rich young man who sought justification to dispose of what he had and give it to the poor and thereby follow Christ. Is that warning now forgotten?

Jesus purified the temple when it had become a haven for thieves. Is that no precedent for the Church?

Jesus was nursed in a shed, did not follow the occupation of his father Joseph but became an itinerant, had no place to sleep, sought out the poor and disadvantaged, and blessed them many times and in many ways. He was seldom welcomed among the affluent; by all accounts He was poor Himself in every worldly sense, and declared that money belongs to Caesar. Where the Church and the people of the Church forsake His poverty, is not Christ thereby foresworn?

Although money and the property which money begets accomplishes, in America, fabulous and terrifying feats, no camel has yet passed through the eye of a needle.

After all, the price, in money, of the life of Christ was thirty coins.

The Making of Socialist Consciousness

The Socialist Revolution—**Editorial**

What is the most effective means for distributing the wealth and resources of a particular society? In examining this question it is necessary to consider the traditional assumptions that are made by both capitalistic and socialistic theorists in considering the question of the proper distribution of a nation's wealth and

Reprinted by permission of the publisher. *Socialist Revolution*, January/ February 1970.

resources. It is of primary importance to consider the use and ownership of the means of production in a particular society as a major point of conflict between these two theoretical systems. A basic Marxist contention was that capitalism would inevitably destroy itself because of specific unresolvable conflicts within its own system. One of the key conflicts is in the area of the central value placed on private property in the capitalist system and the use made of profit gained from the exploitation of one's property in one form or another. The chief objective of the capitalist system is to maximize one's profit from the ownership of goods and resources and to exploit other members of the system in order to increase one's share of the property and resources available in a society. Within the capitalist system the human and natural resources of a society are exploited for profit rather than for the general good of the society.

The essential appeal of socialism, at least in theory, lies in its demand for social and economic equity through state ownership of the means of production for the purpose of achieving a more balanced distribution of the goods and services available in a society. Capitalism has sought to counter the idealism of the socialist position by arguing that every citizen may advance himself by becoming an exploiter of property himself and thereby becoming a more effective capitalist within his own right. Capitalism does not view social equality and the equity of goods and services as a birthright, but rather these are viewed as acquired properties in the struggle for survival within a highly competitive and atavistic social system.

It must be remembered, however, that the purer theoretical forms of both socialism and capitalism do not exist anywhere in the world. Both systems, when applied, contain major distortions and deviations from the stated theoretical models. However, across the world, the struggle continues between the two ideologies of socialism and capitalism in terms of which system is most effective in providing greater equity and more meaningful life styles for the bulk of the population within a particular society. In considering these issues one needs to consider the following questions. Which system provides the fairest equity in terms of goods and services to its citizens? Which system is the least destructive and the most humane in providing a meaningful life for all of its citizens? Which system offers its citizens the most in the way of personal liberty and potential for a more complete human life?

The concept of private property is an important educational idea. It is not only basic to the economic distinction between capitalism and socialism, but it has repercussions throughout school-related areas. Since property separates social classes in America, it also has an effect on schools which reflect those classes. The elite private preparatory school and Ivy League college have historically been a haven for the propertied class. Recent democratizing moves

have partially opened these schools to certain select members of
lower classes, but the aura of property remains. The ghetto school
in the poorest neighborhood is open to all but suffers dramatically
from financial, social, and cultural starvation. Even within standard
public schools there is a social class separation resulting from
differences in manner of dress, type of transportation, housing,
and entertainment. Special costs charged in free public schools for
dances, athletic events, extra curricular activities, and even books
in many states continue property distinctions. The free lunch
program is often operated like a charity program with its attendant
lack of dignity.

In two brief centuries, the capitalist mode of production penetrated
and transformed the entire world. Whole peoples became dependent in
almost every area of their lives upon capitalist property relations—
they became proletarianized. World capitalism, dominated today by a
few owners of the giant, international corporations, by constantly
revolutionizing the productive forces, produced vast amounts of material goods. Simultaneously, capitalism produced a world-wide revolutionary movement determined to destroy capitalist property relations
themselves.

Capitalist expansion, containment, and counter-revolution.
National liberation and socialist revolution. These words try to express
the antagonistic social relations created by, and inherent in the world
capitalist social order. As Marx foresaw, world capitalism tears itself
apart through its internal contradictions—private ownership of the
means of production against the social character of production; production for profit against production for use.

Capitalism created productive forces—material goods and scientific, technical, and administrative skills and knowledge that are the
pre-condition for the abolition of alienated labor and the exploitation
of man by man. Simultaneously, capitalism created production relations that hinder the full development of the productive forces, above
all else, the most important productive force—freely developed individual men and women.

At present, within world capitalism as a whole, the ruling class in
the developed countries appropriates the greatest share of the world
social product of the world proletariat. And everywhere in the "Third
World" developing national liberation struggles and revolutionary
movements oppose this exploitation, and begin the arduous task of
developing their countries economically, politically and culturally.

Within the developed capitalist societies, large scale corporate
capital dominates the economy and the polity, determining the rhythm
of capital accumulation, the deployment of technology, the govern-

ment budget—indeed, social needs themselves, on the basis of one criterion: profit. It then satisfies these needs profitably. But even in "prosperous" Europe and North America, even in these "democracies" and "welfare states" of "middle class" workers, capitalist society is rent by social antagonisms signifying the possibilities of socialist revolution.

These antagonisms are rooted in the nature of bourgeois society. The bourgeois revolutions were made in order to realize the individual, particular interests of the bourgeoisie—to exploit labor, alienate land, expand and control markets for the sake of capital accumulation. The bourgeoisie came together and fought as a class in order to expand and protect the exploitative social relations they had begun to develop within the feudal social order. They then established a basis for social order which was itself private—bourgeois property to which all men had "rationally" to adjust. But, the bourgeoisie was compelled to represent its own particularized interests as the common interests of all members of society in order to replace the feudal ruling class. In Marx's words, "they appeared not as a class, but as the representative of the whole of society." The bourgeoisie legitimated its triumph by creating liberal democracy—democratic forms of class rule. Its formal political equality masked the economic inequality upon which bourgeois rule rested.[1]

Further, the bourgeoisie equated the private accumulation of capital, the expanded reproduction of material goods, with the public interest and the common good. As a class, it measured individual achievement by material prosperity, and the health of society by economic development. The ideology of commodity accumulation became crucial for the identification of bourgeois class interests with the interests of society as a whole.

Integral to the rise of the bourgeoisie, capitalist development integrated world-wide production relations through imperialism—first, mercantile expansion; second, the imperialism of free-trade; finally, imperialism as the expression of the interests of monopoly capital. World-wide capitalist integration and imperialism produced economically developed and economically underdeveloped poles. The first were concentrated in North America, Europe and Japan; the second were concentrated in Asia, Africa and Latin America.[2] Capitalism also

[1] See Richard Lichtman, "The Facade of Equality in Liberal Democratic Theory," *Socialist Revolution* (January/February 1970), p. 85.

[2] cf. Paul Baran, *The Political Economy of Growth*, (New York, 1957). There are a number of studies of specific countries and regions which detail Baran's general theory. See, eg., Andrew Gunder Frank, *Capitalism and Under-*

created regions of underdevelopment within the developing, industrial metropoles; within the underdeveloping, nonindustrial peripheries, capitalism produced small pockets of development.

The underdeveloped regions are characterized by an emphasis on raw material production, dependence on one or a handful of raw material exports and foreign control of industry. Most significant for revolutionary theory, an independent or national industrial bourgeoisie does not exist. Unlike the bourgeoisie of the economically advanced countries, the comprador classes of the "Third World" (including the black bourgeoisie in the United States) have been unable to identify their interests with those of society. Their identification with foreign capital (or white capital in the United States) undercuts their claim to represent the national (or black community) interest. More important, they are unable to satisfy the criterion by which bourgeois sovereignty is justified. Everywhere they have failed to produce on-going national economic, political and cultural development. By the standards of bourgeois rule, the comprador classes have proven themselves failures. In their own countries, the people see them as parasitic rather than as representative. Their real failures in the economic sphere, which are rooted in the capitalist mode of production, have vitiated their attempts to rule ideologically, and compelled them to resort to coercion, force and terror.[3] For this reason, revolution is always imminent in the underdeveloped regions.

Many of the guiding ideas of the developing revolutionary movements, as well as those movements which have already come to power, are bequeathed to the revolution by the bourgeoisie itself, which has failed to fulfill its own promises. The most important of these ideas is economic development, which can be accomplished only through socialism in the underdeveloped poles of world capitalism. There, the revolutionary movement appears as the true national "class," alone able to begin the work of a ruling class.

In addition, the path to power through immediate armed struggle is already staked out by the reliance of the comprador ruling class on coercion and force exercised by itself and in alliance with imperialism. Thus, the primacy of armed struggle and the primacy of economic development in the revolutionary movements of the "Third World" stem from the same origin, and consist of part of the same process: the underdevelopment of capitalism.

---

development in Latin America; Historical Studies of Chile and Brazil (New York, 1967); Clifford Geertz, *Agricultural Involution*; James O'Connor, *The Origins of Socialism in Cuba*, (Ithaca, New York, 1969).

[3] This is true for *political* rule; the *social* discipline exercised by the wages system is itself the foundation of "non-coercive" rule in all capitalist societies.

What, then, is the meaning of socialism in those countries that have broken free from the world capitalist system? How did socialism transform the metro-colony of old Russia, the partial economic dependencies of pre-revolutionary Vietnam, Korea and Eastern Europe and the total economic satellite of Cuba? How did socialism remake China—fragmented into a thousand pieces by imperialism—while resisting its total integration into the world market? The governments of the socialist countries, no matter how they came to power, continue to emphasize economic development as the key to the social well-being of their peoples. The *class* meaning of individual well-being (material wealth) and social progress (economic development) was discarded, but the *societal* meaning of these expressions remained fundamentally unchanged. Thus, material underdevelopment limited cultural and political development.

As long as the underdeveloped regions are compelled to concentrate energy on economic development, the full realization of human freedom must await the further development of the productive forces. The realm of freedom can be attained only when social relations need no longer be subordinated to economic development. For the world proletariat, this realm can be approached only through socialist revolution in the developed countries.

A small, well-integrated, bourgeoisie—the corporate ruling class —dominates the developed countries. Its ruling practice of private accumulation has produced vast material wealth. It uses this record of economic growth and material abundance to sanction its claim to represent, in its own interests, the interests of society. Corporate capital has thus satisfied its own criterion of success. Because of this success, the world view of corporate capital has been rendered credible and ruling class imperatives appear as basic morality, social decency and common sense. Alienated labor appears as the only kind of labor; consumption as the highest form of life activity. Poverty and exploitation are defined as minor, remediable concomitants of economic growth, which further growth will eliminate. In short, except in the underdeveloped "internal colonies," the corporate ruling class in developed societies rules primarily through ideological means, precisely because its root idea shaped and therefore corresponds with reality.

The material wealth that justifies capital's ideological domination has been produced by, and has in turn produced, a world proletariat characterized by a disparity of social condition and consciousness: capitalist exploitation and oppression reflects a disparity of evils. World-wide, the social condition of the proletariat encompasses Rio de Janeiro *favelas*, South African mining towns surrounded by barbed wire, the shanty towns of capital's cheap labor havens in Hongkong,

Formosa, Puerto Rico, the barracks of Caribbean sugar workers. Within the developed countries, the condition of the proletariat includes the shacks of Italian construction laborers in the Swiss Alps, the high rises outside of Paris, the new shopping centers in provincial Europe, the crowded streets of suburban Tokyo, the American subdivision, the black ghetto, the computerized factory and the sweat shop, the traffic jam, the new recreation-slums of the Yosemite floor. Is it any wonder that an international class-consciousness has emerged only in erratic and self-contradictory ways?

The revolutionary task of our time is to unite this heterogeneity around opposition to the corporate ruling class and to develop its particularized grievances into explicit socialist consciousness and practice by demonstrating their common root in capitalist property relations. This in turn requires revolutionary theory that encompasses both the specific situation and the concrete, historial occasion of the entire world proletariat. Revolutionary theory mediates between and unites individual feelings, introspective understanding, social vision, historical consciousness, and political strategies and tactics.

Such theory is necessary for the proletariat to understand and fulfill its dual task: the abolition not only of the bourgoisie, but also of alienated labor and class society. In the process of revolution, the proletariat is not fulfilling its present existence as a class; it is repudiating itself.

For this reason, socialist revolution in developed countries requires both a degree of self-consciousness and a theory of history that was lacking in the bourgeois revolution, and in underdeveloped socialist revolutions in the "Third World." There is nothing external to man that can lay the basis for developed socialist society in the way that private property lays the basis for capitalist society. Developed socialist society will be rooted in the only "property" proletarians have —their human capacities as social beings to rebuild and manage society. The revolution which finally establishes world socialism will be made by proletarians fully aware of themselves as *social* beings.

This historical self-understanding is necessary not only in the struggle to destroy the corporate ruling class, but also capitalist production relations—alienated labor—which have still to be overcome in the underdeveloped socialist countries, and which define exploitation in capitalist society. And to win the socialist revolution, the struggle against the ruling class requires as well a struggle against those instrumental, manipulative, and oppressive social relations—racism, nationalism, chauvinism, and authoritarianism—as capitalism produces them in all spheres of life. It is the struggle against these capitalist social relations that provides the condition for a united movement toward a common destiny.

Bourgeois society, built upon the ideals of individualism and self-interest, has by its very nature turned people against each other. Integral to capitalist production relations, men and women are forced to dissemble, ideas are cut off from feelings, and direct intimate social relations put one at an economic, social, and political disadvantage. Historical self-understanding must therefore serve to uncover the social nature of man, the realization of which is impossible in bourgeois society, and upon the basis of which a proletarian revolution will be made. In the most profound sense, the proletariat has not one enemy, but two—the ruling class and itself. In the absence of a humanizing militancy and a militant humanism, in the absence of a fierce common hatred for the common enemy, and a fiercer common love for the proletariat as a whole, history will degenerate into barbarism.

The revolutionary movement in developed capitalist societies inherits few guiding ideas from the past. "Third World" revolutionary movements know what they want, because they know what they need: economic development, the prerequisite for political and cultural development. In the developed countries, there are few existing guidelines for the socialist revolution; quite the contrary, the proletariat does not want what it needs today, does not need what it wants, and must discover what it wants to need.[4]

In developed capitalist society, many still assume that capitalism is capable of meeting human needs. For people to comprehend the magnitude of this failure, to *feel* this failure without feeling anxiety and hopelessness, requires that concrete experience, including emotional experience, be informed by theoretical understanding. In societies in which production is quintessentially *social*, the social character of individual experience is extraordinarily complex and deep-rooted. Each individual act has a variety of social meanings, which many skills and much knowledge of history and of oneself are required to reveal. Because the ideological hegemony of the bourgeoisie depends upon the core idea of commodity accumulation, the prime requisite for socialist revolution is the redefinition of well-being, of abundance, in theory and practice. This requires historical comprehension: the synthesis of self-consciousness and social consciousness.

[4] This seemingly metaphysical formulation of the problem is in fact real. Paul Baran used these particular words to describe the condition of the working class in the United States. A specific example is: auto workers produce cars, and also the need for cars. But auto workers are not self-conscious of the fact that they are producing needs, as well as the objects which satisfy these needs. Put another way, workers do not have any choice of what they *want* to need. Collective control over transportation may produce a *want* for a different *need*—e.g. decentralization, public transportation, the merging together of work, recreation, and residence, etc.

The task will not be easy. By virtue of its concentration of capital, the corporate ruling class has been able to concentrate ideological resources. A prime task of revolutionary organizing then consists of the struggle against the bourgeois world-view, including the idea that it is in society's interest that the ruling class monopolizes these resources. Thus, the arena of struggle today is not only the streets and the factory. It is also the university, the public schools, the church, the labor union, the television stations, the publishing houses, the shopping center, the home—wherever men and women reproduce bourgeois ideas and bourgeois social relations.

In the past, opposition to bourgeois ideological rule has often been vaporous, sentimental, idealistic, utopian, divorced from the social existence of the proletariat: that is, opposition to the bourgeois world-view has never risen from cultural dissent into revolutionary theory. The bourgeois idea—that capitalism would produce material wealth—proved largely correct, except during depressions, especially during the Great Depression when the business classes lost much of their moral authority, and except for the condition of the subproletariat. Alternatives to bourgeois definitions of well-being and the good life that were glimpsed by only a few artists and intellectuals appeared utopian in the onrush of material production and were swept aside. The great majority of proletarians were too confined by the mundane struggle for survival to contemplate alternative world-views and practice, and to struggle for them.

Today, however, capitalist expansion faces a world-wide anti-imperialist movement, which recognizes that capitalism has generated economic underdevelopment rather than development in the "Third World," that has compressed the space for capitalist penetration. At home, the inability of capitalist production to expand without recourse to massive expenditures on objects for waste and destruction is now obvious, not only to a few Marxist economists, but to a large number of people. Further, there are signs that the basic economic contradiction of capitalism, which has extended beyond the factory and office, and has been partly displaced to the "Third World," Europe, the state, and the sub-proletariat at home, is once again reappearing at the point of direct production.

Even more important, *the meaning of abundance and the good life themselves are being redefined by larger and larger sections of the proletariat*. Today, masses of people are repudiating the bourgeois definition of abundance—the very meaning of life under capitalism. They, and we, are thus engaged in a common project, and self-consciously or unself-consciously are beginning to negate bourgeois ideological hegemony itself.

section TWO

Radical Morality

"Conventional morality is a drab morality,
in which the only fatal thing is to be
conspicuous."
—John Dewey

"What is moral is what you
feel good after and what is
immoral is what you feel bad
after."
—Ernest Hemingway

chapter 3

Religion

Jesus Christ may be a superstar today, but he was a prophet without honor in his own time. Which is to say that in religion, as in other areas, radicalism is relative. Today's orthodoxy is an accumulation of past heresies. Christianity incurred the terrible wrath of the emperor Diocletian, but it became the state religion under his immediate successor Constantine. The man who is martyred for distorting revealed Truth may subsequently be sainted for his inspired exegesis. Conversely, yesterday's religious values may be out of favor today. Maria Goretti was canonized as recently as 1950 because she had suffered death rather than submit to the sexual advances of her assailant. Today's church fathers are likely to consider Maria's overreaction an embarrassment to the faith, better explained in psychiatric than religious terms. Similarly, "puritan" is now a popular put-down, and not even middle America cares to be thought *that* straight.

The Word is geographically as well as historically variable. There are, after all, those "weird" religions in the East. In a society as religiously pluralistic as that of the United States, the geographic dimension can reduce to the distance between two people. Everyone is someone else's heretic. Indeed, everyone is a heretic to *most* everyone else.

The ways of dealing with religious radicals are also relative to time and place. Someone who refuses to recant an extreme position in these "enlightened" times runs the risk of being committed to a mental hospital, but he does not have to fear a hideous death. Today's adulterer does not suffer the public humiliation of a scarlet letter, although he may undergo the prolonged aggravation of alimony. However, there are countries where juries still refuse to convict a cuckold who visits mayhem on his wife's lover and/or his wife. Occasionally, one also reads reports from Latin countries of wedding nights that end in murder because the bride could not convince the groom that he was the first. On the other hand, polygyny (multiple wives) is still widely practiced in Africa, and polyandry (multiple husbands) has been practiced in Tibet and parts of India and Ceylon.

In a cosmopolitan culture most heresy ceases to be a sufficient condition of religious radicalism. Because the odds are so evenly balanced, we have to disregard each other's lesser heresies. The word heretic becomes an archaism. Gradually intolerance comes to be a worse sin than many of its objects. Intolerance becomes the new heresy: The people to really watch out for are the ones with burning zeal—nobody likes a fanatic.

Thus, the opportunities for religious radicalism have been diminished. It is difficult to deviate in a land of indulgent and somewhat indifferent minorities. Nevertheless, there are convictions which most of these minorities hold in common. In the West there is a widely shared belief in a personal God who issued ten universally applicable commandments. Some of the heated religious controversies of recent years were kindled by authoritative challenges to these basic articles of faith. Atheism has been propounded by theologians in the "God is dead" movement, and selective compliance with the Ten Commandments has been recommended by clerical leaders of the "situation ethics" movement. The radicalism inherent in these challenges is compounded by the stature of the challengers.

The characteristics of Christ himself have been subjected to radical re-interpretation, again by people of prestige in religious communities. For Christians, the denial of Christ's divinity is the most drastic of these revisions. However, Christ's genealogy and ideology have also been recast from traditional conceptions to the point where Christ now serves as soul brother and role model for black militants. For those on the right, Christ functions as the J. Edgar Hoover of yesteryear, who rooted out evil and thwarted Godless ideologies. Bible Belt America becomes the new promised land, where God's will is done on earth as it is in heaven.

The conventional means by which belief is derived and expressed in Western religion are also being renounced. Rationalism and ritualism are replaced by subjectivism and personalism. Some manifestations of these phenomena have been imported from the East—Zen Buddhism being a notable example. Others, like Pentecostalism, are revivals of primitive Christianity.

This, then, is an age of exploration in religion, as it is in other cultural spheres. There is a toleration, if not a receptivity, for much of this quest and its yield. And yet the traditional boundaries are being transgressed often enough that for many people this has become an age of religious crisis. However, crises can provoke thought as well as paralyze it, and the purpose of education is to exploit the former potentiality. This cannot be done if schools shun religion through an overly-cautious interpretation of church-state separation, nor can it be done if schools limit themselves to presenting inoffensive glosses on the major religions, and neither can it be done if schools continue to teach religiously-based moral principles as though they were self-evident truths.

School should be a place for the analysis of assumptions, religious and other. How else will students be educated to live examined lives? A consideration of unpopular religious views constitutes a test of popular belief. In addition, it widens the range of alternatives from which students can choose in constructing their own religious foundations. To be kept ignorant and fearful of these alternatives makes freedom of religion a mockery.

God Is Dead

William Hamilton

William Hamilton, one of the leading theologians in the "God is dead" movement, is co-author (with Thomas Altizer) of *Radical Theology and the Death of God*. In the following article which shook the religious community, Hamilton contends that American theologians really do not believe in God: They have no sense of God's immanence. In addition, they are alienated from the church and are no longer interested in the theologizing enterprise itself. However, they keep up appearances while waiting, somewhat indifferently, for their faith to be restored. A loving involvement with their fellow humans is the only "religion" that currently makes sense to them.

Hamilton's article suggests that religious doubt and disbelief are as natural conditions as belief is popularly assumed to be. Agnosticism and atheism should also be accorded respect since they too are religious positions sincerely held, and ones for which considerable evidence can be marshalled. A general acknowledgement to this effect might make it possible to get beyond saccharine tolerance (for theists only) and insipid ecumenism to classroom consideration of ultimate religious questions. To be sure, some students will lose their family faith in whole or part, but to conclude that they can only be worse for this is to echo the absolutist arrogance which haunts the history of religion. Some students may develop an appreciation for the majesty of their religion which they never had before, but it will be tempered by the realization that their religion was erected, after all, on faith in the undemonstrable.

I

Perhaps we do not know and should not try to know what "theology" is going to look like tomorrow, for we do not really know what either church or world is going to look like tomorrow. But there are ways of finding out *what is happening to the theologian*, if not to theology, and some of these things are interesting and odd.

There is, for example, a common feeling among a good many pursuers of theology that the time of European hegemony is at an end; that while we will always be working on and even loving our German and Swiss betters, the thing of being a Christian in America today is so wildly *sui generis* that our most precious clues are no longer expected to come from a *Zitschrift* or a *Dogmatik*. Perhaps the American theologian is guilty, subtly guilty because of his lack of a humanistic scholarly tradition, or more obviously guilty because he helped out in the bombing raids twenty years ago. It is more likely, I think, that this declaration of independence is neither guilt nor pride, but—as in that other Declaration of Independence—the familiar American innocence coming to the fore. In any case, guilty or innocent or both, the American theologian today is likely to be saying, like the poor lady in the TV commercial, "Please, Mother, I would rather do it myself!"

Non-theological observers have been saying for some time that America is a place and a people without a past and without a future, or, more exactly, without a sense of having a past and without a sense of being able to count on a stable future. To put the point a little more theologically, America is the place that has travelled furthest along the road from the cloister to the world that Luther and the Reformation mapped out. We are the most profane, the most banal, the most utterly worldly of places. Western Europe is positively numinous with divine substance compared to us, and even the Communist world has a kind of spiritual substance and vitality that we are said to lack. Both the academic sabbatical leave and the conventional summer vacation bear witness to the American's need to go abroad to look for something he has not found at home.

But let us try to be more precise and even more theological. The Christian way of talking about the sense of time past and time future is to talk about faith and hope and love. Faith is the way the Christian affirms the past and appropriates the meaning of certain past events deemed to be significant. Just how faith does this is the subject of a very lively debate right now in Protestant circles. Living as the Protestant must, without the Mass, how can a past event become a present reality for him? By imaginative meditation on the biblical stories, by participation in the church as the community of memory, by the Lord's Supper, by a leap? It is concern with just this problem that leads some today to speak of the problem of hermeneutics as the critical theological issue of our day.

Hope is the way of declaring one's future to be open and assured, while love is the way of standing before your neighbor in the present moment. Taking faith, hope, and love together, one gets the feeling that the American theologian can really live in only one of them at a time, perhaps even only one in a lifetime. If this is so, and if it is also so that as an American he is fated to be a man without a sense of past or of future, it may follow that the theologian of today and tomorrow is a man without faith, without hope, with only the present and therefore only love to guide him.

Of these three propositions, so vulnerable and precarious, and to some extent falsified whenever any reader chooses to blurt out, "Why, it's not like that for me at all," the most alluring, interesting, and defensible is the one that speaks of the faithlessness of the theologian. Let me try to state what I mean by this. I am pretty sure I am describing something that is the case. Nor am I inclined to view with alarm, for I am convinced that this is something that ought to be, not just a sad inevitability. We should not only acknowledge, but welcome *this* faithlessness.

II

What does it mean to say that the theologian in America is a man without faith? Is he therefore a man without God? It would seem to follow. He has his *doctrine* of God, several no doubt, and all correct. But that is surely not the point. He really doesn't believe *in* God, whatever that means, or that there is *a* God, or that God *exists*. It is not just that he is fashionably against idols or opposed to God as a Being or as part of the world. It is God himself he has trouble with. Can one stand before God in unbelief? In what sense is such a man "before God"? Faith, or trusting in God, ought to produce some palpable fruits. The theologian may sometimes see these, but never in himself. Something has happened. At the center of his thoughts and meditations is a void, a disappearance, an absence. It is sometimes said that only a wounded physician can heal.

Some other pertinent questions can be raised. Does the theologian go to church? This is a banal kind of question, but we need this form of the question because the answer is "no." He may, in the past, have concealed this "no" from himself by escaping into church work, speaking to church groups, preaching at church or college, slaking his thirst for worship and word in more protected communities. But now he is facing up to this banal answer to the banal question and he wills to say "no" openly.

It used to be otherwise. Before, the theologian would distinguish between God, Christendom, Christianity, and church, so that a different balance of "yes" and "no" could be uttered to each. Now he finds himself equally alienated from each of the realities represented by the four terms, and he says his "no" to each.[1]

The quality of the theologian's "no" to the church differs from the impressive, if verbose, debate now being waged by the church's sociological pundits. In this debate the issue is drawn between a kind of strident despair and grim hope. This game, among the "in" score-keepers, is posted as Bergerism vs. Martyism. The Ecclesiastical Broadcasting Company reports that Martyism is leading, while the Student Broadcasting Company gives Bergerism the edge. Both agree, of course, that it is two out, the last of the ninth. The theologian, however, is neither despairing nor hopeful about the church. He is not interested, and he no longer has the energy or interest to answer ecclesiastical questions about "What the Church Must Do to Revitalize Itself." Altizer writes that "contemporary theology must be alienated from the church. . . . [and] the theologian must exist outside the Church, he can neither proclaim the Word, celebrate the sacraments, nor rejoice in the presence of the Holy Spirit: before contemporary theology can become itself, it must first exist in silence."[2]

One can choose his own language here, as it may happen to fit: the theologian does not and cannot go to church; he is not interested; he is alienated (for a tenser word); he must live outside. He is not thereby a happier man, nor is he a troubled one. He is neither proud nor guilty. He has just decided that this is how it has to be, and he has decided to say so.

III

An even funnier question casts a strange light on our theologian. Does he write books in systematic theology? The answer to this, oddly, is an almost unambiguous "no." If you mean, does he sit down and decide that he'd better do a theological book, the answer is a clear "no." What he does is first to get his doctoral dissertation published. If this is good, as it often is, he can get quite a few years of professional mileage from it, defending it, clarifying, writing articles on

[1] In an impressive, helpful, and profoundly important article, Thomas J. J. Altizer of Emory University has argued against the fashionable Christian radicalism which, for purposes of a selective criticism, distinguishes between Christendom, Christianity and church. "America and the Future of Theology," *Antaios*, September, 1963.

[2] *Op. cit.*

relevant material that has come out since. From then on he speaks and writes as he is asked. Editors, ecclesiastics, institutions, and other scholars then take over, and assign him set subjects that they think he would be interested in. In this way he can get a reputation for being skilled and interested in a field that he has no interest in whatever. Along these lines, the gulf between what he wants to do and what he does grows wider and funnier as the years pass, as he moves through the stages of being "young" and "promising" to whatever comes after that. His books, if any, are either private love-letters (or hate-letters) to fellow guild members or lecture series that offer an extra $500.00 for publication. Anything serious he manages will probably be in articles.

This leads directly to another question. What does the theologian read? Does he read religious books in hard covers? Less and less, perhaps not at all, except when he has a free copy for review or a bibliography to prepare. He has been unable to read books of sermons for a long time, and he has recently found that he practically never reads a book of theology for the sheer fun of it. He reads a lot of paperbacks, and a lot of articles and reviews. Just as theological writing is less and less being put into books, the theologian is reading fewer and fewer books. One wonders quite seriously if there is any long-range future for hard-cover religious book publishing, apart from church materials, reference works, and perhaps textbooks.

Speaking of reading, is this theologian reading the Bible? Of course, he is forced into a kind of affable semi-professional relationship with Scripture in his daily work. His Bible is not exactly a dust-collector. But the rigorous systematic confronting of Scripture, expecting the Word of God to be made manifest when one approaches it with faith or at least with a broken and contrite heart, this has gone. Perhaps because he is without both faith and the truly contrite heart, the Bible is a strange book that does not come alive to him as it is supposed to. There are still some pieces of it that come alive, to be sure; he is not sure why or how. This psalm, that prophetic call, a piece or two of Job, a bit of a letter, some words of Jesus.

This won't do, to be sure, to have to say that this theologian is alienated from the Bible, just as he is alienated from God and the church. It may not last, this alienation, just as the other forms of it may not last. If it doesn't last, fine; if it does last, it will get rough, and the theologian will have some piercing questions to ask of himself. But there are wrong ways and right ways to overcome this alienation, and for now he has to be honest with himself, with the God before whom he stands in unbelief, and he has to wait.

IV

Let us turn to a couple of more inward, more psychological questions. Perhaps the query can be put in this way: What is this theologian really like? How does he act? Is he consciously or unconsciously dishonest? What is the relation between his public and his private *persona*? I am sure we must exonerate the theologian from certain coarse professional faults: he is not overly ambitious for position or even notice; he is not moving in the direction I am sketching so that he can be seen by men or because of some special delight he has *épater le bourgeois*. Like all men, he lives in a public and in a private sphere, and like most men he works hard to keep the first from overpowering the second. On his public and professional side he is likely to make use of two different masks. One is a modestly devout one, earnest and serious, and this he uses for his teaching and church work. The other is a modestly worldly mask for his non-religious friends and for the forms of their common life. Sometimes he deliberately decides to interchange the masks, and wears the worldly mask for a church talk, a lecture, or even a sermon here or there. This leads to some harmless fun, and he is careful to see that everybody enjoys himself. Sometimes he dons the devout mask for his worldly friends and their parties, and this too is quite harmless, for his friends understand and even sometimes admire his willingness to stand up for his rather odd beliefs.

But back in the private realm, he is coming more and more to distrust this kind of manipulation. God—this much he knows—is no respecter of persons or *personae* or masks, and the theologian really knows that he is neither mask. He knows that his rebellion and unbelief is both deeper and uglier than his bland worldly mask suggests, and he knows also (a bit less assuredly) that his devout mask is too vapid. To be a man of two masks is, he knows, to be less than honest. Thus, he has had to come out into the open about his faithlessness even though he may suspect and hope that beneath it is a passion and a genuine waiting for something that may, one day, get transformed into a kind of faith even better than what he has willed to lose.

Is this theologian alone, or does he live in a community that needs and nourishes him? He is not alone, but he does not ordinarily live in a true community. He rarely gets close enough to anybody to identify him as a member of this community, but he knows there is no place under the sun where a member of this community may not be found. Members may, of course, even be found in the church.

The problem is not, as might be suspected, that he has no doctrine of the church; the problem is with the doctrine of the church he does have. Professionally he finds himself working with three quite different understandings of the church, but only the third really makes genuine sense to him, and it is far too imprecise to be very helpful.

The first understanding of the church states that it is to be defined by the classical marks of the church—unity, holiness, catholicity, apostolicity. In his ecumenical work or in the emerging Roman Catholic–Protestant dialogue, he is compelled to see the church in this way. The second way reminds him that the church is found where the Word of God is preached and the sacraments rightly administered. This doctrine of the church is most congenial to his own theology and theological vocation. He has always been drawn to a theology of the Word, and he has had moments when he has felt that theology might, after all, be able to minister to the church's proclamation.

But somehow along the way he has had to come to define the church in a third way: the church is present whenever Christ is being formed among men in the world. This is a very vague way of describing his feeling about the community, for now it has no outlines, no preaching, sacraments, or liturgy.

V

One final question needs to be asked: What is tomorrow's theologian doing *now?* The answer comes in two parts, the first related to what we have called his loss of God, of faith, of church. In the face of all this, he is a passive man, trusting in waiting, in silence, and even in a kind of prayer for the losses to be returned. He does not do this anxiously, nor does he impress us as a particularly broken or troubled sort of person. If it is true that he is somehow without hope as well as without faith, he is not in despair about himself. His waiting is more docile and patient and has little of existential moodiness in it. There is, of course, no single Christian doctrine which he affirms or grasps with guileless joy, but for all of his acute sense of loss, he has an overwhelmingly positive sense of being in and not out; that even in his unbelief he is somehow home and not in a far country. He may, of course, be deceived about this. But you might find him saying, for example: "As long as the Gethsemane prayer stands there somehow close to the center of things, I can stand there. If it should have to go, I might have to go too."

Thus it appears that the theologian is both a waiting man and a praying man. While this is true, he cannot quite yet be written off by wiser heads, younger or older.

The second part of the answer to the question "What is the theologian doing now?" has to do not with the loss of faith but with the presence of love. His faith and hope may be badly flawed, but his love is not. It is not necessary to probe the cultural, psychological, or even marital reasons for this, but simply to note it as a fact. It is interesting to see how this works out in a particular theological area—let us take Christology.

The theologian is sometimes inclined to suspect that Jesus Christ is best understood not as either the object or ground of faith, and not as person, event, or community, but simply as a place to be, a standpoint. That place is, of course, alongside the neighbor, being for him. This may be the meaning of Jesus' true humanity, and it may even be the meaning of his divinity, and thus of divinity itself. In any case, now—even when he knows so little about what to believe—he does know *where to be*. Today, for example, he is with the colored community in its struggle (he will work out his own understanding of what "being with" must mean for him), working and watching, not yet evangelizing. He is also with all sorts of other groups: poets, critics, psychiatrists, physicists, philosophers. He is not in these places primarily to make something happen—a new solution to the science-religion problem or a new theological literary criticism—but just to be himself and to be attentive as a man and therefore as a theologian. This is what his form of love looks like. It is a love that takes place in the middle of the real world, the ugly, banal, godless, religious world of America today.

He has been drawn, then, to these worldly places by love (not by apologetics or evangelism), and it is his hope that in such places his faithlessness and dishonesty may be broken. His love is not a secure and confident one, and thus it is not condescending. It is not, therefore, what some men call *agape*. It is a broken love, one that is needy and weak. It is thus a little like what men call *eros*. To be sure, his whole project may be swept away in a moment, if it can be shown that the theologian is just fleeing from one kind of religion-as-need-fulfillment to another. Perhaps someone will be able to show him that his weak and needy love has some points of connection with the love of the Cross.

Dietrich Bonhoeffer is, of course, deeply involved in this portrait I have been drawing. Have we discovered this in him, and then in ourselves; or in ourselves, and then rejoiced to find it in him? I think the second is nearer the truth. It does seem clear, in any case, that as Western Europe turns away from Bonhoeffer as a theological mentor, we in America need not be apologetic in refusing to follow that refusal, and in welcoming his fragmentary help. We could begin with these words:

Atonement and redemption, regeneration, the Holy Ghost, the love of our enemies, the cross and resurrection, life in Christ and Christian discipleship—all these things have become so problematic and so remote that we hardly dare any more to speak of them. . . . So our traditional language must perforce become powerless and remain silent, and our Christianity today will be confined to praying for and doing right by our fellow men. Christian thinking, speaking and organization must be reborn out of this praying and this action.[3]

[3] "Thoughts on the Baptism of D. W. R.," in *Letters and Papers from Prison*, by Dietrich Bonhoeffer, Macmillan, N. Y., 1963, pp. 187 f.

The Black Messiah

Albert B. Cleage, Jr.

Albert Cleage is a graduate of Wayne State University and Oberlin Graduate School of Theology. He has been co-pastor of the famous inter-racial Fellowship Church of San Francisco. The following article is taken from a sermon given by the Rev. Cleage at his Shrine of the Black Madonna in Detroit. The position developed is that the Israelite nation of the Scriptures was a predominantly black nation, that Jesus was black, and that God, in whose image man is created, is also black. The further point is made that God's message, as expressed in the Old Testament and the life of Christ, concerns an active social morality and not the morality of individualism and passivity which allows people to be divided and enslaved.

The interpretation of Christ's life which Cleage gives is strikingly similar to that given by William Hamilton. In the past few years there have been several studies of Christ which portray him as a social activist and sometimes as a political revolutionary. The studies have intensified the historical controversy that has always

From *The Black Messiah* by Albert B. Cleage, Jr., © Sheed and Ward, Inc., 1968. Reprinted with permission.

surrounded the life of Christ. They also raise intriguing questions about the selection and interpretation of historical data. There may be no better figure around whom to construct a course in the historical method than Jesus. Why is he presented in such startling contrasts by so many different people?

It would be interesting to know if Cleage's interpretations have affected the bland treatments of Christianity in world history courses. Perhaps Cleage's version is becoming the official line in black schools with the standard rendition continuing to prevail in white schools—a tragedy for all concerned.

I address my remarks to those who believe in the Movement but who do not believe in the Christian Church because they do not understand that the Movement is the Christian Church in the 20th Century and that the Christian Church cannot truly be the church until it also becomes the Movement. So then, I would say to you, you are Christian, and the things you believe are the teachings of a Black Messiah named Jesus, and the things you do are the will of a black God called Jehovah; and almost everything you have heard about Christianity is essentially a lie.

You have been misled. Christianity for you has been misinterpreted. That which you believe to be Christianity, the theology and philosophy of history which you reject, is not Christianity. The Christianity which we see in the world today was not shaped by Jesus. It was put together by the Apostle Paul who never saw Jesus, and given form and shape during the Middle Ages when most of the hymns were written, the hymns which for the most part enunciate white supremacy. "Fairest Lord Jesus." Most of the famous religious pictures that you see were painted between the fourteenth and the seventeenth centuries by white artists. When Dutch artists painted religious pictures, everything looks just like it all happened in Holland. When French artists painted religious pictures, the biblical characters look French.

But we didn't realize this when we looked at our Sunday School literature as children. When we turned the pages and always saw a white Jesus, when we saw pictures of a white God pointing down at creation, we didn't realize that these were not statements of fact but statements by white men depicting what they wanted to believe was true. I say, what they wanted to believe was true, because essentially they knew that white men did not create Christianity. They borrowed it, more bluntly, they stole it. In fact, of all the peoples on earth, the one people who have never created a religion worthy of the name religion are white people.

All religions stem from black people. Think of them for a moment. The Muslim religion, the Buddhist religion, the Jewish religion, the Christian religion, they all come from parts of the world dominated by non-white peoples. The white man's religion was the primitive religion of the pagans with a pantheon of gods throwing thunderbolts and cavorting about heaven and earth, filled with lust and violence. To the Romans, religion was the deification of the Emperor. They had no God. They believed that whoever could take power must be God, and they worshipped him. The white man has never created a genuine religion. He has only borrowed religions from non-white peoples.

It's important for us to understand this because the civilization around us is not ours. We are sojourners in a strange land, and we have been taught what someone else wanted us to know. So what we have been taught about Christianity is not what Christianity is, but what white people wanted us to believe. The white man captured the religion of a Black Nation, the revelations of a Black God, the teachings of a Black Messiah, and he has used them to keep black men enslaved. We are the chosen people in a religious sense, in a historic sense, and this I will try to develop for you. The time has come for us to reclaim our God, our prophet, and our power. . . .

Abraham, the father of Israel was a Chaldean. Look at your map of this part of the world, and you will find that there was very little likelihood that the Chaldeans were white. Abraham went out from Chaldea to build for himself and for his family a new way of life. In going out, he declared that he had received a revelation from God, and had made a covenant with God, and that God had selected him to build a Nation. This was the beginning of Israel. He went out from the Chaldean city of Ur into Africa. He went down into Egypt and dwelt in Egypt among the Egyptians. Now if there is any question in your mind about whether or not the Egyptians were black you have only to look at the Sphinx, the drawings and the inscriptions from Egypt. Recent studies prove that many of the Pharaohs were black or Negroid. Only the American white man tries to pretend that the Egyptians were white.

Abraham went into Egypt and he lived with the Egyptians and because his wife was beautiful he was afraid to admit she was his wife for fear that someone might want her and kill him. So he said, "She is my sister." And so while he lived in Egypt, his wife was taken by the Egyptian King and he made no protest. Obviously, the relationship between the Egyptians and Abraham and his clan was a very close one. We are at the beginning. There is no question about Abraham and the beginning of the Nation Israel being very closely related to Africa, to the Egyptians and to black people. This is the beginning of the Nation Israel.

The Egyptians were very good to Abraham. They gave him cattle and wealth. He came out of Egypt a wealthy man with many black Egyptian servants with him. The Nation Israel is beginning to develop now as a combination of Abraham, his family and the Egyptians who have been adopted while Abraham was in Egypt. The nature of the relationship can be deduced from the fact that he himself married Hagar, his Egyptian servant, and had a child by her named Ishmael. We still use the word Hagar. We speak of Hagar's children and you know what that means.

Then Sara, his wife, had her own child and got mad and didn't want her son to have to split the inheritance. So she told Abraham to get rid of the child Ishmael. So Hagar and Ishmael were driven out into the desert and God looked down on Hagar and Ishmael and said, "I will protect them and save them because you, Ishmael, will become the father of a great people." Ishmael is traditionally reputed to be the father of the Arabic Nation. Abraham was very closely identified with the black people of Africa.

Later on, there was Moses, born during Israel's Egyptian bondage. Moses is quite obviously, by the biblical story, part Egyptian. His adoption by Pharaoh's daughter does not ring true. Moses is at least half-Egyptian and half-Jewish, and to say that he's half-Egyptian and half-Jewish makes him unquestionably all non-white. This is Moses. We're still dealing with the Nation Israel which is always depicted as a white nation. The Nation Israel was not at any time a white nation. Where could they have picked up any white blood, wandering around Africa? They hadn't even had any contact with white people. Moses married a Midianite, a black woman, and had children.

Israel finally fought its way into Canaan and mixed with the people of Canaan. Those weren't white people either. "People of the land" they called them. The Israelites looked down on them, after a fashion, but that didn't stop them from sleeping with them. And all through the Old Testament you notice every once in a while a prophet rares up and says, "We have got to maintain our purity." And you know what that means. That means that the purity is already gone. There's nothing to maintain. Just as in the South when the white man stands up and talks about maintaining white purity. He wouldn't be talking about it if there was any purity to maintain, and it was exactly the same with the prophets. They looked about and saw that Israel had mixed with the people wherever they went.

When Israel was taken captive into Babylon, they mixed with the people of Babylon, and Babylon was no white nation. They lived with them, intermarried with them, and then the prophets began to write down rules about how God's Chosen People should not mix with other people. At this late date, they were trying to build a sense of identity. They petitioned the king to be permitted to return to Israel. But when they finally received permission to go back, most of the Jews wouldn't go. They were happy and content. They were in business. They had friends, relatives, everything. They didn't want to go back. Only a little handful returned, and when they went back, they looked around and saw the Jews who had remained and said, "These Jews have become people of the land. They're like all of the other people. They've intermarried." And then the prophet stood up and said, "You've got to separate from the people of the land. We must keep the Jews pure."

Now how could you keep them pure? They had mixed in Babylon, they had mixed in Egypt, they had mixed in Canaan. What was there to keep pure? And yet they tried to issue a pronouncement, "You've got to separate." But it was ridiculous and impossible. It was as impossible to separate the Jews from the people of the land as it was to maintain segregation in the South after nightfall. It could not be done. Israel was a mixed-blood, non-white nation. What usually confuses you is the fact that the Jews you see today in America are white. Most of them are the descendants of white Europeans and Asiatics who were converted to Judaism about one thousand years ago. The Jews were scattered all over the world. In Europe and Russia, they converted white people to Judaism. The Jews who stayed in that part of the world where black people are predominant, remained black. The conflict between black Jews and white Jews is a problem in Israel today.

Jesus came to the Black Nation Israel. We are not talking now about "God the Father." We are concerned here with the actual blood line. Jesus was born to Mary, a Jew of the tribe of Judah, a non-white people; black people in the same sense that the Arabs were black people, in the same sense that the Egyptians were black people. Jesus was a Black Messiah born to a black woman.

The pictures of the Black Madonna which are all over the world did not all turn black through some mysterious accident. Portraits of the Black Madonna are historic, and today in many countries they are afraid to take the ancient pictures of the Black Madonna out of storage so that people can see them. Only this year in Spain they were afraid to parade with the Black Madonna because they feared that it might have political implications. But the Black Madonna is an historic fact, and Jesus as a Black Messiah is an historic fact.

We might ask why did God choose to send his son (or to come

himself) to the nation Israel? It is a question you should have asked yourself. Why, of all the peoples on earth did he come to these people? Why not to some little group of white people in Europe who were living in caves and eating raw meat? Why did he pick these people? Why? Go back for a moment to the Biblical account of creation, "God created man in his own image." We say that all the time, but what does it mean? If God created man in his own image, what must God look like? I know that if you close your eyes, you see a white God. But if God created man in his own image, then we must look at man to see what God looks like. There are black men, there are yellow men, there are red men, and there are a few, a mighty few, white men in the world. If God created man in his own image, then God must be some combination of this black, red, yellow and white. In no other way could God have created man in his own image.

So if we think of God as a person (and we are taught in the Christian religion to think of God as a person, as a personality capable of love, capable of concern, capable of purpose and of action) then God must be a combination of black, yellow and red with just a little touch of white, and we must think of God as a black God. So all those prayers you've been sending up to a white God have been wasted. In America, one drop of black makes you black. So by American law, God is black, and by any practical interpretation, why would God have made seven-eighths of the world non-white and yet he himself be white? That is not reasonable. If God were white, he'd have made everybody white. And if he decided to send his son to earth, he would have sent a white son down to some nice white people. He certainly would not have sent him down to a black people like Israel.

So we have been misled. We received Christianity as we know it from our slave masters. Most of us didn't have it when we got here. We had lost it. We learned it from our slave masters. The Christianity given to the slaves and used to enslave the continent of Africa, when the white man sent missionaries back over there with guns and with Bibles, is the white man's distortion and corruption of the black man's historic faith. It is this corruption of Christianity which the black man, and especially black young people, is rejecting today.

Let me point out three things which are a part of this rejection. Christianity is essentially and historically concerned with a group, with society, with the community. In the Old Testament and in the Synoptic Gospels, God is concerned with a people, not with individuals. Yet, the slave Christianity that we were taught told us that God is concerned with each individual. And the master told each slave, "If you are a good slave, God is going to take care of you and you will be saved." He didn't tell them that if all you black people love God and fight together, God is going to help you get free from slavery. The group concept is historic Christianity. Individualism is slave Christianity.

The petty personal morality emphasized in the slave Church comes from slave Christianity. God is concerned in the Old Testament and Jesus is concerned in the New Testament with social morality, with how a group of people act, how they take care of each other, whether they're concerned about poverty, whether they're concerned about each other. Whence comes, then, this emphasis upon petty personal morality? Do you smoke? Then you're a sinner. Do you drink? Then you're a sinner. This is slave Christianity. Because this was the emphasis that the slave master wanted to make so that he could use religion to control his slaves.

The other worldly emphasis, where did that come from? That's not in the Old Testament nor in the teachings of Jesus, either. Jesus talked of the kingdom of God on earth. He talked to his followers about building a certain kind of world *here*. In the Old Testament the prophets were concerned with building God's kingdom out of the Nation Israel. Then whence comes this other worldly emphasis? This is slave Christianity. Slave Christianity deliberately emphasized the other world so that we would not be concerned about the everyday problems of this world.

The tremendous confusion in Christianity grows out of the fact that after the death of Jesus, the Apostle Paul began to corrupt his teachings with concepts which were essentially the pagan concepts of the Gentile oppressors. From the Greek and Roman world he borrowed philosophical ideas that had nothing to do with anything that Israel had ever believed or anything that Jesus had ever taught. The Apostle Paul attempted to break the covenant which the Black Nation Israel had with God. He said, "Circumcision is unimportant, all these little rules and laws are unimportant. We must accept everybody." That is why Paul was in conflict with the real disciples who had walked with Jesus and were still in Jerusalem. They said, "We are a people. We have a covenant with God. We believe in certain things, and when you go out and you try to convert the barbarians you are corrupting our faith." History has proven that they were correct. The Epistles of Paul are in direct contradiction to the teachings of the Old Testament. Slave Christianity emphasizes these distortions of the Apostle Paul and denies and repudiates the basic teachings of Jesus Christ and the Black Nation Israel.

The Black Messiah Jesus did not build a Church, but a Movement. He gathered together people to follow him and he sent them out to change the world. He sent out the seventy two-by-two, and he himself went from place to place. He built a Movement, not a Church. Like today's young black prophets, he rejected the institutionalization of religion. He rejected the Church deliberately because he said, "It's wrong, it's hypocritical, and it's opposed to the will of God." He rejected the morality of his time. He rejected the Church of his time. He was a prophet.

He was in the same frame of mind as the young black prophets today who reject Christianity as they see it institutionalized in the slave Church. Jesus tried to minister to the every-day needs of his days and he did this within the loose organizational structure of a Movement. He was a dangerous revolutionary.

In our Scripture lesson this morning we read, first, the account of Jesus' first sermon in Nazareth where he described the things that he had come to do. To give sight to the blind, to give food to the hungry, to take the chains off those who were in bondage. These things he had come to do. To minister to the everyday needs of people. In another scriptural passage we had the account of Jesus going into the Temple. A man whose arm was withered went up to Jesus, and the Scribes and the Pharisees waited to see whether or not Jesus would help the man on the Sabbath Day. Jesus looked angrily at the Pharisees and the Scribes, and he healed the man right there in the Temple because it was more important to help the man than it was to observe the laws of the Sabbath. At another time he said, "The Sabbath was made for man, not man for the Sabbath."

It's peculiar how we could misread the Bible for so long. How could we just keep on singing the same old wrong songs and keep on going through the same old wrong motions when the truth was right there in the Book. People don't really read the Bible. They listen to what somebody tells them. Now, let me tell you, your grandmother and that country preacher down home didn't know all there is to know about Christianity. And if you're going to depend on what they told you, then you're just going to be wrong about almost everything. You've got to go back and look at the Bible itself, read some history books and find out what this Christianity is that you either believe or don't believe. Find out who this Jesus is that you either follow or reject!

The Faith of Our Fathers

Billy James Hargis

Billy James Hargis, the leader of the anti-Communist Christian Crusade, asserts that America is a Christian nation in its heritage and by the beliefs of the vast majority of its citizens. Its Christian character accounts for the nation's greatness. The founding fathers only disestablished churches, not God and the Bible. Unfortunately, the principle of church-state separation has been exaggerated by godless, satanic Communists and their dupes to serve the purposes of imperialistic Communism. American institutions, including the schools, must once again proudly proclaim their Christian foundations.

Hargis strongly implies that there is a complete opposition between Christianity and Communism. The two terms are mutually and utterly exclusive. This, in turn, suggests that Hargis either views Christianity as being necessarily capitalistic or he understands Communism to be essentially atheistic. Either way, he leaves no room for reconciliation. And since he attributes the growing secularization of American life to a Communist plot, co-existence is also out of the question. The most cheering prospect with which we are left is a relentless pursuit of the Cold War.

It would be instructive to compare Hargis' desire for official re-institutionalization of Christianity with Supreme Court opinions regarding school prayer. Hargis asserts his concern for the rights of religious minorities, but he claims that these rights have been exaggerated to the detriment of the majority. In short, Hargis claims that the Supreme Court's aversion to majority imposition on the minority has actually led it to countenance the opposite—minority imposition on the majority.

Where should one draw the line between majority rule and minority rights in the conduct of public education? If community control in the suburbs permits the inculcation of the WASP ethic,

From Billy James Hargis, *Communist America: Must It Be?* (Tulsa, Okla.: Christian Crusade, 1960), pp. 31–37, 38–39. Reprinted with the permission of the author and publisher.

shouldn't black nationalist majorities in the decentralized school systems of the cities be allowed to indoctrinate students with their ideology? Or must one think in terms of a national ethos as Hargis implies? If so, what are the components of that ethos in addition to Christianity? Hargis would obviously include capitalism. The members of the Kerner Commission on Civil Disorders might feel obliged to include racism.

Our founding fathers did not intend to establish a government that did not recognize God and Jesus Christ, but instead, their vision was to establish government that did not recognize a church or an ecclesiastical body.

Today, the left-wingers and liberals, in far too many instances, interpret separation of church and state, as separation of state and God. This is the opposite of the original meaning of this great principle and doctrine.

Patriotism and Christianity are very close to each other. It is impossible to be a true Christian and not be a true patriot. One who loves God also loves his country. Our forefathers believed in Jesus Christ and in His atoning blood. They talked about their faith in their homes, taught it in the schools as well as in the churches, and sang of it in wilderness brush arbors, tabernacles and camp-meetings.

Our forefathers followed the Biblical admonition of Jesus, "Seek ye first the Kingdom of God and His righteousness and all these other things shall be added unto you." They heeded the warning in Psalms 9:17, "The wicked shall be turned into hell and all nations that forget God." The American dream has had a progressive fulfillment because of the Christian faith of this nation, and because of the religious liberty graciously accorded all men, regardless of their beliefs.

Communism, however, has come along with insistence that America no longer look toward God, but instead toward government. Communism, through its associates, liberalism, progressivism, socialism, and modernism is creating class warfare within America, fomenting hatred, stirring up various so-called "social crises," destroying love of country, perverting morals of young and old, casting aside beloved traditions, banning the Bible from American schools, and in general reducing the proud and free American citizenship to an insignificant, helpless, hopeless pawn of giant government.

America is and always has been a Christian nation. The very

spirit of the American Constitution reflects the teachings of Christ. America was founded by Christians. Every president to date, has been or professed to be a Christian, with perhaps one exception, Thomas Jefferson. The overwhelming majority of American citizens are members of the Christian faith, and these Christian citizens are paying 70 per cent of the nation's taxes.

The United States always has been a Christian nation, willing, ready and able to fight for the right of every man to worship as he pleases. The first constitutional form of government ever signed in all history was signed by forty-one of America's pilgrim fathers. Their laws were molded closely on the Bible. Freedom of divine worship was, for the first time, incorporated in the constitutional laws of a country. In fact, the primary objective of our founding fathers was the discovery and establishment of a land and a nation where they could worship God according to the dictates of their own consciences, and where they could establish homes and rear their children without fear of the iron hand of tyranny.

Never did the founding fathers of America intend that our government become one which denies God. Never did they intend for our government to "shield" our children from the saving knowledge of God's truth by banning the Bible and prayer from the public schools. The first great American president, George Washington, made it clear that it is impossible to govern the world without the Bible.

The Plymouth Colony Law for Education of Children states,

> . . . the good education of children . . . is of . . . benefit to any commonwealth. It is ordered that the Deputies and Select men of every town shall have a vigilant eye to see that all parents and masters so duly endeavor, by themselves or others, to teach their children . . . so much learning as through the blessings of God they may attain, at least to be able to read the Scriptures . . . and in some competent measure to understand the . . . principles of the Christian religion necessary to salvation. . . .

Such was the faith of our fathers—holy faith. They were true to that faith till death, and we hold the same privilege and responsibility. Never in all of America's glorious history has the faith of our fathers been dimmer in the hearts and souls of the sons and daughters of America as today.

The New England Articles of Confederation in 1643, stated, ". . . we all came into these parts of America with one and the same end and aim, namely to advance the Kingdom of our Lord Jesus Christ and to enjoy the liberties of the Gospel in purity with peace. . . ."

Early American settlers signing the Rhode Island Compact in 1638, declared their faith in this manner: "We whose names are underwritten . . . will submit our persons, lives, and estates unto our Lord Jesus Christ, the King of Kings and the Lord of Lords, and to all those perfect and absolute laws of His, given us in His holy word of truth, to be judged and guided thereby."

Our Declaration of Independence proclaims "reliance on the protection of Divine providence." The Thanksgiving Proclamation of the Continental Congress on November 1, 1777, spoke of pleasing God through the merits of Jesus Christ and of "the promotion and enlargement of the kingdom which consisteth in righteousness, peace, and joy in the Holy Ghost." The founders of America had no hesitation, and no shame in acknowledging the Bible as the word of God and as the guide for their nation and their nation's rulers.

The fifty-six courageous men who signed the Declaration of Independence, instantly became criminals in the eyes of the British Crown and were made to suffer untold hardships and persecutions because of their faith. The price of freedom was very great. Yet today, America is in deadly danger of losing its precious freedoms because millions upon millions of its free sons and daughters will not consider their danger nor arouse themselves to take personal and individual responsibility for the saving and preservation of those freedoms.

One of the Declaration signers was John Hart. His thirteen children fled their father's home for their lives; his wife died alone. His large farm was pillaged and his livestock driven away and destroyed. He was a hunted man. He paid a bitter price for freedom. Lewis Morris of New York, a wealthy man and a graduate of Yale University, wrote his name on the parchment. His forest of more than one thousand acres was burned, his home destroyed, and his family forced to flee for their lives. Richard Stockton of New Jersey, a Princeton graduate and lawyer, was arrested, thrown into prison, denied food, and given such brutal treatment that he never recovered his health. His papers and library were burned and his farm laid in ruins. Francis Lewis, another signer, saw his home plundered and wrecked, his business and source of income swept away, and everything he had confiscated.

Our founding fathers were willing to give all they had, even their lives, to obtain the freedoms which we now take for granted and which are gradually being cut away from us. American citizens have become far more interested in what they can get out of government than in what they can give to preserve their Republican form of government. The judgment of God surely will fall more severely upon America than upon other lands because much is required of those who have been granted much. Christian America has gained the most of all the civilized world and, if America falls, the fall of it will be great indeed. The suffering of American people under godless, satanic Communism, will be unparalleled in its horror, brutality and abandon.

Under Communism, no one as an individual can say, "My land, my farm, my home, my automobile, my cattle, or even my dog." As Congressman Wint Smith of Kansas has warned, "Under Communism you cannot possess anything except your picture with a card (with your serial number), your residence and the place where you work by government order. Of course, you would never say, 'This is my country,' because you belong to godless, atheistic, international Communism."

America has become a great nation because its great leaders and its people have believed in God, but godless leaders have infiltrated and subverted practically all phases of the American way of life. The people as a whole are being swept along by the socialists, the liberals, the progressives, the modernists, unwittingly making themselves tools as well as dupes of the international Communist conspiracy, which is active not only in America but in every nation and every land in the world. The end and aim of Communism is world conquest and world enslavement, with America being the grand prize of all.

Seldom are the sacred, patriotic songs of the land of the free such as "America," "The Star Spangled Banner," "America the Beautiful," "God Bless America," and "Faith of Our Fathers," sung in public meetings, colleges, theaters, or even churches anymore because those songs glorify God, bless God, thank God, and praise God "from whom all blessings flow."

In the famous Trinity Church decision of the American Supreme Court in February, 1892, Justice Brewer said, ". . . no purpose of action against religion can be imputed to any legislation, state or national, because this is a religious people." Christianity is and always has been a vital part of the American way of life and the American form of government. There is no other possible explanation for the blessing of America, for in all lands where religious freedom is denied the standard of living is extremely low in contrast with the United States. No nation which denies God has long prospered or endured.

Yet, little by little, decree by decree, America is denying God and turning its face away from the Saviour of the world. On June 10, 1955, the attorney general of California handed down an "opinion" that the Bible and prayer are unconstitutional in California's public schools. The opinion was given by Edmund G. "Pat" Brown, then attorney general.

Mr. Brown said, "Daily prayer . . . might well be a disruptive element which would weaken the moral influence of parents and teachers." Such a view is quite in contrast to the view of the father of our country, George Washington, who said that "religion and morality" were "indispensable supports" for political prosperity, and that "reason and experience both forbid us to expect that national morality can prevail in exclusion of religious principle."

All too many other states have followed the example of California in banning the Bible from the public schools. Wherever the Bible is banned, sooner or later, the "Pledge of Allegiance to the Flag of the United States of America" and the displaying of the flag itself are also discreetly omitted. Thus, are love of God and love of country stifled in the young.

Are we ashamed of our nation? Are we ashamed of our flag? Are we ashamed of our God? Are we ashamed of the faith of our fathers?

America's greatest need in this dark and deadly hour is continuous, prevailing, intercessory prayer. God's divine prescription for the recovery of a nation is found in II Chronicles 7:14: "If my people, which are called by my name, shall humble themselves, and pray, and seek my face, and turn from their wicked ways; then will I hear from Heaven, and will forgive their sins, and will heal their land."

If God's people, which are called by His name, Christians, will remember the faith of their fathers, God will heal their land. America can be saved by doing the opposite to the will of Communists. Instead of turning away from God, turn toward God. As a matter of fact, the antidote to every Communist intrigue is to do the opposite, for all of Communism is based upon a lie.

America is being sold out by treasonous, traitorous leaders. America is being surrendered to the enemy by a deceived people. America's salvation is an immediate return to the faith of our fathers, and the declaration of that faith in the Bible, the word of God. America must return to the faith which proudly declares, "I am not ashamed of the gospel of Christ for it is the power of God unto salvation to everyone that believeth."

America's destruction is in satanic Communism. America's salvation is in the faith of our fathers, in Jesus Christ, the Son of God.

chapter 4

Violence and Pacifism

The problem of an equitable resolution of conflict is perhaps the oldest and most difficult problem faced by human society. The manner in which conflicting ideas and interests are decided is an indication of the nature of justice, social development, and national character present in a particular political form. The rationale, goal, and purpose of violence are to accomodate conflicting interests, and the end result of the violence is to alter an assumed or real inequity or injustice and ultimately achieve once again a state of peace and tranquility. When violence moves beyond the threat stage within the community context, the authority of the state is directly challenged.

A growing concern of our time is that an increasing amount of violence is manifesting itself in our urban centers. Much of this violence is directly tied to the large unresolved conflict of interests inherent in our multi-racial and ethnic social system. Our racial problems involve the deepest kind of human conflict. They involve, on the one hand, a powerful reluctance by the white society and its dominant social and political and economic values to grant a legitimate social and economic status to specific racial and ethnic groups in the society. These groups, on the other hand, have directly challenged the traditional standards and policies of the state because they have felt that alternative means of resolving the racial conflict of interest were not realistic. The state has not shown itself willing or capable up to the present time of resolving the deep and basic conflict of interests which characterize our racial problems in the U.S. The efficacy of political violence has been well demonstrated by the black revolution whose direct action methods openly challenge the apathy and inadequacy of the state's actions in these areas in redressing long-term deeply-rooted human grievance. We are discovering that violence in the modern world reveals itself in many forms. There is the more traditional and obvious violence which directly involves a physical assault upon persons or property. The state does not sanction or legitimitize this use of violence. This kind of direct violence is most frightening and produces the greatest public response. However another form of violence is that kind of deliberate social and economic neglect which produces the worse forms of human degradation and despair. This form of covert violence involves millions of Americans in an endless cycle of poverty, unemployment, neglect, hunger, social and economic exploitation, and ultimate human destruction. This form of covert violence for large population groups is both sanctioned and legitimized by our social system.

Covert violence visited upon children in the educational system includes the chilling of creativity under demands for conformity, the regimentation of learning limited to only those ideas permitted expression in the schools, and the selectivity process of determining which students get the rewards of the school in curriculum, teachers, stimulation, and credentials. The simple examples of requirements to raise two fingers in order to go to the bathroom in elementary schools, of harassment by the vice-principal in charge of discipline for not having a hall pass, of threats by teachers to lower grades for talking too much, and of patrols of teachers policing hallways, lavatories, and cafeterias to enforce school rulings on noise, smoking, and eating suffice to indicate this mental violence.

Physical violence, in practice or in threat, also permeates school settings. School discipline includes the weapon of corporal punishment in most states, and the student populace is well aware of its threat behind each teacher's remonstration. Coaches employ violence as a test of manhood in preparing athletic teams. Students, as the newspapers show, have also been distinguished in their use of violence as a political tactic or against individual teachers and administrators. The language of the school includes violent messages like kicked out of class, but the best examples are in school cheers: "slaughter 'em," "whip 'em," and "stomp 'em."

Violence in one form or another has been an essential component in the resolution of human conflicts in our society. The covert forms of violence which involve brutalizing social and economic life conditions help to foster those human responses which lead to more overt forms of violent action. The direct physical assaults on the community are obvious indications of pathological social and human conditions in the society and a basic questioning of the racist policies of the general society.

The historical problem for men in all societies has been one of choosing techniques or methods both violent and non-violent which will effectively provide them with their share of justice and equal treatment in a particular social system.

We have witnessed in the past half-century the careful development of non-violent techniques as an alternative means of resolving social conflicts. This method as developed and utilized by Gandhi and Martin Luther King has been highly successful in bringing about social change in selected areas of contention. However, the passive resistance method is most effective within a social system which does not legitimitize the use of physical violence on dissenting or non-conforming members of that system. Within the context of American values and traditions it is possible for pacifistic methods of non-violence to achieve quite impressive social changes.

There are hopeful signs that non-violent methods will increasingly be used to resolve social conflicts. If this occurs, violence in all of its ugly forms will be responded to in the future less by violent counter-reaction than by methods of passive resistance and persuasion which hold out new hope for a more human working model for the resolution of human conflict.

Civil Disobedience

Henry David Thoreau

Henry David Thoreau, the American pacifist and dissenter, considered the problem of personal freedom and morality as these conflict with one's duty to the state. His "Civil Disobedience" is one of the most enduring moral examinations of the right to disobey the state when one's moral convictions do not permit acquiescence. Thoreau argues that when one's moral convictions are in conflict with the state and its laws an individual has the right to serve a higher moral authority, namely his personal beliefs and values or God. He argues that the state is not the final arbitrator of its subjects' actions and beliefs. Man has the right and the duty to resist the state when its laws, its powers, and its purposes clearly contravene a higher moral order.

Thoreau makes it clear that it is a duty of a moral man to resist the immoral acts of the state by witholding his support even to the point of breaking the law if necessary to demonstrate his moral revulsion against the actions of the larger society. The larger society may have the legitimate authority to undertake immoral objectives, but they remain morally reprehensible for the individual and he should refuse to cooperate in their undertaking.

One wonders, since school and society are so close, how students can resist the imposition of immoral acts by the school or society. Student rights as citizens are less than those of adults, and students have less independence to accept the responsibilities of their acts. In schools, depending on age and maturity level, the student's ability to fully comprehend the possible consequences of a civilly disobedient act, and thus to make a decision in light of them, is not so clear as an adult's. Since a high school student cannot vote in society to legitimately alter a law or elect a representative, he has little recourse. At the same time, an act of civil disobedience may

Henry David Thoreau, "Civil Disobedience," in *A Yankee in Canada*. Boston: Ticknor and Fields, 1866.

implicate his parents without their consent because of our legal
structure. The consequences he can suffer separately are those the
school imposes, but there are serious questions about the justice of
a school suspension or expulsion as a result of a sit-in in a city hall.

I heartily accept the motto—"That government is best which governs
least"; and I should like to see it acted up to more rapidly and systematically. Carried out, it finally amounts to this, which also I
believe—"That government is best which governs not at all"; and
when men are prepared for it, that will be the kind of government
which they will have. Government is at best but an expedient; but
most governments are usually, and all governments are sometimes,
inexpedient. The objections which have been brought against a standing army, and they are many and weighty, and deserve to prevail, may
also at last be brought against a standing government. The standing
army is only an arm of the standing government. The government itself,
which is only the mode which the people have chosen to execute their
will, is equally liable to be abused and perverted before the people can
act through it. Witness the present Mexican war, the work of comparatively a few individuals using the standing government as their
tool; for, in the outset, the people would not have consented to this
measure.

  This American government—what is it but a tradition, though
a recent one, endeavoring to transmit itself unimpaired to posterity,
but each instant losing some of its integrity? It has not the vitality
and force of a single living man; for a single man can bend it to his
will. It is a sort of wooden gun to the people themselves. But it is not
the less necessary for this; for the people must have some complicated
machinery or other, and hear its din, to satisfy that idea of government which they have. Governments show thus how successfully men
can be imposed on, even impose on themselves, for their own advantage. It is excellent, we must all allow. Yet this government never of
itself furthered any enterprise, but by the alacrity with which it got
out of its way. *It* does not keep the country free. *It* does not settle
the West. *It* does not educate. The character inherent in the American
people has done all that has been accomplished; and it would have
done somewhat more, if the government had not sometimes got in
its way. For government is an expedient by which men would fain
succeed in letting one another alone; and, as has been said, when it is
most expedient, the governed are most let alone by it. Trade and
commerce, if they were not made of India-rubber, would never manage to bounce over the obstacles which legislators are continually

putting in their way; and, if one were to judge these men wholly by the effects of their actions and not partly by their intentions, they would deserve to be classed and punished with those mischievous persons who put obstructions on the railroads.

But, to speak practically and as a citizen, unlike those who call themselves no-government men, I ask for, not at once no government, but *at once* a better government. Let every man make known what kind of government would command his respect, and that will be one step toward obtaining it.

After all, the practical reason why, when the power is once in the hands of the people, a majority are permitted, and for a long period continue, to rule is not because they are most likely to be in the right, nor because this seems fairest to the minority, but because they are physically the strongest. But a government in which the majority rule in all cases cannot be based on justice, even as far as men understand it. Can there not be a government in which majorities do not virtually decide right and wrong, but conscience?—in which majorities decide only those questions to which the rule of expediency is applicable? Must the citizen ever for a moment, or in the least degree, resign his conscience to the legislator? Why has every man a conscience, then? I think that we should be men first, and subjects afterward. It is not desirable to cultivate a respect for the law, so much as for the right. The only obligation which I have a right to assume is to do at any time what I think right. It is truly enough said, that a corporation has no conscience; but a corporation of conscientious men is a corporation *with* a conscience. Law never made men a whit more just; and, by means of their respect for it, even the well-disposed are daily made the agents of injustice. A common and natural result of an undue respect for law is, that you may see a file of soldiers, colonel, captain, corporal, privates, powder-monkeys, and all, marching in admirable order over hill and dale to the wars, against their wills, ay, against their common sense and consciences, which makes it very steep marching indeed, and produces a palpitation of the heart. They have no doubt that it is a damnable business in which they are concerned; they are all peaceably inclined. Now, what are they? Men at all? or small movable forts and magazines, at the service of some unscrupulous man in power? Visit the Navy-Yard, and behold a marine, such a man as an American government can make, or such as it can make a man with its black arts—a mere shadow and reminiscence of humanity, a man laid out alive and standing, and already, as one may say, buried under arms with funeral accompaniments, though it may be—

Not a drum was heard, not a funeral note,
  As his corse to the rampart we hurried;
Not a soldier discharged his farewell shot
  O'er the grave where our hero we buried.

The mass of men serve the state thus, not as men mainly, but as machines, with their bodies. They are the standing army, and the militia, jailers, constables, posse comitatus, etc. In most cases there is no free exercise whatever of the judgment or of the moral sense; but they put themselves on a level with wood and earth and stones; and wooden men can perhaps be manufactured that will serve the purpose as well. Such command no more respect than men of straw or a lump of dirt. They have the same sort of worth only as horses and dogs. Yet such as these even are commonly esteemed good citizens. Others —as most legislators, politicians, lawyers, ministers, and office-holders—serve the state chiefly with their heads; and, as they rarely make any moral distinctions, they are as likely to serve the Devil, without *intending* it, as God. A very few, as heroes, patriots, martyrs, reformers in the great sense, and *men*, serve the state with their consciences also, and so necessarily resist it for the most part; and they are commonly treated as enemies by it. A wise man will only be useful as a man, and will not submit to be "clay," and "stop a hole to keep the wind away," but leave that office to his dust at least:—

I am too high-born to be propertied,
To be a secondary at control,
Or useful serving-man and instrument
To any sovereign state throughout the world.

He who gives himself entirely to his fellowmen appears to them useless and selfish; but he who gives himself partially to them is pronounced a benefactor and philanthropist.

How does it become a man to behave toward this American government today? I answer, that he cannot without disgrace be associated with it. I cannot for an instant recognize that political organization as *my* government which is the *slave's* government also.

All men recognize the right of revolution; that is, the right to refuse allegiance to, and to resist, the government, when its tyranny or its inefficiency are great and unendurable. But almost all say that such is not the case now. But such was the case, they think, in the Revolution of '75. If one were to tell me that this was a bad government because it taxed certain foreign commodities brought to its ports, it is most probable that I should not make an ado about it, for I can do without them. All machines have their friction; and possibly this does enough good to counterbalance the evil. At any rate, it is a great evil to make a stir about it. But when the friction comes to have its machine, and oppression and robbery are organized, I say, let us not have such a machine any longer. In other words, when a sixth of the population of a nation which has undertaken to be the refuge of liberty are slaves, and a whole country is unjustly overrun and conquered by a foreign army, and subjected to military law, I think that it is not too soon for honest men to rebel and revolutionize. What makes this duty the more urgent is the fact that the country so overrun is not our own, but ours is the invading army.

Paley, a common authority with many on moral questions, in his chapter on the "Duty of Submission to Civil Government," resolves all civil obligation into expediency; and he proceeds to say, "that so long as the interest of the whole society requires it, that is, so long as the established government cannot be resisted or changed without public inconveniency, it is the will of God that the established government be obeyed, and no longer. . . . This principle being admitted, the justice of every particular case of resistance is reduced to a computation of the quantity of the danger and grievance on the one side, and of the probability and expense of redressing it on the other." Of this, he says, every man shall judge for himself. But Paley appears never to have contemplated those cases to which the rule of expediency does not apply, in which a people, as well as an individual, must do justice, cost what it may. If I have unjustly wrested a plank from a drowning man, I must restore it to him though I drown myself. This, according to Paley, would be inconvenient. But he that would save his life, in such a case, shall lose it. This people must cease to hold slaves, and to make war on Mexico, though it cost them their existence as a people.

In their practice, nations agree with Paley; but does any one think that Massachusetts does exactly what is right at the present crisis?

> A drab of state, a cloth-o'-silver sut,
> To have her train borne up, and her soul trail
>   in the dirt.

Practically speaking, the opponents to a reform in Massachusetts are not a hundred thousand politicians at the South, but a hundred thousand merchants and farmers here, who are more interested in commerce and agriculture than they are in humanity, and are not prepared to do justice to the slave and to Mexico, *cost what it may*. I quarrel not with far-off foes, but with those who, near at home, cooperate with, and do the bidding of, those far away, and without whom the latter would be harmless. We are accustomed to say, that the mass of men are unprepared; but improvement is slow, because the few are not materially wiser or better than the many. It is not so important that many should be as good as you, as that there be some absolute goodness somewhere; for that will leaven the whole lump. There are thousands who are *in opinion* opposed to slavery and to the war, who yet in effect do nothing to put an end to them; who, esteeming themselves children of Washington and Franklin, sit down with their hands in their pockets, and say that they know not what to do, and do nothing; who even postpone the question of freedom to the question of free trade, and quietly read the prices-current along with the latest advices from Mexico, after dinner, and, it may be, fall asleep over them both. What is the price-current of an honest man and patriot today? They hesitate, and they regret, and sometimes they petition; but they do nothing in earnest and with effect. They will wait, well disposed, for others to remedy the evil, that they may no longer have it to regret. At most, they give only a cheap vote, and a feeble countenance and Godspeed, to the right, as it goes by them. There are nine hundred and ninety-nine patrons of virtue to one virtuous man. But it is easier to deal with the real possessor of a thing than with the temporary guardian of it.

All voting is a sort of gaming, like checkers or backgammon, with a slight moral tinge to it, a playing with right and wrong, with moral questions; and betting naturally accompanies it. The character of the voters is not staked. I cast my vote, perchance, as I think right; but I am not vitally concerned that that right should prevail. I am willing to leave it to the majority. Its obligation, therefore, never exceeds that of expediency. Even voting *for the right* is *doing* nothing for it. It is only expressing to men feebly your desire that it should prevail. A wise man will not leave the right to the mercy of chance, nor wish it to prevail through the power of the majority. There is but little virtue in the action of masses of men. When the majority shall at length vote for the abolition of slavery, it will be because they are indifferent to slavery, or because there is but little slavery left to be abolished by their vote. *They* will then be the only slaves. Only *his* vote can hasten the abolition of slavery who asserts his own freedom by his vote.

I hear of a convention to be held at Baltimore, or elsewhere, for the selection of a candidate for the Presidency, made up chiefly of editors, and men who are politicians by profession; but I think, what is it to any independent, intelligent, and respectable man what decision they may come to? Shall we not have the advantage of his wisdom and honesty, nevertheless? Can we not count upon some independent votes? Are there not many individuals in the country who do not attend conventions? But no: I find that the respectable man, so called, has immediately drifted from his position, and despairs of his country, when his country has more reason to despair of him. He forthwith adopts one of the candidates thus selected as the only *available* one, thus proving that he is himself *available* for any purposes of the demagogue. His vote is of no more worth than that of any unprincipled foreigner or hireling native, who may have been bought. O for a man who is a *man*, and, as my neighbor says, has a bone in his back which you cannot pass your hand through! Our statistics are at fault: the population has been returned too large. How many *men* are there to a square thousand miles in this country? Hardly one. Does not America offer any inducement for men to settle here? The American has dwindled into an Odd Fellow—one who may be known by the development of his organ of gregariousness, and a manifest lack of intellect and cheerful self-reliance; whose first and chief concern, on coming into the world, is to see that the almshouses are in good repair; and, before yet he has lawfully donned the virile garb, to collect a fund for the support of the widows and orphans that may be; who, in short, ventures to live only by the aid of the Mutual Insurance company, which has promised to bury him decently.

It is not a man's duty, as a matter of course, to devote himself to the eradication of any, even the most enormous wrong; he may still properly have other concerns to engage him; but it is his duty, at least, to wash his hands of it, and, if he gives it no thought longer, not to give it practically his support. If I devote myself to other pursuits and contemplations, I must first see, at least, that I do not pursue them sitting upon another man's shoulders. I must get off him first, that he may pursue his contemplations too. See what gross inconsistency is tolerated. I have heard some of my townsmen say, "I should like to have them order me out to help put down an insurrection of the slaves, or to march to Mexico;—see if I would go"; and yet these very men have each, directly by their allegiance, and so indirectly, at least, by their money, furnished a substitute. The soldier is applauded who refuses to serve in an unjust war by those who do not refuse to sustain the unjust government which makes the war; is applauded by those whose own act and authority he disregards and sets at naught; as if the state were penitent to that degree that it hired one to scourge it while it sinned, but not to that degree that it left off sinning for a moment. Thus, under the name of Order and Civil Government, we are all made at last to pay homage to and support our own meanness. After the first blush of sin comes its indifference; and from immoral it becomes, as it were, *un*moral, and not quite unnecessary to that life which we have made.

The broadest and most prevalent error requires the most disinterested virtue to sustain it. The slight reproach to which the virtue of patriotism is commonly liable, the noble are most likely to incur. Those who, while they disapprove of the character and measures of a government, yield to it their allegiance and support are undoubtedly its most conscientious supporters, and so frequently the most serious obstacles to reform. Some are petitioning the state to dissolve the Union, to disregard the requisitions of the President. Why do they not dissolve it themselves—the union between themselves and the state—and refuse to pay their quota into its treasury? Do not they stand in the same relation to the state that the state does to the Union? And have not the same reasons prevented the state from resisting the Union which have prevented them from resisting the state?

How can a man be satisfied to entertain an opinion merely, and enjoy *it?* Is there any enjoyment in it, if his opinion is that he is aggrieved? If you are cheated out of a single dollar by your neighbor, you do not rest satisfied with knowing that you are cheated, or with saying that you are cheated, or even with petitioning him to pay you your due; but you take effectual steps at once to obtain the full amount, and see that you are never cheated again. Action from principle, the perception and the performance of right, changes things and relations; it is essentially revolutionary, and does not consist wholly with anything which was. It not only divides states and churches, it divides families; ay, it divides the *individual,* separating the diabolical in him from the divine.

Unjust laws exist: shall we be content to obey them, or shall we endeavor to amend them, and obey them until we have succeeded, or shall we transgress them at once? Men generally, under such a government as this, think that they ought to wait until they have persuaded the majority to alter them. They think that, if they should resist, the remedy would be worse than the evil. But it is the fault of the government itself that the remedy is worse than the evil. *It* makes it worse. Why is it not more apt to anticipate and provide for reform? Why does it not cherish its wise minority? Why does it cry and resist before it is hurt? Why does it not encourage its citizens to be on the alert to point out its faults, and *do* better than it would have them? Why does it always crucify Christ, and excommunicate Copernicus and Luther, and pronounce Washington and Franklin rebels?

One would think, that a deliberate and practical denial of its authority was the only offense never contemplated by government; else, why has it not assigned its definite, its suitable and proportionate penalty? If a man who has no property refuses but once to earn nine shillings for the state, he is put in prison for a period unlimited by any law that I know, and determined only by the discretion of those who placed him there; but if he should steal ninety times nine shillings from the state, he is soon permitted to go at large again.

If the unjustice is part of the necessary friction of the machine of government, let it go, let it go: perchance it will wear smooth— certainly the machine will wear out. If the injustice has a spring, or a pulley, or a rope, or a crank, exclusively for itself, then perhaps you may consider whether the remedy will not be worse than the evil; but if it is of such a nature that it requires you to be the agent of injustice to another, then, I say, break the law. Let your life be a counter friction to stop the machine. What I have to do is to see, at any rate, that I do not lend myself to the wrong which I condemn.

As for adopting the ways which the state has provided for remedying the evil, I know not of such ways. They take too much time, and a man's life will be gone. I have other affairs to attend to. I came into this world, not chiefly to make this a good place to live in, but to live in it, be it good or bad. A man has not everything to do, but something; and because he cannot do *everything*, it is not necessary that he should do *something* wrong. It is not my business to be petitioning the Governor or the Legislature any more than it is theirs to petition me; and if they should not hear my petition, what should I do then? But in this case the state has provided no way: its very Constitution is the evil. This may seem to be harsh and stubborn and unconciliatory; but it is to treat with the utmost kindness and consideration the only spirit that can appreciate or deserves it. So is all change for the better, like birth and death, which convulse the body.

I do not hesitate to say, that those who call themselves Abolitionists should at once effectually withdraw their support, both in person and property, from the government of Massachusetts, and not wait till they constitute a majority of one, before they suffer the right to prevail through them. I think that it is enough if they have God on their side, without waiting for that other one. Moreover, any man more right than his neighbors constitutes a majority of one already.

The New American Militarism

General David Shoup

The impact of the military and its allied defense industries on American life since World War II has been significant. A new military-industrial complex has emerged to the extent that President Eisenhower could bring public attention to its threat to American democracy. Despite the warnings, increased military budgets have had effective industrial lobbying and a lack of general concern. In a number of ways democratic and social welfare goals have been subordinated to military objectives and priorities. Obsolescent military equipment still uses vast sums of public wealth. Development of weapons systems with capacities far beyond those necessary for defense have soaked up millions of dollars. Internal military bickering, budget padding, and industrial cost overrun that boost predicted costs into profit-making windfalls tap the public till. Clandestine military operations and intelligence surveillance of civilians are hidden military costs in other government budgets. Pentagon public relations have received television notoriety for their salesmanship efforts at public expense.

General Shoup, the former commander of the United States Marine Corps, has been a major critic of the unchecked growth of military power and its increasing dominance of foreign policy. As a military person, General Shoup's criticisms are more radical than they may seem. The military tends to be a close-knit, self-protective institution. Seldom do military personnel stand against the encroaching militariness of American life.

More than half of our tax dollars support the massive, proliferating military establishment. Military might now includes political and economic power. Much of the quality of American life is influenced by the military. General Shoup suggests that we have been manipulated by the sales job of the military to believe that highly complex socio-economic problems around the world can be most efficiently solved by the application of an American military presence.

Since schools assist in providing the manpower and the social mentality for the military forces, the level and nature of militarism in society have considerable impact on education. Student uprisings against recruiting on campuses, the few draft counseling courses in high schools, and the lack of course work on war prevention illustrate this relationship. Study of the negative American involvement in Vietnam was unheard of in schools until well after the general public had begun to recognize our mistakes. Schools contribute to American militarism in a variety of ways.

On one level the educational implications for militarism rest in the fight over priorities in financial support between education and defense. Despite great educational needs in a democratic society, the federal budget is overloaded with commitments to war-related activities. Early federal education assistance often tied defense and education in order to gain passage. The Morrill Act of 1862, providing for land grant colleges, was tied to national defense through ROTC requirements. During the 1950s the major federal aid bill was titled the National Defense Education Act.

At another level the schools assist in the continuance of a military mentality by such activities as an emphasis on military history and military heroes in textbooks and curricula, requirements of patriotic exercises and assemblies, and quasi-military orientations in physical education, school organization, and administration. In addition, the lack of opportunity for students to examine critically sacrosanct social topics like American militarism perpetuates a society which fails to fully consider the kinds of questions General Shoup proposes.

America has become a militaristic and aggressive nation. Our massive and swift invasion of the Dominican Republic in 1965, concurrent with the rapid buildup of U.S. military power in Vietnam, constituted an impressive demonstration of America's readiness to execute military contingency plans and to seek military solutions to problems of political disorder and potential Communist threats in the areas of our interest.

This "military task force" type of diplomacy is in the tradition of our more primitive, pre-World War II "gunboat diplomacy," in which we landed small forces of Marines to protect American lives and property from the perils of native bandits and revolutionaries. In those days the U.S. Navy and its Marine landing forces were our chief means, short of war, for showing the flag, exercising American power, and protecting U.S. interests abroad. The Navy, enjoying the freedom of the seas, was a visible and effective representative of the nation's sovereign power. The Marines could be employed ashore "on such other duties as the President might direct" without congressional approval or a declaration of war. The U.S. Army was not then used so freely because it was rarely ready for expeditionary service without some degree of mobilization, and its use overseas normally required a declaration of emergency or war. Now, however, we have numerous contingency plans involving large joint Air Force–Army–Navy–Marine task forces to defend U.S. interests and to safeguard our allies wherever and whenever we suspect Communist aggression. We maintain more than 1,517,000 Americans in uniform overseas in 119 countries. We have 8 treaties to help defend 48 nations if they ask us to—or if we choose to intervene in their affairs. We have an immense and expensive military establishment, fueled by a gigantic defense industry, and millions of proud, patriotic, and frequently bellicose and materialistic citizens. How did this militarist culture evolve? How did this militarism steer us into the tragic military and political morass of Vietnam?

Prior to World War II, American attitudes were typically isolationist, pacifist, and generally anti-military. The regular peacetime military establishment enjoyed small prestige and limited influence upon national affairs. The public knew little about the armed forces, and only a few thousand men were attracted to military service and careers. In 1940 there were but 428,000 officers and enlisted men in the Army and Navy. The scale of the war, and the world's power relationships which resulted, created the American military giant. Today the active armed forces contain over 3.4 million men and women, with an additional 1.6 million ready reserves and National Guardsmen.

America's vastly expanded world role after World War II hinged upon military power. The voice and views of the professional military people became increasingly prominent. During the postwar period, distinguished military leaders from the war years filled many top positions in government. Generals Marshall, Eisenhower, MacArthur, Taylor, Ridgeway, LeMay, and others were not only popular heroes but respected opinion-makers. It was a time of international readjustment; military minds offered the benefits of firm views and problem-solving experience to the management of the nation's affairs. Military procedures—including the general staff system, briefings, estimates of the situation, and the organizational and operational techniques of the highly schooled, confident military professionals—spread throughout American culture.

World War II had been a long war. Millions of young American men had matured, been educated, and gained rank and stature during their years in uniform. In spite of themselves, many returned to civilian life as indoctrinated, combat-experienced military professionals. They were veterans, and for better or worse would never be the same again. America will never be the same either. We are now a nation of veterans. To the 14.9 million veterans of World War II, Korea added another 5.7 million five years later, and ever since, the large peacetime military establishment has been training and releasing draftees, enlistees, and short-term reservists by the hundreds of thousands each year. In 1968 the total living veterans of U.S. military service numbered over 23 million, or about 20 percent of the adult population.

Today most middle-aged men, most business, government, civic, and professional leaders, have served some time in uniform. Whether they liked it or not, their military training and experience have affected them, for the creeds and attitudes of the armed forces are powerful medicine, and can become habit-forming. The military codes include all the virtues and beliefs used to motivate men of high principle: patriotism, duty and service to country, honor among fellowmen, courage in the face of danger, loyalty to organization and leaders, self-sacrifice for comrades, leadership, discipline, and physical fitness. For many veterans the military's efforts to train and indoctrinate them may well be the most impressive and influential experience they have ever had—especially so for the young and less educated.

In addition, each of the armed forces has its own special doctrinal beliefs and well-catalogued customs, traditions, rituals, and folklore upon which it strives to build a fiercely loyal military character and esprit de corps. All ranks are taught that their unit and their branch of the military service are the most elite, important, efficient, or effective in the military establishment. By believing in the superiority and importance of their own service they also provide themselves a degree of personal status, pride, and self-confidence.

As they get older, many veterans seem to romanticize and exaggerate their own military experience and loyalties. The policies, attitudes, and positions of the powerful veterans' organizations such as the American Legion, Veterans of Foreign Wars, and AMVETS, totaling over 4 million men, frequently reflect this pugnacious and chauvinistic tendency. Their memberships generally favor military solutions to world problems in the pattern of their own earlier experience, and often assert that their military service and sacrifice should be repeated by the younger generations.

Closely related to the attitudes and influence of America's millions of veterans is the vast and powerful complex of the defense industries, which have been described in detail many times in the eight years since General Eisenhower first warned of the military-industrial power complex in his farewell address as President. The relationship between the defense industry and the military establishment is closer than many citizens realize. Together they form a powerful public opinion lobby. The several military service associations provide both a forum and a meeting ground for the military and its industries. The associations also provide each of the armed services with a means of fostering their respective roles, objectives, and propaganda.

Each of the four services has its own association, and there are also additional military function associations, for ordnance, management, defense industry, and defense transportation, to name some of the more prominent. The Air Force Association and the Association of the U.S. Army are the largest, best organized, and most effective of the service associations. The Navy League, typical of the "silent service" traditions, is not as well coordinated in its public relations efforts, and the small Marine Corps Association is not even in the same arena with the other contenders, the Marine Association's main activity being the publication of a semi-official monthly magazine. Actually, the service associations' respective magazines, with an estimated combined circulation of over 270,000, are the primary medium serving the several associations' purposes.

Air Force and Space Digest, to cite one example, is the magazine of the Air Force Association and the unofficial mouthpiece of the U.S. Air Force doctrine, "party line," and propaganda. It frequently promotes Air Force policy that has been officially frustrated or suppressed within the Department of Defense. It beats the tub for strength through aerospace power, interprets diplomatic, strategic, and tactical problems in terms of air power, stresses the requirements for quantities of every type of aircraft, and frequently perpetuates the extravagant fictions about the effectiveness of bombing. This, of course, is well coordinated with and supported by the multibillion-dollar aerospace industry, which thrives upon the boundless desires of the Air Force. They reciprocate with lavish and expensive ads in every issue of *Air Force*. Over 96,000 members of the Air Force Association receive the magazine. Members include active, reserve, retired personnel, and veterans of the U.S. Air Force. Additional thousands of copies go to people engaged in the defense industry. The thick mixture of advertising, propaganda, and Air Force doctrine continuously repeated in this publication provides its readers and writers with a form of intellectual hypnosis, and they are prone to believe their own propaganda because they read it in *Air Force*.

The American people have also become more and more accustomed to militarism, to uniforms, to the cult of the gun, and to the violence of combat. Whole generations have been brought up on war news and wartime propaganda; the few years of peace since 1939 have seen a steady stream of war novels, war movies, comic strips, and television programs with war or military settings. To many Americans, military training, expeditionary service, and warfare are merely extensions of the entertainment and games of childhood. Even the weaponry and hardware they use at war are similar to the highly realistic toys of their youth. Soldiering loses appeal for some of the relatively few who experience the blood, terror, and filth of battle; for many, however, including far too many senior professional officers, war and combat are an exciting adventure, a competitive game, and an escape from the dull routines of peacetime.

It is this influential nucleus of aggressive, ambitious professional military leaders who are the root of America's evolving militarism. There are over 410,000 commissioned officers on active duty in the four armed services. Of these, well over half are junior ranking reserve officers on temporary active duty. Of the 150,000 or so regular career officers, only a portion are senior ranking colonels, generals, and admirals, but it is they who constitute the elite core of the military establishment. It is these few thousand top-ranking professionals who command and manage the armed forces and plan and formulate military policy and opinion. How is it, then, that in spite of civilian controls and the national desire for peace, this small group of men exert so much martial influence upon the government and life of the American people?

The military will disclaim any excess of power or influence on their part. They will point to their small numbers, low pay, and subordination to civilian masters as proof of their modest status and innocence. Nevertheless, the professional military, as a group, is probably one of the best organized and most influential of the various segments of the American scene. Three wars and six major contingencies since 1940 have forced the American people to become abnormally aware of the armed forces and their leaders. In turn the military services have produced an unending supply of distinguished, capable, articulate, and effective leaders. The sheer skill, energy, and dedication of America's military officers make them dominant in almost every government or civic organization they may inhabit, from the federal Cabinet to the local PTA.

The hard core of high-ranking professionals are, first of all, mostly service academy graduates: they had to be physically and intellectually above average among their peers just to gain entrance to an academy. Thereafter for the rest of their careers they are exposed to constant competition for selection and promotion. Attrition is high, and only the most capable survive to reach the elite senior ranks. Few other professions have such rigorous selection systems; as a result, the top military leaders are top-caliber men.

Not many industries, institutions, or civilian branches of government have the resources, techniques, or experience in training leaders such as are now employed by the armed forces in their excellent and elaborate school systems. Military leaders are taught to command large organizations and to plan big operations. They learn the techniques of influencing others. Their education is not, however, liberal or cultural. It stresses the tactics, doctrines, traditions, and codes of the military trade. It produces technicians and disciples, not philosophers.

The men who rise to the top of the military hierarchy have usually demonstrated their effectiveness as leaders, planners, and organization managers. They have perhaps performed heroically in combat, but most of all they have demonstrated their loyalty as proponents of their own service's doctrine and their dedication to the defense establishment. The paramount sense of duty to follow orders is at the root of the military professional's performance. As a result the military often operate more efficiently and effectively in the arena of defense policy planning than do their civilian counterparts in the State Department. The military planners have their doctrinal beliefs, their loyalties, their discipline—and their typical desire to compete and win. The civilians in government can scarcely play the same policy-planning game. In general the military are better organized, they work harder, they think straighter, and they keep their eyes on the objective, which is to be instantly ready to solve the problem through military action while ensuring that their respective service gets its proper mission, role, and recognition in the operation. In an emergency the military usually have a ready plan; if not, their numerous doctrinal manuals provide firm guidelines for action. Politicians, civilian appointees, and diplomats do not normally have the same confidence about how to react to threats and violence as do the military.

The motivations behind these endeavors are difficult for civilians to understand. For example, military professionals cannot measure the success of their individual efforts in terms of personal financial gain. The armed forces are not profit-making organizations, and the rewards for excellence in the military profession are acquired in less tangible forms. Thus it is that promotion and the responsibilities of higher command, with the related fringe benefits of quarters, servants, privileges, and prestige, motivate most career officers. Promotions and choice job opportunities are attained by constantly performing well, conforming to the expected patterns, and pleasing the senior officers. Promotions and awards also frequently result from heroic and distinguished performance in combat, and it takes a war to become a military hero. Civilians can scarcely understand or even believe that many ambitious military professionals truly yearn for wars and the opportunities for glory and distinction afforded only in combat. A career of peacetime duty is a dull and frustrating prospect for the normal regular officer to contemplate.

The professional military leaders of the U.S. Armed Forces have some additional motivations which influence their readiness to involve their country in military ventures. Unlike some of the civilian policy-makers, the military has not been obsessed with the threat of Communism per se. Most military people know very little about Communism either as a doctrine or as a form of government. But they have been given reason enough to presume that it is bad and represents the force of evil. When they can identify "Communist aggression," however, the matter then becomes of direct concern to the armed forces. Aggressors are the enemy in the war games, the "bad guys," the "Reds." Defeating aggression is a gigantic combat-area competition rather than a crusade to save the world from Communism. In the military view, all "Communist aggression" is certain to be interpreted as a threat to the United States.

The armed forces' role in performing its part of the national security policy—in addition to defense against actual direct attack on the United States and to maintaining the strategic atomic deterrent forces—is to be prepared to employ its *General Purpose Forces* in support of our collective security policy and the related treaties and alliances. To do this it deploys certain forces to forward zones in the Unified Commands, and maintains an up-to-date file of scores of detailed contingency plans which have been thrashed out and approved by the Joint Chiefs of Staff. Important features of these are the movement or deployment schedules of task forces assigned to each plan. The various details of these plans continue to create intense rivalries between the Navy-Marine sea-lift forces and the Army–Air Force team of air-mobility proponents. At the senior command levels parochial pride in service, personal ambitions, and old Army-Navy game rivalry stemming back to academy loyalties can influence strategic planning far more than most civilians would care to believe. The game is to be ready for deployment sooner than the other elements of the joint task force and to be so disposed as to be the "first to fight." The danger presented by this practice is that readiness and deployment speed become ends in themselves. This was clearly revealed in the massive and rapid intervention in the Dominican Republic in 1965 when the contingency plans and interservice rivalry appeared to supersede diplomacy. Before the world realized what was happening, the momentum and velocity of the military plans propelled almost 20,000 U.S. soldiers and Marines into the small turbulent republic in an impressive race to test the respective mobility of the Army and the Marines, and to attain overall command of "U.S. Forces Dom. Rep." Only a fraction of the force deployed was needed or justified. A small 1935-model Marine landing force could probably have handled the situation. But the Army airlifted much of the 82nd Airborne Division to the scene, included a lieutenant general, and took charge of the operation.

Simultaneously, in Vietnam during 1965 the four services were racing to build up combat strength in that hapless country. This effort was ostensibly to save South Vietnam from Viet Cong and North Vietnamese aggression. It should also be noted that it was motivated in part by the same old interservice rivalry to demonstrate respective importance and combat effectiveness.

The punitive air strikes immediately following the Tonkin Gulf incident in late 1964 revealed the readiness of naval air forces to bomb North Vietnam. (It now appears that the Navy actually had attack plans ready even before the alleged incident took place!) So by early 1965 the Navy carrier people and the Air Force initiated a contest of comparative strikes, sorties, tonnages dropped, "Killed by Air" claims, and target grabbing which continued up to the 1968 bombing pause. Much of the reporting on air action has consisted of misleading data or propaganda to serve Air Force and Navy purposes. In fact, it became increasingly apparent that the U.S. bombing effort in both North and South Vietnam has been one of the most wasteful and expensive hoaxes ever to be put over on the American people. Tactical and close air support of ground operations is essential, but air power use in general has to a large degree been a contest for the operations planners, "fine experience" for young pilots, and opportunity for career officers.

The highly trained professional and aggressive career officers of the Army and Marine Corps played a similar game. Prior to the decision to send combat units to South Vietnam in early 1965, both services were striving to increase their involvement. The Army already had over 16,000 military aid personnel serving in South Vietnam in the military adviser role, in training missions, logistic services, supporting helicopter companies, and in Special Forces teams. This investment of men and matériel justified a requirement for additional U.S. combat units to provide local security and to help protect our growing commitment of aid to the South Vietnam regime.

There were also top-ranking Army officers who wanted to project Army ground combat units into the Vietnam struggle for a variety of other reasons; to test plans and new equipment, to test the new air-mobile theories and tactics, to try the tactics and techniques of counterinsurgency, and to gain combat experience for young officers and noncommissioned officers. It also appeared to be a case of the military's duty to stop "Communist aggression" in Vietnam.

The Marines had somewhat similar motivations, the least of which was any real concern about the political or social problems of the Vietnamese people. In early 1965 there was a shooting war going on and the Marines were being left out of it, contrary to all their traditions. The Army's military advisory people were hogging American participation—except for a Marine Corps transport helicopter squadron at Danang which was helping the Army of the Republic of Vietnam. For several years young Marine officers had been going to South Vietnam from the 3rd Marine Division on Okinawa for short tours of "on-the-job training" with the small South Vietnam Marine Corps. There was a growing concern, however, among some senior Marines that the Corps should get involved on a larger scale and be the "first to fight" in keeping with the Corps's traditions. This would help justify the Corps's continued existence, which many Marines seem to consider to be in constant jeopardy.

The Corps had also spent several years exploring the theories of counterinsurgency and as early as 1961 had developed an elaborate lecture-demonstration called OPERATION CORMORANT, for school and Marine Corps promotion purposes, which depicted the Marines conducting a large-scale amphibious operation on the coast of Vietnam and thereby helping resolve a hypothetical aggressor-insurgency problem. As always it was important to Marine planners and doctrinaires to apply an amphibious operation to the Vietnam situation and provide justification for this special Marine functional responsibility. So Marine planners were seeking an acceptable excuse to thrust a landing force over the beaches of Vietnam when the Viet Cong attacked the U.S. Army Special Forces camp at Pleiku in February, 1965. It was considered unacceptable aggression, and the President was thereby prompted to put U.S. ground combat units into the war. Elements of the 3rd Marine Division at Okinawa were already aboard ship and eager to go, for the Marines also intended to get to Vietnam before their neighbor on Okinawa, the Army's 173rd Airborne Brigade, arrived. (Actually the initial Marine unit to deploy was an airlifted antiaircraft missile battalion which arrived to protect the Danang air base.) With these initial deployments the Army-Marine race to build forces in Vietnam began in earnest and did not slow down until both became overextended, overcommitted, and depleted at home.

For years up to 1964 the chiefs of the armed services, of whom the author was then one, deemed it unnecessary and unwise for U.S. forces to become involved in any ground war in Southeast Asia. In 1964 there were changes in the composition of the Joint Chiefs of Staff, and in a matter of a few months the Johnson Administration, encouraged by the aggressive military, hastened into what has become the quagmire of Vietnam. The intention at the time was that the war effort be kept small and "limited." But as the momentum and involvement built up, the military leaders rationalized a case that this was not a limited-objective exercise, but was a proper war in defense of the United States against "Communist aggression" and in honor of our area commitments.

The battle successes and heroic exploits of America's fine young fighting men have added to the military's traditions which extol service, bravery, and sacrifice, and so it has somehow become unpatriotic to question our military strategy and tactics or the motives of military leaders. Actually, however, the military commanders have directed the war in Vietnam, they have managed the details of its conduct; and more than most civilian officials, the top military planners were initially ready to become involved in Vietnam combat and have the opportunity to practice their trade. It has been popular to blame the civilian administration for the conduct and failures of the war rather than to question the motives of the military. But some of the generals and admirals are by no means without responsibility for the Vietnam miscalculations.

Some of the credibility difficulties experienced by the Johnson Administration over its war situation reports and Vietnam policy can also be blamed in part upon the military advisers. By its very nature most military activity falls under various degrees of security classification. Much that the military plans or does must be kept from the enemy. Thus the military is indoctrinated to be secretive, devious, and misleading in its plans and operations. It does not, however, always confine its security restrictions to purely military operations. Each of the services and all of the major commands practice techniques of controlling the news and the release of self-serving propaganda: in "the interests of national defense," to make the service look good, to cover up mistakes, to build up and publicize a distinguished military personality, or to win a round in the continuous gamesmanship of the interservice contest. If the Johnson Administration suffered from lack of credibility in its reporting of the war, the truth would reveal that much of the hocus-pocus stemmed from schemers in the military services, both at home and abroad.

Our militaristic culture was born of the necessities of World War II, nurtured by the Korean War, and became an accepted aspect of American life during the years of cold war emergencies and real or imagined threats from the Communist bloc. Both the philosophy and the institutions of militarism grew during these years because of the momentum of their own dynamism, the vigor of their ideas, their large size and scope, and because of the dedicated concentration of the emergent military leaders upon their doctrinal objectives. The dynamism of the defense establishment and its culture is also inspired and stimulated by vast amounts of money, by the new creations of military research and matériel development, and by the concepts of the Defense Department-supported "think factories." These latter are extravagantly funded civilian organizations of scientists, analysts, and retired military strategists who feed new militaristic philosophies into the Defense Department to help broaden the views of the single service doctrinaires, to create fresh policies and new requirements for ever larger, more expensive defense forces.

Somewhat like a religion, the basic appeals of anti-Communism, national defense, and patriotism provide the foundation for a powerful creed upon which the defense establishment can build, grow, and justify its cost. More so than many large bureaucratic organizations, the defense establishment now devotes a large share of its efforts to self-perpetuation, to justifying its organizations, to preaching its doctrines, and to self-maintenance and management. Warfare becomes an extension of war games and field tests. War justifies the existence of the establishment, provides experience for the military novice and challenges for the senior officer. Wars and emergencies put the military and their leaders on the front pages and give status and prestige to the professionals. Wars add to the military traditions, the self-nourishment of heroic deeds, and provide a new crop of military leaders who become the rededicated disciples of the code of service and military action. Being recognized public figures in a nation always seeking folk heroes, the military leaders have been largely exempt from the criticism experienced by the more plebeian politician. Flag officers are considered "experts," and their views are often accepted by press and Congress as the gospel. In turn, the distinguished military leader feels obliged not only to perpetuate loyally the doctrine of his service but to comply with the stereotyped military characteristics by being tough, aggressive, and firm in his resistance to Communist aggression and his belief in the military solutions to world problems. Standing closely behind these leaders, encouraging and prompting them, are the rich and powerful defense industries. Standing in front, adorned with service caps, ribbons, and lapel emblems, is a nation of veterans—patriotic, belligerent, romantic, and well intentioned, finding a certain sublimation and excitement in their country's latest military venture. Militarism in America is in full bloom and promises a future of vigorous self-pollination—unless the blight of Vietnam reveals that militarism is more a poisonous weed than a glorious blossom.

Militant Non-Violence

William Sloan Coffin, Jr.

William Sloan Coffin is the chaplain at Yale University and a prominent and consistent critical dissenter against American policies in Vietnam. Mr. Coffin is an advocate of the non-violent technique of passive resistance as developed by Gandhi and Thoreau and Martin Luther King, and he believes that moral persuasion, resolution, and love are more effective as methods of changing hostile and violent behavior. The central purpose of the non-violent approach is to change the traditional style and form of achieving social and political change through political violence to higher and more humanistic form whereby producing a significant evolutionary change in conflict-resolution methodology. The highest form of masculinity does not have to be expressed through physical and political violence as has been traditionally the case, for it is possible for man to use reason, persuasion, and moral argument rather than the traditional methods of physical attack and political destruction which have been the traditional forms. Dr. Coffin hopes violence can be eventually eliminated as acceptable political methodology by demonstrating that non-violence is a more viable and more rational means of achieving social change. This approach to non-violent methodology involves knowledge of the methods and theory of non-violent approach to social change and consists of militant and humane methods of moral persuasion.

There is the possibility that the new form of militant non-violent approach to social change could provide an alternative approach to social problems which could eliminate the physically inhuman destructive aspects that have been routinely used in the

Reprinted by permission of the publisher, *Motive*, January 1970.

past. It is through the civilizing aspects of man's development that we gage his progress as human being rather than his primitive and animalistic tendencies to slaughter and destruction of his fellow human beings.

The school's responsibilities in this area include an examination of the components of violence and the social value of violent resolution of conflict. Studies of the nature and history of cultural differences in and alternatives to violence are certainly suitable subjects for schools. At the present time, however, schools which deal with war prevention are so few as to be scarcely known, while those which deal with war include virtually every school. A revision in the way schools look at societal violence may also open the door to a consideration of non-violence in the handling of students. Coffin speaks directly of education in his definition of non-violence.

Non-violence badly needs redefinition. Non-violence should mean not only a refusal to do another physical harm, but also a determination not to violate the integrity of any human being, our own integrity included.

According to this definition we all come out pretty violent, and first of all toward ourselves. For we love policies of repression: self-denial in place of self-discovery and self-fulfillment, moralistic terrorism in place of ethical persuasion. Instead of bringing into the full light of day the ambivalences that are part of the human equipment, we hide them. In every relationship of love there is hate, in every expression of altruism some self-advantage is being sought—but instead of examining, we repress. But these policies of repression are wrong if only because the subconscious has no digestive tract. What goes down must come up, and it usually does so in the form of displaced violence. Thus older folk who violently repress their sexuality become violent when they see the present permissiveness of the young. People who repress their ethical natures become violent when others make claims on their consciences. Middle class youth becomes violent toward middle class values because it cannot quite take leave of the class it forswears.

The result is disaster. As Freud once observed acidly, "It is a good thing men do not love their neighbors as themselves; if they did they would kill them." And that seems to be what we're up to a good deal of the time.

The point is that it is all right to have ambivalent feelings. It is wrong to pretend not to have them. It is wrong to have pretensions of innocence when in the sullied stream of human life holiness is man's only option. As "whole" and "holy" have the same root, holiness can be defined as the effort to bring into one integrated and dedicated whole the sensual, logical and ethical aspects of our nature; our past, present and future; our race, nationality and class. And holiness is possible given the certainty of God's love.

But let us go on with this theme of non-violence and recognize that as with individuals, so with social structures: they can be outwardly orderly yet inwardly violent. And if violence means violating human integrity, then without hesitation, we must call violent any university, business, government or social structure that condemns human beings to hopelessness and helplessness, to less than human existence. Further it is clear that people concerned with non-violence must show not only compassion for the victims of violence but also a determination to change the structures of society that make them objects of compassion. Let religious folk note well Colin Williams' splendid statement that it is no longer possible to distinguish between a personal conversion experience and a change in social attitudes.

That is why Elijah was so determined, despite the personal risk, to confront Ahab. And when Ahab called him the disturber of Israel, Elijah properly retorted that it was Ahab who was the disturber of Israel's peace, for his rule rejected more than it reflected the commandments of God. In other words Ahab's kingdom was an established disorder, and as Augustine later wrote, "What are . . . kingdoms without justice but large bands of robbers?"

What we need to recognize is Gandhi's truth that exploitation is the essence of violence, that violence in its cruelest form is not blue collar or no collar, but white collar; not individual and messy, but organized and efficient, antiseptic and profitable. The violent ones are less the mugging drug addicts that inhabit slum tenements than the modern-day Ahabs who occupy pentagonal palaces, skyscrapers like the Ling tower, the house that weapons built, and who never see blood unless their secretaries have a nosebleed.

To see how violent a world we live in, we have only to engage in an exercise of imagination: There are now three billion people on this planet. Reduce these peoples proportionately to a town of 1,000 and 60 will be Americans, 940 the rest of the world's population. The 60 Americans will control half the total income of the town. The 60 Americans will enjoy on an average fifteen times as much of all material goods as the rest of the citizens. The 60 Americans will enjoy a life expectancy of 71 years while the 940 on an average will die before they are 40.

Now we can see how ridiculous it is to define violence in physical terms alone. For a man killed by a bullet is no less dead than a man who has died from a disease resulting from eradicable poverty. When you stop to think of it, poverty is no longer inevitable; therefore it is intolerable. It is no more a private tragedy; it is now a public crime.

But there are other forms of violence and death, the kinds suffered by the 60 Americans. American production is now powerfully oriented toward consumption. And as consumption seems almost limitless, so too appears production. But to produce something, something else has to be destroyed, and the evidence of destruction is all about us. "Modern production," write two commentators, "has obscured the sun and the stars, and it has made the cities unliveable. It chews up great forests and drinks whole lakes and rivers, and it consumes men's religions and traditions and makes nonsense of their notions of the aims of education. It periodically slays heaps of men in war, and it daily mangles the spirits of millions of others in meaningless labor."

O for a President who could repeat, in place of cliches whose application has long since ceased, these words of the poet-king so eerie in their timeliness:

The bay trees in our country are all wither'd
And meteors fright the fixed stars of heaven;
The pale-fac'd moon looks bloody on the earth
And lean-look'd prophets whisper fearful change.

But what is to be done—non-violently? One obvious thing is to speak Elijah's truth that we dwell in a land of idol worshippers. Like Willy Loman we have the wrong dreams. The wrongness comes through most poignantly when talking with blue-collar workers who, unlike blacks today and unlike whites during the Depression, are not excluded from the American pie; they are part of the American dream. Only what kind of a dream is it to return from spirit-mangling work to payments on the car, a mortgage on the house, stultifying TV programs, an over-heated teen-age daughter and a D-in-English car-smashing son? But who, particularly in the Church, has had the candor and courage to tell them of their wrong dreams, to tell them that the wonders of man do not consist in consumer goods, to tell them that their wretchedness is interior and therefore that it is wrong to seek to scapegoat long-haired students, liberal professors, the Vietcong, the UN?

In its most dangerous form, idol worshipping is reflected in the government, and we need not bother with the obvious examples today. Like many of you I read Robert Kennedy's account of the Cuban missile crisis and was greatly impressed by the President's restraint.

But the true hero of the story—if hero there be—is Nikita Khrushchev, for President Kennedy himself privately admitted (and unfortunately the admission is not in the book) that had he as an American President withdrawn missiles as did Khrushchev, he would have been impeached.

Secretary Rusk succinctly summed up the story: we were eyeball to eyeball, and the other fellow blinked. Most Americans thought this kind of manliness impressive. But what impresses me is that if High Noon encounters with nuclear weapons represent manliness, then we simply have to reinvent manhood.

And this, I think, is what non-violence is really all about: a new kind, or perhaps a New Testament kind, of manhood, patterned after the person of Jesus.

I have only begun to think about this new kind of manhood, but this much at least seems clear. If the aim of non-violence is reconciliation and healing, both for the individual and society, then the emphasis must be not on being right but on being loyal to a truth that is good for all. It is not we who must prevail but a truth that is as true for our adversaries as it is for us. Clearly this demands an openness to, a willingness to learn from our adversaries. (Actually a refusal to learn from another always reflects doubts about one's own position.) In short, the fight is for everyone. Every confrontation should offer opportunities, as Gandhi would say, "for all to rise above their present conditions." And this means we should avoid words or acts which inhibit the awakening of a decent response and only confirm us in our self-righteousness and self-pity.

It is at this point that words such as "pig," "nigger" and "honky" are not helpful. And it is at this point that physical violence is unhelpful. I can consider myself the equal of a man threatening me with violence, but I have trouble considering myself his equal if I am threatening him. (This, of course, is not to ignore the distinction between the violence of the oppressor and the violence of the oppressed.)

But openness to an adversary does not mean acquiescence in any evil in which he may be involved. Non-violence has nothing to do with passivity; it has everything to do with resistance. So if a man is opposed to the war in Vietnam, he should naturally refuse to have anything to do with it and go to jail rather than enter the Army. If he opposes the draft he should not register for it provided he has thought through all the consequences of his action for himself and others. For until the adversary in power knows that non-violent men are willing to suffer for their beliefs, he will not be truly willing to listen to them, knowing he can count on their ultimate acquiescence to his power if not to his opinion. Of this we have had endless examples in recent years.

Somehow we have to combine a quality of openness with a quality of determination. We have to fight racial and class enemies, yet never as personal enemies. We have to become twice as militant and twice as non-violent, twice as tough and twice as tender, as only the truly strong can be tender.

That is why a Communion service is so meaningful to me. "After the same manner he took the cup, after he had supped saying, 'This cup is the new covenant in my blood.'" That's what we need— a new covenant with God and with Christ for a new kind of manhood. To this new covenant we must devote a great deal of thought. Perhaps we should inscribe on the exit doors of the church these words of Daedalus: "I go forth . . . to forge in the smith of my soul the uncreated conscience of my race."

chapter 5

Sexuality

The sexual revolution has become so popular that it threatens its own existence as a radical movement. A rapid transition in sexual taboos has taken place in America and other areas of western culture, although the changes appear to have occurred in subjects of public conversation rather than in behaviors of individuals. In the past two decades the Puritan tradition of silence on sexual matters has been strongly challenged and perhaps broken. It is permissable, even encouraged, for people to discuss sexual hangups, sexual deviation, sexual pleasure, and sexual morality. High circulation family magazines like *Time*, *Life*, *Newsweek*, and *McCalls* regularly include articles on sexual topics that would have shocked even World War II parents. Television exploits sex as a subject through sensuous advertising, documentaries, and interviews on talk shows. Even established religions have undertaken public programs of discussion on sexual matters. The venerable Catholic Church is struggling over issues of sexuality: birth control, priestly celibacy, nuns in miniskirts.

The old standards in sexual radicalism are still in vogue despite the popular success of open sex discussion. Free love advocates tear at the notions of monogamous families and single sex objects. Prevalent social ostracism of illegitimate children and their mothers is still an issue, although schools are no longer a primary social institution for carrying out that ostracism. Abortion and its attendant moral problems continues as a topic of discussion, though now laws have been modified and the discussions are more public. Premarital sexual intercourse, promiscuity, and prostitution are all openly debatable subjects. Pornography is now a topic for presidential commissions and academic discourse. Venereal disease remains a social problem, but clinics now advertise their availability and confidentiality for treatment. Coeducation arguments have progressed beyond admission policies in previously all-male or all-female colleges to questions of joint dormitory accommodations and facilities. These areas of radical viewpoint have become more open to inquiry and, perhaps, less radical. They also represent the acceptance of bisexuality and cultural traditions of expected sexual behavior. Since accurate data on actual sex behaviors are almost impossible to obtain, the sex revolution may reside in the openness of subject and not in dramatic change in practices.

The newer expressions of radical ideas in sexuality challenge bisexuality and the traditional norms of sex relations. Unisex, the term coined to identify a movement toward indistinguishable sex characteristics in hair style, dress, and mannerism, is an example of a newer confrontation with older forms. Lesbianism and male homosexuality have jointly supported a social movement titled "Gay Liberation" in an attempt to drastically change the society's view of sexual separation along lines different from the norm. The "Women's Liberation" movement raises social and political questions about a society based on male domination. These radical ideas are not entirely new, but they are different from the areas of attack in sex matters that have been standard in American society.

Sex education is another area that has recently been under attack for various reasons. Some of the dissidents see sex education as a part of a Communist plot to foster decadence in western culture. Others see it as a move having the potential of destroying families by making sex an institutional matter. Still others dislike the idea of exposure of young minds to subjects that may create psychic damage. And still another group protests sex education as being inadequate and too moralistic, bound in the biology of reproduction and the morality of ascetics.

Sex roles, except for procreation, are culturally determined. There are societies in which the female is dominant, aggressive in sexual activities, and the family provider, while males are docile, receptive, and housekeepers. Cultural roles are learned in a variety of ways. Imitation of role models, reward and punishment for behaviors, and formal schooling each contribute to learning sex roles. By the time children reach school age they have learned many distinctions between the sexes, but schools augment the myths and facts of early childhood. Separate bathrooms and gyms, differential treatment of girls and boys by teachers, and peer pressures to conform in sex-role behavior are examples of this augmentation. High-school social activities enhance sex-role differentiation whether by football teams, pom-pom girls, or school dances. Current movements toward long hair for boys and pants for girls have upset traditional sex-role relationships, and schools have reacted by resistance and reluctance. The school shoulders burdensome responsibilities in sexual morality as it protects the values of an old, though often hypocritical, order and confronts the new generations in their desires to test and change the values.

Should broad scale sexual revolution develop not only in areas such as abortion and venereal disease but also in regard to societal sex relationships like unisex and women's liberation, education would be one of the focal points for reform.

Recommendations of the U.S. Commission on Obscenity and Pornography

One does not normally expect government commissions, whose membership typically includes the most solid of establishment figures, to propose radical changes in society. There is an expectation that commissions will propose change because they would be considered derelict to recommend nothing. But the changes proposed by government-appointed committees and commissions tend to stay well within the norms of society. It is true that many recommendations, however bland, come to no result because they only represent political window dressing for public consumption, would jeopardize certain interests who lobby effectively against them, or are simply ignored by being filed away in the archives. It is also true that some commissions, currently including those which studied violence and civil rights, have made dramatic and forthright statements to the public and have become sources for continuing debate over American values. This latter group of appointed bodies, however, are surely in the minority.

One recent commission had the distinction of being appointed to study that murky and treacherous area of sexual morality and to propose recommendations regarding pornography and obscenity. Surely those appointing such a group would have expected a report that would uphold the American tradition of sexual secrecy, innuendo, and see-through Puritan morality. The report might be expected to shift slightly toward the "new morality" but to still chastise those evil doers who thrive in the flesh markets producing or consuming porno.

The following selection of recommendations made by this commission shows that the report is not a revolutionary document advocating free love, group sex, or family dissolution. Its radicalism lies in its reasoned and articulate expression against governmentally legislated morality and for adequate education about sex. There is no emotional diatribe against promiscuity or for premarital sex experience. Yet this commission report contains a radically different

The Report of the Commission on Obscenity and Pornography. Washington, D.C.: U.S. Government Printing Office, September 1970.

view of the government's involvement in sexual morality—moving it from repression and censorship to education and openness. It is one of the few reports that has earned public disclaimers from the President and other government officials.

It is clear from the notes showing dissent by several members of the commission that these recommendations were not unanimous. Some dissenting members produced minority reports which are included in the complete commission report. Sexual morality continues to be an area of considerable dispute. The implications for education are forcefully presented in the first set of recommendations presented.

I. Non-Legislative Recommendations

The Commission believes that much of the "problem" regarding materials which depict explicit sexual activity stems from the inability or reluctance of people in our society to be open and direct in dealing with sexual matters. This most often manifests itself in the inhibition of talking openly and directly about sex. Professionals use highly technical language when they discuss sex; others of us escape by using euphemisms—or by not talking about sex at all. Direct and open conversation about sex between parent and child is too rare in our society.

Failure to talk openly and directly about sex has several consequences. It overemphasizes sex, gives it a magical, nonnatural quality, making it more attractive and fascinating. It diverts the expression of sexual interest out of more legitimate channels, into less legitimate channels. Such failure makes teaching children and adolescents to become fully and adequately functioning sexual adults a more difficult task. And it clogs legitimate channels for transmitting sexual information and forces people to use clandestine and unreliable sources.

The Commission believes that interest in sex is normal, healthy, good. Interest in sex begins very early in life and continues throughout the life cycle although the strength of this interest varies from stage to stage. With the onset of puberty, physiological and hormonal changes occur which both quicken interest and make the individual more responsive to sexual interest. The individual needs information about sex in order to understand himself, place his new experiences in a proper context, and cope with his new feelings.

The basic institutions of marriage and the family are built in our society primarily on sexual attraction, love, and sexual expression. These institutions can function successfully only to the extent that they have a healthy base. Thus the very foundation of our society rests upon healthy sexual attitudes grounded in appropriate and accurate sexual information.

Sexual information is so important and so necessary that if people cannot obtain it openly and directly from legitimate sources and through accurate and legitimate channels, they will seek it through whatever channels and sources are available. Clandestine sources may not only be inaccurate but may also be distorted and provide a warped context.

The Commission believes that accurate, appropriate sex information provided openly and directly through legitimate channels and from reliable sources in healthy contexts can compete successfully with potentially distorted, warped, inaccurate, and unreliable information from clandestine, illegitimate sources; and it believes that the attitudes and orientations toward sex produced by the open communication of appropriate sex information from reliable sources through legitimate channels will be normal and healthy, providing a solid foundation for the basic institutions of our society.

The Commission, therefore, presents the following positive approaches to deal with the problem of obscenity and pornography.

1. *The Commission recommends that a massive sex education effort be launched.* This sex education effort should be characterized by the following:

a) its purpose should be to contribute to healthy attitudes and orientations to sexual relationships so as to provide a sound foundation for our society's basic institutions of marriage and family;

b) it should be aimed at achieving an acceptance of sex as a normal and natural part of life and of oneself as a sexual being;

c) it should not aim for orthodoxy; rather it should be designed to allow for a pluralism of values;

d) it should be based on facts and encompass not only biological and physiological information but also social, psychological, and religious information;

e) it should be differentiated so that content can be shaped appropriately for the individual's age, sex, and circumstances;

f) it should be aimed, as appropriate, to all segments of our society, adults as well as children and adolescents;

g) it should be a joint function of several institutions of our society: family, school, church, etc.;

h) special attention should be given to the training of those who will have central places in the legitimate communication channels— parents, teachers, physicians, clergy, social service workers, etc.;

i) it will require cooperation of private and public organizations at local, regional, and national levels with appropriate funding;

j) it will be aided by the imaginative utilization of new educational technologies; for example, educational television could be used to reach several members of a family in a family context.

The Commission feels that such a sex education program would provide a powerful positive approach to the problems of obscenity and pornography. By providing accurate and reliable sex information through legitimate sources, it would reduce interest in and dependence upon clandestine and less legitimate sources. By providing healthy attitudes and orientations toward sexual relationships, it would provide better protection for the individual against distorted or warped ideas he may encounter regarding sex. By providing greater ease in talking about sexual matters in appropriate contexts, the shock and offensiveness of encounters with sex would be reduced.

2. *The Commission recommends continued open discussion, based on factual information, on the issues regarding obscenity and pornography.*

Discussion has in the past been carried on with few facts available and the debate has necessarily reflected, to a large extent, prejudices and fears. Congress asked the Commission to secure more factual information before making recommendations. Some of the facts developed by the Commission are contrary to widely held assumptions. These findings provide new perspectives on the issues.

The information developed by the Commission should be given wide distribution, so that it may sharpen the issues and focus the discussion.

3. *The Commission recommends that additional factual information be developed.*

The Commission's effort to develop information has been limited by time, financial resources, and the paucity of previously existing research. Many of its findings are tentative and many questions remain to be answered. We trust that our modest pioneering work in empirical research into several problem areas will help to open the way for more extensive and long-term research based on more refined methods directed to answering more refined questions. We urge both private and public sources to provide the financial resources necessary for the continued development of factual information so that the continuing discussion may be further enriched.

The Federal Government has special responsibilities for continuing research in these areas and has existing structures which can facilitate further inquiry. Many of the questions raised about obscenity and pornography have direct relevance to already existing programs in the National Institute of Mental Health, the National Institute of Child Health and Human Development, and the United States Office of Education. The Commission urges these agencies to broaden their concerns to include a wider range of topics relating to human sexuality, specifically including encounters with explicit sexual materials.

4. *The Commission recommends that citizens organize themselves at local, regional, and national levels to aid in the implementation of the foregoing recommendations.*

The sex education effort recommended by the Commission can be achieved only with broad and active citizen participation. Widespread discussion of the issues regarding the availability of explicit sexual materials implies broad and active citizen participation. A continuing research program aimed at clarifying factual issues regarding the impact of explicit sexual materials on those who encounter them will occur only with the support and cooperation of citizens.

Organized citizen groups can be more constructive and effective if they truly represent a broad spectrum of the public's thinking and feeling. People tend to assume, in the absence of other information, that most peoples' opinions are similar to their own. However, we know that opinions in the sexual realm vary greatly—that there is no unanimity of values in this area. Therefore, every group should attempt to include as wide a variety of opinion as is possible.

The aim of citizen groups should be to provide a forum whereby all views may be presented for thoughtful consideration. We live in a free, pluralistic society which places its trust in the competition of ideas in a free market place. Persuasion is a preferred technique. Coercion, repression and censorship in order to promote a given set of views are not tolerable in our society.

II. LEGISLATIVE RECOMMENDATIONS

On the basis of its findings, the Commission makes the following legislative recommendations. The disagreements of particular Commissioners with aspects of the Commission's legislative recommendations are noted below, where the recommendations are discussed in detail. Commissioners Link, Hill, and Keating have filed a joint dissenting statement. In addition, Commissioners Keating and Link have submitted separate remarks. Commissioners Larsen and Wolfgang have filed statements explaining their dissent from certain Commission recommendations. A number of other Commissioners have filed short separate statements.[1]

In general outline, the Commission recommends that federal,

[1] Commissioners Joseph T. Klapper, Morris A. Lipton, G. William Jones, Edward D. Greenwood and Irving Lehrman.

state, and local legislation should not seek to interfere with the right of adults who wish to do so to read, obtain, or view explicit sexual materials.[2] On the other hand, we recommend legislative regulations upon the sale of sexual materials to young persons who do not have the consent of their parents, and we also recommend legislation to protect persons from having sexual materials thrust upon them without their consent through the mails or through open public display.

The Commission's specific legislative recommendations and the reasons underlying these recommendations are as follows:

A. Statutes Relating to Adults

The Commission recommends that federal, state, and local legislation prohibiting the sale, exhibition, or distribution of sexual materials to consenting adults should be repealed. Twelve of the 17 participating members[3] of the Commission join in this recommendation.[4] Two additional Commissioners[5] subscribe to the bulk of the Commission's Report, but do not believe that the evidence presented at this time is sufficient to warrant the repeal of all prohibitions upon what adults may obtain. Three Commissioners dissent from the recommendation to repeal adult legislation and would retain existing laws prohibiting the dissemination of obscene materials to adults.[6]

The Commission believes that there is no warrant for con-

----

[2] The term explicit sexual materials is used here and elsewhere in these recommendations to refer to the entire range of explicit sexual depictions or descriptions in books, magazines, photographs, films, statuary, and other media. It includes the most explicit depictions, or what is often referred to as "hard-core pornography." The term, however, refers only to sexual *materials*, and not to "live" sex shows, such as strip tease or on-stage sexual activity or simulated sexual activity. The Commission did not study this phenomenon in detail and makes no recommendations in this area. See Preface to this Report.

[3] Commissioner Charles H. Keating, Jr., chose not to participate in the deliberation and formulation of any of the Commission's recommendations.

[4] Commissioner Edward E. Elson joins in this recommendation only on the understanding that there will be prior enactment of legislation prohibiting the public display of offensive sexual materials both pictorial and verbal, that there will be prior enactment of legislation restricting the sales of explicit sexual materials to juveniles, and that there be prior public and governmental support for the Commission's nonlegislative recommendations before such repeal is enacted.

[5] Commissioners Irving Lehrman and Cathryn A. Spelts.

[6] Commissioners Morton A. Hill, S. J., Winfrey C. Link, and Thomas C. Lynch.

tinued governmental interference with the full freedom of adults to read, obtain or view whatever such material they wish. Our conclusion is based upon the following considerations:

1. Extensive empirical investigation, both by the Commission and by others, provides no evidence that exposure to or use of explicit sexual materials play a significant role in the causation of social or individual harms such as crime, delinquency, sexual or nonsexual deviancy or severe emotional disturbances. This research and its results are described in detail in the Report of the Effects Panel of the Commission and are summarized above in the Overview of Commission findings, pp. 23. Empirical investigation thus supports the opinion of a substantial majority of persons professionally engaged in the treatment of deviancy, delinquency and antisocial behavior, that exposure to sexually explicit materials has no harmful causal role in these areas.

Studies show that a number of factors, such as disorganized family relationships and unfavorable peer influences, are intimately related to harmful sexual behavior or adverse character development. Exposure to sexually explicit materials, however, cannot be counted as among these determinative factors. Despite the existence of widespread legal prohibitions upon the dissemination of such materials, exposure to them appears to be a usual and harmless part of the process of growing up in our society and a frequent and nondamaging occurrence among adults. Indeed, a few Commission studies indicate that a possible distinction between sexual offenders and other people, with regard to experience with explicit sexual materials, is that sex offenders have seen markedly *less* of such materials while maturing.

This is not to say that exposure to explicit sexual materials has no effect upon human behavior. A prominent effect of exposure to sexual materials is that persons tend to talk more about sex as a result of seeing such materials. In addition, many persons become temporarily sexually aroused upon viewing explicit sexual materials and the frequency of their sexual activity may, in consequence, increase for short periods. Such behavior, however, is the type of sexual activity already established as usual activity for the particular individual.

In sum, empirical research designed to clarify the question has found no evidence to date that exposure to explicit sexual materials plays a significant role in the causation of delinquent or criminal behavior among youth or adults.

2. On the positive side, explicit sexual materials are sought as a source of entertainment and information by substantial numbers of American adults. At times, these materials also appear to serve to

increase and facilitate constructive communication about sexual matters within marriage. The most frequent purchaser of explicit sexual materials is a college-educated, married male, in his thirties or forties, who is of above average socio-economic status. Even where materials are legally available to them, young adults and older adolescents do not constitute an important portion of the purchasers of such materials.

3. Society's attempts to legislate for adults in the area of obscenity have not been successful. Present laws prohibiting the consensual sale or distribution of explicit sexual materials to adults are extremely unsatisfactory in their practical application. The Constitution permits material to be deemed "obscene" for adults only if, as a whole, it appeals to the "prurient" interest of the average person, is "patently offensive" in light of "community standards," and lacks "redeeming social value." These vague and highly subjective aesthetic, psychological and moral tests do not provide meaningful guidance for law enforcement officials, juries or courts. As a result, law is inconsistently and sometimes erroneously applied and the distinctions made by courts between prohibited and permissible materials often appear indefensible. Errors in the application of the law and uncertainty about its scope also cause interference with the communication of constitutionally protected materials.

4. Public opinion in America does not support the imposition of legal prohibitions upon the right of adults to read or see explicit sexual materials. While a minority of Americans favors such prohibitions, a majority of the American people presently are of the view that adults should be legally able to read or see explicit sexual materials if they wish to do so.

5. The lack of consensus among Americans concerning whether explicit sexual materials should be available to adults in our society, and the significant number of adults who wish to have access to such materials, pose serious problems regarding the enforcement of legal prohibitions upon adults, even aside from the vagueness and subjectivity of present law. Consistent enforcement of even the clearest prohibitions upon consensual adult exposure to explicit sexual materials would require the expenditure of considerable law enforcement resources. In the absence of a persuasive demonstration of damage flowing from consensual exposure to such materials, there seems no justification for thus adding to the overwhelming tasks already placed upon the law enforcement system. Inconsistent enforcement of prohibitions, on the other hand, invites discriminatory action based upon considerations not directly relevant to the policy of the law. The latter alternative also breeds public disrespect for the legal process.

6. The foregoing considerations take on added significance because of the fact that adult obscenity laws deal in the realm of speech and communication. Americans deeply value the right of each individual to determine for himself what books he wishes to read and what pictures or films he wishes to see. Our traditions of free speech and press also value and protect the right of writers, publishers, and booksellers to serve the diverse interests of the public. The spirit and letter of our Constitution tell us that government should not seek to interfere with these rights unless a clear threat of harm makes that course imperative. Moreover, the possibility of the misuse of general obscenity statutes prohibiting distributions of books and films to adults constitutes a continuing threat to the free communication of ideas among Americans—one of the most important foundations of our liberties.

7. In reaching its recommendation that government should not seek to prohibit consensual distributions of sexual materials to adults, the Commission discussed several arguments which are often advanced in support of such legislation. The Commission carefully considered the view that adult legislation should be retained in order to aid in the protection of young persons from exposure to explicit sexual materials. We do not believe that the objective of protecting youth may justifiably be achieved at the expense of denying adults materials of their choice. It seems to us wholly inappropriate to adjust the level of adult communication to that considered suitable for children. Indeed, the Supreme Court has unanimously held that adult legislation premised on this basis is a clearly unconstitutional interference with liberty.

8. There is no reason to suppose that elimination of governmental prohibitions upon the sexual materials which may be made available to adults would adversely affect the availability to the public of other books, magazines, and films. At the present time, a large range of very explicit textual and pictorial materials are available to adults without legal restrictions in many areas of the country. The size of this industry is small when compared with the overall industry in books, magazines, and motion pictures, and the business in explicit sexual materials is insignificant in comparison with other national economic enterprises. Nor is the business an especially profitable one; profit levels are, on the average, either normal as compared with other businesses or distinctly below average. The typical business entity is a relatively small entrepreneurial enterprise. The long-term consumer interest in such materials has remained relatively stable in the context of the economic growth of the nation generally, and of the media industries in particular.

9. The Commission has also taken cognizance of the concern of many people that the lawful distribution of explicit sexual materials to adults may have a deleterious effect upon the individual morality of American citizens and upon the moral climate in America as a whole. This concern appears to flow from a belief that exposure to explicit materials may cause moral confusion which, in turn, may induce antisocial or criminal behavior. As noted above, the Commission has found no evidence to support such a contention. Nor is there evidence that exposure to explicit sexual materials adversely affects character or moral attitudes regarding sex and sexual conduct.

The concern about the effect of obscenity upon morality is also expressed as a concern about the impact of sexual materials upon American values and standards. Such values and standards are currently in a process of complex change, in both sexual and nonsexual areas. The open availability of increasingly explicit sexual materials is only one of these changes. The current flux in sexual values is related to a number of powerful influences, among which are the ready availability of effective methods of contraception, changes of the role of women in our society, and the increased education and mobility of our citizens. The availability of explicit sexual materials is, the Commission believes, not one of the important influences on sexual morality.

The Commission is of the view that it is exceedingly unwise for government to attempt to legislate individual moral values and standards independent of behavior, especially by restrictions upon consensual communication. This is certainly true in the absence of a clear public mandate to do so, and our studies have revealed no such mandate in the area of obscenity.

The Commission recognizes and believes that the existence of sound moral standards is of vital importance to individuals and to society. To be effective and meaningful, however, these standards must be based upon deep personal commitment flowing from values instilled in the home, in educational and religious training, and through individual resolutions of personal confrontations with human experience. Governmental regulation of moral choice can deprive the individual of the responsibility for personal decision which is essential to the formation of genuine moral standards. Such regulation would also tend to establish an official moral orthodoxy, contrary to our most fundamental constitutional traditions.[7]

[7] Commissioner Thomas D. Gill has amplified his position with reference to this finding as follows: Legislation primarily motivated by an intent to establish or defend standards of public morality has not always been, as the Report

Therefore, the Commission recommends the repeal of existing federal legislation which prohibits or interferes with consensual dis-

---

of the Commission would have it, inappropriate, unsound, and contrary to "our most unsound," and contrary to "our most fundamental constitutional traditions."

In fact for at least 140 years after its adoption, the Constitution never appears to have been considered a barrier to the perpetuation of the belief held in the 13 original colonies that there was not only a right but a duty to codify in law the community's moral and social convictions. Granted homogeneous communities and granted the ensuing moral and social cohesiveness implied in such uniformity of interest the right of these solid and massive majorities to protect their own values by legislation they deemed appropriate went unchallenged so long as it did not impinge upon the individual's right to worship and speak as he pleased.

Only in the 20th century has an increasingly pluralistic society begun to question both the wisdom and the validity of encasing its moral and social convictions in legal armour, and properly so, for if all laws to be effective must carry into their implementation the approval of a majority, this is peculiarly and all importantly the case with laws addressed to standards of morality, which speedily become exercises in community hypocrisy if they do not embody the wishes and convictions of a truly dominant majority of the people.

The Commission's studies have established that on a national level no more than 35% of our people favor adult controls in the field of obscenity in the absence of some demonstrable social evil related to its presence and use.

The extensive survey of the prosecutorial offices of this country gives added affirmation of the principle that acceptable enforcement of obscenity legislation depends upon a solid undergirding of community support such as may be and is found in the smaller, more homogeneous communities, but is increasingly difficult to command in the largest urban areas where the divisiveness of life leads to splintered moral and social concepts. In effect this report tells us that where you have substantial community concern you don't require the law, but lacking such concern, the law is a substitute of uncertain effectiveness.

If, then, legal rules controlling human conduct are designed to emphasize and reinforce society's moral convictions only in those areas where the pressures for transgression are the greatest and the resulting social consequences the most serious, there is a notable lack of justification for such intervention in the Commission's findings as to the magnitude of the public's concern and the efficacy of the enforcement of current obscenity laws. As has so often occurred, an approach which was both defendable and workable in one era has become vulnerable and suspect in another.

Fairness, however, requires that despite these formidable considerations something more be said and therein is to be found the primary reason for this individual statement. It is by no means certain that the Commission's national study, accurate as it has every reason to be in presenting a national concensus, has an equal validity in depicting the group thinking of a given geographical tribution of "obscene" materials to adults. These statutes are: 18 U.S.C. Section 1461, 1462, 1464, and 1465; 19 U.S.C. Section 1305; and 39 U.S.C. Section 3006.[8] The Commission also recommends the repeal of existing state and local legislation which may similarly prohibit the consensual sale, exhibition, or the distribution of sexual materials to adults.

---

area, state, or community. It is believable, therefore, that notwithstanding the findings in the national reports, and quite consistent with them, there well may be found geographical pockets of homogeneous conviction, various regional, state, and local units where the requisite massive majority support essential for the legal codification of community standards does exist. My concurrence in the recommendation for the abolition of obscenity controls for consenting adults is not intended to express my disapproval of the right of any such group, so constituted, to challenge and attempt to override the substantial findings of law and fact which the Commission has determined to be persuasive in order to sustain their own deeply and widely held beliefs: a very considerable body of legislation in this country rests on just such a base of moral and social traditions.

It is a base, however, which is being undercut and eroded by the currents of the time and because this is so it may not now upon fair and objective examination be found to be of sufficient dimensions to sustain its burden.

[8] The broadcasting or telecasting of explicit sexual material has not constituted a serious problem in the past. There is, however, a potential in this area for thrusting sexually explicit materials upon unwilling persons. Existing federal statutes imposing criminal and civil penalties upon any broadcast of "obscene" material do not adequately address this problem because they do not describe with sufficient specificity what material would be prohibited, or under what conditions. Hence, the repeal of these statutes is recommended, upon the understanding that the Federal Communications Commission either already has, or can acquire through legislation, adequate power to promulgate and enforce specific rules in this area should the need arise.

Gay Liberation

Red Butterfly Publications

Homosexuality is not a new phenomenon, though it is still considered sexually deviate in the United States. Scandals related to homosexuality or lesbianism discovered among famous people are favorite subjects for exposé stories. An entire subculture with distinct language forms, signals, and liaison locations exists in major cities of the world. Standard comedian repertoires include gay jokes and routines. Fears of the social consequences of homosexuality drive some to excessive displays of masculinity or femininity. The strong social morality against homosexuals has developed legal restraints that keep such practices underground.

Recent public response to other liberation movements has encouraged homosexuals to take their case to the people. The Gay Liberation Front, patterned after other revolutionary insurgent groups, organized to pursue a revolution in sexual morality. Although the subject is still less than popular, gay liberation marches, pamphlets, and protests have become more public. The "closet queens" are raising radical social questions about the traditional sexual morality in this country.

Education, as an institution that assists in the socialization of youth, is changed by alterations in sex attitudes and behaviors. If the Gay Liberation movement is successful, schools may have to rethink their regulations regarding sex-related activities. Teaching about sexual behaviors in ancient times as well as contemporary literature may become more honest but more volatile. School dances and hallway romancing in the traditions of old Siwash High may look shockingly different to alumni and faculty. At the same time school may become less traumatic for those who deviate from the norm in sexual interest. Additionally, if educational institutions can more openly study sex, morality, and deviation, it may discover

Red Butterfly Publications, the source for this piece, are produced by the Gay Liberation Front. GLF developed as a radical homosexual movement during the 1960s. They have engaged in demonstrations, public appearances, and protests regarding the treatment of homosexuals, male and female, in America.

more appropriate avenues for those who wish to come into mainstream sexual life from its fringes. Studies of sexuality and deviation are still fraught with emotionalism and concepts of sinfulness.

An Approach to Liberation

The movement for liberation in America is practical humanism. It is the concrete, political expression of the stifled desires of all those victimized and exploited in our society. The movement translates desires into demands and needs into programs for struggle. The movement's starting point is the actual situation of all those under social and economic oppression. Its goal is to free our lives from bondage based on race, sex, sexual expression, economic class position—a bondage which results from the present structure of American society. Liberation means to seize control over our own lives and destinies, to begin to build a truly free society which will positively encourage the development of all its participants.

As human beings we are unique among animals in having a largely unspecified potential. Besides the basic biological needs for food, water and rest, we have needs which are specifically human and subject to conscious development: the need for relationship, the need to create and build. We are all erotic beings. We experience our lives as a striving for realization and satisfaction. We experience our lives sexually, as enlivened by beauty and feeling. At base we have a need for active envolvement and creation, the need to give form and meaning to our environment and ourselves.

Society is the environment of human life. Society is a system of roles or patterns of behavior which form and regulate the lives of each individual member. These roles extend to all aspects of behavior; they are learned, not innate, and to a great extent form the lives and characters of all those in society. The social roles, in turn, are largely dictated by the economic system, the way a society produces and distributes the fundamental necessities of life. We must judge a society by how well it fosters the full human development of all its members, given the material circumstances of the environment and the level of available technology.

The system of roles we call American society is presently organized around the needs and requirements of the prevailing economic system, capitalism. American capitalism has produced vast wealth and industrial power. But it has failed to provide a good and rational life for large numbers of our people. Capitalism does not directly and consciously operate to serve human needs. Profit-making is the dynamic of the system, and human requirements are left for fulfillment to the "invisible hand" of the market—or, more realistically, the hand of the welfare state.

Moreover, the kind of social roles necessitated by capitalism are not conducive to the kind of social flexibility and spontaneity which could make liberation a reality. We are saddled with the exploitation of labor, poverty amid abundance, ecological disaster, and imperialist wars such as those in Viet Nam and Laos. Work is a task most Americans must perform for survival, a task over whose direction they have no control. The creation of concrete value through labor can never become a human need and source of fulfillment so long as its product belongs to someone other than the producer. Yet this situation constitutes the base of American economic life. The competitive drive of capitalist society forces on all of us an ethic of accumulation and egocentrism, stifling growth and enrichment through enjoyment and cooperation.

Sexuality too is constricted. It is bent into an aspect of life apart from the active and creative functions of society. Sexuality is structured into the narrow channel of the nuclear family. Competition and exclusive possession, traits of the marketplace, are extended to erotic relations among persons. The oppression of homosexuals in America flows from this restriction and containment of human sexual potential within certain narrow roles. Labels, such as homo-, hetero- and bi-sexual, indicate the rigidity of the forms of relating under which we live. Like women, both male and female homosexuals suffer from sex-typing (homosexuals are supposed to be neurotic, weak, irresponsible, etc. *because* they are gay), with practical harassment and exploitation as a result.

Our oppression as homosexuals stems from the same source as that of other repressed groups: the restrictive competitive social roles necessitated by a capitalist economy and a ruling elite. Our liberation can only be achieved by replacing this humanly wasteful and destructive system by a genuine democracy, which would include taking rational control of the economy to serve human needs, and opening cultural development and leisure to all. The realization of this basic social transformation is a necessity if we are to advance humanly, if we are to be able to realize the rich potentials of our sexuality for relationships of all kinds, for bringing new energy and vision to the creation of a more human world.

Gay Liberation is a process of struggle, of forming our unvoiced needs into political and social demands. Gay Liberation cannot mean mere "toleration" for homosexuals. It must result in the transformation of existing social relations, the breakdown of straight definitions of relationships such as male supremacy, the subjugation of women, sexual exclusivity, etc. It necessitates the evolution of new, more fluid patterns of relating based on cooperation and sharing. Gay Liberation presupposes a free, consciously controlled social life, a goal we share with all other oppressed groups directly. We must declare our demands concretely and struggle for them. We must likewise join with all others who suffer from the narrow, profit-bent social and economic machinery of our society. We extend fraternal support to all liberation struggles and invite the participation of all in ours.

GAY LIBERATION AND THE MOVEMENT

Gay Liberation is a very new concept. Some movement activists seem to be in conflict and confused over how to relate to the emerging Gay Liberation movement. As radical analyses of Gay Liberation are just beginning to appear (this pamphlet is a first effort) it is difficult for many to fit it meaningfully into a framework of radical thought.

Some younger activists, and some older ones, have immediately grasped the validity and relevance of Gay Liberation. Women's Liberation groups have generally seen how Gay Liberation is related to their struggle. Gay Liberation and Women's Liberation are such closely related issues that neither can be fully understood without reference to the other.

Self-denial has undoubtedly played a part in the lives of many movement people. We can understand a somewhat puritanical attitude towards sex on their parts. Self-denial should not, however, be accompanied by an uncritical acceptance of the superstitions, religious taboos, and prejudices of bourgeois culture.

Words like "faggot" and "cocksucker" have been used to attack ruling class figures and political tendencies opposed to one's own. Use of the words has been defended as "street rhetoric." This is crap. These words are vicious and demeaning, and their use reduces millions of gay people to a less than human status.

Gay people have been systematically, if not democratically, excluded from certain political groups. This practice also must stop.

Basically we make two points to the movement:

1) Homosexual acts between freely consenting partners harm no one, and are a natural and completely human form of behavior. The Revolution cannot be just or complete if our rights as full human beings are not recognized. We call upon our comrades to be progressive in sexual matters also, as we include ourselves in the Brotherhood of Man. An injury to one is an injury to all.
2) We feel that our oppression is due, not merely to ignorance and superstition, but to the interest and ideologies of an authoritarian

capitalist society. Sexual repression is one means used to maintain class domination in an unfree society. Sexual liberation cannot succeed within the framework of reactionary society. At the same time, the struggle for sexual liberation is a necessary part of making the Revolution by any means necessary.

Perhaps with the emergence of a classless society, we shall also enter into a *labelless* society—one that will be free of the stereotypes that divide people and perpetuate the privileges of the few over the needs of the many.

We will not stop, nor will our straight friends, in the fight for the liberation of all, no matter what superstitions must be conquered. No one need give up anything for Gay Liberation except his own prejudice. We are not asking for our rights as human beings, but demanding them. We will not be satisfied with anything less than freedom.

ALL POWER TO THE OPPRESSED PEOPLES!
POWER TO ALL THE PEOPLE!

A Manifesto for Sexual Revolution

Kate Millett

Kate Millett has become well known through publication of her analysis of literary figures titled *Sexual Politics*. As a professor at Barnard College, spokeswoman for women's liberation causes on television interview shows, participant in activities supported by the liberation movement, and writer of provocative articles, Millett has become a dominant leader in the field. The following manifesto was written to outline the reasons for and proposals of the movement.

She charges that women's education has been inferior by

Reprinted by permission of the author. From *Notes from the Second Year: Women's Liberation*. New York: Radical Feminism, 1970.

design and non-powerful by intent. For those new to the study of education, it should be noted that women were entirely excluded from education at the secondary and college level during early periods of American history. Separate colleges for women were established through the efforts of Emma Hart Willard and other leaders of women's rights during the nineteenth century, yet male education continued to get preferential treatment in financing, choice of professional curricula, and educational expectation. Women in the twentieth century have not yet moved into equal status with regard to educational opportunities. The professions, except for public school teaching, continue to be male dominated, and women are neither admitted to nor encouraged to pursue studies in professional and graduate education to the extent that bright men are.

School guidance counselors and teachers contribute to this sexual discrimination by discouraging capable girls with scientific or male-dominated profession interests. Females must become even more competitive than their male educational counterparts in order to secure comparable admission, placement, and advancement.

When one group rules another, the relationship between the two is political. When such an arrangement is carried out over a long period of time it develops an ideology (feudalism, racism, etc.). All historical civilizations are patriarchies: their ideology is male supremacy.

Oppressed groups are denied education, economic independence, the power of office, representation, an image of dignity and self-respect, equality of status, and recognition as human beings. Throughout history women have been consistently denied all of these, and their denial today, while attenuated and partial, is nevertheless consistent. The education allowed them is deliberately designed to be inferior, and they are systematically programmed out of and excluded from the knowledge where power lies today—e.g., in science and technology. They are confined to conditions of economic dependence based on the sale of their sexuality in marriage, or a variety of prostitutions. Work on a basis of economic independence allows them only a subsistence level of life—often not even that. They do not hold office, are represented in no positions of power, and authority is forbidden them. The image of woman fostered by cultural media, high and low, then and now, is a marginal and demeaning existence, and one outside the human condition—which is defined as the prerogative of man, the male.

Government is upheld by power, which is supported through consent (social opinion), or imposed by violence. Conditioning to an ideology amounts to the former. But there may be a resort to the latter at any moment when consent is withdrawn—rape, attack, sequestration, beatings, murder. Sexual politics obtains consent through the "socialization" of both sexes to patriarchal policies. They consist of the following:

1) the formation of human personality along stereotyped lines of sexual category, based on the needs and values of the master class and dictated by what he would cherish in himself and find convenient in an underclass: aggression, intellectuality, force and efficiency for the male; passivity, ignorance, docility, "virtue," and ineffectuality for the female.
2) the concept of sex role, which assigns domestic service and attendance upon infants to all females and the rest of human interest, achievement and ambition to the male; the charge of leader at all times and places to the male, and the duty of follower, with equal uniformity, to the female.
3) the imposition of male rule through institutions: patriarchal religion, the proprietary family, marriage, "The Home," masculine oriented culture, and a pervasive doctrine of male superiority.

A Sexual Revolution would bring about the following conditions, desirable upon rational, moral and humanistic grounds:

1) the end of sexual repression—freedom of expression and of sexual mores (sexual freedom has been partially attained, but it is now being subverted beyond freedom into exploitative license for partriarchal and reactionary ends).
2) Unisex, or the end of separatist character-structure, temperament and behavior, so that each individual may develop an entire— rather than a partial, limited, and conformist—personality.
3) re-examination of traits categorized into "masculine" and "feminine," with a total reassessment as to their human usefulness and advisability in both sexes. Thus if "masculine" violence is undesirable, it is so for both sexes, "feminine" dumb-cow passivity likewise. If "masculine" intelligence or efficiency is valuable, it is so for both sexes equally, and the same must be true for "feminine" tenderness or consideration.
4) the end of sex role and sex status, the patriarchy and the male supremacist ethic, attitude and ideology—in all areas of endeavor, experience, and behavior.
5) the end of the ancient oppression of the young under the patriarchal proprietary family, their chattel status, the attainment of the human rights presently denied them, the professionalization and therefore improvement of their care, and the guarantee that when they enter the world, they are desired, planned for, and provided with equal opportunities.
6) Bisex, or the end of enforced perverse heterosexuality, so that the sex act ceases to be arbitrarily polarized into male and female,

to the exclusion of sexual expression between members of the same sex.

7) the end of sexuality in the forms in which it has existed historically
—brutality, violence, capitalism, exploitation, and warfare—that it may cease to be hatred and become love.

8) the attainment of the female sex to freedom and full human status after millenia of deprivation and oppression, and of both sexes to a viable humanity.

chapter 6

Drugs

To enhance the quality of existence is the purpose of life. Changing the chemistry of the body is a time-honored way by which man has sought to fulfill this purpose. His actions have been impelled by discontent and curiosity and hope. The consequences of chemical alteration have deepened discontent, exceeded hope, and quickened curiosity.

To those for whom the world is too much, drugs supply the serenity of blunted sensibility; to others for whom the senses are too dull, drugs deliver the exhilaration of heightened awareness. In either case, the experience which is produced can be radiated through space and time, witness the "Kubla Khan" of Coleridge. Thus, drugs are a blessing for individuals, for society, and for posterity.

Regretfully, it is a mixed blessing. Drugs kill people as well as pain. The power of drugs to liberate the mind is still surpassed by their power to shackle. Chemical warfare is not an enterprise designed for the universal dissemination of joy. The horrendous potential of drugs was keenly recognized in the alarm which greeted the news that Yippies were talking of slipping LSD into the Chicago water supply during the 1968 Democratic national convention.

And yet the drug explosion is as inexorable as the knowledge explosion, of which it is a part. An enormously endowed research industry is devoted to the proliferation of drugs. Just as drugs are a way of life for millions of people, they are a means of livelihood for other millions. Already projected for early marketing are pills that will strengthen the memory, or improve reading ability, or moderate specific emotions.

The interpretations and recommendations related to the drug phenomenon cover a wide range of political persuasions. At one extreme are those who believe that the human body is private not public property. Therefore, the consumption of drugs is essentially personal business, not subject to official regulation.

At a different remove are those who have convinced themselves that drug usage is promoted by pro-Communist elements as part of a conspiracy to undermine the republic.

And, of course, there are the prophets of the drug culture itself, who trumpet chemistry as the way to reestablish contact with primeval human values while also giving the mind dominion over vast new realms of experience.

Schools have become loci for socially proscribed drugs, as well as forums for legally mandated indoctrination against these drugs. In consequence, the school atmosphere, as it relates to drugs, fluctuates between furtiveness and hysterical negativism. Each side *knows* that the other is wrong, but neither side attends to what the other is saying. Those who defend the use of illegal drugs are dismissed as too naïve for credibility or too drug-crazed for objectivity. Those who deplore the use of these drugs are discounted as too misinformed to understand or too uptight to experiment or, worst of all, too faithless to be honest with the younger generation. Dogmatic reductionism and *ad hominem* argumentation have become the intellectual *modus operandi* for dealing with the drug phenomenon. School is turned into a place where protagonists confront each other rather than the evidence.

Drugs and the Law

Donald M. Dozer

Donald Dozer, professor of history at the University of California, Santa Barbara, argues that individuals have the right to harm themselves, and laws should be enacted only to keep people from hurting others. Thus, drug usage, like alcohol consumption, is a matter of private morality not a subject for legislative regulation. Official efforts to halt a shifting morality lead to tyranny or to unenforceable laws that breed contempt for law itself.

Dozer's position is in line with the new wave of libertarian thought in America, especially among college students. The libertarians hold that, in most cases, individuals understand their needs and can satisfy them better than government. Even when this is not so, the government's role remains essentially negative—to keep people from interfering with the freedom of others. And it would be ludicrous for government to do that which it is charged with preventing others from doing. No group, however large or official, has any right to mold other groups or individuals to its taste. The libertarian position, then, attempts to provide legal protection for all those who would do "their own thing."

The ramifications of the libertarians' position, and Dozer's in particular, are far reaching indeed. If the freedom which the libertarians accredit to people is extended to or claimed by students, the high school will become a different place than it is now. Students will be able to get stoned on the premises, so long as they do so in nooks and crannies where the smoke will not affect others. But it really won't be necessary for drug users to slip off to a quiet corner of the building, since compulsory school attendance is clearly contrary to libertarian principles.

Some authors who are in sympathy with young people fear that the young are already suffering from a freedom so great that it is oppressive. Educators will have to grapple with the problem of how much self-direction is satisfying and beneficial to individual students.

Reprinted by permission of the publisher, *The Freeman*, March 1970.

Marijuana, LSD, barbiturates, amphetamines, and now the cyclamates have become targets of legal extermination. When marijuana is found growing on our hillsides or in a neglected crevice of a downtown building it must be attacked with hoe and shovel and destroyed under the surveillance of police authorities. The zeal of the national government to prevent the importation of marijuana has produced a border crisis with Mexico. Tobacco has been proved to be a serious offender against the health of our people. Will the new crusaders, acting in the name of the public welfare, now mobilize and march with hoes and shovels against the dread plants ranged in militant phalanx in the fields of Marlboro country?

A young college student seeking escape from the ordeal of modern living brews himself a jimson weed broth on his hot plate and after hallucinogenic contortions dies. Will the law now undertake to extirpate all jimson weeds from the countryside and clamp a quarantine on it at the borders of the nation? And the possibility must not be overlooked that seeds of these *plantes noires* may be carried across the border by birds, which obviously therefore must be brought under the surveillance of the immigration authorities.

A half century ago the United States undertook by law to prevent the sale and use of intoxicating beverages and as a result produced a nation of informers, bootleggers, lawbreakers, and drunkards. In panicked anxiety we adopted a policy of paternalistic authoritarianism which is now repeating itself as another periodic spasm of concern to be our brother's keeper. Now police officers are given instruction in detecting the smell of marijuana smoke, and they snoop outside the apartments of suspected users in an effort to catch a whiff drifting through windows or over transoms.

Inviolability of Free Choice or Social Control through Law

The central idea of the law in the nineteenth century was the importance and, derivatively, the inviolability of the free individual will. But the law has come increasingly to involve itself not only in protecting individual life but in assuring to the individual a productive and satisfying life. All this is being done under the modern postulate, so well expressed by Dean Roscoe Pound, that "the risk of misfortune to individuals is to be borne by society as a whole," and consequently society must assume the obligation to prevent misfortune to individuals even when committed by their own hand.[1]

[1] Roscoe Pound, *Social Control Through Law*, 2nd printing (Hamden, Conn.: Archon Books, 1968), p. 116.

This places the state squarely in the position of being the guardian of the morals of each individual in society who may engage in acts harmful to no one but himself. In such cases the state may even impose punishment without proving that his act produced any harm to himself. The tendency in this direction, it appears, increases with the growth of the consensus society, with the expansion of the agencies of responsiveness between citizens and the instrumentalities of government, in short with the coercive facilities available to society.

What, then, is the stake that society has in the preservation of the life of an individual citizen? Is it obliged to see to it that no individual harms himself even though he may wish to do so? Should government rightly assume any role in the enactment and enforcement of sumptuary legislation, that is legislation affecting the appetites, dress, and health of individuals?

These questions lie close to the heart of responsible civilian government. They impinge directly upon the problem of the optimum relationship between the individual and society, a perennial problem in our human situation. Legal restraints which are couched in too repressive language may be tempered by administrative discretion, which in turn may give rise to inequities in the application of the law, or such restraints may, on the other hand, be judged to necessitate rigorous enforcement action, even to the calling out of troops and the imposition of military controls with consequences fatal to consensual government. For, significantly, the limitations upon individual freedom are bracketed under the police power opening the way inexorably to the establishment of the police state.

LIMITED USE OF FORCE

It has been the persistent objective of the champions of freedom to limit the area within which the law, construed as the force of society, may impinge upon the individual. The basic principle of a free society, as defined by John Stuart Mill, is that "mankind are greater gainers by suffering each other to live as seems good to themselves than by compelling each to live as seems good to the rest." The individual is entitled as of right to enjoy legal noninterference with his natural freedom.

We are living in a period marked by a wide dichotomy between law and morals when law is seeking to replace morals as the cement of society. The justice that is sought is to be achieved, it is thought, through the force of state action, by the acts of a society which is politically organized. This society, as it perceives its moral values slipping away, seeks to establish canons of value through legal enactment and to constrain all members of society to follow them. The law has thus extended its domain to become an instrument of ethical behavior and social change.

The lawmaker and the moralist are alike actuated by a more or less ideal conception of what life should be and of what makes for order and progress in society. Their conception may or may not bear much relationship to the actual conditions of living, but to the extent that it soars far away from those conditions it forfeits both its credibility and its social force. And when the lawmaker and the moralist, having thus divorced themselves from reality, assume a command role, they find that their conception, however beautiful, is unattainable except through the application of force. Narrow is the line that separates the dogmatist who argues that what is is unequivocally right and the dogmatist who insists that what is is unequivocally *not* right— between him who insists that the state can do no right and him who insists that the state can do no wrong.

SELF-EXECUTING LEGISLATION

The only effective legislation is self-executing. This truism is as applicable to the moral as to human law. When it is ignored or violated, the law itself ceases to be a force making for order, and it yields place to a politicized society which operates in accordance with prejudice and whim and which exerts moral force only because it possesses physical power. Those, then, who would impose sumptuary restrictions upon human conduct are dissolving the concept of law into an instrument of social control and social order. They are thus creating insoluble problems of enforcement.

"Moral populism," to use H.L.A. Hart's phrase, "is a necessary cohesive factor in any society as implying a hard-core moral consensus. It becomes a threat to that society when it undertakes to use law to enforce that consensus and thus impose itself forcibly upon the minority."[2] This is one of the things which government must not be allowed to do. Much of the student unrest today is directed against the excessive intrusion of the law into areas where it has no business to be.

The law as such will not and cannot be expected to produce that voluntary restraint which alone will develop a moral citizenry, a citizenry dedicated to that better way envisioned by the moralists. "Virtue," as Malcolm Muggeridge has observed, "should be implicit rather than explicit." It should be "revealed in living" rather than in laws.

[2] H. L. A. Hart, *Law, Liberty and Morality* (Stanford, California: Stanford University Press, 1963), p. 79.

WARDS OF SOCIETY

The law, therefore, must not concern itself with victimless crimes. Society must not hold an individual accountable for actions which do not harm anyone but himself. Restrictions on the highway speed of motor vehicles are imposed, it may be assumed, not for the purpose of preventing drivers from injuring themselves or from destroying their property interest in their vehicles, but rather exclusively for the purpose of preventing drivers from committing physical injury to others and causing an increase in insurance rates. To argue the contrary is to hold that society is entitled to assure the function and to claim the product of every individual in society as of interest to it and that society will be prejudiced by his loss.

If government bases its action upon such a claim, namely, the functional usefulness of human life and the corresponding obligation of society to protect the physical integrity of the person, then does not society possess the corollary obligation to enhance the social utility of the individual even against his will, that is, to promote a state-defined virtue? Under this proposition the state can resort to almost any method of dealing with individuals on the plea of the good of the state, thus opening up the way broadly for completely paternalistic government. It would then be obliged, for example, to judge attempted suicide to be as heinous as murder, and the person who only half succeeds in a suicide attempt should be punished after recovering.

Legislative enactment cannot successfully rebut the daily legislation of the people. In this context, as Dr. Margaret Mead has pointed out, the legal prohibitions against the use of marijuana are doing greater damage than the harmful effects on those who use marijuana. The broader the ambit of the law, the greater is the danger of building a society of force. Ironically, therefore, the stronger the attempt to create a system of reason, the greater is the danger of creating a system that indulges in arbitrary action and responds only to impulse. In the attempt to impose sumptuary regulations we come dangerously near to championing the proposition that coercion must be used to maintain the moral status quo and to eliminate deviations from it. But we must face the consequent fact that the act of thus freezing a moral system at a given moment in time will arrest even those processes of social changes which are judged wholesome by the mass of society. Surely an indisputable prerequisite to the maintenance of a civilized society is to maintain optimum conditions for the fullest possible realization of the idea of liberty in human experience.

The traffic in drugs which have been proved dangerous to human life ought to be prohibited, for when the "pusher" peddles his wares he is harming others—his customers. But the mere use of such drugs or the fact of an individual's being in a place where such drugs are being used by others should by no means be punishable. These acts must be regarded as individual rights which are beyond the concern and business of the law. If an individual or a group of consenting adults find pleasure in sitting around and using drugs, which all the evidence shows will harm them, their action should be no concern of the law, however flagrantly it may flaunt public morality.

In short, narcotic and hallucinogenic drugs present a serious challenge to the moral forces in society; but they must not be allowed to become a major preoccupation of the law. Punitive laws ought to be designed to curb only the patently antisocial actions of the almost infinitesimally small minority of the members of any society who, if not curbed, will destroy that society. When they go beyond that limit and undertake to define other human actions as misdemeanors, felonies, and crimes, they stimulate in the heart of every man the desire to commit the very offenses which they purport to prohibit.

LSD—Weapon of Subversion

Frank Capell

This article originally appeared in *The American Mercury*, which was founded in 1924 by H. L. Mencken and George Jean Nathan. However, the Mencken-Nathan publication was without the strong anti-Semitic and anti-Negro biases that characterize *The American Mercury* today. Frank Capell is editor and publisher of *The Herald of Faith*, newsletter of the fundamentalist Christian sect The Pillar of Fire.
    In his article Capell weaves a web of circumstantial evidence to support his contention that subversive elements may be using LSD as a means of weakening national resolve against the encroach-

Reprinted by permission of the publisher from *The American Mercury*, Vol. 104, Spring 1968.

ments of Communism. He recalls Timothy Leary's role in propagandizing for the drug and notes that left-wingers, alleged Communists, and strange people like Norman Mailer have supported Leary. He also points out that Communists have long had a diabolical interest in such debilitating drugs as fluoride.

The Capell piece illustrates the dilemma between the citizen's duty to speak out and his obligation to keep quiet. Is Capell performing a patriotic service or is he fear-mongering? If one declines to use a public forum to parade his barely supportable fears, might not the swift flow of events bring about that which is feared before a more persuasive warning can be issued? It may be that Americans are now sufficiently skeptical and sophisticated that one can trust them to make their own critical judgments and should not deprive them of the opportunity to do so. One may also have an obligation to himself to subject his ideas to public scrutiny.

For the foregoing to be possible, a market place for ideas must exist. There is an especially cogent reason why the school should function as such a bazaar: It is the socially designated place for citizens to acquire the ability to make critical judgments.

"The city exposed to a successful LSD attack presumably will cease to function. The inhabitants will be so bemused with the odd things that are happening to them and their neighbors that for half a day an aggressor force could take over without substantial resistance."

"A saboteur could carry enough in an overcoat pocket to produce serious temporary effects on all the inhabitants of a megapolis if only he could distribute it equally. The contents of a two-suiter piece of luggage will hold an amount sufficient to disable every person in the United States."

These frightening conclusions are not the statements of a "right-wing extremist," but are the result of a serious ten-year study made by Prof. Sidney Cohen, M.D., of the University of California Medical School, who is Chief of Psychosomatic Medicine at the U.S. Veterans Hospital in Los Angeles. They are set forth in his book, *The Beyond Within*.

LSD is known as an hallucinogen or vision producer. According to expert researcher Dr. Cohen, this drug, which literally immobilizes from normal consciousness, is so potent that 300,000 adult doses can be obtained from one ounce. Two pounds, he states, evenly distributed would mentally dissociate every man, woman and child in Greater New York for an eight hour period.

Much of the credit for the fantastic spread of the use of LSD among college students coast to coast is attributed to individuals like Dr. Leary and Dr. Alpert. The publicity which followed and Dr.

Leary's justification for its use received national publicity. Thereafter Dr. Leary, a former Roman Catholic who became a convert to Hinduism, established the Castalia Foundation, a "utopian" colony with headquarters in a 64-room building resembling a Bavarian castle located at Millbrook, N.Y. Dr. Leary had previously headed an organization called International Foundation for Internal Freedom, which organization under his direction conducted experiments with hallucinogenic drugs on inmates of a Massachusetts correctional institution. Commenting on Dr. Leary's experiments and activities with his International Foundation for Internal Freedom, psychiatrist Cohen stated, "Much can be learned from the efforts of I.F.I.F. to introduce psychedelic chemicals into the American culture."

Dr. Leary, who has become known as the principal spokesman for the LSD cult, was arrested in Laredo, Texas in December, 1965. The following March, he was convicted in the Federal court on changes of illegal transportation of marijuana (from Mexico to U.S.) and sentenced to thirty years in prison. In April, 1966, he was again arrested on charges of possessing narcotics when police raided the Castalia Foundation Building and found narcotics in an upstairs bedroom. *Time* magazine of April 29, 1966 quoted Dr. Leary as having told an audience during a lecture entitled, "The Politics and Ethics of Ecstasy," that some one-million Americans have already had psychedelic experiences. The approach of Dr. Leary to the problem has been one of promoting the use of the drug and then justifying its use by quoting figures which make it seem legitimate through its wide use.

An LSD Conference was held in San Francisco in June, 1966, by the University of California Extension Division. Dr. Leary, one of the speakers, estimated that 2 million doses of LSD would be introduced into California during the month of June, 1966. He stated he personally had taken LSD 131 times. In describing the effects of the drug, Dr. Leary stated, "The LSD trip is best understood as a religious pilgrimage, the LSD kick is best understood as ecstasy, and LSD panic is nothing short of a spiritual crisis." By contrast, psychiatrist Dr. William Frosch, another speaker, who has had considerable experience treating patients who took LSD, stated he noticed a loss of social inhibition, lessening of ambition, greater love of fellow man, etc. "None of our patients," he said, "turned to organized religion after taking the drug."

Dr. Frosch told a *Time* magazine writer the number of steady users in New York City had doubled from 5,000 to 10,000 in the past year. He stated there are three basic reactions caused by LSD ranging from merely frightening to the development of permanent psychosis. "We have called these," he said, "panic reactions, reappearance of the drug symptoms without reingestion of the drug, and overt, prolonged psychosis." He described the spontaneous return of LSD illusions up to a year after the people involved had last taken the drug.

The promotion of LSD by Dr. Leary and others has resulted in a widespread use of the drug, so great that estimates vary from one to several million users. As head of the LSD cult, Dr. Leary has many important friends and supporters. After Dr. Leary's conviction on narcotics charges, a defense committee was set up called the Timothy Leary Defense Fund with an office at 40 Exchange Place, New York, N.Y. Among those supporting Dr. Leary in paid advertisements for fund donations has been Jules Feiffer, cartoonist who has supported many left-wing causes, including anti-war in Vietnam groups, Turn Towards Peace, Peace parades, etc. His work is used often by left-wing pacifist groups. Guy Endore, another supporter, has been identified as a member of the Communist Party, according to published reports, by a witness in 1951 and another in 1952.

Norman Mailer, the author, is an additional Dr. Leary supporter. Mailer is best known for his books *White Negro*, *The Naked and the Dead* and similar "off-beat" type books and writings. He was arrested on one occasion when he tried to kill his wife. He was a supporter of pro-Castro elements who were trying to sell the American public on the Cuban murderer as a "Robin Hood," and agrarian reformer.

EXPERIMENTS ON TROOPS

Dr. Cohen has written that troops have been exposed to the hallucinogenic drugs without their knowledge or permission. He stated they were quite unaware of their abnormal state and could not follow simple commands or perform ordinary tasks with an acceptable degree of accuracy. Dr. Cohen stated, "A further way in which these drugs (LSD) might conceivably be exploited is their secret administration to one or several of the critical civilian and military decision-makers of a nation. This would not necessarily have the goal of producing disastrous decisions, because the system of checks and counterchecks on crucial judgments tends to neutralize the disturbed thinking of a single man or of a small group. Rather, it might aim at demoralizing the country. Witnessing the mental collapse of the leaders from spaced doses of a psychotomimetic agent would be disheartening. Confidence would be impaired, and those empowered to manage the nation might begin to question the sanity of all their colleagues."

Dr. Cohen wrote, "A review of the advantages of LSD as an incapacitating agent will help understanding of the interest of the military in this esoteric chemical. It can be cheaply and easily made. Its enormous potency would be an important factor in wartime use."

LSD Weakens Will

An indication of the weakening of the will to resist caused by LSD will be found through the experiments of Dr. Eric Kast who used the drug on 80 patients expected to die within weeks or months from malignant diseases. Dr. Kast stated the LSD created "acceptance and surrender to the inevitable loss of control" among the dying— while with most patients "this control is anxiously maintained and fought for."

The use of LSD by students and adults alike has had a demoralizing effect. Users are inclined to join pseudo religious cults; they also frequently use other drugs as well; and there appears to be a general breakdown of integrity and morality. The liberal professors who are defending its use are the same who support left-wing causes and radical peace movements. The Federal Government has made several financial grants for medical and psychiatric research with LSD and there is no need for the universities to be flooded with the drug under "Research Project" excuses. In the meantime, a tremendous number of young men are using or have used this drug which could make them unreliable as armed forces draftees. The presence of the drug and its potency constitutes a continuing danger to our country since whole cities can be made helpless by the placing of a relatively small amount in their water supply systems. Yet only three states so far have passed laws to control its manufacture and use and no inquiry has been made (or at least made public) regarding the huge quantities made at Weitzman Institute in Israel and smuggled into the U.S.

The International Communist Conspiracy has long manifested its interest in the use of drugs and has conducted extensive experiments on human beings. It has been well established that drugs have been used to extract false confessions from innocent people accused of crimes against communist police states. It would be naive to assume that the communists do not have a deep seated interest in LSD and its potential as a "Weapon for Destruction."

LSD in Water Supply

Oliver Kenneth Goff, a militant anti-communist, who had been a member of the Communist Party under the name of John Keats, testified before a government committee that public drinking water is being fluoridated against the wishes of American citizens who should have the right not to have their reservoirs poisoned.

A portion of a sworn affidavit signed by Goff, reads as follows:

"While a member of the Communist Party, I attended Communist underground training schools outside the city of New York. . . . We were trained . . . the art of poisoning water supplies. We discussed quite thoroughly the fluoridation of water supplies and how we were using it in Russia as a tranquilizer in the prison camps. The leaders of our school felt that if it could be induced into the American water supply, it would bring about a spirit of lethargy in the nation; where it would keep the general public docile during a steady encroachment of Communism."

The Federal Government which is so concerned about American citizens swallowing extra vitamin tablets is encouraging the use of poison (fluoride) in public water supplies and ignoring the sale and use of LSD. The Food and Drug Administration which spends millions and uses police state methods to harass health food and vitamin firms should start taking some interest in cutting off the flow of LSD which has reached alarming proportions from coast to coast and which causes "instant insanity" (in some cases permanent of recurrent).

The drug LSD presents a serious and continuing threat to our national security, as a source of immobilizing whole cities through its use in water supplies. It is also weakening the will of our young people and breaking down moral standards. It is truly a weapon of destruction, more dangerous than the atom bomb and the nuclear "holocaust" that worries (?) the left-wingers and peaceniks.

The Cosmic Courier

Timothy Leary

In this article Timothy Leary, guru of the drug culture and former Harvard psychologist, alternates between details of a visit from a

Reprinted by permission of publisher, *Other Scenes*, October 1970.

rambling, turned-on friend and his own occasionally ecstatic chron-
icle of the LSD phenomenon. Leary believes the disseminators of
LSD are holy outlaws because they provide people with revelatory
religious experiences that can serve as an antidote to nuclear madness. He recounts the efforts of himself and others to spread the
chemical gospel and maintains that the new social forms which
would result from successful proselytizing are the real reasons for
establishment opposition to LSD.

The gap between Leary's position and that of the previous
article is mind-blowing, even if Leary does lend support to some of
Capell's suspicions. Despite the huge disparity between the two
articles, the same issue is raised by both. For if Capell is irre-
sponsibly promoting fear, isn't Leary doing the same thing with
hope? If students can be exposed to Capell's alarm, why not to
Leary's rhapsodizing? Or does pessimism entail less risk than optimism? Some may find the Leary message more dangerous because
it is more seductive. It beguiles with its promise of euphoric escape
from the ordinary everyday experience that the young especially
find depressing.

Leary's career subsequent to this article has taken him to jail,
from which he escaped, and then into political asylum in Algeria,
from whence he issues statements invoking the violent overthrow of
the American system. However, he does not appear to have had
any more success persuading his Algerian hosts of the value of LSD
than he did the American authorities.

---

*Rosemary and I had been waiting for him for five hours. He's
always and deliberately erratic about appointments. Science fiction
James Bond paranoia. Throw off police surveillance. Suddenly I could
feel his presence. A telepathic hit. He really does emit powerful
vibrations. A minute later his boots drummed on the walk.*

*He looked tired, pale but the furry, quick animal tension was
still there. Black leather sleeveless jacket. Wide sleeved multi-colored
theatrical shirt. Jangling bells. The magician. The electronic wizard.*

*He had been up several days working in his laboratory and was
coming off an acid high. He wanted to be warm.*

*Rosemary and I built up the fire, lit candles and fell out on a
low divan. O. paced the floor in front of us. He's not tall and he likes
to stay above his listeners, higher than anyone else, moving while they
rest.*

*He started a three hour rap about energy, electronics, drugs,
politics, the nature of God and the place of man in the Divine system.
Laughing at his own brilliance, turning himself on, turning us on
Einsteinian physics and Buddhist philosophy translated into the fast,
right, straight rhythm of acid rock hip.*

The television folk-heroes of today are the merry outlaws of the past. The television Robin Hoods of the future, the folk-heros of the 21st Century, will be the psychedelic drug promotors of the 1960's. A good bet for romantic immortality is God's Secret Agent A.O.S.3—acid-king, LSD millionaire, test-tube Pancho Villa—the best known of a brand of dedicated, starry-eyed chemical crusaders who outwitted the wicked, gun-toting federals and bravely turned on the land of the young and the free to the electronic harmony of the future.

In the daily press the Reagans and Romneys merit the adulatory headlines. The O.'s, if mentioned at all, are denounced as sordid criminals. But the simple truth is that the Reagans and Romneys will soon be forgotten. Can anyone remember which Republicans were struggling for the nomination in 1936?

The mythic folk-heroes of our times will be the psychedelic drug outlaws, the science-fiction Johnny Appleseeds who build secret laboratories, scrounge the basic chemicals, experiment, experiment, experiment to develop new ecstasy pills, who test their home-made sacraments on their own bodies and the flesh of their trusting friends, who distribute the precious new waters-of-life through a network of dedicated colleagues, forever underground, hidden, as the mysteries have always been hidden from the hard-eyed agents of Caesar, Pharoh [sic], Herod, Pope Paul, Napoleon, Stalin, Johnson and J. Edgar Hoover.

For the last seven years I have watched with admiration these LSD frontiersmen, the Golden Bootleggers, manufacture and pass on the sacraments. Laughing, wild-eyed, visionary alchemists who seek nothing less than the sudden mind-blowing liberation of their fellow man.

First, of course, there was reluctant Albert Hoffman, of Sandoz, the staid involuntary agent mysteriously selected to give LSD to the human race. But this much I have heard. His first LSD trips were deep, revelatory religious experiences. The establishment press tries to tell us that Hoffman's first sessions were accidental and frightening and freaky. The facts are that Hoffman, a spiritual man, grasped immediately the implications of his discovery and initiated a high-level, ethical, gentleman's conspiracy of philosophically-minded scientists to diseminate [sic] LSD for the benefit of the human race. His tactical mistake (if, indeed, he made one) was to work through the established profusions, failing to see that a complete revision of social form would necessarily follow the use of his discovery.

Rosemary had made tea and put a red sanctuary light on the gold framed madonna. O. paced in front of us like a newly caged animal. (Rosemary, *What kind of animal is O.? Oh, he's furry, warm, nervous, whiskers twitching, ears alert, carnivorous but gentle. Like a squirrel, but bigger. Perhaps a badger or a racoon. They are very intelligent.*)

O. *preaching*: *Oh man, how beautifully it all fits together. Dig, the first atomic fission occurred in December 1942.*

Is that the one in the Chicago squash court?

Yeah. Now dig. The Van Allen belt is a thick blanket of electronic activity protecting this planet. What is the earth? A core of molten metals, covered by a thin layer of soft, vulnerable, organic tissue. Life nibbling away, nibbling away at the rock beneath. All life on this planet is a delicate network unified. Each living form feeding on the others. And being eaten. The Van Allen belt is the higher intelligence—protecting earth from lethal solar radiation and it's in touch with every form of living intelligence on the earth—vegetable, animal, human.

I laughed. O., you are so orthodox. Our Father who art in Heaven above! I pointed upwards. He really is up there, huh? Thy Kingdom come, thy will be done on earth as it is in the Van Allen belt!

O. *didn't stop to acknowledge my comment. Somehow he records neurologically what I say and re-programs it and prints it back out to me in endless tapes of electronic poetry but O. never listens.*

Now dig, the Supreme intelligence sees that man has rediscovered atomic energy. Wow! We gotta stop those cats before they disrupt the whole living network. The only thing DNA fears is radiation. That's why the Van Allen belt is there.

OK, now get this. Four months after the first fission Hoffman accidentally, ha ha, rediscovers LSD which is now psycho-active.

Rediscovers?

Yeah, man. Actually Hoffman first synthesized LSD in 1938 but it gave no hit. No turn-on. Now why is it that Hoffman handles LSD in 1938 and nothing happens and then in 1943, three months after atomic energy is released, he puts his finger on lysergic acid and gets flipped out. What happened? Did Hoffman suddenly get careless? Or had LSD suddenly been changed into a psychedelic chemical? Competent chemists just don't change their handling compounds. Hoffman's techniques are standard.

O.'s *eyes are dancing and he's laughing and his hands and body are moving. He was a ballet dancer once before he started making drugs.*

Now dig. The atomic fission in December 1942 changed the whole system of energy in this solar system. The higher intelligence decides to make a few simple changes in the electronic structure of

some atoms and ZAP! We have LSD an incredibly powerful sub-
stance that is the exact antidote to atomic energy. People take LSD
and FLASH! They get the message and start putting things back in
harmony with the Great Design. Stop war. Wear flowers. Conserva-
tion. Turning on people to LSD is the precise and only way to keep
war from blowing up the whole system.

Hoffman's plan was to persuade square psychiatrists and medical researchers to use LSD. But, of course, it never happens that
way. The respectable researchers were afraid. They didn't get the
point. So the first far-out, messianic apostle-alchemist of the psychedelic age was a rum-drinking, snake-oil-fundamentalist-bible-belt sales-
man type named Al Hubbard. Like O., Al Hubbard is a legendary,
behind-the-scene operator whose brilliance was deliberately shielded
behind a veil of rumor. This much is known. In the 1950's Al Hubbard
was turned-on to LSD and got the message at once. He had made
money in uranium mining during the forties and saw the connection
right away. (Do you?) Then this incredible shaman playing the role
of an uneducated, coarse, blustering, Roman Catholic hill-billy boozer
proceeded to turn-on several dozen top sophisticated scientists and
show them the sacramental meaning of LSD.

When the medical associations complained about non-medics
dispensing drugs, Al chuckled and bought a doctor's degree from a
diploma store in the South for fifty dollars and as Doctor-Tongue in
cheek Hubbard was accepted admiringly by Psychiatrist Osmond,
Scientist Hofer, and Aldous Huxley, philosopher Heard and even
Sidney Cohen of UCLA. Al Hubbard was the first psychedelic tactician
to see that supply-control of the drug would be a key issue in the
future so he kept up a mysterious schedule of procurement-distribu-
tion flights. East Coast–West Coast–East Europe–West Europe, bargaining, wheedling, swapping to build up the first underground supply
of the most precious substance the world has ever known. The current
retail price of LSD $20,000 to $50,000 a gram. A million dollars an
ounce.

Hubbard's plan was to have a chain of medically approved
LSD clinics throughout the country. It was a brilliant Utopian Ameri-
can-businessman stroke of genius and would have, among other things,
ended the threat of war on this planet but Hubbard failed to realize
that spiritual revelations and Buddhist Ecstasies were the last thing
that the medical associations and government bureaus were going to
approve, and the International Foundation for Advanced Studies, his
pilot clinic in Menlo Park, California (which turned-on several hundred of the most influential people in the San Francisco Bay Area)

was ruthlessly closed by the F.D.A. in spite of its impressive psychiatric and medical credentials. So Al Hubbard dropped out, disappeared and was reincarnated in the new form of Dr. Spaulding.

It was a grey, cold, winter day in 1962. Dick Alpert and I took the day off from Harvard and flew in Dick's plane to New York. Dick's father was President of the New Haven Railroad and the cop under Grand Central saluted as we got into the huge black Cadillac, with the license plate NHRR, which was equipped with two way radio and an extra set of wheels to run on tracks. We headed south to visit a chemical factory. Going through the water-front-mafia section of Jersey City I had to laugh. Two Harvard professors driving in a black limousine thru the dark slum-city to score drugs which would change the world.

In the wood-panelled conference room of Sandoz Laboratories the top pharmaceutical executives laughed uneasily. We are a medical drug house. How can we market an ecstasy pill to be used by God-seekers? The Vice-President grinned. Let's say LSD isn't a drug. Let's call it a food and bottle it like coca-cola! The company lawyer's reflex frown. As a food it still must be licensed by the F.D.A. and they think medical.

The conference was a failure. They were sympathetic but weren't going to lose their AMA-FDA respectability by releasing LSD to the public. We shook hands and Dick said, "Well, Gentlemen, we'll have to do your marketing for you." And we all laughed.

One of the crew-cut executives escorted us down to the car. On the elevator he suddenly pulled a pill bottle out of his pocket and shoved it in my hand. "I've taken LSD. I know what's happening. Here's five grams. Don't say where you got it. Use it wisely."

By this time (1962) we had set up a loose but effective distribution system for free LSD. A University psychologist in the mid-west. A God-intoxicated business-man in Atlanta. A few God-loving ministers and rabbis. David Solomon, at that time editor of the jazz magazine *Metronome*. Allen Ginsberg. Dozens of holy psychiatrists. All giving psychedelics to people they knew were ready for the trip. A responsible network of friends.

Everytime our supplies would run low a new shaman-alchemist would appear.

Like Bernie and Barnie, the flipped-out desert holymen, who had been taking the peyote trip with the Indians for years and writing crazy brilliant illiterate books on telepathy and accelerated learning through LSD. Bernie claimed to have mastered the German language in two acid sessions. They had learned how to make LSD which they distributed in rubber-stopped bottles, a strange brown elixir with curious green seaweed strands. They sold the sacrament at bargain rates to dozens of famous people in California before they were treacherously betrayed to the feds. They didn't get along well with their defense attorneys and built their case around an insane plot to get the judge and jury to taste their brew which would have revolutionized jurisprudence forever. But the judge recoiled in horror and gave them nineteen years sentences which they jumped. God be with you beloved guides wherever you are.

Sometime later (the exact date must be kept vague) I was lecturing in a college town. A note to my hotel. Please call a Doctor Spaulding. Urgent. Had to see me after the lecture.

He was a distinguished looking man in his fifties. One of the ten leading chemists in the country. Big-boned, handsome, jolly, athletic scholar type.

He drove his car with strange jungle caution, checking the rearview mirror, doubling around blocks. He drove to the middle of a deserted super-market parking lot and stopped the car. Cloak and dagger. He came right to the point. He had taken LSD several times. He knew what it would do. He also knew that the government was alarmed. A lot of high level people had turned-on and knew that LSD was a religious experience. But they were worried. Big power struggle over control of drugs in Washington. The Narcotics bureau of the Treasury department wanted to keep all drugs illegal, to step up law enforcement, add thousands of T-men, G-men and narks to the payroll. On the other hand the medics and scientists in the government wanted the FDA to handle all drugs including heroin, pot, LSD. Make it a medical matter. Would I make a deal? Would I tell the FDA all I knew about the black market and smash the underground distribution of LSD? If I co-operated I'd be guaranteed research approval to use LSD. We have to help the FDA get control of the drugs. Then marijuana and LSD would be legal for licensed use. But we had to keep the kids from getting LSD or the hard-line-cop faction in Washington would get the anti-LSD legislation they wanted. If I didn't cooperate I'd be busted.

I looked at him and laughed. Not a chance. This is a country of free citizens. LSD and marijuana are none of the government's business to give or take away. If it's a choice I'd rather have the kids using LSD than the doctors. Kids are holier. And if it's a choice between becoming a government informer or get busted I'll go to jail.

Dr. Spaulding laughed knowing. O.K. I had to make the offer

but I knew you wouldn't scare. But you should know that a big government crackdown is coming. All the sources of LSD would be sealed off. You better stock up. How much do you have on hand now?

Not much. A few thousand doses.

How much LSD can you use?

I looked at him in surprise. He starts out like a fed and now he's offering me acid.

He saw my look and started to explain. A few of us saw this coming several years ago. We started stockpiling the raw lysergic acid base. We have the largest supply of LSD in the world. More than Sandoz, more than Red China, more than our defense department. We want to give it away to responsible people who won't try to profit by it and who can get it out to the people. O.K. How much can you distribute in one year?

The scene was surrealistic. This famous, eminently respectable professor offering to set us up with unlimited supplies of acid. It was hard to keep from laughing. I asked him one question, Why?

Oh you know why, Tim. Can you see any hope for this homicidal, neurologically crippled species other than a mass religious ecstatic convulsion? O.K. How much do you want?

We can get rid of two hundred grams in a year. That's two million doses.

Dr. Spaulding nodded. Fine. You'll receive a four year supply —1000 grams in the next few weeks. Each package will contain a hundred grams of LSD powder. Get scales to put it in doses. Keep it sterile. Alcohol or even vodka. Dilute it down. If you can't get a pill machine, dilute it down and drop it on sugar cubes.

He started the car and drove back to my hotel. How many people are you distributing to this way? Not many, he answered. In chemistry, every process has to develop at its own natural tempo. We have enough LSD stored now to keep every living American turned on for several years.

That was the only time I met Dr. Spaulding. A week later the acid began arriving at Millbrook—in brown manila envelopes and hollowed out books mailed from different cities throughout the country. In hardly any time at all we have given away ten million doses.

It was ten in the evening by now. Rosemary and I were starved. O. was still too high to be hungry but he was responding telepathically to our stomach pangs. Organic matter nibbling the granite, Galaxies feeding each other.

O., do us a favor and don't mention eating, O.K.? We haven't had supper yet.

O. *was spinning us along an epic-poem trip through the levels of creation. He can really tell it. I've studied with the wisest sages of our times—Huxley, Heard, Lama Govinda, Sri Krishna Prem, Alan Watts and I have to say that A.O.S.3, college flunk-out, who never wrote anything better (or worse) than a few rubber checks, has the best up-to-date perspective of the Divine Design.*

To begin with he begins where they all begin at the beginning. He had taken the full LSD trip, hurled down through his cellular reincarnations, disintegrated beyond life into pulsing electron grids, whirled down beyond atomic form to that unitary center that is one, pure, radiant humming vibration. Yin. Yin. Yin. Yang. Yang. Yang.

O's. face was glowing and he was screaming that full throated God-cry that was torn from the lungs of Moses and shrieked by San Juan de la Cruz and which Rosemary and I heard most recently just after our sunrise wedding on the desert mountain top near Joshua Tree bellowed by the bone-tissue blood trumpet of Ted Marckland— the eternal, unmistakable cry of the man who has heard God's voice and shouted back in joyous, insane acceptance. If you've ever opened your ears to any one who has surrendered wide-eyed to the sound of God you know what I mean.

O. shook his head and laughed. I can't say it in words. God, man. I've got to learn a musical instrument so I can really say what it sounds like.

Yes, O. carries the official stamp on his skin's passport that he has been where all the great mystics have been—that point where you see it and hear it all and know it all belongs together. But how can you describe an electronic rhythm of which 5 billion years of our planetary evolution is just one beat? O. is in the same position as every returned visionary—grabbing at ineffective words. But check O's prophetic credentials. High native intelligence coupled with a photographic memory. Solid grasp of electronics. Absorbed biological texts. Knows computer theory. Has hung out with the world's top orientalists and Hindu scholars. Has lived with and designed amplifiers for the farthest out rock band. As a sniffing, alert, inquisitive mammal of the 20th century he has poked his quivering, whiskered nose into all the dialects and systems by which man attempts to explain and divine.

Throughout history the alchemist has always been a magical awesome figure. The potion. The elixir. The secret formula. Experimental metaphysics. Those old alchemists weren't really trying to transmute lead to gold. That's just what they told the federal agents. They were actually looking for the philosopher's stone, the waters of life. The herb, root, vine, seed, fruit, powder that would turn-on, tune-in and drop-out.

And every generation or so someone would rediscover the key. And the key is always chemical. Consciousness is a chemical process. Learning, sensing, remembering, forgetting are alterations in a bio-chemical book. Life is chemical. Matter is chemical.

O.'s bells jingling as he gesticulates. Everything is hooked together with electrons. And if you study how electrons work you learn how everything is hooked up. You are close to God. Chemistry is applied theology.

The alchemist-shaman-wizard-medicine man is always a fringe figure. Never part of the conventional social structure. It has to be. In order to listen to the shuttling, whispering ancient language of energy (long faint sighs across the milennia) you have to shut out the noise of the market place. You flip yourself out deliberately. Voluntary holy alienation. You can't serve God and Caesar. You just can't.

That's why the wizards who have guided and inspired human destiny by means of revelatory vision have always been socially suspect. Always outside the law. Holy outlaws. Reckless courageous outlaws. Folklore has it that forty-three federal agents were assigned to O.'s case before he was arrested on the day before Christmas, 1967. They have to stop this wildman with jingling bells or he'll turn-on the whole world. O's Christmas acid could have stopped the war.

Messianic certainty. O. is the most moralistic person I have ever met. Everything is labelled, good or bad. Every human activity is either right or wrong. He is, in short, a nagging, preaching, intolerable puritan. Right to O. is what is natural, healthy, harmonious. Right gets you high. Wrong brings you down.

Meat is good. Man is a carnivorous animal, but eat your meat rare.

Vegetables are bad. They are for smoking, not eating. God (or the DNA code) designed ruminants and cud-chewers to eat leaves. And man to eat their flesh.

Psychedelic drugs are good.

Alcohol is bad. Unhealthy, dulling, damaging to the brain. A down trip. O. explains this in ominous chemical warnings. I always feel guilty drinking a beer in front of him.

Showers are good. Clean.

Baths are bad. You soak in your own dirt and your soft pores sponge up foul debris in a lukewarm liquid ideal nutrient for germs.

Rock and roll is good.

Science fiction is bad. Screws up your head. Takes you on weird trips.

Long hair is good. Sign of a free man.

Short hair is bad. Mark of a prisoner, a cop, or a wage-slave.

Smoking is bad.

Marijuana is good.

Sex is good.

Sexual abstinence is insane.

O. is now sitting against the wall talking quietly. The red glow flickers on his round glasses. He is a mad saint.

At the higher levels of energy, beyond even the electronic, there is no form. Form is pure energy limiting itself. Form is error.

On one trip they (I'll refer to "they" for lack of a better term), the higher intelligence, beckoned me to leave the living form and to merge with the eternal formless which is all form and I was tempted. Eternal ecstasy. But I declined regretfully. I wanted to stay in this form for a while longer.

Why?

Oh, to make love. Balling is such a friendly tender human thing to do.

How about eating, O.?

Oh yes, that's tender too.

O.K. Lets go to a restaurant.

O. is a highly conscious man. He is aware at all times of who he is and what's what. Aware of his mythic role. Aware of his past incarnations. Aware of his animal heritage which he wears, preeningly and naturally like a pure forest creature. His sense of smell. O. carefully selects and blends perfumes for himself and his friends. Your nose always recognizes O. Oh, some sandlewood, a dash of musk, a touch of lotus, a taste of civet.

I talked to him once on the phone after a session. He was in his customary state of intense excitement. Listen, man, I saw clearly my mystic karmic assignment. I am merlin. I'm a mischevious alchemist. A playful redeemer. My essence name is A.O.S.3.

Like any successful wizard A.O.S.3 is a good scientist. Radar-sensitive in his observations. Exacting, meticulous, pedantic about his procedures. He has grandiose delusions about the quality of his acid. "Listen, man, LSD is a delicate, fragile molecule. It responds to the vibrations of the chemist."

He judges acid and other psychedelics with the fuffy, patronizing skill of a Bordeaux wine taster. He is less than kind to upstart rival alchemists. But no jeweler, gold-smith, painter, sculptor was ever more scrupulous about aesthetic perfection than A.O.S.3.

And like any good journeyman messiah his sociological and political perceptions are arrow straight. As do all turned-on persons, O. agonizes over the pollution of air and water, the rape of the soil, man's vengeful disruption of the living fabric. He, as well as anyone, sees the mechanization. The robotization.

Metal is good. It performs its own technical function. Metal has individuality, soul.

Plastics are evil. Plastic copies the form of plant, mineral, metal, flesh but has no soul.

O.'s life is a fierce protest against the sickness of our times which inverts man and nature into a frozen brittle plastic. Only a turned-on chemist can appreciate the horror, the ultimate blasphemous horror of plastic.

O. is unique. He is himself. His life is a creative struggle for individuality. He longs for a social group, a linkage of minds modelled after the harmonious collaboration of cells and organs of the body. He wants to be the brains of a social love body. The ancient utopian hunger. Only a turned-on chemist can appreciate God's protein plan for society.

A.O.S.3 is that rare species. A realized, living, breathing, smelling, balling, laughing, working, scolding man. A ridiculous conceited fool, God's fool, dreaming of ways to make us all happy, to turn us all on, to love us and be loved.

chapter 7

Racism

The most dramatic change in American society since World War II has been the development of the Black Revolution. This revolution sought to redress the major social, economic, and moral injustices which had been perpetuated against the blacks since their arrival in America. Black and white problems for the first time in our history began to be openly discussed and basic changes were actively sought.

Both black and white leaders began to confront and examine the destructive social and economic conditions which had been the common heritage for blacks as well as other ethnic groups in American society.

A new black militance developed and demanded a greater share and participation in the economic and social rewards of the society. The black revolution was the forerunner of the other major social criticisms and disruptions in the social system. The demonstration and criticisms of our social institutions will undoubtedly continue to increase both in degree and effectiveness until some basic and important changes occur in American life. It is possible that the changes that take place may increase human freedom and social equity for all Americans or may result in the lessening of the existing freedoms. The repressive and anti-democratic force may result from the continuous criticisms and demonstration. In recent years we have witnessed both a movement toward greater freedom for minority groups as well as toward a repressive and punishment motif for the militant actions of the more radical groups.

There are few societies in which the establishment group in power seeks to deliberately lessen its own power and control and to increase the social and economic leverage of the rejected members of a particular social system.

Since the American economy is extraordinarily reinforcing for those who conform to and accept the dictates of the social-economic order, it would be bizarre to expect the same property conscious individuals to suddenly abandon their life long pursuit of material goods and services which the system so efficiently provides. These individuals, like most ruling classes, are extremely well insulated from the social and economic realities which on a routine basis, maim, crush, and destroy the potential of millions of members of racial and ethnic groups in American society. Historically, most of the immigrant ethnic groups coming to the United States had to demand and fight for their share of social and economic justice. In the same manner, the blacks, the Mexicans, the Puerto Ricans, and the American Indians are beginning to demand and to fight for their fair share of the returns of the system.

It would probably be naïve to assume that the leadership for these necessary changes would come from the main-line establishment group. Even though individuals in this group occasionally show active concern for the minority groups, it is far more realistic to expect the effective changes to come from leaders within their own ethnic groups.

For many ethnic groups in the United States, assimilation into the general national life has been fairly successful; however, specific minority groups have been isolated and rejected on a long-term basis from the main stream of American life. This isolation involves a deliberate rejection by the establishment group in the society. It involves a whole set of interlocking prejudices, rituals, laws, and taboos which serve as a facade to mask the basic racist attitudes and values which are a routine part of the American value system. They are racist values and attitudes which are learned on a conditioned basis throughout the child's developmental history.

The blacks, the Mexican Americans, the American Indians, the Puerto Ricans, and the migrant workers have not succeeded in their attempts to enter the American system and gain the heavy rewards offered by the system. They have not been able to receive the economic opportunities or the political equality and freedom which are routinely present for most ethnic groups in the society. The ultimate viability of the democratic experiment in America will in part be answered by the resolution of this question. The question is simply whether or not the large population of so-called minority groups in the United States will ever be effectively admitted on an equal basis in all areas of social, economic, and political life.

The United States will continue to have great difficulty in finding acceptance throughout the world, both in traditional Western nations and in the emerging, underdeveloped countries, until this critical question is fully resolved. Until this question is resolved, it is nonsense to promote the myth that we are a democratic and egalitarian social system. For the repression and the exploitation of vast population groups, numbering 30 to 40 million individuals, makes it an absurdity to pretend that the humanistic values we preach represent anything more than a public sham and a dreary form of self-conceit. What is finally happening is that the facade and the hypocrisy are no longer sufficient devices to fool the large minority groups into remaining acquiescent and subordinate in the socio-economic system. They are demanding an equal relationship in all aspects of human life, and until that demand is reasonably and humanely answered, it is ridiculous for us to continue to play our sanctimonious empire games overseas and to continue to accept routinely the basic and extensive corruption of our internal society.

Deep-rooted, volatile racial antagonisms which are often beyond the reach of reason and moral persuasion routinely exist at all levels of our social system. Long established racial stereotypes are extensively held by both blacks and whites, and these in turn tend to crystallize into attitudes and behaviors which focus on the weaknesses and failures of both racial groups. There is a growing awareness by the white establishment of its long-term destruction and injustice to the blacks and other racial and ethnic minorities. This awareness should help to foster other forms of acceptable behavioral styles which in turn may lead to greater black liberation and complete integration for those racial and ethnic groups who are not presently accepted into the system.

The paramount task for Americans at this time is to find ways of bringing our political and social idealism into closer accord with the realities of American life. Enormous contradictions and incongruities have been a major and a basic part of our American heritage. The democratic myth and the facade of social and economic equality for all groups in the social system has been heavily perpetuated and fostered by the school system, by school teachers, and by educational values and methods which have been carefully chosen to present only a showcase picture of American life. The schools have played a major destructive role in the evolving of a more genuinely democratic life process. They have chosen to be more conservative, more frightened, and more cautious than almost any of the political groups in the community. Their role as critics and evaluators of the culture has been completely bypassed, and in its place they have chosen the parochialism and the insularity of those who maintain, control, and run the school system. The schools have chosen to become a subservient, conforming member of the system. At the present time, they aggressively and reluctantly refuse to recognize the major changes which are taking place in the social system, and in every possible way they are attempting to limit the growth of the democratic experiment. Instead of providing an exciting and effective arena for social change, which the schools could help to initiate, they are in most every school system fighting a last ditch battle against the forces of social and economic change.

Schools are not institutions where freedom of thought is desired, nor are they centers for the exchange of libertarian ideas and ideals. They are rather places where a dreary kind of passivity and fear is learned, and where the cheapest kind of chauvinism and patriotic rubbish is routinely presented to the students as a realistic picture of life in these United States. It is really a tragic condition; our schools could be one of the most exciting and intellectually active aspects of American life instead of places in which our children's minds and spirits are deliberately crippled for life. Instead of a vital and creative force in our culture, our schools have become an obsolete and dysfunctional component within the democratic process. If meaningful change is to take place within the American community to make the system move toward those values and concerns which are so grossly absent at the present time, it is vitally necessary that our public schools be radically altered.

The gross social and economic contradictions which have become a routine part of our social system can no longer be ignored completely as they have been in the past. The vast difference between the public facade of democracy and the reality beneath the facade must finally be resolved, either toward becoming more truly a democracy or moving toward the negative alternative of a more complete totalitarianism.

The critical problem for all Americans for the remainder of the century is to find alternative solutions to the major social and economic inequities which are a routine part of our social system. Our wide scale social pathology requires a resolution to these great conflicts. At some point we will have to stop the dishonesty and hypocrisy which have long characterized our domestic and foreign policy. Some of the major questions which must be faced in the future are: (1) What role should the educational institutions play in the development of greater human and racial understanding in the United States? (2) How can the churches implement their moral teachings so that moral persuasion becomes a major vehicle for the needed changes? (3)

How can government institutions redress the grievances of the vast minority groups while the mainline political groups are persuaded of the importance of these changes? (4) What are the best methods of utilizing both black and white militancy in bringing about those positive social changes which are essential if the democratic experiment is to survive?

Potentials for Race War

Julius Lester

Critical revolutionary writings which present radical solutions to
the American racial problem have become abundant. The passionate style of much of this writing reflects a deep emotional commitment to extreme white or black militance. Julius Lester's article
presents such a picture of tragic racial conflict in this society. He
argues that race war and the destruction of American society are
not only possibilities inherent in the present system, but they are
also his recommendations for action to resolve key racial problems.
He writes in a style which conveys his deep personal anger and
conviction, similar in many respects to the writings of LeRoi Jones,
Eldridge Cleaver, and others. Lester has accepted Franz Fanon's
analysis of the racial issue which suggests that violence is needed as
a liberating and cathartic force in order for the black man's identity
to be reborn.

Lester assumes that black power will eventually bring about a
major racial war, creating conditions for the rebirth of the black
people in America and resulting in the rebuilding of a new black
community. This new community will be more committed to certain American ideals with a greater respect for all men in the social
system and a more humanistic society. Mr. Lester's view is shared
by many black militants who do not believe that racism is solved by
gradualness or "all deliberate speed." They advocate revolution and
necessary violence in order to correct this social cancer.

School bus bombings, club-carrying white pickets who threaten
black children going to previously white schools, increasing activities of the KKK, and police shootings of black college students
suggest that many white militants might also accept Lester's call to
arms as an opportunity to engage in wholesale slaughter in a race
war. Education may well be the tinder box in this volatile environment.

It is clear that America as it now exists must be destroyed. There is no other way. It is impossible to live within this country and not become a thief or a murderer. Young blacks and young whites are beginning to say NO to thievery and murder. Black Power confronts White Power openly, and as the SNCC poet Worth Long cried: "We have found you out, false-faced America. We have found you out!"

Having "found you out," we will destroy you or die in the act of destroying. That much seems inevitable. To those who fearfully wonder if America has come to the point of a race war, the answer is not certain. However, all signs would seem to say yes. Perhaps the only way that it might be avoided would be through the ability of young white radicals to convince blacks, through their actions, that they are ready to do whatever is necessary to change America.

The race war, if it comes, will come partly from the necessity for revenge. You can't do what has been done to blacks and not expect retribution. The very act of retribution is liberating, and perhaps it is no accident that the symbolism of Christianity speaks of being washed in Blood as an act of purification. Psychologically, blacks have always found an outlet for their revenge whenever planes have fallen, autos have collided, or just every day when white folks die. One old black woman in Atlanta, Georgia, calmly reads through her paper each day counting the number of white people killed the previous day in wrecks, storms, and by natural causes. When the three astronauts were killed in February, 1967, black people did not join the nation in mourning. They were white and were spending money that blacks needed. White folks trying to get to the moon, 'cause it's there. Poverty's here! Now get to that! Malcolm X spoke for all black people when a plane full of Georgians crashed in France: "Allah has blessed us. He has destroyed twenty-two of our enemies."

It is clearly written that the victim must become the executioner. The executioner preordains it when all attempts to stop the continual executions fail. To those who point to numbers and say that black people are only ten percent, it must be said as Brother Malcolm said: "It only takes a spark to light the fuse. We are that spark."

Black Power is not an isolated phenomenon. It is only another manifestation of what is transpiring in Latin America, Asia, and Africa. People are reclaiming their lives on those three continents and blacks in America are reclaiming theirs. These liberation movements are not saying give us a share; they are saying we want it all! The existence of the present system in the United States depends upon the United States taking all. This system is threatened more and more each day by the refusal of those in the Third World to be exploited. They are colonial people outside the United States; blacks are a colonial people within. Thus, we have a common enemy. As the Black Power movement becomes more politically conscious, the spiritual coalition that exists between blacks in America and the Third World will become more evident. The spiritual coalition is not new. When Italy invaded Ethiopia in 1938, blacks in Harlem held large demonstrations protesting this. During World War II, many blacks were rooting for the Japanese. Blacks cannot overlook the fact that it was the Japanese who were the guinea pigs for the atomic bomb, not the Germans. They know, too, that if the U.S. were fighting a European country, it would not use napalm, phosphorus and steel-pellet bombs, just as they know that if there had been over one hundred-thousand blacks massed before the Pentagon on October 21, 1967, they would not have been met by soldiers with unloaded guns. In fact, they know they would never have been allowed to even reach the Pentagon.

The struggle of blacks in America is inseparable from the struggle of the Third World. This is a natural coalition—a coalition of those who know that they are dispossessed. Whites in America are dispossessed also, but the difference is that they will not recognize the fact as yet. Until they do, it will not be possible to have coalitions with them, even the most radical. They must recognize the nature and character of their own oppression. At present, too many of them recognize only that they are white and identify with whites, not with the oppressed, the dispossessed. They react against being called "honky" and thereby establish the fact that they are. It is absolutely necessary for blacks to identify as blacks to win liberation. It is not necessary for whites. White radicals must learn to nonidentify as whites. White is not in the color of the skin. It is a condition of the mind: a condition that will be destroyed. It should be possible for any white radical to yell "honky" as loud as a black radical. "Honky" is a beautiful word that destroys the mystique surrounding whiteness. It is like throwing mud on a sheet. Whiteness has been used as an instrument of oppression; no white radical can identify himself by the color of his skin and expect to fight alongside blacks. Black Power liberates whites also, but they have refused to recognize this, preferring to defend their whiteness.

Black Power is not anti-white people, but is anti anything and everything that serves to oppress. If whites align themselves on the side of oppression, then Black Power must be antiwhite. That, however, is not the decision of Black Power.

For blacks, Black Power is the microscope and telescope through which they look at themselves and the world. It has enabled them to focus their energies while preparing for the day of reckoning. That day of reckoning is anticipated with eagerness by many, because it is on that day that they will truly come alive. The concept of the black man as a nation, which is only being talked about now, will become reality when violence comes. Out of the violence will come the new nation (if the violence is successful) and the new man. Frantz Fanon wrote that "For the colonised people this violence, because it constitutes their only work, invests their characters with positive and creative qualities. The practice of violence binds them together as a whole, since each individual forms a violent link in the great chain, a part of the great organism of violence which has surged upwards in reaction to the settler's violence in the beginning. The groups recognize each other and the future nation is already indivisible. The armed struggle mobilises the people; that is to say, it throws them in one way and in one direction."[1]

It is obvious, of course, that White Power will not allow Black Power to evolve without trying to first subvert it. This is being attempted. This attempt will fail and White Power will have no choice but to attempt to physically crush Black Power. This is being prepared for, with intensive riot-control training for the National Guard, chemicals for the control of large crowds, and concentration camps. It is to be expected that eventually black communities across the country will be cordoned off and a South African passbook system introduced to control the comings and goings of blacks.

At the moment, though (but, oh, how short a moment is), the tactic is one of subversion. Particular attention and energy is being given toward the subversion of SNCC. An inordinate number of SNCC men have received draft notices since January of 1967. Another tactic has been the calling of court cases to trial that have lain dormant for two or three years, cases that in many instances had been forgotten by SNCC. The most sophisticated tactic has been the legal maneuvers the government has used to keep SNCC's chairman, H. Rap Brown, confined to Manhattan Island, thus preventing him from traveling around the country and speaking. Having accomplished that, the government now seems content to take its own good time about bringing Brown's cases up for trial.

Black Power, however, will not be denied. America's time is not long and the odds are on our side.

Black Power seeks to destroy what now is, but what does it

[1] Frantz Fanon, *The Wretched of the Earth.* New York: Grove Press, 1965, p. 73.

offer in replacement? Black Power is a highly moral point of view, but its morality is one that sees that a way of life flows from the economic and political realities of life. It is these that must be changed. Mrs. Ida Mae Lawrence of Rosedale, Mississippi, put it beautifully when she said, "You know, we ain't dumb, even if we are poor. We need jobs. We need houses. But even with the poverty program we ain't got nothin' but needs. . . . We is ignored by the government. The thing about property upset them, but the things about poor people don't. So there's no way out, but to begin your own beginning, whatever way you can. So far as I'm concerned, that's all I got to say about the past. We're beginning a new future."

In his 1966 Berkeley speech, Stokely Carmichael put it another way.

> Our vision is not merely of a society in which all black men have enough to buy the good things of life. When we urge that black money go into black pockets, we mean the communal pocket. We want to see money go back into the community and used to benefit it. We want to see the cooperative concept applied in business and banking. . . . The society we seek to build among black people is not a capitalistic one. It is a society in which the spirit of community and humanistic love prevail. The word love is suspect; black expectations of what it might produce have been betrayed too often. But those were expectations of a response from the white community, which failed us. The love we seek to encourage is within the black community, the only American community where men call each other "brother" when they meet. We can build a community of love only where we have the ability and power to do so; among blacks.

Those whites who have a similar vision and want to be a part of this new world must cast down their bucket where they are. If this kind of a world is as important and as necessary for them as it is for us, they must evolve an approach to their own communities. We must organize around blackness, because it is with the fact of our blackness that we have been clubbed. We therefore turn our blackness into a club. When this new world is as totally necessary for whites as it is for blacks, then maybe we can come together and work on some things side by side. However, we will always want to preserve our ethnicity, our community. We are a distinct cultural group, proud of our culture and our institutions, and simply want to be left alone to lead our good, black lives. In the new world, as in this one, I want to be known, not as a man who happens to be black, but as a black man. With that knowledge I can visit the graves of my slave foreparents and say, "I didn't forget about you . . . those hot days you worked in the fields, those beatings, all that shit you took and just grew stronger on. I'm still singing those songs you sang and telling those tales and passing them on to the young ones so they will know you, also. We will never forget, for your lives were lived on a spider web stretched over the mouth of hell and yet, you walked that walk and talked that talk and told it like t.i. is. You can rest easy now. Everything's up-tight."

The old order passes away. Like the black riderless horse, boots turned the wrong way in the stirrups, following the coffin down the boulevard, it passes away. But there are no crowds to watch as it passes. There are no crowds, to mourn, to weep. No eulogies to read and no eternal flame is lit over the grave. There is no time, for there are streets to be cleaned, houses painted, and clothes washed. Everything must be scoured clean. Trash has to be thrown out. Garbage dumped and everything unfit, burned.

The new order is coming, child.

The old is passing away.

Black Power

Stokely Carmichael and Charles V. Hamilton

Few phrases have elicited dramatic responses in as wide an area as "Black Power." Fear, repression, pride, and an evolving black identity have derived much of their strength from the Black Power movement. Several other minority groups have adopted the term as a referent for their own social and political ends. We now have Red Power, Teacher Power, Women's Power, Student Power, and People Power. Carmichael and Hamilton use a political science model to examine how the long-term white power system has held the blacks in social and economic bondage. They propose an alternative program of black self-determination and black identity as a means of achieving Black Power and a more complete form of equality in the decision-making process in the overall society. They view the schools as a major negative force in perpetuating black inequality. They feel that the schools will have to be radically revamped in terms of curriculum content, teacher training, and what they assume to be its essentially white racist orientation.

The adoption of the concept of Black Power is one of the most legitimate and healthy developments in American politics and race relations in our time. The concept of Black Power speaks to all the needs mentioned in this chapter. It is a call for black people in this country to unite, to recognize their heritage, to build a sense of community. It is a call for black people to begin to define their own goals, to lead their own organizations and to support those organizations. It is a call to reject the racist institutions and values of this society.

The concept of Black Power rests on a fundamental premise: *Before a group can enter the open society, it must first close ranks.* By this we mean that group solidarity is necessary before a group can operate effectively from a bargaining position of strength in a pluralistic society. Traditionally, each new ethnic group in this society has found the route to social and political viability through the organization of its own institutions with which to represent its needs within the larger society. Studies in voting behavior specifically, and political behavior generally, have made it clear that politically the American pot has not melted. Italians vote for Rubino over O'Brien; Irish for Murphy over Goldberg, etc. This phenomenon may seem distasteful to some, but it has been and remains today a central fact of the American political system. There are other examples of ways in which groups in the society have remembered their roots and used this effectively in the political arena. Theodore Sorensen describes the politics of foreign aid during the Kennedy Administration in his book *Kennedy*:

> No powerful constituencies or interest groups backed foreign aid. The Marshall Plan at least had appealed to Americans who traced their roots to the Western European nations aided. But there were few voters who identified with India, Columbia or Tanganyika [p. 351].

The extent to which black Americans can and do "trace their roots" to Africa, to that extent will they be able to be more effective on the political scene.

A white reporter set forth this point in other terms when he made the following observation about white Mississippi's manipulation of the anti-poverty program:

> The war on poverty has been predicated on the notion that there is such a thing as a community which can be defined geographically and mobilized for a collective effort to help the poor. This theory has no relationship to reality in the deep South. In every Mississippi county there are two communities. Despite all the pious platitudes of the moderates on both sides, these two communities habitually see their interests in terms of conflict rather than cooperation. Only when the Negro community can muster enough political, economic and professional strength to compete on somewhat equal terms, will Negroes believe in the possibility of true cooperation and whites accept its necessity. En route to integration, the Negro community needs to develop a greater independence—a chance to run its own affairs and not cave in whenever "the man" barks—or so it seems to me, and to most of the knowledgeable people with whom I talked in Mississippi. To OEO, this judgment may sound like black nationalism. . . .[1]

The point is obvious: black people must lead and run their own organizations. Only black people can convey the revolutionary idea—and it is a revolutionary idea—that black people are able to do things themselves. Only they can help create in the community an aroused and continuing black consciousness that will provide the basis for political strength. In the past, white allies have often furthered white supremacy without the whites involved realizing it, or even wanting to do so. Black people must come together and do things for themselves. They must achieve self-identity and self-determination in order to have their daily needs met.

Black Power means, for example, that in Lowndes County, Alabama, a black sheriff can end police brutality. A black tax assessor and tax collector and county board of revenue can lay, collect, and channel tax monies for the building of better roads and schools serving black people. In such areas as Lowndes, where black people have a majority, they will attempt to use power to exercise control. This is what they seek: control. When black people lack a majority, Black Power means proper representation and sharing of control. It means the creation of power bases, of strength, from which black people can press to change local or nation-wide patterns of oppression—instead of from weakness.

It does not mean *merely* putting black faces into office. Black

[1] Christopher Jencks, "Accommodating Whites: A New Look at Mississippi," *The New Republic* (April 16, 1966).

visibility is not Black Power. Most of the black politicians around the country today are not examples of Black Power. The power must be that of a community, and emanate from there. The black politicians must start from there. The black politicians must stop being representatives of "downtown" machines, whatever the cost might be in terms of lost patronage and holiday handouts.

Black Power recognizes—it must recognize—the ethnic basis of American politics as well as the power-oriented nature of American politics. Black Power therefore calls for black people to consolidate behind their own, so that they can bargain from a position of strength. But while we endorse the *procedure* of group solidarity and identity for the purpose of attaining certain goals in the body politic, this does not mean that black people should strive for the same kind of rewards (i.e., end results) obtained by the white society. The ultimate values and goals are not domination or exploitation of other groups, but rather an effective share in the total power of the society.

Nevertheless, some observers have labeled those who advocate Black Power as racists; they have said that the call for self-identification and self-determination is "racism in reverse" or "black supremacy." This is a deliberate and absurd lie. There is no analogy—by any stretch of definition or imagination—between the advocates of Black Power and white racists. Racism is not merely exclusion on the basis of race but exclusion for the purpose of subjugating or maintaining subjugation. The goal of the racists is to keep black people on the bottom, arbitrarily and dictatorially, as they have done in this country for over three hundred years. The goal of black self-determination and black self-identity—Black Power—is full participation in the decision-making processes affecting the lives of black people, and recognition of the virtues in themselves as black people. The black people of this country have not lynched whites, bombed their churches, murdered their children and manipulated laws and institutions to maintain oppression. White racists have. Congressional laws, one after the other, have not been necessary to stop black people from oppressing others and denying others the full enjoyment of their rights. White racists have made such laws necessary. The goal of Black Power is positive and functional to a free and viable society. No white racist can make this claim.

A great deal of public attention and press space was devoted to the hysterical accusation of "black racism" when the call for Black Power was first sounded. A national committee of influential black churchmen affiliated with the National Council of Churches, despite their obvious respectability and responsibility, had to resort to a paid advertisement to articulate their position, while anyone yapping "black racism" made front-page news. In their statement, published in the *New York Times* of July 31, 1966, the churchmen said:

> We, an informal group of Negro churchmen in America, are deeply disturbed about the crisis brought upon our country by historic distortions of important human realities in the controversy about "black power." What we see shining through the variety of rhetoric is not anything new but the same old problem of power and race which has faced our beloved country since 1619.
>
> . . . The conscience of black men is corrupted because having no power to implement the demands of conscience, the concern for justice in the absence of justice becomes a chaotic self-surrender. Powerlessness breeds a race of beggars. We are faced with a situation where powerless conscience meets conscienceless power, threatening the very foundations of our Nation.
>
> We deplore the overt violence of riots, but we feel it is more important to focus on the real sources of these eruptions. These sources may be abetted inside the Ghetto, but their basic cause lies in the silent and covert violence which white middle class America inflicts upon the victims of the inner city.
>
> . . . In short, the failure of American leaders to use American power to create equal opportunity in *life* as well as *law*, this is the real problem and not the anguished cry for black power.
>
> . . . Without the capacity to participate with power, i.e., to have some organized political and economic strength to really influence people with whom one interacts, integration is not meaningful.
>
> . . . America has asked its Negro citizens to fight for opportunity as *individuals*, whereas at certain points in our history what we have needed most has been opportunity for the *whole group*, not just for selected and approved Negroes.
>
> . . . We must not apologize for the existence of this form of group power, for we have been oppressed as a group and not as individuals. We will not find our way out of that oppression until both we and America accept the need for Negro Americans, as well as for Jews, Italians, Poles, and white Anglo-Saxon Protestants, among others, to have and to wield group power.

It is a commentary on the fundamentally racist nature of this society that the concept of group strength for black people must be articulated—not to mention defended. No other group would submit to being led by others. Italians do not run the Anti-Defamation League of B'nai B'rith. Irish do not chair Christopher Columbus Societies. Yet when black people call for black-run and all-black organizations, they are immediately classed in a category with the Ku Klux Klan. This is interesting and ironic, but by no means surprising: the society does not expect black people to be able to take care of their business, and there are many who prefer it precisely that way.

In the end, we cannot and shall not offer any guarantees that Black Power, if achieved, would be non-racist. No one can predict human behavior. Social change always has unanticipated consequences. If black racism is what the larger society fears, we cannot help them. We can only state what we hope will be the result, given the fact that the present situation is unacceptable and that we have no real alternative but to work for Black Power. The final truth is that the white society is not entitled to reassurances, even if it were possible to offer them.

We have outlined the meaning and goals of Black Power; we have also discussed one major thing which it is not. There are others of greater importance. The advocates of Black Power reject the old slogans and meaningless rhetoric of previous years in the civil rights struggle. The language of yesterday is indeed irrelevant: progress, non-violence, integration, fear of "white backlash," coalition. Let us look at the rhetoric and see why these terms must be set aside or redefined.

One of the tragedies of the struggle against racism is that up to this point there has been no national organization which could speak to the growing militancy of young black people in the urban ghettos and the black-belt South. There has been only a "civil rights" movement, whose tone of voice was adapted to an audience of middle-class whites. It served as a sort of buffer zone between that audience and angry young blacks. It claimed to speak for the needs of a community, but it did not speak in the tone of that community. None of its so-called leaders could go into a rioting community and be listened to. In a sense, the blame must be shared—along with the mass media—by those leaders for what happened in Watts, Harlem, Chicago, Cleveland and other places. Each time the black people in those cities saw Dr. Martin Luther King get slapped they became angry. When they saw little black girls bombed to death *in a church* and civil rights workers ambushed and murdered, they were angrier; and when nothing happened, they were steaming mad. We had nothing to offer that they could see, except to go out and be beaten again. We helped to build their frustration.

We had only the old language of love and suffering. And in most places—that is, from the liberals and middle class—we got back the old language of patience and progress. The civil rights leaders were saying to the country: "Look, you guys are supposed to be nice guys, and we are only going to do what we are supposed to do. Why do you beat us up? Why don't you give us what we ask? Why don't you straighten yourselves out?" For the masses of black people, this language resulted in virtually nothing. In fact, their objective day-to-day condition worsened. The unemployment rate among black people increased while that among whites declined. Housing conditions in the black communities deteriorated. Schools in the black ghettos continued to plod along on outmoded techniques, inadequate curricula, and with all too many tired and indifferent teachers. Meanwhile, the President picked up the refrain of "We Shall Overcome" while the Congress passed civil rights law after civil rights law, only to have them effectively nullified by deliberately weak enforcement. "Progress is being made," we were told.

Such language, along with admonitions to remain non-violent and fear the white backlash, convinced some that that course was the *only* course to follow. It misled some into believing that a black minority could bow its head and get whipped into a meaningful position of power. The very notion is absurd. The white society devised the language, adopted the rules and had the black community narcotized into believing that that language and those rules were, in fact, relevant. The black community was told time and again how *other* immigrants finally won *acceptance*: that is, by following the Protestant Ethic of Work and Achievement. They worked hard; therefore, they achieved. We were not told that it was by building Irish Power, Italian Power, Polish Power or Jewish Power that these groups got themselves together and operated from positions of strength. We were not told that "the American dream" wasn't designed for black people. That while today, to whites, the dream may *seem* to include black people, it cannot do so by the very nature of this nation's political and economic system, which imposes institutional racism on the black masses if not upon every individual black. A notable comment on that "dream" was made by Dr. Percy Julian, the black scientist and director of the Julian Research Institute in Chicago, a man for whom the dream seems to have come true. While not subscribing to "black power" as he understood it, Dr. Julian clearly understood the basis for it:

> The false concept of basic Negro inferiority is one of the curses that still lingers. It is a problem created by the white man. Our children just no longer are going to accept the patience we were taught by our generation. We were taught a pretty little lie—excel and the whole world lies open before you. *I obeyed the injunction and found it to be wishful thinking.* (Authors' italics)[2]

[2] *The New York Times* (April 30, 1967), p. 30.

A key phrase in our buffer-zone days was non-violence. For years it has been thought that black people would not literally fight for their lives. Why this has been so is not entirely clear; neither the larger society nor black people are noted for passivity. The notion apparently stems from the years of marches and demonstrations and sit-ins where black people did not strike back and the violence always came from white mobs. There are many who still sincerely believe in that approach. From our viewpoint, rampaging white mobs and white night-riders must be made to understand that their days of free head-whipping are over. Black people should and must fight back. Nothing more quickly repels someone bent on destroying you than the unequivocal message: "O.K., fool, make your move, and run the same risk I run—of dying."

When the concept of Black Power is set forth, many people immediately conjure up notions of violence. The country's reaction to the Deacons for Defense and Justice, which originated in Louisiana, is instructive. Here is a group which realized that the "law" and law enforcement agencies would not protect people, so they had to do it themselves. If a nation fails to protect its citizens, then that nation cannot condemn those who take up the task themselves. The Deacons and all other blacks who resort to self-defense represent a simple answer to a simple question: what man would not defend his family and home from attack?

But this frightened some white people, because they knew that black people would now fight back. They knew that this was precisely what *they* would have long since done if *they* were subjected to the injustices and oppression heaped on blacks. Those of us who advocate Black Power are quite clear in our own minds that a "non-violent" approach to civil rights is an approach black people cannot afford and a luxury white people do not deserve. It is crystal clear to us—and it must become so with the white society—*that there can be no social order without social justice.* White people must be made to understand that they must stop messing with black people, or the blacks *will* fight back!

Next, we must deal with the term "integration." According to its advocates, social justice will be accomplished by "integrating the Negro into the mainstream institutions of the society from which he has been traditionally excluded." This concept is based on the assumption that there is nothing of value in the black community and that little of value could be created among black people. The thing to do is siphon off the "acceptable" black people into the surrounding middle-class white community.

The goals of integrationists are middle-class goals, articulated primarily by a small group of Negroes with middle-class aspirations or status. Their kind of integration has meant that a few blacks "make it," leaving the black community, sapping it of leadership potential and know-how. Those token Negroes—absorbed into a white mass— are of no value to the remaining black masses. They become meaningless show-pieces for a conscience-soothed white society. Such people will state that they would prefer to be treated "only as individuals, not as Negroes"; that they "are not and should not be preoccupied with race." This is a totally unrealistic position. In the first place, black people have not suffered as individuals but as members of a group; therefore, their liberation lies in group action. This is why SNCC—and the concept of Black Power—affirms that helping *individual* black people to solve their problems on an *individual* basis does little to alleviate the mass of black people. Secondly, while color blindness may be a sound goal ultimately, we must realize that race is an overwhelming fact of life in this historical period. There is no black man in this country who can live "simply as a man." His blackness is an ever-present fact of this racist society, whether he recognizes it or not. It is unlikely that this or the next generation will witness the time when race will no longer be relevant in the conduct of public affairs and in public policy decision-making. To realize this and to attempt to deal with it does not make one a racist or overly preoccupied with race; it puts one in the forefront of a significant *struggle*. If there is no intense struggle today, there will be no meaningful results tomorrow.

"Integration" as a goal today speaks to the problem of blackness not only in an unrealistic way but also in a despicable way. It is based on complete acceptance of the fact that in order to have a decent house or education, black people must move into a white neighborhood or send their children to a white school. This reinforces, among both black and white, the idea that "white" is automatically superior and "black" is by definition inferior. For this reason, "integration" is a subterfuge for the maintenance of white supremacy. It allows the nation to focus on a handful of Southern black children who get into white schools at a great price, and to ignore the ninety-four percent who are left in unimproved all-black schools. Such situations will not change until black people become equal in a way that means something, and integration ceases to be a one-way street. Then integration does not mean draining skills and energies from the black ghetto into white neighborhoods. To sprinkle black children among white pupils in outlying schools is at best a stop-gap measure. The goal is not to take black children out of the black community and expose them to white middle-class values; the goal is to build and strengthen the black community.

"Integration" also means that black people must give up their identity, deny their heritage. We recall the conclusion of Killian and Grigg: "At the present time, integration as a solution to the race problem demands that the Negro foreswear his identity as a Negro." The fact is that integration, as traditionally articulated, would abolish the black community. The fact is that what must be abolished is not the black community, but the dependent colonial status that has been inflicted upon it.

The racial and cultural personality of the black community must be preserved and that community must win its freedom while preserving its cultural integrity. Integrity includes a pride—in the sense of self-acceptance, not chauvinism—in being black, in the historical attainments and contributions of black people. No person can be healthy, complete and mature if he must deny a part of himself; this is what "integration" has required thus far. This is the essential difference between integration as it is currently practiced and the concept of Black Power.

The idea of cultural integrity is so obvious that it seems almost simple-minded to spell things out at this length. Yet millions of Americans resist such truths when they are applied to black people. Again, that resistance is a comment on the fundamental racism in the society. Irish Catholics took care of their own first without a lot of apology for doing so, without any dubious language from timid leadership about guarding against "backlash." Everyone understood it to be a perfectly legitimate procedure. Of course, there would be "backlash." Organization begets counterorganization, but this was no reason to defer.

The so-called white backlash against black people is something else: the embedded traditions of institutional racism being brought into the open and calling forth overt manifestations of individual racism. In the summer of 1966, when the protest marches into Cicero, Illinois, began, the black people knew they were not allowed to live in Cicero and the white people knew it. When blacks began to demand the right to live in homes in that town, the whites simply reminded them of the status quo. Some people called this "backlash." It was, in fact, racism defending itself. In the black community, this is called "White folks showing their color." It is ludicrous to blame black people for what is simply an overt manifestation of white racism. Dr. Martin Luther King stated clearly that the protest marches were not the cause of the racism but merely exposed a long-term cancerous condition in the society.

The Chicano Struggle

The following documents developed by an independent Chicano party illustrate the clear relationship between power and education. The La Raza Unida Party was formed for the purpose of pursuing the goals and grievances discussed in these documents. The statement of rationale for such a party and the additions suggested for the Plan de Aztlan were prepared by Antonio Camejo, who was a candidate for California Superintendent of Public Instruction, and Froben Lozada, Chairman of the Latin and Mexican-American Studies Department at Merritt College, Oakland, California. The original Plan de Aztlan, named for land in the Southwest which was seized by the United States during the Mexican war, was passed at the First Annual Chicano Youth Conference in 1969.

    Schools, as these documents show, have become important means for demonstrating power. Community control, curricular changes to reflect racial or nationality interests, and manipulation of minority groups by school authorities are all sources of power conflict. The political components of education are evident in daily newspapers. Schools have been used to oppress and restrict people through class, race, and sex discrimination, but they are also seen as potential agents to alleviate injustice, immorality, and inhumanity. This peculiar quality of education keeps it in power turmoil.

In order to organize our struggle for the liberation of La Raza we need a political organization. A mass, independent Chicano political party is an indispensable vehicle for mobilizing La Raza in day to day struggles.

What should be the nature of such a party? What could it realistically hope to accomplish in the immediate future and also in the long run?

An independent Chicano political party must reject the liberal approach of vendidos [sellouts] like Democrat Henry B. Gonzales (Texas). The Republican and Democratic parties are controlled from

top to bottom by the millionaires who profit from the oppression of
La Raza. Neither of these parties, completely devoted to the capitalist
system, can serve the interests of our people. They are our enemies
and liberation will involve a struggle against both capitalist parties.

Those who attempt to work within either the Democratic or
Republican Party can only become tools of the racist power structure.
They are like the vendidos of old who went begging "con el sombrero
en la mano" [with hat in hand] for more crumbs from our oppressors.
Against these present day malinches [roughly in English: Uncle
Toms] we counterpose a complete break from the Democratic and
Republican parties with the cry, "ni un minuto mas de rodillas!"
[not another minute on our knees].

Although the majority of Chicanos who vote, vote Democratic,
there is already a growing awareness of the futility of this line of
action. An example of the possibilities for an independent Chicano
party is La Raza Unida Party in South Texas. The response which this
party has gotten from thousands of Chicanos in Texas shows the
tremendous potential for an independent Chicano party winning our
people over to the strategy which can further our fight for self-
determination.

La Raza Unida is struggling for the support of the overwhelming majority of Chicanos in southwest Texas counties where we
constitute 85 to 95 per cent of the population. They did not start out
with the support of the majority of our people. No party has ever
started out with the majority of the people it hoped to mobilize. The
majority must be won through struggle and education.

A mass, independent Chicano political party could turn American politics upside down and inside out. The strength of the Democratic Party comes from the support it receives from a combination of
sizable oppressed groups—the trade unions, the unemployed, the pen-
sioners and retirees, and especially the great majority of the Black and
Chicano people. The coalition of these forces with the wealthy Democrats is not based on any political principles or identity of interests,
but rather on the belief that this coalition can win elections. The
massive defection of Chincano voters would create an immediate
crisis for all the elements in this coalition, not only in Aztlan, but
nationally. Without the Chicano vote, the Democrats would be
unable to carry whole sections of Aztlan, as well as some large
cities outside of Aztlan. The Democratic Party's growing incapacity
to win nationally would break up this coalition, encouraging Black
people and the labor movement to consider independent political
action.

Old alignments will disintegrate and new ones will be formed. An independent Chicano political party will therefore not only be the best way to promote and protect our welfare, but will also create the possibility of forging new alliances with other oppressed groups.

An independent Chicano party will engage in mass actions around the demands of La Raza. Such a party will raise the political consciousness of our people on the streets and during elections by struggling around the demands and concepts of El Plan de Aztlan. Many such demands have already appeared on the doors of courthouses, on banners flying in demonstrations of our people from Chicago to San Francisco, Tierra Amarillo, Denver, East Los Angeles, Crystal City, San Antonio—all over Aztlan. The struggle for demands relating to community control of the schools, bilingual education, equality of the Spanish language, enforcing the treaty of Guadalupe-Hidalgo, and other demands directed at the liberation of our people will have to become the very heart of any Chicano party.

Most of our people still see no alternative to the two capitalist parties. Our task is to destroy the illusions our people have that either capitalist party can serve the interests of the Chicano people. Our job is to win our people, not write them off. Our job is to politicize them, to mobilize them, to expose the hypocrisy and lies of the capitalist rulers. We must not jump so far ahead that our people are not able to bridge the gap between present reality and the future we point to. No small band of armed men, no matter how dedicated or sincere, can substitute themselves for the actions of the masses of our people. The masses are the real makers of history. The Chicano party is the vehicle to mobilize them.

For La Raza Unida Party in Texas to win mass support it had to do a lot of difficult and tedious groundwork over several years. Independent political action will not lead immediately to a nationwide party with a mass base. This will take time and the necessary preliminary educational work to explain to people its potential. We will have to gather dedicated activists who could begin to popularize El Plan de Aztlan. In some areas of Aztlan, independent Chicano parties will be able to get on the ballot, as in South Texas, wherever there are conscious people to carry out the necessary work. The skeleton of the party must first be created before we can build the flesh and muscle of real mass support and influence. Electoral victory, even in areas where La Raza is a majority, will not come immediately. Our people in the barrios, the ranchos, the campos, the pueblos, and in the factories will demand proof of our seriousness before they act. They will not come over at once but will be won over through struggles initiated by our party and the partial victories in which it shows itself capable of leading masses. Our people will slowly gain confidence in our party as the authoritative voice of their needs and aspirations.

Many difficulties will have to be dealt with. The ruling class will not stand idly by and watch their two-party system undermined. They will use every trick at their disposal. Chicano faces will appear on Democratic and Republican tickets. Chicano mayors and city officials controlled by the Democrats will make their appearance, all in an attempt to disorient our people. The ruling class will use the dual tactic of concession and repression. They will attempt to frame up our leaders and activists and we will have to fight them at every turn for our right to organize our party without continual harassment, Chango [cop] brutality and killings. They will also attempt to buy off leaders with lucrative (for them) job offers in some "poverty" (pacification) program. But if we answer each such attempt by challenging their hypocrisy and exposing their actions before our people, we will gain in strength. The only effective defense against repressive measures is the mobilization of the Chicano community, as was done in the case of Baltazar Martinez in Denver. First and foremost we will have to keep the independence of the Chicano party as a principle of struggle.

We have a great deal to do, but the time to start is today, not tomorrow. Real progress towards self-determination will begin on the day we reinforce our grito: "Ya Basta" [Enough!] and move through independent political action toward complete liberation.

The Plan of Aztlan

El Plan Espiritual de Aztlan sets the theme that the Chicanos (La Raza de Bronze) must use their nationalism as the key or common denominator for mass mobilization and organization. Once we are committed to the idea and philosophy of El Plan de Aztlan, we can only conclude that social, economic, cultural and political independence is the only road to total liberation from oppression, exploitation and racism. Our struggle then must be for the control of our barrios [neighborhoods], campos [countryside], pueblos [villages], lands, our economy, our culture, and our political life. El Plan commits all levels of Chicano society—the barrio, the campo, the ranchero [rancher], the writer, the teacher, the worker, the professional—to La Causa.

Nationalism

Nationalism as the key to organization transcends all religious, political, class and economic factions or boundaries. Nationalism is the common denominator that all members of La Raza can agree upon.

Organization Goals

1. Unity—in the thinking of our people concerning the barrios, the pueblo, the campo, the land, the poor, the middle class, the professional—all committed to liberation of La Raza.

2. Economy—economic control of our lives and our communities can only come about by driving the exploiter out of our communities, our pueblos, and our lands and by controlling and developing our own talents, sweat, and resources. Cultural background and values which ignore materialism and embrace humanism will contribute to the act of cooperative buying and the distribution of resources and production to sustain an economic base for healthy growth and development. Lands rightfully ours will be fought for and defended. Land and realty ownership will be acquired by the community for the people's welfare. Economic ties of responsibility must be secured by nationalism and the Chicano defense units.

Addition—The urban Chicano worker represents about 85 per cent of our population. We must support and extend the struggle of Chicano workers. The Chicano worker confronts the exploiting employer, but also the racist union bureaucrats who ride rough-shod over the unions. We are exploited as workers, but also oppressed because of our brown skin, our culture and language. The following demands can help focus the struggle on the job and in the unions:

A. Equality of the Spanish language in all places of employment and business.
B. Rank and file democratic control of the unions. The elimination of all racist practices in the labor movement.
C. Preferential hiring and promotion for Chicanos and other oppressed peoples, including access to all training programs and supervisory posts.
D. For an escalator clause in all union contracts to assure automatic wage increases with the rising cost of living.
E. For a 30-hour week with no reduction in pay to spread the available jobs.
F. Support to Chicano caucuses in the unions.

3. Education—must be relative to our people, i.e., history, culture, bilingual education, contributions, etc. Community control of our schools, our teachers, our administrators, our counselors, and our programs.

Addition—The entire educational system is now used as a means to oppress us, to destroy our culture, to channel us into the degrading roles assigned to us by the Anglos. We struggle to turn the educational institutions into a resource for the liberation of Aztlan, for the development of Chicano culture and language. We thus raise these basic demands:

A. We must control the schools of our community from the kindergartens to the universities, including the trade schools and job training programs.
B. Our control must be exercised by totally autonomous concilios [councils] elected by La Raza.
C. Tracking must be abolished.
D. We demand full political rights for organization and dissemination of political ideas and the right of struggle without victimizations in the high schools.
E. La Raza students and parents must control all disciplinary matters involving our youth, including in schools where La Raza is not the majority.
F. Chicano studies programs controlled by Chicano students, faculty, and the community must be established to develop our culture and our educational system.
G. All university complicity with the oppression of our brothers and sisters in Latin America, Asia, and Africa must end.
H. We demand that the Spanish language be placed on an equal footing with English in all educational institutions. To rob our language is to strip us of our dignity. We demand bilingual education that applies not only to Chicano studies, Latin American and Mexican literature and history, but to all disciplines: art, music, science, job training, mathematics, history, and the teaching of English as a second language.

4. *Institutions*—shall serve our people by providing the service necessary for a full life and their welfare on the basis of restitution, not handouts or beggar's crumbs. Restitution for past economic slavery, political exploitation, ethnic and cultural psychological destruction and denial of civil and human rights. Institutions in our community which do not serve the people have no place in the community. The institutions belong to the people.

Addition—The struggle for community control encompasses all the immediate demands of our struggles and at the same time takes these questions up at the root—the control of our community by the Anglo power structure. Posing the question of power, this demand is profoundly revolutionary and relates to the consciousness of La Raza.

A struggle for control of the different institutions of the community can be the focal point for this stage of the struggle. By control of the community we do not mean "decentralization" or the giving up of the struggle for Aztlan, but to integrate our struggle in our communities with the struggle for nationhood. We advance the following demands that can be raised in this struggle:

A. Community control over all institutions of the community: schools, hospitals, libraries, welfare agencies, police, fire departments, etc.
B. The establishment of concilios de La Raza to administer these institutions and our communities. These concilios shall be democratically elected.
C. The community must control (with no strings attached) all government, church, and private foundation funds granted to "community action programs."
D. The schools should provide free breakfast and lunch for all school children from the vast stores of food kept under lock and key.

Americans: Red and Black

Vine Deloria

The original early Americans, Indians, have had a tragic history of ethnic relations with white men. From open ranges to closed reservations the red man has succumbed to America's "Manifest Destiny." The ideals of love, brotherhood, and civil rights which permeate our religious, ethical, and legal culture have consistently been overshadowed by fear and property considerations when it comes to Indians. Initial fear of the natives, apparently unfounded if we are to believe the stories of Indian assistance to white settlers, and land speculation for economic exploitation became the guideposts for treatment of Indian groups. American history books still recall, presumably as a significant act of white superiority, the trading of Manhattan Island for trinkets. One must pause to wonder

Reprinted with permission of The Macmillan Company from *Custer Died for Your Sins* by Vine Deloria. Copyright © 1969 by Vine Deloria, Jr.

at this time in history about the wisdom of that trade, but it sym-
bolized the continuing relationship between those who saw land as
private investment potential and those who did not.

In the course of the white man's relations with blacks and
reds, there have been both mental and physical skirmishes. Slave
ships and plantations are in this history, as are frontier wars and
desolate segregated reservations. Although both red and black have
shared in the white legacy, they are separate and different. Vine
Deloria, an Indian, writes of the relation of black to red and of
both to white. Since education has been one of the areas of white
blindness to serious ethnic disadvantage, it may be unlikely that
improved education is an answer. Some of our attempts to educate
minorities have actually been attempts to rob them of their own
culture. Such is the case with Indians. In addition, the treatment of
minorities in the traditional American school curriculum and
textbook blots out any serious consideration of their dissent from
or contributions to the emerging American society.

Civil Rights has been the most important and least understood movement of our generation. To some it has seemed to be a simple matter of fulfilling rights outlined by the Constitutional amendments after
the Civil War. To others, particularly church people, Civil Rights has
appeared to be a fulfillment of the brotherhood of man and the
determination of humanity's relationship to God. To those opposing
the movement, Civil Rights has been a foreign conspiracy which has
threatened the fabric of our society.

For many years the movement to give the black people rights
equal to those for their white neighbors was called Race Relations.
The preoccupation with race obscured the real issues that were
developing and meant that programs devised to explore the area of
race always had a black orientation.

To the Indian people it has seemed quite unfair that churches
and government agencies concentrated their efforts primarily on the
blacks. By defining the problem as one of race and making race refer
solely to black, Indians were systematically excluded from consideration. National church groups have particularly used race as a means
of exploring minority-group relations. Whatever programs or policies
outlined from national churches to their affiliates and parishes were
generally black-oriented programs which had been adapted to include
Indians.

There was probably a historical basis for this type of thinking.
In many states in the last century, Indians were classified as white by
laws passed to exclude blacks. So there was a connotation that Indians might in some way be like whites. But in other areas, particularly

marriage laws, Indians were classified as blacks and this connotation really determined the role into which the white man forced the red man. Consequently, as far as most Race Relations were concerned, Indians were classified as non-whites.

There has been no way to positively determine in which category Indians belong when it comes to federal agencies. The Bureau of Indian Affairs consistently defined Indians as good guys who have too much dignity to demonstrate, hoping to keep the Indian people separate from the ongoing Civil Rights movement. Other agencies generally adopted a semi-black orientation. Sometimes Indians were treated as if they were blacks and other times not.

The Civil Rights Commission and the Community Relations Service always gave only lip service to Indians until it was necessary for them to write an annual report. At that time they always sought out some means of including Indians as a group with which they had worked the previous fiscal year. That was the extent of Indian relationship with the agency: a paragraph in the annual report and a promise to do something next year.

Older Indians, as a rule, have been content to play the passive role outlined for them by the bureau. They have wanted to avoid the rejection and bad publicity given activists.

The Indian people have generally avoided confrontations between the different minority groups and confrontations with the American public at large. They have felt that any publicity would inevitably have bad results and since the press seemed dedicated to the perpetuation of sensationalism rather than straight reporting of the facts, great care has been taken to avoid the spotlight. Because of this attitude, Indian people have not become well known in the field of inter-group and race relations. Consequently they have suffered from the attitudes of people who have only a superficial knowledge of minority groups and have attached a certain stigma to them.

The most common attitude Indians have faced has been the unthoughtful Johnny-come-lately liberal who equates certain goals with a dark skin. This type of individual generally defines the goals of all groups by the way he understands what he wants for the blacks. Foremost in this category have been younger social workers and clergymen entering the field directly out of college or seminary. For the most part they have been book-fed and lack experience in life. They depend primarily upon labels and categories of academic import rather than on any direct experience. Too often they have achieved positions of prominence as programs have been expanded to meet needs of people. In exercising their discretionary powers administratively, they have run roughshod over Indian people. They have not wanted to show their ignorance about Indians. Instead, they prefer to place all people with darker skin in the same category of basic goals, then develop their programs to fit these preconceived ideas.

Since the most numerous group has been the blacks, programs designed for blacks were thought adequate for all needs of all groups. When one asks a liberal about minority groups, he unconsciously seems to categorize them all together for purposes of problem solving. Hence, dark-skinned and minority group as categorical concepts have brought about the same basic results—the Indian is defined as a subcategory of black.

Cultural differences have only seemed to emphasize the white liberal's point of view in lumping the different communities together. When Indians have pointed out real differences that do exist, liberals have tended to dismiss the differences as only minor aberrations which distinguish different racial groups.

At one conference on education of minority groups, I once mentioned the existence of some three hundred Indian languages which made bicultural and bilingual education a necessity. I was immediately challenged by several white educators who attempted to prove that blacks also have a language problem. I was never able to make the difference real to them. For the conference people the point had again been established that minority groups all had the same basic problems.

Recently, blacks and some Indians have defined racial problems as having one focal point—the White Man. This concept is a vast oversimplification of the real problem, as it centers on a racial theme rather than on specific facts. And it is simply the reversal of the old prejudicial attitude of the white who continues to define minority groups as problems of his—that is, Indian problem, Negro problem, and so on.

Rather than race or minority grouping, non-whites have often been defined according to their function within the American society. Negroes, as we have said, were considered draft animals, Indians wild animals. So too, Orientals were considered domestic animals and Mexicans humorous lazy animals. The white world has responded to the non-white groups in a number of ways, but primarily according to the manner in which it believed the non-whites could be rescued from their situation.

Thus Orientals were left alone once whites were convinced that they preferred to remain together and presented no basic threat to white social mores. Mexicans were similarly discarded and neglected when whites felt that they preferred to remain by themselves. In both cases there was no direct confrontation between whites and the two groups because there was no way that a significant number of them could be exploited. They owned little; they provided little which the white world coveted.

With the black and the Indian, however, tensions increased over the years. Both groups had been defined as animals with which the white had to have some relation and around whom some attitude must be formed. Blacks were ex-draft animals who somehow were required to become non-black. Indeed, respectability was possible for a black only by emphasizing characteristics and features that were non-black. Indians were the ex-wild animals who had provided the constant danger for the civilizing tendencies of the invading white. They always presented a foreign aspect to whites unfamiliar with the western hemisphere.

The white man adopted two basic approaches in handling blacks and Indians. He systematically excluded blacks from all programs, policies, social events, and economic schemes. He could not allow blacks to rise from their position because it would mean that the evolutionary scheme had superseded the Christian scheme and that man had perhaps truly descended from the ape.

With the Indian the process was simply reversed. The white man had been forced to deal with the Indian in treaties and agreements. It was difficult, therefore, to completely overlook the historical antecedents such as Thanksgiving, the plight of the early Pilgrims, and the desperate straits from which various Indian tribes had often rescued the whites. Indians were therefore subjected to the most intense pressure to become white. Laws passed by Congress had but one goal—the Anglo-Saxonization of the Indian. The antelope had to become a white man.

Between these two basic attitudes, the apelike draft animal and the wild free-running antelope, the white man was impaled on the horns of a dilemma he had created within himself.

It is well to keep these distinctions clearly in mind when talking about Indians and blacks. When the liberals equate the two they are overlooking obvious historical facts. Never did the white man systematically exclude Indians from his schools and meeting places. Nor did the white man ever kidnap black children from their homes and take them off to a government boarding school to be educated as whites. The white man signed no treaties with the black. Nor did he pass any amendments to the Constitution to guarantee the treaties of the Indian.

The basic problem which has existed between the various racial groups has not been one of race but of culture and legal status. The white man systematically destroyed Indian culture where it existed, but separated blacks from his midst so that they were forced to attempt the creation of their own culture.

The white man forbade the black to enter his own social and economic system and at the same time force-fed the Indian what he was denying the black. Yet the white man demanded that the black conform to white standards and insisted that the Indian don feathers and beads periodically to perform for him.

The white man presented the *problem* of each group in contradictory ways so that neither black nor Indian could understand exactly where the problem existed or how to solve it. The Indian was always told that his problem was one of conflicting cultures. Yet, when solutions were offered by the white man, they turned out to be a reordering of the legal relationship between red and white. There was never a time when the white man said he was trying to help the Indian get into the mainstream of American life that he did not also demand that the Indian give up land, water, minerals, timber, and other resources which would enrich the white men.

The black also suffered from the same basic lie. Time after time legislation was introduced which purported to give the black equal rights with the white but which ultimately restricted his life and opportunities, even his acceptance by white people. The initial Civil Rights Act following the thirteenth, fourteenth, and fifteenth amendments was assumed to give the blacks equal rights with "white citizens." In fact, it was so twisted that it took nearly a century to bring about additional legislation to confirm black rights.

In June of 1968 the Supreme Court finally interpreted an ancient statute in favor of blacks in the matter of purchasing a house. Had the right existed for nearly a century without anyone knowing it? Of course not, the white had simply been unwilling to give in to the black. Can one blame the black athletes at the recent Olympic Games for their rebellion against the role cast for them by white society? Should they be considered as specially trained athletic animals suitable only for hauling away tons of gold medals for the United States every four years while equality remains as distant as it ever was?

It is time for both black and red to understand the ways of the white man. The white is after Indian lands and resources. He always had been and always will be. For Indians to continue to think of their basic conflict with the white man as cultural is the height of folly. The problem is and always has been the adjustment of the legal relationship between the Indian tribes and the federal government, between the true owners of the land and the usurpers.

The black must understand that whites are determined to keep him out of their society. No matter how many Civil Rights laws are passed or how many are on the drawing board, the basic thrust is to keep the black out of society and harmless. The problem, therefore, is not one of legal status, it is one of culture and social and economic mobility. It is foolish for a black to depend upon a law to make acceptance of him by the white possible. Nor should he react to the rejection. His problem is social, and economic, and cultural, not one of adjusting the legal relationship between the two groups.

When the black seeks to change his role by adjusting the laws of the nation, he merely raises the hope that progress is being made. But for the majority of blacks progress is not being made. Simply because a middle-class black can eat at the Holiday Inn is not a gain. People who can afford the best generally get it. A socio-economic, rather than legal adjustment must consequently be the goal.

But the understanding of the racial question does not ultimately involve understanding by either blacks or Indians. It involves the white man himself. He must examine his past. He must face the problems he has created within himself and within others. The white man must no longer project his fears and insecurities onto other groups, races, and countries. Before the white man can relate to others he must forego the pleasure of defining them. The white man must learn to stop viewing history as a plot against himself. . . .

White culture destroys other culture because of its abstractness. As a destroyer of culture it is not a culture but a cancer. In order to keep the country from complete divisiveness, separatism must be accepted as a means to achieve equality of personality both for groups and individuals. Separatism can be the means by which blacks gain time for reflection, meditation, and eventual understanding of themselves as a people.

The black needs time to develop his roots, to create his sacred places, to understand the mystery of himself and his history, to understand his own purpose. These things the Indian has and is able to maintain through his tribal life. The Indian now needs to create techniques to provide the economic strength needed to guarantee the survival of what he has.

In a real way, white culture, if there is such, is already doomed to its own destruction. Continual emphasis on racial rather than cultural problems will not only bring down white society but may also endanger ancient Indian society and newly emerging black and Mexican social movements.

The white man has the marvelous ability to conceptualize. He has also the marvelous inability to distinguish between sacred and profane. He therefore arbitrarily conceptualizes all things and understands none of them. His science creates gimmicks for his use. Little effort is made to relate the gimmicks to the nature of life or to see them in a historical context.

The white man is problem-solving. His conceptualizations merge into science and then emerge in his social life as problems, the solutions of which are the adjustments of his social machine. Slavery, prohibition, Civil Rights, and social services are all important adjustments of the white man's social machine. No solution he has reached has proven adequate. Indeed, it has often proven demonic.

White solutions fail because *white* itself is an abstraction of an attitude of mind, not a racial or group reality. The white as we know him in America is an amalgam of European immigrants, not a racial phenomenon. But the temptation has always been present to define groups according to their most superficial aspect. Hence we have white, black, red, and the Yellow Peril. And we are taught to speak of the *Negro problem*, the *Indian problem*, and so forth.

White has been abstracted into a magical nebulous mythology that dominates all inhabitants of our country in their attitudes toward one another. We are, consequently, all prisoners of that mythology so far as we rebel against it. It is our misfortune that our economic system reflects uncritical acceptance of the mythology and that economic movements tend to reinforce the myth.

There is basically nothing real about our economic system. It is neither good nor bad, but neutral. Only when we place connotations on it and use it to manipulate people does it become a thing in itself.

Our welfare system demonstrates better than anything else the means to which uncritical *white* economics can be used. We have all types of welfare programs: old age, disability, aid to dependent children, orphanages, and unemployment. There is continual controversy in the halls of Congress, state legislatures, and city halls over the welfare programs.

Conservatives insist that those receiving welfare are lazy and are getting a free ride at the expense of hard-working citizens. Liberals insist that all citizens have a basic right to life and that it is the government's responsibility to provide for those unable to provide for themselves.

What are we really saying?

Welfare is based upon the norm set up by the Puritans long

ago. A man is defined as a white, Anglo-Saxon Protestant, healthy, ambitious, earnest, and honest, a man whom the Lord smiles upon by increasing the fruits of his labor. Welfare is designed to compensate people insofar as they deviate from that norm. Insofar as a woman has an illegitimate child, she receives compensation. Insofar as a man is disabled, he receives compensation. Insofar as a person is too old to work, he receives compensation.

Welfare buys that portion of a person which does not match the stereotype of the real man. Welfare payments are never sufficient, never adequate. This is because each person bears some relation to the norm and in proportion to their resemblance, they receive less.

When this attitude is applied to groups, it is best seen in the politcial parties. The Republicans represent the best of the white economics. The Democrats represent all of the deviations.

The Republican Party has ostensibly stood for less government as a political philosophical position. But when you listen carefully to the Republicans you do not really hear less government, you hear a strange religion of early Puritan mythology. The Republican Party is in reality the truest expression of America's religion of progress and white respectability. It stands for the white superman who never existed. The peddler's grandson who conquered the unknown by inheriting a department store—such is the basic American religion unmasked. The measure of America's willingness to examine the basis of its existence is to be counted in the number of registered voters who claim to be Republicans.

The measure of truth in the above assertion is the Republican willingness to lose elections rather than depart from cherished doctrines and myths. Only a religion can attract and hold such loyalty.

The other party is something else. Popular conceptions gloss over reality and continue the Rooseveltian myth that the Democrats are the party of the people. The old Roosevelt coalition of labor, minority and ethnic groups, and farmers fails to acknowledge one unpublicized member—the special interests.

More than the Republicans, the Democrats are the party of the special interests. Who else defends the oil-depletion allowance more than the Democrats? Who else creates farm subsidies, tariffs, foreign aid, large development projects? Who else piles special programs on top of special programs? Could the Republicans create the poor as a class in themselves? For, the Republicans know no poor because it is not within their religious comprehension. Nixon's election was the last gasp of this quasi-religious nineteenth-century, Horatio Alger, WASP ethic.

Until 1968 the Democrats won election after election by gathering the rejected into an amalgam of special interests for the sole purpose of splitting the pie which they would then attempt to create. The pie never exists; it is continually being created by the adjustment of the governmental machinery to include additional special interests, while eligible parties participate in the American religion carefully being nurtured by the Republicans in their isolation.

Recent elections tend to show the reality of this analysis. Eisenhower proved that a President was not necessary for the true American religion to progress. Kennedy proved that if enough special interests are combined, even Americans will desert the long-term goals of progress for the immediacy of splitting the pie which was to be created. The New Frontier promised a new chance to be cut in on the action, a short cut into Republican heaven for those groups who had deviated from the norm either by birth, place of origin, or failure to deal themselves in at some previous point in history.

Johnson simply dealt more cards to more people than had ever been dealt before. And his opponent was out preaching salvation by works alone. No wonder there was a religious revolt! The election of 1964 was comparable to the Protestant Reformation, for never had the choices been so clear between faith and works.

Politically, most minority groups have shifted to the Democrats and remained loyal through thick and thin. Margins compiled by blacks, Indians, and Mexicans for Democratic candidates have been incredible. In 1964 it took a strong Indian to support Goldwater in spite of his publicized heroic flights to the Navajo and his superb collection of Hopi Kachina dolls.

The Kennedys increased the normal margins which minority groups gave to the Democrats because of their apparent interest in minority groups. Few members of the Indian community realize or will admit how little the Kennedys really did for Indians. Although the mythology of the Kennedys has made them appear as the only saviors of minority communities, the legislative record compiled by both Jack and Robert Kennedy shows another story.

Jack Kennedy broke the Pickering Treaty and had accomplished little besides the usual Interior Task Force study of Indians before his death. Robert Kennedy did little for Indians legislatively or administratively. He drew some fire and spotlighted some of the problems, but in doing so he practically pre-empted any chance of action because of his many political enemies and their outright rejection of causes he advocated.

Robert Kennedy did prove that race was not the real thing bothering this country and that the turmoil over Civil Rights was misunderstood. He presented himself as a person who could move from world to world and never be a stranger anywhere. His genius was that he personified the best traits of his Irish heritage and made an attempt to define *white* in a different way.

Other people were frightened at Kennedy's obvious attempt to re-create the days of the New Frontier. White mythology sees the kingship as demonic, as against the American religion of ostensible equality.

Indian people loved the idea of Robert Kennedy replacing Jack. For them it was an affirmation of the great war chief from the great family leading his people in his brother's place. Robert Kennedy became as great a hero as the most famous Indian war chiefs precisely because of his ruthlessness. Indians saw him as a warrior, the white Crazy Horse. He somehow validated obscure undefined feelings of Indian people which they had been unwilling to admit to themselves. Spiritually, he was an Indian!

Robert Kennedy's death has completely changed the nature of the Civil Rights movement and has altered the outlook of the American Indian toward American society.

Winds of caution have set in and sails are being trimmed. There appears to be no means by which the cultural crisis can be understood by those outside the group. Indian people are becoming more and more reluctant to consider alternatives. They are becoming distrustful of people who talk equality because they do not see how equality can be achieved without cultural separateness. To the degree that other groups demand material ransoms for peace and order, Indian people are fearful of the ultimate goals of the different movements.

There is no basic antagonism between black and red, or even between red and white. Conflicts are created when Indians feel they are being defined out of existence by the other groups. Historically, each group has its own road to travel. All roads lead to personal and group affirmation. But the obstacles faced by each group are different and call for different solutions and techniques.

While it is wrong and harmful to define all dark-skinned people by certain criteria, it is also wrong to pretend that they have nothing in common. It is what Indians, blacks, and Mexicans have in common and where their differences lie which should be carefully studied.

Time and again blacks have told me how lucky they were not to have been placed on reservations after the Civil War. I don't think they were lucky at all. I think it was absolute disaster that blacks were not given reservations.

Indian tribes have been able to deal directly with the federal government because they had a recognized status within the Constitutional scheme. Leadership falls into legal patterns on each reservation through the elective process. A tribal chairman is recognized by federal agencies, Congressional committees, and private agencies as the representative of the group. Quarrels over programs, rivalry between leaders, defense of rights, and expressions of the mood of the people are all channeled through the official governing body. Indian people have the opportunity to deal officially with the rest of the world as a corporate body.

The blacks, on the other hand, are not defined with their own community. Leadership too often depends upon newspaper coverage. Black communities do not receive the deference tribes receive, because they are agencies in the private arena and not quasi-governmental. Law and order is something imposed brutally from without, not a housekeeping function of the group.

Above all, Indian people have the possibility of total withdrawal from American society because of their special legal status. They can, when necessary, return to a recognized homeland where time is static and the world becomes a psychic unity again.

To survive, blacks must have a homeland where they can withdraw, drop the facade of integration, and be themselves. Whites are inevitably torn because they have no roots, they do not understand the past, and they have already mortgaged their future. Unless they can renew their psychic selves and achieve a sense of historical participation as a people they will be unable to survive.

Already the cracks are showing. The berserk sniper characterizes the dilemma of the white man. Government by selective assassination is already well established as the true elective process.

All groups must come to understand themselves as their situation defines them and not as other groups see them. By accepting ourselves and defining the values within which we can be most comfortable we can find peace. In essence, we must all create social isolates which have economic bases that support creative and innovative efforts to customize values we need.

Myths must be re-examined and clarified. Where they are detrimental, sharp and necessary distinctions must be made. The fear of the unknown must be eliminated. The white mythologizes the racial minorities because of his lack of knowledge of them. These myths then create barriers for communication between the various segments of society.

What the white cannot understand he destroys lest it prove harmful. What the Indian cannot understand he withdraws from. But the black tries everything and fears nothing. He is therefore at liberty to build or destroy both what he knows and what he does not know or understand.

The red and the black must not be fooled either by themselves, by each other, or by the white man. The black has moved in a circle from *Plessy v. Ferguson*, where Separate but Equal was affirmed, to *Brown v. the Board of Education*, where it was denied by the Supreme Court, to Birmingham, Washington, Selma, and the tragedies of Memphis and Los Angeles. Now, Separate but Equal has become a battle cry of the black activists.

It makes a great deal of difference who carries this cry into battle. Is it the cry of a dying amalgam of European immigrants who are plagued by the European past? Or is it the lusty cry of a new culture impatient to be born?

The American Indian meditates on these things and waits for their solution. People fool themselves when they visualize a great coalition of the minority groups to pressure Congress for additional programs and rights. Indians will not work within an ideological basis which is foreign to them. Any cooperative movement must come to terms with tribalism in the Indian context before it will gain Indian support.

The future, therefore, as between the red, white, and black, will depend primarily upon whether white and black begin to understand Indian nationalism. Once having left the wild animal status, Indians will not revert to their old position on the totem pole. Hopefully black militancy will return to nationalistic philosophies which relate to the ongoing conception of the tribe as a nation extending in time and occupying space. If such is possible within the black community, it may be possible to bring the problems of minority groups into a more realistic focus and possible solution in the years ahead.

section THREE

Radical Knowledge

"He that will not apply new
remedies must expect new evils."
—Francis Bacon

"Nothing in education is so
astonishing as the amount of
ignorance it accumulates in the
form of inert facts."
—Henry Brooks Adams

chapter 8

Science and Technology

Two revolutions in the last century made possible a vastly different life style for millions of people. Each revolution fired the other to greater heights and deeper valleys of human existence. One of the radical changes was the industrial revolution; the other was the knowledge revolution. Although historians may argue over which preceded the other, the obvious point is that the mutual dependence of rapidly increasing technological innovation and the speed of knowledge incrementation in science has compounded the impact of present civilization on individuals.

Scientific discoveries relating to properties and propensities of fuels have permitted fantastic technological developments from steam engines to space exploration. Equipment produced by improved technology has provided the means for expanded scientific exploration. As each has opened new avenues for the other, the revolutions have spurted forward. Mankind's harvest from this two-pronged explosion range from slavery under mechanical monsters to freedom from toil, illness, and despair.

Chemical research has produced insecticides, fertilizers, and detergents to increase food production and convenience. Pollution of field, stream, and air by the products of chemists and technicians has not improved life. Technical advances in communications offer instant information as well as untold advantages for propagandizing. Physicists have perfected laser beams for medical use and for instant death on battlefields. Computers, the technological marvel of the last decade, make research faster and easier, while offering rich opportunities for governmental surveillance of otherwise private lives. Space exploration enhances scientist, technician, and nationalist as urban areas crumble from lack of fiscal interest. Advances in science and technology are often matched by declines in human life styles.

The impact of science and technology on human institutions which utilize knowledge is remarkable. An earlier statement that a knowledge revolution had occurred illustrates the influence of science. The revolution has changed the concept of knowledge from essentially humanistic to essentially scientific. Knowledge in earlier times represented general philosophies, ideas about man, explanations of the supernatural, and broad-based beliefs about the proper order of the universe. In all of these areas a strong moral value component directed searches for truth. Scientific exploration during the past century has increasingly become analytic, searching to explain universes in terms of their tiniest parts, and non-value, looking for objective truths regardless of consequences. The two cultures of science and humanities described by C. P. Snow do exist.

Scientific concepts of knowledge influence the social sciences and the humanities, causing each to develop notions of objectivity and analysis. The proliferation of social-scientific studies of minute detail and presumed objectivity is a product of this concept of knowledge. Analytic philosophy, mathematical models of language and history, and computer art are humanities examples, although scientific knowledge has not penetrated the humanities as deeply as it has the social sciences. Accommodations between humanistic and scientific knowledge are now being proposed by scholars who see that neither extreme is adequate in itself. In any case, the knowledge revolution has been science-dominated.

The growth of science and technology has outdistanced man's ability to fully comprehend and manage the phenomena. The time lag between society's adoption of a technical achievement and the perception of its advantages and disadvantages is often considerable. This time lag creates social disorganization and personal alienation in industrial societies. Much of the radicalism expressed represents anxieties about the proper relations of science, technology, and human values.

Education as a producer, organizer, and consumer of scientific and humanistic knowledge is directly involved in any adjustments in the definition of knowledge. The learned temples of graduate schools and research institutes govern the nature of worthy knowledge and the paths to its discovery. Radical concepts of knowledge are not likely to originate in this established environment because prestige, promotion, and security tend to favor utilization of existing models for knowledge. The historic openness of higher education institutions, however, does permit some latitude for dramatic changes in these models, though it tends to come from younger, more radical scholars who pose revisionist interpretations. At least the growth of radical knowledge models depends on acceptability in the halls of academe. Humanistic, scientific, mathematic, and eclectic models have been nurtured in small seminars and low readership journals. Those that gain favor are exported to undergraduate, secondary, and elementary education by a long process of filtration.

Elementary and secondary schools tend to follow the dominant concepts of knowledge by a period known as educational lag. Discoveries occur at one point in time, are translated into useful knowledge at another point, assimilated by the forward thinkers of the society after a period of cultural lag, and adopted by the schools as gospel after educational lag. This means that schools are typically well behind current research and scholarship. The benefits of this phenomenon are stability and time-testedness. The disadvantages are a loss of currency and a lack of vitality. This chapter provides differing vantage points for analyzing present concepts of knowledge.

Technocracy and the Counter Culture

Theodore Roszak

The development of advanced technology and its cohort, the sys-
temized society, has produced the mixed blessings of a potential
technocracy. This technological surge, capable of vast relief of
human suffering, brings the sterile atmosphere so aptly described by
George Orwell in *1984* and Aldous Huxley in *Brave New World*.
Technocracy assumes the superiority of experts and specialists who
can make the giant machine operate. The role of education in a
technocracy is obvious.

    Theodore Roszak, an historian who has some skepticism about
the historiography of periods, has described the counter-culture
as a radical minority group resisting the infusion of technocracy.
He states that technological development transcends political and
economic boundaries of capitalism and collectivism. It can, therefore, not be ascribed to right-wing or left-wing ideologies. In the
following piece, the preface to Roszak's book, he poses the new
confrontation of technocracy and its alternatives.

As a subject of study, the counter culture with which this book deals
possesses all the liabilities which a decent sense of intellectual caution
would persuade one to avoid like the plague. I have colleagues in
the academy who have come within an ace of convincing me that no
such things as "The Romantic Movement" or "The Renaissance" ever
existed—not if one gets down to scrutinizing the microscopic phenomena of history. At that level, one tends only to see many different
people doing many different things and thinking many different
thoughts. How much more vulnerable such broad-gauged categoriza-
tions become when they are meant to corral elements of the stormy

contemporary scene and hold them steady for comment! And yet that elusive conception called "the spirit of the times" continues to nag at the mind and demand recognition, since it seems to be the only way available in which one can make even provisional sense of the world one lives in. It would surely be convenient if these perversely ecto-plasmic *Zeitgeists* were card-carrying movements, with a headquar-ters, an executive board, and a file of official manifestoes. But of course they aren't. One is therefore forced to take hold of them with a certain trepidation, allowing exceptions to slip through the sieve of one's generalizations in great numbers, but hoping always that more that is solid and valuable will finally remain behind than filters away.

All this is by way of admitting openly that much of what is said here regarding our contemporary youth culture is subject to any num-ber of qualifications. It strikes me as obvious beyond dispute that the interests of our college-age and adolescent young in the psychology of alienation, oriental mysticism, psychedelic drugs, and communitarian experiments comprise a cultural constellation that radically diverges from values and assumptions that have been in the mainstream of our society at least since the Scientific Revolution of the seventeenth century. But I am quite aware that this constellation has much matur-ing to do before its priorities fall into place and before any well-developed social cohesion grows up around it.

At this point, the counter culture I speak of embraces only a strict minority of the young and a handful of their adult mentors. It excludes our more conservative young, for whom a bit less Social Security and a bit more of that old-time religion (plus more police on the beat) would be sufficient to make the Great Society a thing of beauty. It excludes our more liberal youth, for whom the alpha and omega of politics is no doubt still that Kennedy style. It excludes the scattering of old-line Marxist youth groups whose members, like their fathers before them, continue to tend the ashes of the proletarian revolution, watching for a spark to leap forth. More importantly, it excludes in large measure the militant black young, whose political project has become so narrowly defined in ethnic terms that, despite its urgency, it has become for the time being as culturally old-fash-ioned as the nationalist mythopoesis of the nineteenth century. In any event, the situation of black youth requires such special treatment as would run to book length in its own right.

If there is any justification for such exceptions in a discussion of youth, it must be that the counter cultural young are significant enough both in numbers and in critical force to merit independent attention. But from my own point of view, the counter culture, far more than merely "meriting" attention, desperately requires it, since I am at a loss to know where, besides among these dissenting young people and their heirs of the next few generations, the radical discontent and innovation can be found that might transform this disoriented civilization of ours into something a human being can identify as home. They are the matrix in which an alternative, but still excessively fragile future is taking shape. Granted that alternative comes dressed in a garish motley, its costume borrowed from many and exotic sources—from depth psychiatry, from the mellowed remnants of left-wing ideology, from the oriental religions, from Romantic *Weltschmerz*, from anarchist social theory, from Dada and American Indian lore, and, I suppose, the perennial wisdom. Still it looks to me like all we have to hold against the final consolidation of a technocratic totalitarianism in which we shall find ourselves ingeniously adapted to an existence wholly estranged from everything that has ever made the life of man an interesting adventure.

If the resistance of the counter culture fails, I think there will be nothing in store for us but what anti-utopians like Huxley and Orwell have forecast—though I have no doubt that these dismal despotisms will be far more stable and effective than their prophets have foreseen. For they will be equipped with techniques of inner-manipulation as unobtrusively fine as gossamer. Above all, the capacity of our emerging technocratic paradise to denature the imagination by appropriating to itself the whole meaning of Reason, Reality, Progress, and Knowledge will render it impossible for men to give any name to their bothersomely unfulfilled potentialities but that of madness. And for such madness, humanitarian therapies will be generously provided.

There may be many readers for whom the issues raised in this book will seem meaningless as gibberish. It is not easy to question the thoroughly sensible, thoroughly well-intentioned, but nevertheless reductive humanism with which the technocracy surrounds itself without seeming to speak a dead and discredited language. Especially so if one admits—as I do (*pace* the doctrinaire eschatology of old and new left)—that it may well lie within the capability of the technocracy to utilize its industrial prowess, its social engineering, its sheer affluence, and its well-developed diversionary tactics, to reduce, in ways that most people will find perfectly acceptable, all the tensions born of disorganization, privation, and injustice which currently unsettle our lives. (Note that I do not say it will *solve* the problems; but rather, like adjustive psychotherapy, it will cunningly soothe the neurotic hurt.) The technocracy is not simply a power structure wielding vast material influence; it is the expression of a grand cultural imperative, a veritable mystique that is deeply endorsed by the populace. It is therefore a capacious sponge able to soak up prodigious quantities of discontent and agitation, often well before they look like anything but amusing eccentricities or uncalled-for aberrations. The question therefore arises: "If the technocracy in its grand procession through history is indeed pursuing to the satisfaction of so many such universally ratified values as The Quest for Truth, The Conquest of Nature, The Abundant Society, The Creative Leisure, The Well-Adjusted Life, why not settle back and enjoy the trip?"

The answer is, I guess, that I find myself unable to see anything at the end of the road we are following with such self-assured momentum but Samuel Beckett's two sad tramps forever waiting under that wilted tree for their lives to begin. Except that I think the tree isn't even going to be real, but a plastic counterfeit. In fact, even the tramps may turn out to be automatons . . . though of course there will be great, programmed grins on their faces.

A Marxist View of Science and Technology

World Marxist Review—Editorial

Although Roszak's book, *The Making of a Counter Culture*, argues that technology is neither capitalistic nor collectivistic, each ideology uses the issues raised by science and technology for political gain. The competition over which nation produced a specific scientific invention is widely covered in the media. The race for space exploration as a display of which social system is superior is another example.

Scientific conferences are as commonplace as international crises. The exploitation of science, technology, and education by political and economic ideology is evident in this report of a scientific meeting.

Reprinted by permission of the publisher, *World Marxist Review*, December 1969.

This article argues that socialist educational systems are not afflicted by crises related to the production of technically-educated people, while capitalistic countries have continuing peril. This presupposes a form of educational engineering that has not been palatable to many Americans. Our approach has been one of shortages producing higher salaries and subsidized educational programs as enticements. Some argue that we have overproduced technically proficient people now and are starting to suffer the crisis of insufficient employment. It appears to be an example of engineers designing their own obsolescence.

An effect of the scientific and technological revolution, the closer interaction between science and technology is making a deep impact on man's way of life and the destiny of social classes, countries, and mankind generally. Not surprisingly, therefore, this was the theme of a symposium held under the auspices of the World Federation of Scientific Workers last September in Bratislava, Czechoslovakia.*

Some 60 scientists attended the symposium from all continents, submitting more than 40 papers and communications on subjects ranging from the computer systems in research and technology (by S. Lavrov, Corresponding Member, USSR Academy of Sciences) to the history of science in particular countries.

Despite the diversity of professional, philosophical and political viewpoints represented, the symposium reflected *the growing common concern of scientists for the social problems arising from the expanding interaction of science and technology*, and it is this particular aspect that we have chosen to examine here.

WHY THE "DOUBLE FACE" OF SCIENCE AND TECHNOLOGY?

For years the forced pace of scientific and technological progress has been evoking a strange mixture of both optimistic and pessimistic forecasts about man's future. There arose the notion, for example, that technico-scientific growth has two faces—a benign one and one contorted in a tragic grimace. Apart from the desired effects, the invasion of the many spheres of life by science and technology has yielded some undesirable consequences, perils, difficulties and apparently insoluble problems. One cause of this is gnoseological,

* The World Federation of Scientific Workers was founded in London in 1946. Its first President was Frederic Joliot-Curie. The Federation has affiliated organizations in 27 countries and corresponding members in another 26. Professor Pierre Biquard, of France, is Secretary General.

stemming from the limited knowledge of the scientist or engineer, for it is difficult, sometimes impossible, to anticipate the long-term consequences of technico-scientific innovations, consequences which make themselves felt years, maybe generations, later. Technical systems, while introducing harmony and lessening the entropy in one sphere or relationship, create disharmony and greater entropy in others, adding to the complexity of foreseeing the long-term effects on man's somatic and psychic faculties.

The main cause, however, is purely social. Not all speakers, it is true, were able to probe it with equal insight. Hilary Rose and G. Oliver, two young Britons, denounced the militarist orientation in technico-scientific development, but, in our view, abstracted themselves from the social realities in placing the blame for the flagrant abuses solely on "bureaucrats" and "technocrats." Admittedly, Hilary Rose made the point, and rightly so, that "pure economism," the urge for an "end of ideology," the "escape" to the realm of irrational emotion, which facilitates application of scientific achievement to man's detriment, were inept and dangerous. Architect Oliver spoke of the inhumanity of the technical solutions of vital social problems that did not reckon with man's daily needs, casting him as a passive observer.

The causes of the many pernicious effects of technico-scientific advance in Japan were examined by Professor Shobei Shiota, who pointed out that industrial production in his country had increased by 245 per cent between 1958 and 1967 and that today Japan's gross national income ranks second in the capitalist world as a result of the application of science and technology. The concomitant, he added, was that the public hazards of technical growth were greatest in his country. Pollution of air and water, noise and vibration, and the so-called "traffic warfare" were a new blight and, above all, for the poorer sections of the population. In the industrial areas of Osaka and Yokkaichi, for example, sufferers from chronic bronchitis are twice, even three times, more numerous than elsewhere, and the medical profession attests that air pollution is the most likely indirect cause of pulmonary emphysema and lung cancer. The "logic of enterprise" presents lethal dangers, causing industrial injuries and poisoning with harmful industrial waste. Professor Shiota pinpointed the main reason why the serious social problems, the hazards to health and life, are so acute in present-day Japan. The culprit: *monopoly capital, which, in its profit-seeking, rapaciously exploits the country's land, resources, science and technology.* The victims are the workers, farmers and other wage-earners, their "suffering amid prosperity" aggravated by the political, economic and military dependence on U.S. imperialism.

A deep-going study of the interaction of science and technology was made by Professor Juergen Kuczynski of the German Democratic Republic, who stressed the importance of social science for the growth of the productive forces and the relations of production. The continuous and harmonious development of social science, he said, responding to the objective needs of the times, is possible only through a faithful and consistent utilization of Marxism. Elucidating the trends in industry and society and materializing under the leadership of the working class in socialist production relations, Marxist science assures the optimum scope for a benign growth of technology and the natural sciences.

The "Engineer's Oath"—Will It Help?

The symposium applauded with understanding and sympathy a short film showing Engineer M. W. Thring's ingenious inventions to help the housewife and the handicapped, to relieve man of many difficult, dangerous and unpleasant operations.

Thring suggested that all qualified engineers should take a Hippocratic oath to apply their skills only to projects that contribute to the coexistence of all human beings in peace and human dignity. "I vow," says the oath suggested by Thring, "to struggle through my work to minimize the danger and strain to individuals, pollution of earth, air or water, destruction of natural beauty, wild life and natural resources, noise and invasion of privacy." Thring classified the machines designed to satisfy the needs of a "creative society," which he contrasted with the "affluent society" ruled by acquisitiveness and the urge "to keep up with the Joneses."

Scientists, Thring said, should acknowledge their guilt for the harm and hazards to which man is exposed these days. Yet he rejected political action to combat the abuses. The only effective way, he held, was to appeal to the decency, the code of morals of the present-day science and technology, to public opinion, to the humanist solidarity of scientists and engineers.

While accepting the importance of decency and humanism, many speakers described Thring's approach as obviously insufficient. Not because, as Hilary Rose deplored, too few scientists today prefer to be burned at the stake rather than renounce the truth. The key is mainly in the socio-class structure of the modern world, in which the historically outdated exploiter is ready to go to all lengths, not short of starting a nuclear world war, for the sake of his dividends.

The scientist and technician can make technico-scientific progress serve the needs of mankind to the fullest extent only in alliance with all other working people, primarily, the working class, declared A. Gaegle, representing the French General Union of Administrative Workers and Engineers. To deliver science and technology from dangerous anti-humanistic tendencies, said Professor W. Hoffman, Federal Germany, scientists must fight against the rule of military-industrial complexes, for the liberation of the progressive classes, the working sections of society, from the power of monopoly capital.

Will the "Science Critic" Help?

Science journalist Maurice Goldsmith, director of the London School of Science Foundation, submitted the case for the "science critic."

Referring in particular to the political and scientific scene in Britain, he maintained that neither politicians nor scientists have an overall grasp of the state and significance of modern science. Nor can they acquire that grasp, Goldsmith said, until the "science critic" appears in their midst as an "integrator" of the various branches of knowledge, dispensing competent advice to the government and thereby assuring a competent science policy. Popular science, he said, was out of date and should give way to a "public understanding of science and public appreciation of the impact of science." He assigned to the "science critic" the job of interpreting the social significance of science to the non-scientist, so that "people understand its poetry and cease to be afraid of it."

Goldsmith's is a peculiar concept of the professional middleman between science, politics and society. Though excellently reasoned and, in a way, original, it does not appear sound, for it is not aimed at producing the basic social conditions for the elaboration of a genuine science policy, but merely at improving a professional division of labor that presumes the immutability of society's division into a political and scientific elite, on the one hand, and a mass of "uninitiated," on the other. That Goldsmith is perturbed at the technocratic trends and warns against the peril of a "technological fascism" does not, objectively, make his conception any the less narrow.

Taking issue with the idea of replacing popular-science writing with "science critics," Dr. S. Lilley, of Nottingham University, said: what we need is not so much the "science critic," but that whole generations become critics of science.

Could Goldsmith's "science critic" exercise a substantial influence on the scientific and technical knowledge of the public at large or, for that matter, on government policy under a social system based on the private interests of those who own the means of production?

Effective and truly scientific criticism of social development is practicable only by an organized movement of the working people, led by the working class, the basic interests of which coincide with the objective requirements of scientific, technical and social progress.

The Crisis in Education

Sustained growth of science and technology requires a rapid growth of scientific and technical personnel. The increasing shortage of this personnel and *the crisis in higher education* was examined with deep concern by speakers from the developed capitalist countries and Third World countries. In some countries, they noted, young people are visibly less interested in scientific and technical disciplines. Universities experience a dearth of competent instructors. The blame, among other things, lies with the deficiencies in primary and secondary education—the shortage of schools, the outdated textbooks, the low salaries and skills of teachers. Prof. Humberto Barrera, Chile, noted that even rough estimates place the proportion of adult illiterates in Latin America at over 30 per cent, with sixty and even eighty per cent in the case of some countries. Prof. Samir K. Thabet, Lebanon, observed that in his country, one of the most enlightened in the Middle East, curricula were, until 1969, modelled on old French programs, dating to 1927. In most universities in the Arab countries, he added, the student-to-teacher ratio is 200:1.

Some developed capitalist countries try to eliminate the personnel shortage by draining off brains from other countries, among others also from developing countries, doing the latter untold harm. However, "importing" scientists is not a dependable source of technico-scientific progress. An instructive example, taken by Dr. Lilley from the history of British organic chemistry, shows that at one time Britain's synthetic-dyes industry availed itself extensively of the "brain drain" method, employing German chemists, who, however, returned promptly when favorable prospects were offered them in their homeland, leaving Britain for some years without even one professor of organic chemistry.

To combat the crisis in education, progressive instructors and public leaders in some capitalist countries are campaigning for more allocations and searching for new models. Hilary Rose referred briefly to the attempts in her country to establish "free universities," to join which young people pass no entrance examinations nor present education certificates. However, these and other similar measures will not remove the contradictions between the objective needs of technico-scientific development and the limited possibilities of the social system in which higher education is still very much the privilege of definite social strata. And it is in this contradiction that is rooted the crisis in education, aggravated by modern technico-scientific growth.

Scientific socialism alone removes the element of social privilege from education. In the socialist countries, Professor Lavrov pointed out, the exploitation of man by man has been eliminated, creating thereby the main social prerequisite for unrestricted growth of education for all.

The advance made in higher education in the Polish People's Republic was the theme of Dr. Przeciszewski's paper. In 1963–64, Poland surpassed France, Italy and Japan, treading close on the heels of the United States, for the number of graduates of technical, agricultural and medical higher educational establishments per 10,000 population.

The German Democratic Republic has outstripped higher education in West Germany in many important aspects. The same progress is being made also by the other socialist countries. To be sure, this does not mean that the educational system in socialist society is not in need of improvement. Professor I. Altenbach, for example, devoted his contribution to the third higher school reform in the GDR, aimed at substantially improving education and integrating it in the social system of developed socialism. Academician Ishlinsky (USSR) spoke of the training of science personnel in the USSR, where instruction and training is closely combined with research.

The socialist educational system is not afflicted by crisis. It is a dependable source of talent for the growth of science and technology, a fact borne out by the increasing technico-scientific potential and the visibly higher educational and cultural level of the working people in the socialist countries.

Many interesting ideas were expressed at the Bratislava symposium about the intrinsic laws regulating the development of the fundamental and technical sciences, international cooperation of scientists and engineers and the state and future of technico-scientific progress in Third World countries. Many of the problems posed have still to be solved, both in theory and practice. Yet despite the diversity of attitudes and opinions, the tenor of the symposium centered on *the responsibility of scientists and engineers for the social consequences of the interaction of science and technology* in the modern world. It stimulated the search for, and definition of, this responsibility.

Intellectual Property

Fidel Castro

One concept of knowledge that has had widespread agreement is
that it represents power. The nation which has superior scientific
know-how has capacities to inflict its will on others. A group that
knows how to manipulate financial transactions can affect sizable
portions of the economy. An individual who knows the means of
demagogic expression and persuasion can control populations.

This concept of knowledge as power carries an implication
for knowledge as property. The ability to control the discovery or
communication of knowledge is one way of maintaining power. A
corollary is that the individual who produces knowledge should be
able to protect that property. A second corollary is that the property
which has potentials for improving the human condition belongs
not to any individual or nation, but to mankind. Fidel Castro presents a view on intellectual property which is radically different
from that found in the legal framework of America.

The following is an excerpt from Fidel Castro's May Day 1967 speech
to the scholarship students of the Guane-Mantua region of Cuba. In
this address Fidel emphasized that the basis of the socialist conception
of work is cooperation, as opposed to individual competition and gain
in capitalist society. As part of the policy of cooperation, Fidel set forth
his government's attitude toward copyright laws.

Radio, television, movies, the press, magazines, apparently we do not
know how to use them as efficiently as we could, just as we previously
didn't know how to utilize practically anything else as efficiently as we
could.

But, fortunately, we have been learning in these years, and
therefore we are beginning to understand how to do things better.
And we also hope that in the area of providing information to the
people we are also learning and are going to improve.

Reprinted from *CAW!* (an SDS publication), February 1968.

So many things! Speaking of any one of these deficiencies recalls something we were able to prove in the mountains of Oriente not long ago. That was that with all the publishing houses we have in this country, with all the workers who work in these publishing houses, with all the paper that they use, not one single book had been published in this country for the farmers. And you went into a store in the mountains and found books on philosophy. This does not in any way mean that philosophy is something to be underestimated, but those farmers were not about to study matters of deep philosophy. They were interested in books on agriculture, books on mechanization, books on a whole series of subjects. One day I asked a man in charge of a store what kind of books he had and which ones were sold. The answer was: "Well, we have a lot of books by Marx and Angel." "Marx and Angel? Ah, I see, Marx and Engels."

So there were books on political philosophy, books of every kind, and we asked ourselves: "What are these books doing here?" And the problem was simply that no books were printed in this country for our farmers. Nor for our students either, for that matter.

Fortunately, this is now practically a thing of the past and for quite some time now all the books our students needed have been printed and a Book Institute has been organized that is doing a great deal of printing, taking full advantage of the abundant human resources and machinery we have at hand in the printing field. And perhaps we shall also learn to make better use of our paper.

At times, millions of copies of certain works were printed only to be submitted—as Marx would say—to the devastating criticism of moths and mice—since there was no demand for them and they were simply stored.

Should it surprise us then that many of the things accomplished by our people today are not publicized, when not even many of the great accomplishments of humanity were publicized, when even elementary matters of agricultural technology were not made available to our agricultural workers and farmers and technical matters were not brought before our students nor did our students have text books?

Of course, the solution was not an easy one. It became necessary to make a decision that we considered revolutionary. There exists a thing known as "intellectual property." In these matters of property we are increasingly less experienced. In the past, everything was "property, property and more property." No other concept was better known, more publicized or more sacred than that of private property. Everything was private. Possibly the ground on which you are now sitting was once very "private." The houses, the land, the mountains, the sky, the sea, everything was private—even the sea, the seas surrounding Cuba, because every vessel that crossed those seas was a private vessel.

Well, these are all becoming things of the past. Our entire new generation is becoming more and more familiar with a different concept of property and is beginning to look upon all those things as goods of general use and as goods that belong to the whole of society. The air, it is true, could not be said to be private, for the simple reason that there was no way to get hold of all of it and enclose it in a carafe. Had it been feasible, the air would have been taken over in the same way that the landgrabbers took over the land. But better the air in their control than food. Air was available to everyone, because it could not be bottled up, but food was not available to all because the land that produced it was not in the hands of the people.

Among all of the other things that were appropriated, there was one, very "sui generis," called intellectual property. You will say: but that is abstract property. Yes, it is abstract property. And strangely enough, air could not be bottled up, yet, nevertheless, something as abstract as intellectual property could be shut up in a kind of bottle.

What do we mean by intellectual property? It is well enough understood. But, in case anyone is not familiar with it, it is, simply, the property of anything that emanates from the intelligence of individuals, of a group of individuals—a book, for example; any book of a technical nature or a novel.

I want to make it quite clear—because I do not want to earn the enmity of the intellectuals; in the first place, because it would be unjustified enmity—that this should by no means be taken as disregard for the merit, the value, even the right to survive of those who produce this type of spiritual goods. Very well. But, what happens? Those property rights over intellectual possessions—following custom, following a system that prevailed in the world until very recently, following the influence of the whole capitalist concept of society—those intellectual possessions were subject to purchase and sale.

And, naturally, some—and, in general, many—of the creative intellects were badly paid; many have gone hungry. Anyone who reads, for example, the biography of Balzac, who was one of the great novelists of the last century, must be moved by the poverty in which that good man lived. In general, many of the great creative geniuses have gone hungry because they had no backing. Many products of the intellect have been highly valued years after the death of their authors. Many men whose works have gained fame and immortality later, were completely ignored while they lived.

Persons producing works of intellect have generally lived in poverty. They have lacked the support of society and have often had to sell their intellectual productions at any price.

And in what circumstances, in what conditions, did we find ourselves? We were an underdeveloped country, completely lacking in technical knowledge; a country lacking technology and technicians; a country that had to begin by taking on the task of teaching one million citizens to read and write; a country that had to begin establishing technical schools, technological institutes, schools of all kinds from primary to university level; a country that had to undertake the training of tens of thousands, of hundreds of thousands of skilled workers and technicians in order to emerge from poverty and underdevelopment; a country that had to make up the centuries of backwardness that burdened us. When a country like ours sets itself the task of recovering all that lost time, when it proposes to create better living conditions for the people, when it proposes to overcome poverty and underdevelopment, it must then invest every cent, a large part of its limited resources, in construction, in purchasing means of production, factories, equipment. At the same time that we had to make countless investments, we were faced with difficulties in educating the people.

Why? Because as our citizens learned to read and write, as all children began to attend school, as the number of sixth grade graduates topped the 50,000 mark and reached 60,000, 70,000, and 80,000, as more students entered the technological institutes and the universities, and as we aspired to defeat underdevelopment and ignorance, we needed an ever-increasing number of books. And books were—and are—very costly.

Because of the existing copyright concepts, we found that, in order to satisfy the demand for books, we had to spend tens of millions of pesos on their purchase, often paying for them most dearly. But in practice it is very difficult to determine exactly what is copyright; copyright belonged no longer to the authors but to those who had paid hard cash on the market for these products of the intellect, at any price, generally a low one. Those who exercised a monopoly over books had the right to sell them at the price they deemed suitable. We had to arrive at a decision, a defiant one, indeed, but a fair one. Our country, in fact, decided to disallow copyrights.

What does this mean? We feel that technical knowledge ought to be the patrimony of all mankind. To our way of thinking, whatever is created by man's intelligence ought to be the patrimony of all men.

Who pays royalties to Cervantes and to Shakespeare? Who pays the inventors of the alphabet; who pays the inventors of numbers, arithmetic, mathematics? In one way or another, all of mankind has benefited from, and made use of, those creations of the intellect that man has forged throughout history. When the first primitive man took a stick in his hands to knock down a piece of fruit from a tree, mankind began to benefit from a creation of the intelligence: when the first human being emitted a grunt that was the precursor of a future language, mankind began to make use of that product of man's intelligence.

That is, all, or rather the vast majority of man's creations have been amassed throughout thousands of years. And all mankind feels entitled to enjoy those creations of the intellect; everyone feels entitled to enjoy all that past generations have produced in other periods of history. How is it possible today to deny man, hundreds of thousands of human beings—no, not hundreds of thousands, but hundreds of millions and thousands of millions of human beings, who live in poverty, in underdevelopment, to deny the access to technology to those thousands of millions of human beings who need it for something as elemental as feeding themselves, something as elemental as living?

Naturally, to adopt such a decision generally involves incurring the enmity of those whose interests are affected. Often copyrights are ignored, and it is done secretly, surreptitiously, without admitting it. We are not going to adopt that procedure. We state that we consider all technical knowledge the heritage of all mankind and especially of those peoples that have been exploited. Because where is there hunger, underdevelopment, ignorance, a lack of technical knowledge? Right there, in all those regions of the world where men were criminally exploited for centuries by colonialism and imperialism.

Technical books are generally printed in developed countries. And then the poor countries, the countries that have been exploited for centuries, have virtually no access to that technical knowledge, when for centuries they have been stripped of many of the resources with which, equipped with modern technology, they could have been developed.

In the United States there are many thousands of technical books. We have begun by announcing an end to intellectual copyrights on all technical books from the United States. And we state our unequivocal right to reprint all U.S. technical books that we feel will be useful to us.

It is clear that we don't have to offer any excuses to justify this. We feel justified in printing U.S. technical books, entitled to this, at least in compensation for the harm they have tried to do this country. Well, then, we will bypass copyright in relation to the United States; but we, independent of those circumstances, consider as a right of our people—of all the underdeveloped peoples—the use of all technical knowledge that is available throughout the world, and we therefore consider ourselves entitled to print any book of a technical nature that we need for our development, that we need in the training of our technicians.

And what will we give in exchange? We feel it a duty of society to help, to stimulate. We feel it a duty of society to protect all intellectual creators. I don't mean protect them; perhaps that is not the correct concept. We feel that our intellectual creators must take their place in society with all the rights of outstanding workers.

Cuba can and is willing to compensate all its intellectual creators; but, at the same time, it renounces—renounces internationally —all the copyrights that it is entitled to.

Not many technical books are published in this country, but, for example, we have produced a great deal of music that is enjoyed all over the world.

And in the future, in all intellectual fields, our people will produce more and more. As of now, we announce our renunciation of all copyrights relating to our intellectual property and, with Cuban intellectual producers protected by the Cuban government, our country renounces all its copyrights relating to intellectual property. That is, our books may be reprinted freely in any part of the world, while we, on the other hand, assume the right to do the same. If all countries did the same, humanity would be the beneficiary.

However, this is utopian. It is impossible to think that a capitalist country would do this. But if all countries did exactly the same, in exchange for the books that each country created, for the books published, or rather written in a given country, that country, by renouncing its copyrights to those books, could acquire the rights to the books written in every other country of the world.

Naturally, we cannot assume that this will happen. But, for our part, we can state that this will be our stand on the problem of copyrights. And we believe that it is correct to state this frankly, no matter who may be discomfited.

We can, naturally, come to mutually convenient agreements with any country, they sending us their books published in large editions, and we sending them our books published in large editions. Any type of exchange of already published books, any type of agreement of this sort, we can do perfectly well, meeting the convenience of any country. But this will be the policy that we shall follow. We shall do the same with what are called "patents." We, for our part, it is true, have not yet invented great things or many things, and it is not a matter of our planning to become inventors, but any gadget that we do invent will be at the disposal of all humanity, as well as any success in the technical field, any success in the agricultural field.

And it should be said that we have high hopes in these fields. Yes, we expect to have considerable success. It will not be long before many people in many parts of the world will have to turn their eyes toward what we are doing here, to see how this country, situated in a tropical zone, solves many of the agricultural problems still unsolved in other tropical countries of the world. Because, above all, poverty has been mainly confined to the tropical countries; there are practically no tropical countries in the so-called developed areas of the world. And we, beyond any possibility of doubt, will be in the vanguard of agriculture among the tropical zones of the world and our solutions, our techniques, will be available to all who care to learn from them.

It is known, for example, that our Institute of Sugar Cane Investigations is carrying on research to obtain new and improved cane varieties. Very well: each time that we obtain a new variety of cane, we, a cane-producing country, will put this knowledge at the disposal of every other cane-producing country interested in that variety. We shall not stoop to weak and miserly egoism.

No! We shall not concern ourselves with questions of competition.

If in the poultry sector, for example, we develop a variety of fowl that lays more eggs than another or produces more meat than another, this knowledge will be placed at the disposal of all other peoples. If with the massive programs we are carrying out in livestock genetics, we obtain superior specimens, new breeds of animals or, within existing breeds varieties with singular characteristics, this knowledge will be placed at the disposal of all who need it, and even the means to acquire these specimens—by artificial insemination or by any other method. This holds true for any field of agriculture. We shall not concern ourselves with questions of competition.

Because the concept of competition belongs to a world of hunger, because competition belongs to an underdeveloped world, because competition belongs to a world where hunger and poverty have become institutions. Because, what is competition, after all; it is that fight among producers of one same product for a limited market. When competition appears, the fight appears, too; it is not the fight to feed all the needy, but the fight to feed those who are able to buy. In our country there were surpluses of many products, because production was geared not to needs, but to the market. People without a penny in their pockets didn't count. There could be surpluses of coffee, milk, meat and citrus fruits: anything, because how were people without money going to buy?

And in the midst of the job scarcities, in the midst of chaos, anarchy and limitations of a capitalist economy, there could be surpluses of anything; because there was a greater surplus of unemployed than of goods, a surplus of those without either a penny in their pockets or the means to earn one, and who, consequently, didn't count. Hundreds of millions of people in this world live in poverty and suffer malnutrition.

This idea of competition will have to disappear in tomorrow's world. Because, just as our people produce today not for the market but for their needs—that is, domestically, we attempt to produce what is necessary and not what can be sold—in tomorrow's world all nations will have to work on that same basis.

This, of course, can only happen when colonialism and imperialism have disappeared from the face of the earth. And we know that there are needs to be filled in this world, that there will always be a need for whatever we produce, and that someone will always produce the things that we need. Therefore, the advantages from our agricultural development; therefore, our thrust towards mass application of technology in the gigantic development of our plans for different branches of production, so that our production may both fill our needs and meet demands abroad. We know that all we produce will always be useful to someone else, and that other countries can do likewise: produce things that are useful to us. But, beginning with the domestic market, we will produce everything we need, as much milk as we need, and the day that we have more than enough milk we will not begin to throw it away. What have many capitalist countries been doing in the last decades? There is a surplus of coffee, they burn coffee; they have a surplus of other products and they burn them and throw them away, and the restrictions . . . We do not suffer from these ills. If we have a surplus of milk one day we will ask ourselves what the average consumption is and we will either lower the price or we will give the milk away free.

chapter 9

The Arts

Artists, whether expressing ideas in stone, oil, print, or voice, appear to maintain an individuality that transcends both establishment systems and revolutionary movements. There are obvious exceptions like painters whose patrons exert control over that they paint, writers who extol the virtues of the present conditions because they are afraid to lose privilege or reward, and architects who design for the market and commissions rather than for themselves. The general public view of artists, however, is that they are permitted virtually total freedom to express their individual ideas and to be as radical as they wish. Western society assumes that artists are peculiar, but desirable people to retain so long as they do not seek power. As Dwight MacDonald has noted, the mass culture dotes on the artistic temperament to the point of nearly smothering the artist with requests for public displays of avant-gardism. This tolerance, not complete but certainly extensive in America, has given artists the opportunity to produce radically different works in both message and media. It has also kept artists out of the mainstream of decision-making in society. The artistic reputation for anarchy in self-determination has left them alienated from social decisions and revolutionary leadership.

Many artists engage in political radicalism and many protect the values of the status quo, but seldom is an artist seen as a political or economic leader. Artists are not considered for places on major commissions dealing with social issues. Artists as a group are not easily identified by political ideologies or labeled as anything but eccentrics. They tend, as radicals, to be individuals and not affiliated with mass movements. They tend, as moderates, to be suppliers of the mass culture with limited access to power. An artist as a radical is presumably rebelling against a tradition which prides itself on individuality and latitude of expression. The social revolutionary, on the other hand, rebels against a tradition of compromise, group think, and massive apathy. It is sometimes difficult, then, to blend art with general revolutionary movements.

The artist and his works are usually tolerated but largely ignored. There appears to be little fear of the power of art to persuade large numbers of people toward radical causes. Art can and does shock the public and anger groups, but it is not normally seen as a part of a social movement. Nudism on the stage may produce repressive censorship and be decried by some as a symptom of moral decay, but rarely is it considered a major thrust of a threatening radicalism. There are political movements, however, which use art and artists as ploys in their campaigns. Nationalistic art and charges of contra-nationalistic forms of artistic expression are examples of this. The arts can be powerful as revolutionary tools, but often the artist is enveloped by the society and his impact is muffled. Schools and museums are good institutions to act as mufflers for the moderates in society.

Art, as it is typically taught in the schools, loses its social impact. Art classes are separate from those dealing with social issues. Art works are used selectively in history and literature studies to illustrate the period, not the divergent ideas. Art is taught for appreciation or for skill but not as a form of social protest and dialogue. Schools tend to view art and artists as devoid of social content and comment.

Nationalism vs. Pimp Art

LeRoi Jones

Artistic expression and nationalism are seldom considered to be
synonymous, but there are periods and places where the artist
expresses the national will and where nationalism determines artistic
expression. LeRoi Jones, the playwright, discusses black nationalism and its relation to black culture, white culture, and revolutionary
art.

Education, a cultural as well as national institution, has a
stake in both aspects of Jones' thesis. Schools have begun to
emphasize black studies as a result of the civil rights and black
militant movements. Readings in Chapters 2 and 8 indicate the
failings and responsibilities of education in adequately and accurately presenting ethnic studies. Jones, an articulate spokesman for
black separatism, presents an analysis of black nationalism and its
relation to art forms. Schools have been instruments of nationaliza-
tion using white models for citizenship. Nationalistic education is
being modified to include ethnic group history, literature, and arts,
but not to foster multi-nationalism. Disparities in the views of those
who see the school as a melting pot institution based on premises
of national unity and those who see it as a means for enriching
ethnic diversity and pluralism create a continuing battleground.

New talk of Black Art reemerged in America around 1964. It was the
Nationalist consciousness reawakened in Black people. The sense of
identity, and with that opening, a real sense of purpose and direction.
The sense of who and what we were and what we had to do.

We began to understand with the most precise consciousness
that we were beings of a particular race and culture, whatever our
experience. And that finally if we were to be saved we must be saved

totally, as a race, because the death battle raging around and through us was an actual death struggle between two cultures.

Warfare between that which generates and signifies life and that which is death. As a confusing adjunct to this real war minces "ThE reVolUTioN" within white society, to make Allen Ginsberg and/or Fulton Sheen comfortable with John Bull's grandson. And that is, will happen. (If you don't have on red, white and blue bellbottoms you must be neckit!)

And all of the above can get in on the vague, integrated, plastic, homosexual "reVolUTioN" . . . a conglomeration of words, degeneracy, and fake pseudo "act." But for Black people it was (is) critical that we begin to focus on National Liberation, which is what we always meant when we were conscious, National Liberation, the freeing of one nation (culture) from the domination of another.

This was the truth we felt and found, and this is the path we still pursue. Malcolm said (to us) "if you love revolution, you love Black Nationalism." And this consciousness is coming into strong fruition, this legacy of, and movement through, nationalism. Fanon added, "the concept of nation and culture are inseparable. If you talk about nation you talk about culture." The ways and means of a people, how they live, and what they remember of that life. Their value system. Not merely singing and dancing, or wearing dashikis, though all life function is to some extent part of a creative motif. Whether war or cornbread. It is a creation of some sensibility. It issues out of some value system. The largest sensibility we deal with now is the national sensibility. *To free the nation is at the same time to free the culture, i.e., the way of life of* . . .

The largest creation, the most exacting manifestation of Euro-American (white) creative motif is, right now, Viet Nam. An Absurd White-Comedy. The Ethos (characteristic life-style) of Euro-America is death, about death, and/or dead, or the worship of. Beckett is the prize winner cause he tell about it so cool.

But Nationalism was the move away from this death and degeneracy. To draw away from the dead body, and its spirit. (As Toure says, "decolonialization is not only to get rid of the colonizer, but his spirit as well.") Black Art was first the restoration of LIFE and the restoration of HOPE, that all of the humans would survive the reign of the beasts. But we learned that we could only survive by evolving a different value system from the beast value system. Whether social or aesthetic, they are exactly the same. The films of Warhol, when they are about anything are about sucking people off. (They are exact replicas of American Sensibility.) This can be high art, to people who are interested in sucking people off. But that will not liberate Black people. Campbell's soup cans will not. Some more materialism, if you can dig it, the worship of *things* . . . sacred to a nation, indicative of that nation's spirit . . . an artificial commodity.

The Art is The National Spirit. That manifestation of it. Black Art must be the Nationalist's vision given more form and feeling, as a raiser to cut away what is not central to National Liberation. To show that which is. As a humanistic expression Black Art is a raiser, as a spiritual expression it is itself raised. And these are the poles, out of which we create, to raise, or as raised.

The great deluge of nakedness and homosexuality, is a "revolution" within the Euro-Am meaning world. The great dope "revolution." All these will change the mores of Euro-Am, they already have. That "revolution" will succeed. But it is not the revolution we spoke of. Though the energy unleashed by our own Black swiftness serves to power the jr. cracker's cry of "reVolUTioN." (Witness SDS blackfist minstrel show. Or Rock.) But the Nationalist does not confuse this marxbros type changeover, from old to young white boy, not a regeneration but simply a change of generation in degeneration . . . the Nationalist does not confuse this with National Liberation. So the hand grows shakier. We "support" the white revolutoin of dope and nakedness because it weakens the hand that holds the chain that binds Black people. But we must not confuse the cry of young white boys to be in charge of the pseudo destruction of America (with a leisure made possible by the same colonialism) with our own necessity. Just because the slavemaster has long hair and smokes bush does nothing to change the fact that he is and will be the slave master until we, yes, *free ourselves*.

And just as the young white boy could pick up "reVolUTioN" and apply it to his desires, so could some Negroes uncommitted to Nationalism, so emotionally committed to their masters were they, be harnessed as showcase "Black Artists" whose real function was the perpetuation of white cultural imperialism in quaint black face, even funnier, like rag time, in white face over black face over Negro Skin over White Mind. That's heavy ain't it? And where we said Black Art, Negroes with grants were set-up in Soul Food Thea-tuhs to hustle ears, and nostrils, and plenty of I's, in place of the righteous food of the Spirit. Skin was (is) hustled as content. The content was, like Eddie Albee, pizen. The content, was (is) like National Football League Quarterbacks, white.

Black Art is the change of content to the survival of a race and culture, as itself. It is John Coltrane not Mantan Moreland disguised as Lawrence Welk disguised as Mantan Moreland, The Elder

Ward of the White State who long ago convinced himself he was Flash Gordone.

In Black Ritual Art, it is Bullins, and Milner, and Garrett, and Marvin X, Yusef Iman, Rob Penny, Furaha, Katibu, Yusef Rahman, Damu, Mchochezi, and Hilary, Barbara Teer, National Black Theater, early Boissiere, Norman Jordan and innumerable young brothers and sisters in Black communications satellites all over the planet.

If the artist is the raised consciousness, and this is what the Black Artist strives to be, the raised consciousness of a people. Precise. Specific. From the particular to the general to the universal to the cosmic, and on back to the single instance of love in the west market street barber shop. (But the Black Man is an artist when he realizes the profundity of his specific placement in the world and seeks to render it into intelligibility to make it meaningful by describing it with his life. There is no such thing as Art and Politics, there is only life, and its many registrations.) If the artist is the raised consciousness then all that he touches, all that impinges on his consciousness, must be raised. We must be the will of the race toward evolution. We must demand the spiritual by being the spiritual. THE LARGEST WORK OF ART IS THE WORLD ITSELF. The potential is unlimited. The consciousness of men themselves must be raised. The creation of Cities. Of Institutions. Governments. Treaties. Ceremonies. Public Rituals of The Actual World. The Nation. These are the only things worthy of the true Black Artist's consciousness. The Recreation of the Actual World. Garvey the artist. Malcolm the artist. Toure the artist. Nyerere the artist. Karenga the artist. &c. In order for the creations of the idea world to be valid they must speak as Karenga says Collectively, Functionally, and Committedly. That is Black Art must be Collective, i.e., the spirit of the whole Nation. It must be Functional, it must have a function in the world to Black people. It must also Commit Black people to the struggle for National Liberation.

But just as robot kneegrows, lustful winduptoys, created by massa in response to the power of Black Nationalism, mack around the pseudo "liberated zones" of America being black, as Weldon Smith says, "for a quick f——", in for instance literature, theater, graphics, &c., so there are these same pimps, like the dream fulfillment numbers of panting whiteladies who feared the peeholes would dry up under the sudden late SNCC, late Malcolm decamp of young Black people from out the various villages, Haight-Ashburys, &c, existing in the main area of "the movement" itself.

Frankly the Panthers, no matter the great amounts of sincere but purposefully misled brothers, getting shotup because some nigger was emotionally committed to white people, are extreme examples of PimpArt gone mad. It is a spooky world when the Negro Ensemble Theater and The Black Panther Party (post Huey) can both suddenly exist as large manipulative symbols of white power and white ideology.

Around the time of Malcolm's death, a Nationalistic spirit moved Black people. There was a sense of Umoja (Unity) that seemed to band us all together against the devil. But with the incarceration of Huey, and the move by Cleaver into the chief strategist's seat, the Panthers turned left on Nationalism, and turned left on Black people. And the love of Beverly Axelrod has left terrible Marx on the dirty Lenin Black people have been given by some dudes with some dead 1930's white ideology as a freedom suit. Instead of ol' swishy Bayard Rustin now we gets violent integrationists. Wow!

So the blunt negativism and plain out whiteness of PimpArt, which would kill us for wanting freedom. Which will show itself on the stage. Or show itself weekend weekout in the streets, by misguided dudes who think by saying "Pick Up The Gun," that the devil will wither up and die, or just by picking up that literal gun, without training, using the same sick value system of the degenerate slavemaster, the same dope, the same liquor, the same dying hippy mentality, that they will liberate all the slave peoples of the world. NO.

It will be a Black Ideology of Change, as perhaps an aggregate of world information, that will free us. Lenin, Marx and Trotsky, or O'Neill, Beckett, and the Marat-Sade dude, are just the names of some more "great white men," there are other dudes who will give you other lists like Washington, Jefferson, Adams, or Paul McCartney, Cream, Grateful Dead, or Mozart, Pinky Lee and the fag with the health tv show. They are just lists of white people.

I can learn from anybody and anything. I could learn something from a pile of Nixon under a stoop. But I will not confuse my identity with its. This is the Nationalist's position. We must survive (and this is the only way we *will* survive) as a nation, as a culture. We are against the "depersonalization of African Culture" (to quote Toure again). But we must understand that Black as Karenga says is Color (race), Culture, and Consciousness. And Black Art, and any movement for National Liberation, must be all three, if they are to be legitimate.

We know we are Black race, we can look at ourselves, tho I guess there are still dudes who really want to be something other than Black . . . I think I read about some dude who thought he was an Indian, which would really be weird, like a white mind in a blood's head with an Indian mask on. Can you dig it? That Black is easy, the racial one. The second Black is the culture. Surely you know the difference between John Coltrane and Lawrence Welk. Or DaVinci and Benin. Or myself in my green vine coming around the corner and Robert Lowell. Or between James Brown and Big Brother or Mozart's Mother. Its some difrunce man. I know you know. The attitude that is the culture. Simply, the way people live. The way they bees, feeling. The conglomerate concretization of their feelings, as religion, politics, history, social organization, economic organization, creative motif, and ethos—how they doos it.

Black as consciousness, is the knowledge that we are Black by race and Black by culture, and that we must benefit Black by living, if our life is to have positive meaning. Brother JB is a good example. When he sang "America," he was still Black as color, the song was an example of Afro-American culture, an R&B song for sure, but it did not have the consciousness of Black, so it could not be called Black. To sing lies about America is not beneficial to the Black Nation, therefore it is not conscious of Blackness. It is white manipulation, like a Cocacola commercial on a soul station. Colored Form, and like PimpArt, white content.

So the neo leftist bloods confusing the struggle, they are colored by form but with white content. Dignifying a deathmotion that had been laid to rest many of us thought, only to see it rise Bela Lugosi style to suck some negroes' blood.

But the rationale is always just a plastic transparent nutout suit to cover the old commitment to whiteness. To white ideas and to white meat. Most of these negroes who will call Nationalists racists just feel a draft because they are sleeping white. Racism is a theory, as life motif, of why something is inferior, check out Herodotus and The Teutonic Origins theory of White first, with the rest of life sloping off xenophobically down the scale to bad us. We are not racists, when we accuse white people it is based on still observable phenomena. No theories. We did not make up colonialism, slavery, slumdeath and murder to justify Nationalism. We are not Nationalists because of the devil. We would be Nationalists if there were no devil.

Surrealism and the Revolution

Franklin Rosemont

That artists have fired the imaginations of patriots and insurgents
is beyond question. Every American schoolchild has seen the famous
painting of the "Boston Massacre," and most have inferred (incor-
rectly) that it really was a massacre and actually happened as
painted. There are numerous other examples, but they are examples
using realism in art. Soviet artists portray strong workingmen creating the new society, and WPA painters during the depression
provided similar murals for the United States.

Surrealism in art, however, has been considered decadent,
amoral, and evil but not popularly seen as a part of a political
movement. Franklin Rosemont writes of this problem for surrealists
and their role in the social revolution. The possibilities of surrealism
in education—building design, teaching materials, and curriculum
and human interaction—are mind-boggling.

Imagine a school designed by Salvador Dali, most popular of
the surrealists. The building might have walls on only one side, and
they would be distorted in perspective, giving the impression of
great length stretching beyond visual comprehension. Of course, the
school clock would droop languidly over one edge of the roof and
run down the side of the wall. Classrooms might have wire-strung
partitions of varying heights and a blowing sheer curtain that blurs
vision out a window. Instead of George Washington's portrait by
the principal's office, one would find a three-dimensional skeleton
embellished with ornaments. The educational thrust of the school
would be to fire the creative spirit of children by uniting the dream
world and the physical world. The present rational base for education would be replaced by a passionate, sensual base.

Rosemont, a regional editor for *Radical America*, wrote this
editorial to pose the relation of art to society.

Reprinted by permission of the publisher, *Radical America*, January
1970.

Forty-five years after the appearance of the first *Surrealist Manifesto*, the revolutionary aims and principles of surrealism remain almost completely misunderstood in the English-speaking world. It would require easily a thousand pages to merely catalogue, as succinctly as possible, the distortions, mis-statements, obfuscations, derisions and lies directed against the surrealist movement since 1924. Again and again we are told, for example, that surealism is only an artistic and literary movement; or that it is exclusively French; or that it somehow "disappeared" as a movement during the second World War. Critics of the most varied and seemingly incompatible persuasions have formed a veritable holy alliance to exorcise the surrealist spectre, openly avowing their common unrelenting opposition to this essentially new and disquieting menace.

But surrealism knows well the reasons why it must be attacked. The bourgeois protagonists of "art-for-art's-sake" (including its recent incarnations under the names Pop, Op, Minimal Art, etc.) despise the surrealist movement because of its solidarity with the cause of proletarian revolution, its adherence to the principles of marxism-leninism. Thus too the priest Montague Summers, who tries to convince us that "God is the only Reality," is insulted by the "intimacy . . . between surrealism and communism," and judges surrealism guilty of "crass materialism," of being "unmystical" and "unromantic," and of denying the supernatural. Sarte and Camus, while climbing the ladder of literary and philosophical success, also found it auspicious to fulminate against the surrealist insurrection: their invertebrate polemics against André Breton are classics of incomprehension and calumniation. Stalinists, for their part, pretend to see in surrealism only decadence, "idealism" and even mysticism, doubtless because the surrealists have never succumbed to the bureaucratic superficiality of so-called "socialist" realism. The liberal humanist Herbert Muller absurdly reduces surrealism to a "glorification of the irrational, the unconscious," and accordingly manages to read into it similarities with —of all things—fascism. Renegades from surrealism such as S. Dali (better known as Avida Dollars), P. Waldberg, Marcel Jean and J.-J. Lebel also add their mediocre resources to this rampant idiocy. Finally, even Theodor W. Adorno, whose indisputable intellectual qualifications would have led us to expect greater accuracy in this regard, permitted himself to write that "it is doubtful if any of the surrealists ever read Hegel"—a statement which, considering the obvious and immense influence the author of the *Phenomenology* and the *Logic* began to exert on the surrealists as early as the late 1920s, must be counted as plainly and demonstrably false. (The example of Adorno suffices to indicate how the consensus of confusion is reinforced and perpetuated by the casual errors and misinformed ignorance of genuinely intelligent thinkers.)

Surrealism itself arises here and now to challenge and destroy the lying insinuations leveled against it, as well as to combat the overwhelming lack of reliable information which has hitherto confined the subject to a few academic specialists and columnists for the Sunday supplements. This surrealist intervention, raising its voice in the English language, intends to correct the stultifying procession of misconceptions not only by elementary critical techniques of clarification and polemic, but above all by exemplary manifestations of the ineluctable spirit of surrealist adventure, discovery and revelation.

Let us make clear at the very beginning that it is the fundamental aim of the surrealist movement to diminish and ultimately to dispose of completely the appalling contradictions between dream and waking life, desire and reality, the unconscious and the conscious; to "transform the world" (in the words of Marx), to "change life" (in the words of Rimbaud), to create a society of freedom and exaltation, of "poetry made by all," according to Lautréamont's unparalleled watchword. Let us also make clear, to dispel in advance certain misunderstandings, that surrealism fully recognizes that the liberation of the mind requires thoroughgoing social liberation (that is, the emancipation of the working class) and consequently situates itself unhesitatingly "in the service of the Revolution."

Doubtless, however, many serious revolutionaries will approach this surrealist compilation with considerable misgivings, expecting to find here nothing more than a new fashion following in the dismal wake of existentialism, happenings, psychedelics, "post-scarcity" anarchism, McLuhanism, rock 'n' roll mysticism, pop astrology and other essentially theological distractions of a hysterical middle class entering a new period of capitalist crisis. A radical activist might well ask what it is, precisely, that surrealism brings to the revolutionary movement; in what way, with what weapons, does it strengthen the cause of proletarian emancipation? Such questions are, in themselves, entirely legitimate. But they are too often asked of us with an attitude of egocentric arrogance which only too clearly reveals an underlying bad faith. Let me emphasize, meanwhile, that we do not claim for ourselves any "artistic" privileges: we contribute to the best of our abilities to current political struggles and are prepared at any and all times to act decisively on the side of the proletariat, even to take up arms, to serve in the Red Army in order to destroy once and for all the loathesome reign of the bourgeoisie. But as surrealists our essential contribution to the revolutionary cause lies elsewhere, and it would constitute for us an act of intellectual and moral evasion to pretend otherwise.

The reader will find [in *Radical America*] sufficient evidence of this surrealist contribution. But this traces, above all, only the initial steps of the surrealist project. In the long run, especially here in the United States, surrealism has the power to decisively dethrone and guillotine the ignoble traditions of positivism-pragmatism-rationalism-humanism which for a century and a half, at least, have stifled the development of revolutionary thought in this country. Rest assured that we will perform this ideological regicide with a smile upon our lips, in homage to Saint-Just, to Nat Turner, to Lenin, to Durruti, to Che Guevara, to their admirable, inestimable severity which is also the severity of the true practice of poetry.

The texts collected are not presented with the customary anthological justifications. Least of all should one expect to find a complete exposition of the surrealist point of view, or any sort of "finished" compilation: surrealist dynamism automatically precludes such pretensions. There is occasion to insist, in fact, on the essentially prefactory (as opposed to conclusive) character of the material. Surrealism is a movement defiantly not shut up in tight definition. [There is] a wide selection of theoretical, critical, poetic and pictorial manifestations of surrealism, mostly dating from the post-war period to serve not only as an antidote to the academic and journalistic propaganda against surrealism, but primarily as an introduction, an initiation, to certain fundamental surrealist principles and preoccupations, as well as to its methods of intervention in various domains of inquiry.

The prefactory character of [the writings] will soon reveal itself in another and more immediate sense, for the present preliminary act of clarification is intended above all to clear the ground for a specifically surrealist journal in the English language. In closest collaboration and solidarity with the international surrealist movement (with comrades in France, Holland, Czechoslovakia, Cuba, Belgium, Portugal, Brazil, Argentina, England, etc.) this journal, to be called ARSENAL: SURREALIST SUBVERSION—the first issue of which is now in preparation—will demonstrate with ruthless incandescence that surrealists today, more than ever, assume the position of "specialists in revolt."

For the cause of freedom remains the brightest star in the eye of man, source of our most ardent hope and focus of the realization of our most splendorous and inexhaustible dreams. Armed with its impassioned dialectic, with Maldoror's six-bladed American knife, surrealism spares no effort in its perpetual unfettering of the human imagination, releasing the most far-reaching and daring forces of inspiration into the theory and practice of total revolution.

Radical Ideas through Science Fiction

Arthur Maglin

The imaginary world with its romantic appeal perhaps plays a
heavy role in the development of radical thought. At least radical
ideas can gain expression through imaginative writing. Arthur Maglin separates science fiction from fantasy and writes of the relationships between radicalism and science fiction. Maglin's thesis of
revolutionary writing in science fiction provides an interesting means
of examining radical writings as these relate to educational practice.

Schools teach selective literature in English courses. Selections
are based on a variety of circumstances: the teacher's knowledge,
the age and interests of students, the availability of materials, the
policies of the district, and the risk-taking stature of those making
selections. Teachers who have had the traditional literature education may be unaware of or disposed against different literary
forms, like science fiction. Students, especially girls who have been
led to believe it is unfeminine, may lack interest in science. Antho-
logies purchased for school use and required by teachers may not
include socially-oriented material. School boards, administrators,
and teachers may regulate against provocative reading material.
And a high level of risk-taking in controversial areas is not a hall-
mark of schoolteachers. These factors tend to keep volatile literature
in politics, race, sex, religion, drugs, economics, and general morality out of the hands of students. Censorship by edict of boards or
tacit agreement of teachers prevents literature deemed radical from
being discussed, while *Silas Marner,* expurgated Mark Twain works,
and Louisa May Alcott's most innocuous stories are well taught.
Radical ideas have gotten into school via Shakespeare, Chaucer,
and Aldous Huxley, but often the social relevance is not discussed.

Science fiction is obviously not a necessary ingredient in literature courses, but social issue literature is surely needed in these
classes.

Reprinted by permission of the publisher, *Radical America,* July/August
1969.

However fantastic art may be, it cannot have at its disposal any other material except that which is given to it by the world of three dimensions and by the narrower world of class society. Even when the artist creates heaven and hell, he merely transforms the experience of his own life into his phantasmagorias, almost to the point of his landlady's unpaid bill.
—Leon Trotsky, *Literature and Revolution*

In an epoch when the continued world rule of the bourgeois order is meeting serious challenges everywhere, a genre of literature has arisen whose most general cultural characteristic is the promotion of speculation about the future of mankind. It should be no surprise that this particular mode of literary expression is either viewed with suspicion or held in contempt by the comfortable literati of the bourgeois academies and journals. That genre, of course, is modern science fiction.

When the subject of science fiction is brought up, the normal reaction of those imbued with the prejudices propagated by means of the bourgeois press and educational structures is to dismiss the whole thing as childish nonsense. There have been exceptions made for such works as George Orwell's *1984* or Aldous Huxley's *Brave New World* or Evgenii Zamyatin's *We*, all of which are readily classified as literature and all of which just happen, also, to bolster the hysterical cold war mentality. Nevertheless, the exceptions are explained as somehow not really science fiction. It is a case of what happens to art in the world of today: new genres are at first ignored, then resisted, and finally the attempt is made to co-opt them. Science fiction finds itself in the anomalous position of being resisted in the main and co-opted where possible. But co-optation presents difficulties since all speculation about the future need not include the continued existence of United States capitalism.

Neocapitalist ideology has only the smallest, ever-tightening margin of room for the expression of great hopes, great dreams, great visions of the future, great goals. In short, it has only the most constricted tolerance for the exercise of the imagination, especially for an enterprise that limits itself to *realistic* extrapolation.

What Science Fiction Is

Science fiction can be considered a sub-category of the broader category of imaginative or speculative fiction, including fantasy as well. Science fiction is not fantasy. It is important to make the distinction between these two branches of imaginative fiction because they have decidedly different functions as literature. Science fiction grapples with and is limited to dealing with materialistic extrapolation from the present to future possibilities, whereas fantasy makes no pretense at reality. The distinguishing mark of fantasy is the assumption within the story of supernaturalistic premises.

Science fiction, unlike fantasy, promotes a social enterprise that inevitably involves a realistic speculation about the future of mankind. It raises questions on the order of: Is the type of society being depicted really possible? Is it better or worse than the one we've got? Is social progress possible?

Moreover, science fiction, again unlike fantasy, encourages an awareness of environmental change and motion. It points out the transitoriness of our present environment, including its political and social along with its scientific and technological aspects. Significantly, the almost universal treatment of racism in the literature of science fiction is in the mode of a passing reflection on the nearly incomprehensible or dimly remembered primitive ways of the past.

Fantasy promotes neither realistic speculation about the future of mankind nor an awareness of the transitoriness of the present. It deals with magic, witchcraft, supernatural entities, life after death and similar subjects in the vein of mysticism. What has been said about fantasy should not be taken to mean that fantasy can never have a social significance. On the contrary, fantasy may or may not have a direct social content just as any other form of literature, as for instance in Poul Anderson's novel *Operation Changeling* (serialized in the May and June 1969 issues of *The Magazine of Fantasy and Science Fiction*). Anderson depicts a make-believe world very similar to our own in all ways except that by and large the laws of magic operate in the place of the laws of physics. Using this context of purest fantasy, Anderson presents us with a reactionary satire on the radical movement (which in the end we learn is the work of the Devil).

In science fiction an obviously exaggerated or unlikely future development is often depicted for the purpose of satirizing or making a direct comment on the present. William Tenn has proven to be especially good at this sort of thing. His short story, "Eastward Ho!" for example, is a direct attack on the racist anti-Indian mythology portrayed in the mass media and the general run of textbooks. Tenn constructs a future situation in which the Indian tribes regain the upper hand on the American continent and the vanishing white man is relentlessly driven from his traditional territories. Unlikely? Yes, but it is not intended to be convincing except as social satire in the vein of: How would you like it if it happened to you? Another Tenn story, "The Masculinist Revolt," projects a future in which the myths of male supremacy and female inferiority get out of hand to the point where women and men divide into masculinist and feminist political parties to contend for the presidency. Tenn expertly exploits all the ashamed male feelings of masculine inadequacy that accompany the propagation of the male supremacist myth, particularly the fear of female dominance. In any case, the future political struggles he depicts are unconvincing as real possibilities, but right to the point as satire.

HISTORY

Modern science fiction might best be called social science fiction and, as such, it can be conveniently dated as having a history dating no further back than 1938. Isaac Asimov separates the history of science fiction into four basic periods: (1) 1815–1926, (2) 1926–1938, (3) 1938–1945, and (4) 1945 to the present.[1] He terms the first era "primitive" because "although the concept of science fiction had been born, the economic basis for the support of science-fiction writers did not yet exist."[2] There was no such thing as a specialist literature in the nineteenth century. Mystery stories, for example, were written simply as fiction by authors who also wrote other types of fiction. Literary specialities are thus an outgrowth of the mass literacy and mass production techniques of the twentieth century.[3]

In 1926, Hugo Gersback founded the first magazine specializing in science fiction and three years later coined the term "science fiction" to describe its contents. Its birth as a "specialized" field was stamped by the fact that Gersback had made it a practice to include some fiction in the earlier factual magazines he had edited, such as *Modern Electrics* and *Science and Invention* and so built up an

[1] Isaac Asimov, "Social Science Fiction," in Reginald Bretnor (ed.), *Modern Science Fiction: Its Meaning and Future*, New York: Coward-McCann, Inc., 1953, p. 168.

[2] *Ibid.*

[3] Alleged pre-nineteenth century science fiction was not at the time it was written very clearly distinguished from fantasy in the minds of either writers or readers for the very good reason that the scientific foundation did not exist to make a voyage to the moon, for instance, any more realistic than a voyage to hell. This fact becomes evident when one reads of Cyrano de Bergerac's various contrivances for reaching the moon which included rising up by means of the evaporation of sacks of morning dew, on the one hand, and by means of something fairly closely resembling a ramjet, on the other. As far as de Bergerac was concerned, the various methods of locomotion were equally credible (or incredible), a conclusion inevitable on the basis of the scientific knowledge of his day. Before the nineteenth century no science fiction was written or could have been written. Asimov's arbitrary choice of 1815 will do as a convenient birthdate.

audience for fiction with a heavy technological bent. The fiction in these earlier magazines and in Gersback's pioneering *Amazing Stories* was overwhelmingly gadget shop stuff, very boring to anyone but the technically minded. Low-level Buck Rogers rock-em sock-em type adventure stories also grew up in this period first as a means of providing a story line for the gadget shop fiction and then as a more and more dominant element in its own right.

However, all this began to change about 1938 when John W. Campbell, Jr., became the editor of *Astounding Stories* magazine. The history of what Asimov has dubbed "social science fiction" can be dated from this year. Campbell began to promote the development of stories that brought the interaction of the characters with their social environments to the fore, which gave science fiction a more interesting, more relevant and more widely appealing role to play.

But it was not until the final phase of science fiction's development (1945 to the present) that it evinced the growing mass awareness of the relevance of the field prompted by the dropping of the atomic bomb on Hiroshima and by the H-bomb, sputnik, manned space flight, as well as automation and cybernetics. In this phase we have increasing amounts of the pablum-for-the-public expressions (or corruptions) of science fiction: monster movies, juvenile TV programs and unimaginative, sloppily written literature.

On the other hand, more and more writers can now support themselves by writing science fiction for a widening market of relatively discriminating readers. Given the quality of art under capitalism, this has led to an increase in the quantity of writing in the field. Writers of science fiction have generally been afflicted with the same problem that writers had in the last century—Charles Dickens, for instance—of being paid by the word. Like piece-work in any industry this has led to an increase in quantity at the expense of quality. With a wider market monetary rewards are greater. Consequently, writers can afford to take the necessary time to achieve higher levels of quality and are, at the same time, more or less forced to do so by the increased competition brought about by the greater financial returns available.

Nevertheless, the mechanics of the literary market have produced a rather anomalous situation for the science fiction genre in relation to literature as a whole. Damon Knight, in his book of critical essays on science fiction, *In Search of Wonder*, points out:

> Cramped and constricted as it is, the science fiction field is one of the best of the very few paying markets for a serious short story writer. The quality magazines publish a negligible quantity

of fiction; slick short stories are as polished and as interchange-able as lukewarm-water faucets; the pulps are gone; the little magazines pay only in prestige.[4]

Why Science Fiction Holds an Attraction for Radicals

Science fiction holds an undeniable attraction for many of those who are dissatisfied with their own time and place. It should not be surprising that a disproportionately high number of radicals are also science fiction enthusiasts. My personal estimate (conservative, I believe) is that at least 5–10% of all young radicals are relatively consistent readers of science fiction. It is, in any case, clear that more radicals proportionately read science fiction than the public generally does.

It is also true that, in one sense at least, science fiction is escapist literature. This is frequently considered the most damning charge levelled against it. Science fiction does provide a vicarious escape from the pressures and problems of capitalist society, including a relief from the unending tedium of its work and study routines. This is also true of every other type of fiction—one escapes the facts of one's own life by entering into the fictions about someone else's. Science fiction does add a unique element of its own to this process of temporary mental liberation: it projects the possibility of a social environment that is more exciting and which possibly provides more of a scope for the individual's creative initiatives.

Sometimes the escapist impulse, a necessary feature of alienated class societies, can be run into dead ends. Detective stories which glorify the shrewdness and moral qualities of policemen. Western stories which propagate racist myths about the American Indians, and orgy stories which revel in the mystical delights of sexuality to the exclusion of all other values are familiar examples of how escape can be channeled into conservative directions. Within the field of science the most frequent type of safe channeling is the space opera, a sort of Western in a space ship with only names and places changed. However, in its current phase science fiction presents a rather encouraging evolution. This may be why hippies as well as radicals are drawn to science fiction in large numbers. Both Kurt Vonnegut's *The Sirens of Titan* and Robert Heinlein's *Stranger in a Strange Land*

---

[4] Damon Knight, *In Search of Wonder: Essays on Modern Science Fiction*, Chicago: Advent Publishers, 1967, p. 116.

have had big vogues in hippy-type circles. (On the other hand, there has only been one novel in the science fiction vein by a hippy about hippies: Chester Anderson's very amusing *The Butterfly Kid*.)

In any case, the argument is frequently raised that modern science fiction is anti-utopian, that it presents us with no hope for a change for the better, that its picture of the future is gloomy and pessimistic, and that its message is that the present is at least better than the future is likely to be, so that you might as well count your blessings while you've got some. There is no doubt that science fiction frequently does present an outlook on the future that is shaped by the pessimism of bourgeois ideology. However, two factors must be taken into consideration.

First, despite the fact that capitalism or some other form of stratified society is generally depicted as the society of the future (and generally in an authoritarian form at that), one tendency in science fiction is to use this social background as the dramatic setting for revolution and an exaltation of the revolutionary. Not to be misleading, it must be readily admitted that most science fiction writers do not write convincingly about revolution. Their idea of a revolution is shaped by their ideological limitations and tends to be somewhat romantic or melodramatic in results.

Second, some of the best writers in the field have written utopian novels and these are among their most famous works. For example, *Stranger in a Strange Land*, by Robert Heinlein, projects an imminent victory at the end of the book of a world-wide communism of integrated personalities ("water brothers"); A.E. van Vogt depicts an operating communist system of sorts made up of men who have been selected out by a testing process from the ranks of mankind in *The World of Null-A*; Isaac Asimov's famous trilogy, *Foundation*, *Foundation and Empire*, and *Second Foundation*, tells the story of the building up of a humane and scientific galactic nation on the ruins of a crumbling empire; and Kurt Vonnegut, Jr., in his satirical novel, *The Sirens of Titan*, depicts the construction of a society where no man takes advantage of any other.

Two works by Cyril Kornbluth will serve to illustrate how the same author can hold contradictory viewpoints about the immediate future and the more distant future with the former being thoroughly reactionary and the latter being pro-socialist. To take the latter first, in *The Syndic*, Kornbluth outlines a working, socialistic society. Everything from economic security to matters of sexual morality and the family system has been moved onto a higher, non-oppressive plane. The novel is definitely utopian in the sense that it is a bit fanciful in its explanation of how this society was brought about; namely, that when the old society became too oppressive the gangster element rallied the masses against it. Thus, the title, which is a play on the words "syndicate" and "syndicalism." Syndic territory is loosely organized by a beneficent and paternalistic clique and the whole population are considered members of the Syndic rather than as citizens because the Syndic does not consider itself a government.

The Syndic was published in 1953. A few years later, Kornbluth wrote *Not This August*, which deals with the nearer future. Here, the United States is taken over and occupied by Soviet and Chinese Communist armies. The people are starved and oppressed. The Chinese are even more ruthless than the Russians. The active part of the plot concerns the hero's efforts to make contact with the underground opposition and the solution involves a missile-launching spaceship built in a secret cavern by a left-over U.S. government research project.

When Kornbluth can write outside the context of present day social realities he can write sympathetically of socialism of a sort. However, a race prejudice and fear of communism cause him to write reactionary stories about the nearer future. It is as much as we can expect. Greater consistency would have to come from radical writers, a scarce breed in the science fiction field.

Utopian and Anti-Utopian Fiction

It should not be assumed that utopian science fiction is necessarily progressive and anti-utopian science fiction necessarily reactionary. Things never work out quite so simply in any field of art. There are reactionary utopian novels, the primary exemplification of this category being Ayn Rand's *Atlas Shrugged*, which depicts a laissez-faire capitalist utopian community composed of a supposed natural elite—the people who allegedly are alone capable of making the decisions that make an economy work. This elite has withdrawn from society to their hidden mountain anti-commune (capitalune?) in protest against creeping socialism. Everything collapses in the United States when they withdraw and we are given to understand that if only the population throws the liberal socialist rascals out and throws itself gratefully on the mercy of the elite, then everything will go smoothly back to normal. Then the dollar sign will become the symbol of the new day for the nation as it already is back in the mountain hideout.

As ridiculous as Ayn Rand's plot outline is—and however one might wish that the capitalists would take her seriously and disappear—she and her numerous followers are dead serious about this unappealing view of society and its future.

There are also positive aspects to anti-utopian fiction from the radical standpoint. The alternatives to basic revolutionary social and political changes ought to be presented, for many of them are theoretically possible, and their presentation can serve as a warning. Jack London's anticipation of fascism in *The Iron Heel* is a novel of this type.

Both utopian and anti-utopian science fiction frequently displays an inadequate grasp of social dynamics. While this is by no means universally the case—Isaac Asimov is almost always an exception to this rule—it is especially unfortunate when one considers how frequently revolution figures as a plot element in science fiction. Still, the very concentration on the subject produces a certain general ferment that produces an occasional outstanding treatment of the subject of revolution. In anti-utopian novels, as Damon Knight points out:

> Revolution is a common theme, not to say a cliché, in stories of this type—so much so that I've often wondered when the FBI is going to get around to compiling an index of science fiction writers. It's very nearly unavoidable, simply because it's the most dramatic sociological process . . .[5]

Anti-utopias almost always remind one of analogously oppressive situations in the present. Sometimes this is the intent of the writer, sometimes not, but the factor is inevitably there. This by itself is not enough to be classified as radical literature in today's world because it is compatible with the anti-communist's desire for a pro-capitalist "revolution," i.e., counter-revolution, in the Soviet Union, China, Cuba, North Vietnam, etc. Nevertheless, it is also compatible with the desire of the revolutionary socialist for a social revolution in the West and a political revolution in the East. Most works are more compatible with the latter viewpoint since most of the future anti-utopias depicted are *capitalist* anti-utopias (just as most of the utopias are socialist utopias), differing from the present mainly by being more clearly authoritarian and oppressive.

Occasionally, there are science fiction novels which definitely lend themselves to the cold war outlook. Although it was not George Orwell's intention, *1984* is one of these. There are mitigating circumstances which allow us to excuse Orwell, of course. When he wrote *1984* in 1948, Stalin was still in power and Hitler was not long out of it. Orwell thought that the whole world was moving towards the type of totalitarianism these figures represented. As Isaac Deutscher has pointed out, "Orwell intended *1984* to be a warning. But the warning

---

[5] Knight, p. 167.

defeats itself because of its underlying boundless despair. Orwell saw totalitarianism as bringing history to a standstill."[6]

The Future Society

In an alienated society people inevitably keep thinking about and longing for the condition of human solidarity. John W. Campbell, Jr., explains how this often works itself out in science fiction:

> In ordinary fiction, the individual is still able to accept the common cultural background as being truth; in science fiction, we can discuss robots or Martians or fiftieth-century people. It's simply a method of ruling out the basic fixed judgments of modern cultural beliefs, scientific beliefs, and everything else.[7]

For one thing unalienated individuals and social systems can be made credible by the devices of science fiction. Non-human intelligent life, robots, and people in the more or less distant future are utilized to depict this sort of personality or society. In Keith Laumer's novel, *Retief's War*, for instance, the nonhuman inhabitants of the planet Quopp live within the framework of a kind of free-wheeling libertarian socialism. The principal problem of the plot is that of preventing counter-revolution instigated by a foreign imperialism in a healthy socialist society. The Quoppina relate to one another in an engagingly innocent and childlike manner. As humans the Quoppina would be difficult for most people to accept; as nonhumans there is no special difficulty in their believability.

Although the situation is improving, a rather sizable portion of the science fiction which gets into print is still not very good. The formula story of the space opera variety still has a weighty representation in what finally gets into print. And it sells, because alienated, frustrated individuals like to act out vicariously the violent triumphs of an all-conquering hero. Sometimes our hero is just shrewd and a good athlete (the Western), sometimes he is just shrewd (the mystery story), sometimes he is just a good athlete (the sports story), and sometimes he is shrewd, a good athlete and armed to the teeth (the space opera).

On the other hand, as I have tried to emphasize, science fiction can have a very rich and subtle content and can be very rewarding

---

[6] Isaac Deutscher, *Russia in Transition and Other Essays*, New York: Coward-McCann, Inc., 1957, p. 244.

[7] John W. Campbell, Jr., "The Place of Science Fiction," in Bretnor, *op. cit.*, pp. 14–15.

as literature. It can also express rather directly a specifically anti-capitalist content. Take Robert Silverberg's *Invaders From Earth*, published in 1958, which describes in convincing detail how a public relations firm is given the job of selling the people of Earth on the desirability of wiping out the first intelligent beings discovered within the Solar System for the profitable benefit of the Extraterrestrial Development and Exploration Corporation. Silverberg projects the realities of the present onto the possibilities of the future and in the process he has produced a work which is an effective indictment of imperialism and its paid apologists.

Science fiction, like any genre, has its superior works and its inferior. At its worst, science fiction can be dull, repetitious and unimaginative. At its best, it can be very much the opposite. In the last analysis, however, modern science fiction is a literary genre which—almost as a whole—reflects the transcience of the present society, the fact that change is in the air.

chapter 10

Social Science

The role of the social scientist in society has been an ambivalent one. He is drawn to the sources of power for intellectual investigation, while he is repelled by the baseness and corruption he uncovers. His training and personal inclinations tend to limit his entrance into the practical world of reality and his engagement directly in the political process. He is called upon for expert opinion but rarely involved in the nitty-gritty activities of social and political life. To the extent that the social scientist exhibits interests in the application of his knowledge, he is viewed with suspicion by both the masses and his colleagues. The masses distrust the social scientist as an intellectual, and the applied social scientist's work is denigrated by the theoretical social scientist. Historically, social intellectuals have helped pave the way for tyrants and have helped sustain them in office. On the other hand, social intellectuals have provided the theoretic underpinnings for social improvements and the political and economic means for putting them into effect. Intellectuals, whether in science, the arts, social science, or the humanities, are an indispensable factor in social change because they provide the ideological conceptualization for different, if not always better, societies.

The proper role of social scientists as intellectuals and social scientists as activists is a critical question. Those who insist that studies of society should be scientific, objective, dispassionate, and remote from the value problems of decision-makers need to share the responsibility for distortion and misuse of social-scientific knowledge at the hands of politicians, mass media, and special interest groups. At the same time, it may be argued that human brutalization and cynical manipulation of the worst sort have also been the products of social-scientific theorizing. Tyrannical dictatorships, mind manipulation, economic exploitation of whole classes of people, and racial genocide have all had social scientists as banner bearers.

The real problem for a society is to find ways to properly utilize the talents of social scientists without becoming subjected to social engineering on the one hand or personal conceits on the other. The most effective use of the abilities of men of reason continues to be a dilemma for governments everywhere. The growth of scientism during the last 250 years has brought about a major transformation in the relationships between scientists of many types and their governments. Science and social science have created a rationale as well as a mythology that has tended to make the public believers in the pervasive value of scientific thought and to ignore much of the anti-human result of scientific endeavors. As social science emulates physical science, there is considerable danger that social control will emulate control of the physical environment.

Another issue of contemporary society is that there is a widening gulf between social-scientific discoveries on the frontiers of knowledge and the common man's shallow awareness of social, economic, and moral choices available in the social system. It appears to be increasingly difficult for average citizens to sort out the dimensions of crucial social issues, examine them critically, obtain relevant information that is relatively untainted by propaganda, and effectively participate in decisions about those issues. It is often a blind choice, following from an assumption that elitist leaders, both intellectual and political, are genuinely pursuing the common good.

The public schools, for a variety of reasons, have refused to play a significant role in correcting this problem, although the schools are the most likely place to bridge the gap between social-scientific knowledge and public awareness of options and issues. Schools have generally chosen to avoid dealing with controversial issues in an open and straightforward way. The treatment of social issues is often seen merely as the means to feed more data into children or to expand the propaganda function of education. The promotion of conformity and passivity in schools turns them into factory-like enterprises designed to produce a standard citizen with stock answers and a disdain for critical thinking. Students are expected to become model consumers of the best and the worst dictates of the system.

The Case for Radical Change

Howard Zinn

Professor Zinn's article asks his university colleagues to reexamine the true objectives of knowledge and its use in a modern society filled with moral and social crises. He asks for concerned participation of academicians in seeking a direct application of their knowledge in the solution of some of our major social problems. He argues for an abandonment of disinterestedness and insularity, hoping it will be replaced by a greater and more basic humanistic interest and concern with the general society. He believes that this is imperatively required if the rapidly accelerated growth of knowledge is to have any real meaning for the modern world. The social sciences must free themselves from the crippling emulation of the physical sciences and realize in a more direct and honest manner that behavioral sciences, as many have argued, are essentially value-based and that practitioners should abandon their prostituted role for a more humane commitment and concern for brutalizing social conditions which are becoming more routine on a daily basis. Meaningful research in the areas of behavioral science should have as its basis values and ethics which will help to humanize and make relevant the uses of knowledge in a civilizing way. Professor Zinn asks his colleagues to devote their research, energies, and resulting knowledge toward changing the world in a positive way, not merely toward understanding it, cataloguing it, or advancing one's professional career through it. The role of the university and the role of accumulated knowledge is being challenged both by the faculty and the students alike in the search for new relevance and new meaning in a chaotic social period.

Zinn states that "Knowledge is a form of power," and submits that force is replaced as a power base in the rise of democracy. The replacement, according to Zinn, is by deception which he declares is synonymous with education. Whether in the university or the elementary school, the holding of secret knowledge by the

Reprinted by permission from *Saturday Review*, October 18, 1969, and the author. © 1969 Saturday Review, Inc.

teachers represents their power over students. If deception and education are the same in terms of maintaining a society which has defects it is unwilling to have examined, then the schools are guilty of more than mere hypocrisy. Zinn calls for a revolutionary change in education by attacking prevalent myths about scholarship and knowledge.

It is time that we scholars began to earn our keep in this world. Thanks to a gullible public, we have been honored, flattered, even paid, for producing the largest number of inconsequential studies in the history of civilization: tens of thousands of articles, books, monographs; millions of term papers; enough lectures to deafen the gods. Like politicians we have thrived on public innocence, with this difference: the politicians are paid for caring, when they really don't; we are paid for not caring, when we really do.

Occasionally, we emerge from the library stacks to sign a petition or deliver a speech, then return to produce even more of inconsequence. We are accustomed to keeping our social commitment extracurricular and our scholarly work safely neutral. We were the first to learn that awe and honor greet those who have flown off into space while people suffer on earth.

If this accusation seems harsh, read the titles of doctoral dissertations published in the past twenty years, and the pages of the leading scholarly journals for the same period, alongside the lists of war dead, the figures on per capita income in Latin America, the autobiography of Malcolm X. We publish while others perish.

The gap between the products of scholarly activity and the needs of a troubled world could be borne with some equanimity as long as the nation seemed to be solving its problems. And for most of our history, this seemed to be the case. We had a race question, but we "solved" it: by a war to end slavery, and by papering over the continued degradation of the black population with laws and rhetoric. Wealth was not distributed equitably, but the New Deal, and then war orders, kept that problem under control—or at least, out of sight. There was turmoil in the world, but we were always at the periphery; the European imperial powers did the nasty work, while we nibbled at the edges of their empires (except in Latin America where our firm control was disguised by a fatherly sounding Monroe Doctrine, and the pose of a Good Neighbor).

None of those solutions is working anymore. The Black Power revolt, the festering of cities beyond our control, the rebellion of students against the Vietnam war and the draft—all indicate that the United States has run out of time, space, and rhetoric. The liberal artifacts that represented our farthest reaches toward reform—the Fourteenth Amendment, New Deal welfare legislation, the U.N. Charter—are not enough. Revolutionary changes are required in social policy.

The trouble is, we don't know how to make such a revolution. There is no precedent for it in an advanced industrial society where power and wealth are highly concentrated in government, corporations, and the military, while the rest of us have pieces of that fragmented power political scientists are pleased to call "pluralism." We have voices, and even votes, but not the means—more crassly, the power—to turn either domestic or foreign policy in completely new directions.

That is why the knowledge industry (the universities, colleges, schools, representing directly $65-billion of the national spending each year) is so important. Knowledge is a form of power. True, force is the most direct form of power, and government has a monopoly on that (as Max Weber once pointed out). But in modern times, when social control rests on "the consent of the governed," force is kept in abeyance for emergencies, and everyday control is exercised by a set of rules, a fabric of values passed on from one generation to another by the priests and the teachers of the society. What we call the rise of democracy in the world means that force is replaced by deception (a blunt way of saying "education") as the chief method for keeping society as it is.

This makes knowledge important, because although it cannot confront force directly, it can counteract the deception that makes the government's force legitimate. And the knowledge industry, which directly reaches seven million young people in colleges and universities, thus becomes a vital and sensitive locus of power. That power can be used, as it was traditionally, to maintain the status quo, or (as is being demanded by the student rebels) to change it.

Those who command more obvious forms of power (political control and wealth) try also to commandeer knowledge. Industry entices some of the most agile minds for executive posts in business. Government lures others for more glamorous special jobs: physicists to work on H-bombs; biologists to work on what we might call, for want of a better name, the field of communicable disease; chemists to work on nerve gas (like that which killed 6,000 sheep in Utah); political scientists to work on counter-insurgency warfare; historians to sit in a room in the White House and wait for a phone call to let them know when history is being made so they may record it. And sometimes one's field doesn't matter. War is interdisciplinary.

Most knowledge is not directly bought, however. It can also

serve the purpose of social stability in another way—by being squandered on trivia. Thus, the university becomes a playpen in which the society invites its favored children to play—and gives them toys and prizes to keep them out of trouble. For instance, we might note an article in a leading journal of political science not long ago, dealing with the effects of *Hurricane Betsy* on the mayoralty election in New Orleans. Or, a team of social psychologists (armed with a fat government grant) may move right into the ghetto (surely the scholar is getting relevant here) and discover two important facts from its extensive, sophisticated research: that black people in the ghetto are poor, and that they have family difficulties.

I am touching a sensitive nerve in the academy now: am I trying to obliterate all scholarship except the immediately relevant? No, it is a matter of proportion. The erection of new skyscraper office buildings is not offensive in itself, but it becomes lamentable alongside the continued existence of ghetto slums. It was not wrong for the Association of Asian Studies at its last annual meeting to discuss some problems of the Ming Dynasty and a battery of similarly remote topics, but *no* session of the dozens at the meeting dealt with Vietnam.

Aside from trivial or esoteric inquiry, knowledge is also dissipated on pretentious conceptualizing in the social sciences. A catch phrase can become a stimulus for endless academic discussion, and for the proliferation of debates that go nowhere into the real world, only round and round in ever smaller circles of scholarly discourse. Schemes and models and systems are invented that have the air of profundity and that advance careers, but hardly anything else.

We should not be surprised then at the volatile demonstrations for black studies programs, or for the creation of new student-run courses based on radical critiques of American society. Students demanding relevance in scholarship have been joined by professors dissenting at the annual ceremonials called Scholarly Meetings: at the American Philosophical Association, a resolution denouncing U.S. policy in Vietnam; at the American Political Science Association, a new caucus making radical changes in the program; at the American Historical Association, a successful campaign removing the 1968 meeting from Chicago to protest Mayor Daley's hooliganism; at the Modern Language Association, the election of a young, radical English teacher as president.

Still we are troubled, because the new urgency to use our heads for good purposes gets tangled in a cluster of beliefs so stuck, fungus-like, to the scholar, that even the most activist of us cannot cleanly extricate ourselves. These beliefs are roughly expressed by the phrases "disinterested scholarship," "dispassionate learning," "objective study," "scientific method"—all adding up to the fear that using our intelligence to further our moral ends is somehow improper. And so we mostly remain subservient to the beliefs of the profession although they violate our deepest feelings as human beings, although we suspect that the traditional neutrality of the scholar is a disservice to the very ideals we teach about as history, and a betrayal of the victims of an unneutral world.

It may, therefore, be worthwhile to examine the arguments for "disinterested, neutral, scientific, objective" scholarship. If there is to be a revolution in the uses of knowledge to correspond to the revolution in society, it will have to begin by challenging the rules that sustain the wasting of knowledge. Let me cite a number of them, and argue briefly for new approaches.

Rule 1: *Carry on "disinterested scholarship."* (In one hour's reading some weeks ago I came across three such exhortations, using just that phrase: in an essay by Walter Lippmann; in the Columbia University Commencement Address of Richard Hofstadter; in an article by Daniel Beil, appearing ironically in a magazine called *The Public Interest.*) The call is naïve, because there are powerful interests already at work in the academy, with varying degrees of self-consciousness.

There is the Establishment of political power and corporate wealth, whose interest is that the universities produce people who will fit into existing niches in the social structure rather than try to change the structure. We always knew our educational system "socialized" people, but we never worried about this, because we assumed our social norms were worth perpetuating. Now, and rightly, we are beginning to doubt this. There is the interest of the educational bureaucracy in maintaining itself: its endowment, its buildings, its positions (both honorific and material), its steady growth along orthodox lines. These larger interests are internalized in the motivations of the scholar: promotion, tenure, higher salaries, prestige—all of which are best secured by innovating in prescribed directions.

All of these interests operate, not through any conspiratorial decision but through the mechanism of a well-oiled system, just as the irrationality of the economic system operates not through any devilish plot but through the mechanism of the profit motive and the market, and as the same kinds of political decisions reproduce themselves in Congress year after year.

No one *intends* exactly what happens. They just follow the normal rules of the game. Similarly with education; hence the need to challenge these rules that quietly lead the scholar toward trivia, pretentiousness, orotundity, and the production of objects: books, degrees, buildings, research projects, dead knowledge. (Emerson is still right: "*Things* are in the saddle, and ride mankind.")

There is no question then of a "disinterested" university, only a question about what kinds of interests the university will serve. There are fundamental humanistic interests—above any particular class, party, nation, ideology—that I believe the university should consciously serve, I assume this is what we mean when we speak (however we act) of fostering certain "values" in education.

The university should unashamedly declare that its interest is in eliminating war, poverty, race and national hatred, governmental restrictions on individual freedom, and in fostering a spirit of cooperation and concern in the generation growing up. It should *not* serve the interests of particular nations or parties or religions or political dogmas. Ironically, the university has often served narrow governmental, military, or business interests, and yet withheld support from larger, transcendental values, on the ground that it needed to maintain neutrality.

Rule 2: *Be objective.* The myth of "objectivity" in teaching and scholarship is based on a common confusion. If to be objective is to be scrupulously careful about reporting accurately what one sees, then of course this is laudable. But accuracy is only a prerequisite. Whether a metalsmith uses reliable measuring instruments is a prerequisite for doing good work, but does not answer the crucial question: will he now forge a sword or a plowshare with his instruments? That the metalsmith has determined in advance that he prefers a plowshare does not require him to distort his measurements. That the scholar has decided he prefers peace to war does not require him to distort his facts.

Too many scholars abjure a starting set of values, because they fail to make the proper distinction between an ultimate set of values and the instruments needed to obtain them. The values may well be subjective (derived from human needs); but the instruments must be objective (accurate). Our values should determine the questions we ask in scholarly inquiry, but not the answers.

Rule 3: *Stick to your discipline.* Specialization has become as absurdly extreme in the educational world as in the medical world. One no longer is a specialist in American government, but in Congress, or the Presidency, or pressure groups: a historian is a "colonialist" or an "early national period" man. This is natural when education is divorced from the promotion of values. To work on a real problem (such as how to eliminate poverty in a nation producing $800-billion worth of wealth each year), one would have to follow that problem across many disciplinary lines without qualm, dealing with historical materials, economic theories, political problems. Specialization insures that one cannot follow a problem through from start to finish. It ensures the functioning in the academy of the system's dictum: divide and rule.

Another kind of scholarly segregation serves to keep those in the university from dealing with urgent social problems: that which divorces fact from theory. We learn the ideas of the great philosophers and poets in one part of our educational experience. In the other part, we prepare to take our place in the real occupational world. In political science, for instance, a political theorist discusses transcendental visions of the good society; someone else presents factual descriptions of present governments. But no one deals with both the *is* and the *ought*; if they did, they would have to deal with how to get from here to there, from the present reality to the poetic vision. Note how little work is done in political science on the tactics of social change. Both student and teacher deal with theory and reality in separate courses; the compartmentalization safely neutralizes them.

It is time to recall Rousseau: "We have physicists, geometricians, chemists, astronomers, poets, musicians, and painters in plenty, but we have no longer a citizen among us."

Rule 4: *To be "scientific" requires neutrality.* This is a misconception of how science works, both in fact and in purpose. Scientists *do* have values, but they decided on these so long ago that we have forgotten them; they aim to save human life, to extend human control over the environment for the happiness of men and women. This is the tacit assumption behind scientific work, and a physiologist would be astonished if someone suggested that he starts from a neutral position as regards life or death, health or sickness. Somehow the social scientists have not yet got around to accepting openly that their aim is to keep people alive, to distribute equitably the resources of the earth, to widen the areas of human freedom, and therefore to direct their efforts toward these ends.

The claim that social science is "different," because its instruments are tainted with subjectivity, ignores the new discoveries in the hard sciences: that the very fact of observation distorts the measurement of the physicist, and what he sees depends on his position in space. The physical sciences do not talk about certainty anymore, but rather about "probability"; while the probabilities may be higher for them than in the social sciences, both fields are dealing with elusive data.

Rule 5: *A scholar must, in order to be "rational," avoid "emo-*

tionalism." (I know one man in Asian studies who was told by university administrators that the articles he wrote upon his return from Vietnam were too "emotional.") True, emotion can distort. But it can also enhance. If one of the functions of the scholar is accurate description, then it is impossible to describe a war both unemotionally and accurately at the same time. And if the special competence of the mind is in enabling us to perceive what is outside our own limited experience, that competence is furthered, that perception sharpened, by emotion. Even a large dose of emotionalism in the description of slavery would merely begin to convey accurately to a white college student what slavery was like for the black man.

Thus, exactly from the standpoint of what intellect is supposed to do for us—to extend the boundaries of our understanding—the "cool, rational, unemotional" approach fails. For too long, white Americans were emotionally separated from what the Negro suffered in this country by cold, and therefore inadequate, historical description. War and violence, divested of their brutality by the prosaic quality of the printed page, became tolerable to the young. (True, the poem and the novel were read in the English classes, but these were neatly separated from the history and government classes.) Reason, to be accurate, must be supplemented by emotion, as Reinhold Niebuhr once reminded us.

Refusing, then, to let ourselves be bound by traditional notions of disinterestedness, objectivity, scientific procedure, rationality—what kinds of work can scholars do, in deliberate unneutral pursuit of a more livable world? Am I urging Orwellian control of scholarly activities? Not at all. I am, rather suggesting that scholars, on their own, reconsider the rules by which they have worked, and begin to turn their intellectual energies to the urgent problems of our time. The true task of education, Alfred North Whitehead cautioned, is to abjure stale knowledge. "Knowledge does not keep any better than fish," he said. We need to keep it alive, vital, potent.

Specifically, we might use our scholarly time and energy to sharpen the perceptions of the complacent by exposing those facts that any society tends to hide about itself: the facts about wealth and poverty, about tyranny in both communist and capitalist states, about lies told by politicians, the mass media, the church, popular leaders. We need to expose fallacious logic, spurious analogies, deceptive slogans, and those intoxicating symbols that drive people to murder (the flag, communism, capitalism, freedom). We need to dig beneath the abstractions so our fellow citizens can make judgments on the particular realities beneath political rhetoric. We need to expose inconsistencies and double standards. In short, we need to become the critics of the culture, rather than its apologists and perpetuators.

The university is especially gifted for such a task. Although obviously not remote from the pressures of business and military and politicians, it has just that margin of leeway, just that tradition of truth-telling (however violated in practice) that can enable it to become a spokesman for change.

This will require holding up before society forgotten visions, lost utopias, unfulfilled dreams—badly needed in this age of cynicism. Those outside the university who might act for change are deterred by pessimism. A bit of historical perspective, some recapitulation of the experience of social movements in other times, other places, while not wholly cheering, can at least suggest possibilities.

Along with inspirational visions, we will need specific schemes for accomplishing important purposes, which can then be laid before the groups that can use them. Let the economists work out a plan for free food, instead of advising the Federal Reserve Board on interest rates. Let the political scientists work out insurgency tactics for the poor, rather than counter-insurgency tactics for the military. Let the historians instruct us or inspire us, from the data of the past, rather than amusing us, boring us, or deceiving us. Let the scientists figure out and lay before the public plans on how to make autos safe, cities beautiful, air pure. Let all social scientists work on modes of change instead of merely describing the world that is, so that we can make the necessary revolutionary alterations with the least disorder.

I am not sure what a revolution in the academy will look like, any more than I know what a revolution in the society will look like. I doubt that it will take the form of some great cataclysmic event. More likely, it will be a process, with periods of tumult and of quiet, in which we will, here and there, by ones and twos and tens, create pockets of concern inside old institutions, transforming them from within. There is no great day of reckoning to work toward. Rather, we must begin *now* to liberate those patches of ground on which we stand—in our classrooms, in our studies—to "vote" for a new world (as Thoreau suggested) with our whole selves all the time, rather than in moments carefully selected by others.

We will be doing this, not in the interest of the rich and powerful, or in behalf of our own careers, but for those who have never had a chance to read poetry or study philosophy, who so far have had to strive alone just to stay warm in winter, to stay alive through the calls for war.

The Intellectual as Charlatan

Eric Hoffer

Eric Hoffer is a uniquely American writer. Mr. Hoffer, without formal education, supported himself as a longshoreman and itinerant worker, educating himself in the public libraries of California. Hoffer has been concerned with the history and the development of the intellectual from the earliest times to the present day. The common thread, he argues, linking the intellectuals throughout history, is a rational search for status, social usefulness, and manipulative power on an intellectual level.

The difference which sets the intellectual apart from his fellow citizens is his superiority and arrogance, so well observed in those who believe they are privy to certain shared truths. The intellectual continually seeks a verification of his knowledge and personal worth through alliances with individuals, governments, and institutions. Hoffer suggests that the intellectual is often the enemy of the free society, whose philosophical basis is the viability and value of ordinary man in administering his own affairs. The implication of ordinary men maintaining the state without intellectuals is an unforgivable affront to the pride and self-esteem of many intellectuals. Although intellectuals are useful in providing creative direction for society, Hoffer warns that their powers should be controlled and regulated, indeed subordinated, to the general will of the society. Anti-intellectualism, which has been such a common theme in American life, is in part a result of the common man's empirically-learned, justifiable fears resulting from centuries of abuse at the hands of intellectually-dominated European regimes.

The growing power of the intellectuals in modern American life, although a natural development within the context of scientific and technological needs in the social system, constitutes a threat which can only be controlled through the proper integration of their talents in such a way that a balance is maintained between the manipulators and their potential victims.

Mr. Hoffer's criticisms about the dangers of intellectuals who possess disporportionate power are interesting because Mr. Hoffer does not consider himself as a traditional member of the intellectual class. He offers himself as an intellectual of the masses who brings to bear his analytic abilities on the problems faced by ordinary men.

Hoffer shows the defects of education when it produces an intellectual elite. He scans the history of societies where education had provided the means for intellectuals to control the masses and where educational institutions were buffers to protect the elites from social demands. The arrogance of intellectuals and their disdain for common people, as Hoffer indicates, is related to notions of the power of knowledge. Schools tend to reinforce the aristocratic values of intellectuals by separating them in classrooms and curricula. Unfortunately, the separations are often based on economic and social status rather than on innate abilities, but even then there is a hierarchy of values perpetuated in the schools that practical skills are worth less than academic subjects. This is a very important question for consideration in discussions of education. What knowledge is of greatest worth?

There is little doubt that the Cold War has quickened the awakening and modernization that are now going on at full blast in Asia and Africa. Communist pressure is accelerating the end of colonial tutelage, and both sides in the Cold War are wooing the emerging new nations with economic and military aid and with ready recognition of their status as sovereign states.

Now, no one can gainsay the fact that in this kind of wooing the United States has not been doing too well. Our generosity, diplomacy, and propaganda have not won for us a marked measure of wholehearted adherence. Our effort, thus far, seems to lack some essential ingredient. Particularly baffling has been the petulant and often sneering response to our unprecedented outpouring of money, food, raw materials, machines, and military aid. Awkwardness or even tactlessness in our manner of giving cannot possibly explain this unexpected reaction.

Much has been written on our failure to gauge the temper and real needs of the people we try to help. It is implied that were our offering of aid comprehensive enough and our manner of giving adequate we would have the world wholly on our side. Yet the more one thinks on the subject the more one realizes that the attitude toward us is not mainly determined by the nature of our policies and our manner of giving.

The baffling response we hear does not originate in the people we try to help but in a group of self-appointed spokesmen and mediators who stand between us and the mass of people. This group is made up of university teachers and students, writers, artists, and intellectuals in general. It is these articulate people who are the source of the rabid anti-Americanism which has been manifesting itself in many countries since the end of the Second World War. One cannot escape the impression that there is a natural antagonism between these "men of words" and twentieth-century America. It is not the quality of our policies which offends them but our very existence. The intellectuals everywhere see America as a threat. Their petulant fault-finding is the expression of an almost instinctive fear, and it is of vital importance that we should understand the nature of this fear.

In almost every civilization we know of, and in Europe, too, up to the end of the Middle Ages, the equivalent of the intellectual was either a member of a ruling elite or closely allied with it. In ancient Egypt and Imperial China the literati were a privileged part of the population. They were magistrates, administrators, and officials of every kind. In India, the uppermost caste of the Brahmins was also the caste of the educated. In classical Greece, the philosophers, dramatists, poets, historians, and artists were also soldiers, sailors, lawmakers, politicians, and men of affairs. In the Roman Empire, there was an intimate alliance between the Greek intellectuals and the Roman men of action. The Romans needed the Greek intellectual —needed him to satisfy their craving for beauty which they could not satisfy by their own creativeness, and needed him also for the management of affairs at home and in the provinces. It was this dependence on the Greek intellectual which eased the spread of Roman rule in the Hellenized part of the Mediterranean world. In Europe, too, during the Middle Ages, most of the educated people were of the clergy and hence members of an elite. But the fifteenth century, which saw the emergence of the modern Occident, also saw a fateful change in the status of the European intellectual.

The catastrophic events of the fourteenth century—the Black Death, which killed off a large part of the population and nearly half of the clergy, and the divisions and disorders of the Papacy—weakened the hold of the Catholic Church on the European masses. This in conjunction with the introduction of paper and printing made it possible for education to escape the control of an all-embracing Church. There emerged a large group of non-clerical teachers, students, scholars, and writers who were not members of a clearly-marked privileged class, and whose social usefulness was not self-evident.

In the modern Occident power was, and still is, the prerogative of men of action—landowners, soldiers, businessmen, industrialists, and their hangers-on. The intellectual is treated as a poor relation and has to pick up the crumbs. He usually ekes out a living by teaching, journalism, or some white-collar job. Even when his excellence as a writer, artist, scientist, or educator is generally recognized and rewarded, he does not feel himself one of the elite.

The intellectual's passionate search for an acknowledged status and a role of social usefulness has been a ferment in the Occident since the days of the Renaissance. He has pioneered every upheaval from the Reformation to the latest nationalist or socialist movement. Yet the intellectual has not known how to retain a position of leadership in the movements and new regimes he has done so much to initiate and promote. He has usually been elbowed out by fanatics and practical men of action. This has been particularly so in the case of the nationalist movements which have pullulated all over the Occident during the past hundred years.

These movements were usually pioneered by poets, writers, historians, scholars, and philosophers who hoped to find in the corporate warmth of the national state their rightful place as bearers of culture, legislators, statesmen, dignitaries, and men of affairs. The practical solid citizens who are now considered the pillars and guardians of patriotism, as a rule, kept shy of nationalist movements in their early stages, but moved in and took over once the movements became going concerns, and the national states began to consolidate. The intellectual was left out in the cold. He was no better off in the national state than in the dynastic state. One has the feeling that the intellectual has since tried to counter this usurpation by shifting his espousal from the national to the Socialist state.

In Asia and Africa, too, the wider diffusion of literacy, due largely to Western influence, gave rise to numbers of unattached men of words. Their search for a weighty and useful life led them, as it did their counterparts in Europe, to the promotion of nationalist and Socialist movements.

Now, although the homelessness of the intellectual is more or less evident in all Western and Westernized societies, it is nowhere so pronounced as in our own common-man civilization. America has been running its complex economy and governmental machinery, and has been satisfying most of its cultural needs without the aid of the typical intellectual. Nowhere has the intellectual so little say in the management of affairs. It is natural, therefore, that the intellectuals outside the United States should see in the spread of Americanization a threat not only to their influence but to their very existence.

It is strange that when we consider the differences between our social order and that of a Communist country we rarely refer to the striking difference in its attitude toward the intellectual. There is no doubt that the intellectual has come into his own in the Communist world. In a Communist country writers, artists, scientists, professors, and intellectuals in general are near the top of the social ladder, and feel no doubt about their social usefulness. They are the ideal of the rising generation. Czelaw Milosz says of the intellectual in the Communist countries that "never since the Middle Ages has he felt himself so necessary and recognized."[1] The people who come over to us from the Communist regimes are mostly men of action—soldiers, diplomats, sportsmen, technicians, and skilled workers. The intellectual, even when he can travel outside the Communist world, rarely takes advantage of the opportunity to escape.

The Communists have always had an acute awareness of the fateful relations between the intellectual and the established order. They are convinced, in the words of Stalin, that "no ruling class has managed without its own intelligentsia." In the Anglo-Saxon world, social stability has been maintained without the wholehearted allegiance of the intellectuals. But, with the advent of the Cold War, the attitude of the intellectual toward the prevailing dispensation has everywhere become a factor in national survival. For in a Cold War words count at least as much as deeds. Our chief handicap in the bidding for souls that is going on in every part of the world has been our lack of words. Our deeds could not prevent a gang of double-talking murderers and slanderers from posturing as saviors of humanity. Only by a masterly use of words could we have evoked a vivid awareness of the loathsomeness of Stalin and his work, and communicated it not only to friends and neutrals, but to the Communists themselves.

Our men of action, however able and well-intentioned, cannot be our spokesmen in the battle for souls. Whatever the hands that guide our policies, the voice that makes itself heard must be the voice of our foremost poets, philosophers, writers, artists, scientists, and professors. Only they can get around the roadblock which bars our way to the dispirited millions everywhere. Just as in time of a hot

---

[1] This is not contradicted by the fact that intellectuals have been imprisoned and liquidated in Communist countries. What the intellectual craves above all is to be taken seriously, to be treated as a decisive force in shaping history. He is far more at home in a society that weighs his every word and keeps close watch on his attitudes than in a society that cares not what he says or does. He would rather be persecuted than ignored.

war there is an automatic rise in our appreciation of men in uniform, so in time of a cold war there must be a general awareness of the vital role the intellectuals have to play in our struggle for survival. And they must be given a share in the shaping and execution of policies which they will be called upon to expound and defend.

The intellectual as a champion of the masses is a relatively recent phenomenon. Education does not naturally waken in us a concern for the uneducated. The distinction conferred by education is more easily maintained by a sharp separation from those below than by a continued excellence of achievement. When Gandhi was asked by an American clergyman what it was that worried him most, he replied: "The hardness of heart of the educated."

In almost every civilization we know of, the intellectuals have been either allied with those in power or members of a governing elite, and consequently indifferent to the fate of the masses. In ancient Egypt and Imperial China the literati were magistrates, overseers, stewards, taxgatherers, secretaries, and officials of every kind. They were in command, and did not lift a finger to lighten the burden of the lower orders. In India the intellectuals were members of the uppermost caste of the Brahmins. Gautama, who preached love of service for others and the mixing of castes, was by birth not an intellectual but a warrior; and the attempt to translate Buddha's teaching into reality was made by another warrior—Emperor Asoka. The Brahmin intellectuals, far from rallying to the cause, led the opposition to Buddhism, and finally drove it out of India. In classical Greece the intellectuals were at the top of the social ladder: philosophers and poets were also legislators, generals, and statesmen. This intellectual elite had an ingrained contempt for the common people who did the world's work, regarding them as no better than slaves and unfit for citizenship. In the Roman Empire, the intellectuals, whether Greek or Roman, made common cause with the powers that be, and kept their distance from the masses. In medieval Europe, too, the intellectual was a member of a privileged order—the Church —and did not manifest undue solicitude for the underprivileged.

In only one society prior to the emergence of the modern Occident do we find a group of "men of words" raising their voices in defense of the weak and oppressed. For many centuries the small nation of the ancient Hebrews on the eastern shore of the Mediterranean did not differ markedly in its institutions and spiritual life from its neighbors. But in the eighth century B.C., owing to an obscure combination of circumstances, it began to develop a most strange deviation. Side by side with the traditional men of words—

priests, counselors, soothsayers, scribes—there emerged a series of extraordinary men who pitted themselves against the ruling elite and the prevailing social order. These men, the prophets, were in many ways the prototype of the modern militant intellectual. Renan speaks of them as "open-air journalists" who recited their articles in the street and marketplace, and at the city gate. "The first article of irreconcilable journalism was written by Amos about 800 B.C." Many of the characteristic attitudes of the modern intellectual—his tendency to see any group he identifies himself with as a chosen people, and any truth he embraces as the one and only truth; the envisioning of a millennial society on earth—are clearly discerned in the prophets. The ideals, also, and the holy causes that the intellectuals are preaching and propagating today were fully formulated during the three centuries in which the prophets were active.

We know too little about these remote centuries to explain the rise of the prophets. The temptation is great to look for circumstances not unlike those which attended the rise of the militant men of words in the modern Occident. One wonders whether a diffusion of literacy in the ninth century B.C. was not one of the factors. It was at about that time that the Phoenician traders perfected the simple alphabet from the complex and cumbersome picture writing of the Egyptians. And considering the close relations which prevailed then between Phoenicians and Hebrews it would not be unreasonable to assume that the latter were quick to adopt the new easy writing. Particularly during the reign of Solomon (960–925 B.C.) the intimate link with Phoenicia and the need for an army of scribes to run Solomon's centralized and bureaucratized administration must have resulted in a sharp rise in the number of literate Hebrews. Such an increase in literacy was fraught with consequences for Hebrew society. In Phoenicia the new alphabet was primarily an instrument of commerce, and the sudden increase in the number of literate persons presented no problem, for they were rapidly absorbed in the far-flung trade organizations. But the chiefly agricultural Hebrew society was swamped by a horde of unemployed scribes when the bureaucratic apparatus crumbled at Solomon's death. The new unattached scribes found themselves suspended between the privileged clique, whose monopoly on reading and writing they had broken, and the illiterate masses, to whom they were allied by birth. Since they had neither position nor adequate employment, it was natural that they should align themselves against established privilege, and become self-appointed spokesmen of their inarticulate brethren. Such at least might have been the circumstances at the rise of the earliest prophets —of Amos the shepherd of Tekoa, and his disciples. They set the pattern, and the road trodden by them was later followed by men of all walks of life, even by Isaiah the aristocrat.

The rise of the militant intellectual in the Occident was brought about not by a simplification of the art of writing but by the introduction of paper and printing. Undoubtedly the Church's monopoly of education was considerably weakened, as I have said, in the late Middle Ages. But it was the introduction of paper and printing that finished the job. The new men of words, like those of the eighth century B.C., were on the whole unattached—allied with neither Church nor government. They had no clear status, and no self-evident role of social usefulness. In the social orders evolved by the modern Occident, power and influence were, and to a large extent still are, in the hands of industrialists, businessmen, bankers, landowners, and soldiers. The intellectual feels himself on the outside. Even when he is widely acclaimed and highly rewarded he does not feel himself part of the ruling elite. He finds himself almost superfluous in a civilization which is largely his handiwork. Small wonder that he tends to resent those in power as intruders and usurpers.

Thus the antagonism between men of words and men of action which first emerged as a historical motif among the Hebrews in the eighth century B.C., and made of them a peculiar people, reappeared in the sixteenth century in the life of the modern Occident and set it apart from all other civilizations. The unattached intellectual's unceasing search for a recognized status and a useful role has brought him to the forefront of every movement of change since the Reformation, not only in the West but wherever Western influence has penetrated. He has consistently sought a link with the underprivileged, be they bourgeois, peasants, proletarians, persecuted minorities, or the natives of colonial countries. So far, his most potent alliance has been with the masses.

The coming together of the intellectual and the masses has proved itself a formidable combination, and there is no doubt that it was largely instrumental in bringing about the unprecedented advancement of the masses in modern times. Yet, despite its achievements, the combination is not based on a real affinity.

The intellectual goes to the masses in search of weightiness and a role of leadership. Unlike the man of action, the man of words needs the sanction of ideals and the incantation of words in order to act forcefully. He wants to lead, command, and conquer, but he must feel that in satisfying these hungers he does not cater to a petty self. He needs justification, and he seeks it in the realization of a grandiose design, and in the solemn ritual of making the word become flesh. Thus he does battle for the downtrodden and disinherited, and for liberty, equality, justice, and truth, though, as Thoreau pointed out, the grievance which animates him is not mainly "his sympathy with his fellows in distress, but, though he be the holiest son of God, is his private ail." Once his "private ail" is righted, the intellectual's ardor for the underprivileged cools considerably. His cast of mind is essentially aristocratic. Like Heraclitus he is convinced that "ten thousand [of the masses] do not turn the scale against a single man of worth" and that "the many are mean; only the few are noble." He sees himself as a leader and master.[2] Not only does he doubt that the masses could do anything worthwhile on their own, but he would resent it if they made the attempt. The masses must obey. They need the shaping force of discipline in both war and peace. It is indeed doubtful that the typical intellectual would feel wholly at home in a society where the masses got their share of the fleshpots. Not only would there be little chance for leadership where people were almost without a grievance, but we might suspect that the cockiness and the airs of an affluent populace would offend his aristocratic sensibilities.

There is considerable evidence that when the militant intellectual succeeds in establishing a social order in which his craving for a superior status and social usefulness is fully satisfied, his view of the masses darkens, and from being their champion he becomes their detractor. The struggle initiated by the prophets in the eighth century B.C. ended, some three hundred years later, in the complete victory of the men of words. After the return from the Babylonian captivity the scribes and the scholars were supreme and the Hebrew nation became "a people of the book." Once dominant, these scribes, like the Pharisees who succeeded them, flaunted their loathing for the masses. They made of the word for common folk, "am-ha-aretz," a term of derision and scorn—even the gentle Hillel taught that "no am-ha-aretz can be pious." Yet these scribes had an unassailable hold on the masses they despised. The noble carpenter from Galilee could make no headway when he challenged the pretension of the solemn scholars, hair-splitting lawyers, and arrogant pedants, and raised his voice in defense of the poor in spirit. He was ostracized and anathematized, and his teachings found a following chiefly among non-Jews. Yet the teachings of Jesus fared no better than the teachings of the prophets when they came wholly into the keeping of

2 In 1935 a group of students at Rangoon University banded themselves together into a revolutionary group and immediately added the prefix "Thakin" (master) to their names.

dominant intellectuals. They were made into a vehicle for the maintenance and aggrandizement of a vast hierarchy of clerks, while the
poor in spirit, instead of inheriting the earth, were left to sink into
serfdom and superstitious darkness.

In the sixteenth century, we see the same pattern again. When
Luther first defied the Pope and his councils he spoke feelingly of
"the poor, simple, common folk." Later, when allied with the German princelings, he lashed out against the rebellious masses with
unmatched ferocity: "Let there be no half-measures! Cut their
throats! Transfix them! Leave no stone unturned! To kill a rebel is to
destroy a mad dog." He assured his aristocratic patrons that "a
prince can enter heaven by the shedding of blood more certainly
than others by means of prayer."

It is the twentieth century, however, which has given us the
most striking example of the discrepancy between the attitude of the
intellectual while the struggle is on, and his role once the battle is
won. Marxism started out as a movement for the salvation of both
the masses and the intellectuals from the degradation and servitude
of a capitalist social order. The *Communist Manifesto* condemned
the bourgeoisie not only for pauperizing, dehumanizing, and enslaving
the toiling masses, but also for robbing the intellectual of his elevated
status. "The bourgeoisie has stripped of its halo every occupation
hitherto honored and looked up to with reverent awe." Though the
movement was initiated by intellectuals and powered by their talents
and hungers, it yet held up the proletariat as the chosen people—the
only carrier of the revolutionary idea, and the chief beneficiary of the
revolution to come. The intellectuals, particularly those who had
"raised themselves to the level of comprehending theoretically the
historical movement as a whole," were to act as guides—as a com-
posite Moses—during the long wanderings in the desert. Like Moses,
the intellectuals would have no more to do once the promised land
was in sight. "The role of the intelligentsia," said Lenin, "is to make
special leaders from among the intelligentsia unnecessary."

The Marxist movement has made giant strides during the past
forty years. It has created powerful political parties in many countries, and it is in possession of absolute power in the vast stretch of
land between the Elbe and the China Sea. In Russia, China, and
adjacent smaller countries, the revolution envisaged by Marxism has
been consummated. What, then, is the condition of the masses and
the intellectuals in these countries?

In no other social order, past or present, has the intellectual so
completely come into his own as in the Communist regimes. Never
before has his superior status been so self-evident and his social use-

fulness so unquestioned. The bureaucracy which manages and controls every field of activity is staffed by people who consider themselves intellectuals. Writers, poets, artists, scientists, professors, journalists, and others engaged in intellectual pursuits are accorded the high social status of superior civil servants. They are the aristocrats, the rich, the prominent, the indispensable, the pampered and petted. It is the wildest dream of the man of words come true.

And what of the masses in this intellectual's paradise? They have found in the intellectual the most formidable taskmaster in history. No other regime has treated the masses so callously as raw material, to be experimented on and manipulated at will; and never before have so many lives been wasted so recklessly in war and in peace. On top of all this, the Communist intelligentsia has been using force in a wholly novel manner. The traditional master uses force to exact obedience and lets it go at that. Not so the intellectual. Because of his professed faith in the power of words and the irresistibility of the truths which supposedly shape his course, he cannot be satisfied with mere obedience. He tries to obtain by force a response that is usually obtained by the most perfect persuasion, and he uses Terror as a fearful instrument to extract faith and fervor from crushed souls.

One cannot escape the impression that the intellectual's most fundamental incompatibility is with the masses. He has managed to thrive in social orders dominated by kings, nobles, priests, and merchants, but not in societies suffused with the tastes and values of the masses. The trespassing by the masses into the domain of culture and onto the stage of history is seen even by the best among the intellectuals as a calamity. Heine viewed with horror the mass society taking shape on the North American continent—"that monstrous prison of freedom where the invisible chains would oppress me even more than the visible ones at home, and where the most repulsive of tyrants, the populace, holds vulgar sway." Nietzsche feared that the invasion of the masses would turn history into a shallow swamp. The masses, says Karl Jaspers, exert "an immense gravitational pull which seems again and again to paralyze every upward sweep. The tremendous forces of the masses, with their attributes of mediocrity, suffocate whatever is not in line with them." To Emerson, the masses were "rude, lame, unmade, pernicious in their demands and influence, and need not be flattered but to be schooled. I wish not to concede anything to them, but to tame, drill, divide and break them up, and draw individuals out of them. . . . If government knew how, I should like to see it check, not multiply, the population." Flaubert saw no hope in the masses: they "never come of age, and will always be at the bottom of the social scale. . . ." He thought it of little importance "that many peasants should be able to read and no longer heed their priests; but it is infinitely important that men like Renan and Littré should be able to live and be listened to."

Renan himself, so wise and humane, could not hold back his loathing for the masses. He thought that popular education, so far from making the masses wiser, "only destroys their natural amiability, their instincts, their innate sound reason, and renders them positively unendurable." After the debacle of 1870 Renan spent several months in seclusion writing his *Philosophical Dialogues*, in which he vented his spleen not on the political and cultural elite which was responsible for France's defeat, but on democracy and the masses. The principle that society exists for the well-being of the mass of people does not seem to him consistent with the plan of nature. "It is much to be feared that the last expression of democracy may be a social state with a degenerate populace having no other aim than to indulge in the ignoble appetites of the vulgar." The purpose of an ideal social order is less to produce enlightened masses than uncommon people. "If the ignorance of the masses is a necessary condition for this end, so much the worse for the masses." He is convinced that a high culture is hardly to be imagined without the full subordination of the masses, and he envisages a world ruled by an elite of wise men possessed of absolute power and capable of striking terror into the hearts of the vulgar. This dictatorship of the wise would have hell at its command; "not a chimerical hell of whose existence there is no proof, but a veritable hell." It would institute a preventive Terror, not unlike that instituted by Stalin sixty years later, "with a view to frighten people and prevent their defending themselves," and it would "hardly hesitate to maintain in some lost district in Asia a nucleus of Bashkirs and Kalmuks, obedient machines, unencumbered by moral scruples and prepared for every sort of cruelty."

It is remarkable how closely the attitude of the intellectual toward the masses resembles the attitude of a colonial functionary toward the natives. The intellectual groaning under the dead weight of the inert masses reminds us of sahibs groaning under the white man's burden. Small wonder that when we observe a regime by intellectuals in action, whether in Russia or in Portugal, we have the feeling that here colonialism begins at home. Nor should it be surprising that liberation movements in the colonies spearheaded by intellectuals result in a passage from colonialism by Whites to colonialism by Blacks.

In the essay on "The Readiness to Work" it has been suggested that the masses are not likely to perform well in a social order shaped and run by intellectuals. Some measure of coercion, even of enslavement, is apparently needed to keep the masses working in such a regime. However, with the coming of automation it may eventually be possible for a ruling intelligentsia to operate a country's economy without the aid of the masses, and it is legitimate to speculate on what the intellectual may be tempted to do with the masses once they become superfluous. Dostoyevsky, with his apocalyptic premonition of things to come, puts the following words in the mouth of an intellectual by the name of Lyamshin: "For my part, if I didn't know what to do with nine-tenths of mankind, I'd take them and blow them up into the air instead of putting them in paradise. I'd only leave a handful of educated people, who would live happily ever afterwards on scientific principles."[3] Now, it is highly unlikely that even the most ruthless intelligentsia would follow Lyamshin's recommendation, though one has the feeling that Mao Tse-tung's unconcern about a nuclear holocaust is perhaps bolstered by the wish to rid his system of millions of superfluous Chinese. There is no reason, however, why a doctrine should not be propounded eventually that the masses are a poisonous waste product that must be kept under a tight lid, and set apart as a caste of untouchables. That such a doctrine would not be alien to the mentality of the Communist intellectual is evident from pronouncements made by Communist spokesmen in East Germany after the rising of 1953. They maintained that the rebellious workers, though they looked and behaved like workers, were not the working class known by Marx, but a decadent mixture of unregenerate remnants of eliminated classes and types. The real workers, they said, were now in positions of responsibility and power. Bertolt Brecht suggested in an ironical vein that since the Communist government has lost confidence in the people, the simple thing to do is to dissolve the people and elect another.

Actually, the intellectual's dependence on the masses is not confined to the economic field. It goes much deeper. He has a vital need for the flow of veneration and worship that can come only from a vast, formless, inarticulate multitude. After all, God himself could have gotten along without men, yet He created them, to be adored, worshiped, and beseeched by them. What elation could the intellectual derive from dominating an aggregation of quarrelsome, backbiting fellow intellectuals? It is, moreover, the faith of the masses which nourishes and invigorates his own faith. Hermann Rauschning quotes a Nazi intellectual: "If I am disheartened and despairing, if I am dead

[3] *The Possessed*, Modern Library edition. (New York: Random House, 1936), p. 411.

beat through the eternal party quarrels, and I go to a meeting and speak to these simple goodhearted, honest people, then I am refreshed again; then all my doubts leave me."

To sum up: The intellectual's concern for the masses is as a rule a symptom of his uncertain status and his lack of an unquestionable sense of social usefulness. It is the activities of the chronically thwarted intellectual which make it possible for the masses to get their share of the good things of life. When the intellectual comes into his own, he becomes a pillar of stability and finds all kinds of lofty reasons for siding with the strong against the weak.

It is, then, in the interest of the masses that the struggle between the intellectual and the prevailing dispensation should remain undecided. But can we justify a continuing state of affairs in which the most gifted part of the population is ever denied its heart's desire, while the masses go on from strength to strength?

Actually, an antagonism between the intellectual and the powers that be serves a more vital purpose than the advancement of the masses: it keeps the social order from stagnating. For the evidence seems clear that a society in which the educated are closely allied with the governing class is capable of a brilliant beginning but not of continued growth and development. Such a society often attains heights of excellence early in its career and then stops. Its history is in the main a record of stagnation and decline. This was true of the ancient river-valley civilizations in Egypt, Mesopotamia, and China, and of the younger civilizations in India, Persia, the Graeco-Roman world, Byzantium, and the world of Islam. We also see that the first step in the awakening of a stagnant society is the estrangement of the educated minority from the prevailing dispensation, which is usually effected by the penetration of some foreign influence. This change in the relations between the educated and the governing class has been a factor in almost every renascence, including that of Europe from the stagnation of the Middle Ages.

The creativeness of the intellectual is often a function of a thwarted craving for purposeful action and a privileged rank. It has its origin in the soul intensity generated in front of an insurmountable obstacle on the path to action. The genuine writer, artist, and even scientist are dissatisfied persons—as dissatisfied as the revolutionary— but are endowed with a capacity for transmuting their dissatisfaction into a creative impulse. A busy, purposeful life of action not only diverts energies from creative channels, but above all reduces the potent irritation which releases the secretion of creativity.

There is also the remarkable fact that where the intellectuals are in full charge they do not usually create a milieu conducive to genuine creativeness. The reason for this is to be found in the role of the noncreative pseudo-intellectual in such a system. The genuinely creative person lacks, as a rule, the temperament requisite for the seizure, the exercise, and, above all, the retention of power. Hence, when the intellectuals come into their own, it is usually the pseudo-intellectual who rules the roost, and he is likely to imprint his mediocrity and meagerness on every phase of cultural activity. Moreover, his creative impotence brews in him a murderous hatred of intellectual brilliance and he may be tempted, as Stalin was, to enforce a crude leveling of all intellectual activity.

Thus it can be seen that the chronic thwarting of the intellectual's craving for power serves a higher purpose than the well-being of common folk. The advancement of the masses is a mere by-product of the uniquely human fact that discontent is at the root of the creative process: that the most gifted members of the human species are at their creative best when they cannot have their way, and must compensate for what they miss by realizing and cultivating their capacities and talents.

The Misuse of Knowledge

Aldous Huxley

One of the most terrifying aspects of the misuse of knowledge by intellectuals in the modern world expresses itself in the "social engineering" techniques, which are aimed at the manipulation of individuals and groups in our social system.

The dehumanization of men through the use of advanced behavioral techniques has been a chief concern of Aldous Huxley for many years. The manipulation and control of population through new techniques, which often do not include inflicting pain or the overt use of coercion, is a central theme of Huxley's *Brave New World*. The ascendency of the behaviorists suggests that men are

simply the product of environmental conditioning, and there has
been a de-emphasis of the role of genetic factors in human growth
which strengthens the proponents of the social engineering viewpoint. The social engineering viewpoint, in an applied societal
model, may be observed in the Soviet Union. Huxley defends the
individual, his uniqueness among all species on the evolutionary
scale, and argues against the erroneous arguments of the behaviorists as they seek to reduce man to a mechanistic response process,
denying completely his uniqueness and complexity.

Man finds himself in danger of being viewed in oversimplistic
terms, and as a result, standardized and manipulated by social
engineers in government and universities who are increasingly using
behaviorist's information in order to expand and increase their
personal power and careers at the expense of the general society.
These individuals argue that all human behavior is subject to behav-
ioristic laws; all one needs to do is simply understand these laws in
order to reshape and reform human behavior. The breed of new
behaviorists are more concerned with the power their technology
implies than they are with an objective scientific understanding of
human behavior. Gross ignorance masquerading under the guise of
science and technical language is a modern phenomena threatening
individuality and freedom everywhere. Huxley warns us of the
dangers involved in a dogmatic behaviorism and indicates that we
should be careful of the dangers of science which lacks a value basis
and pretends to be a new solution to man's complex problems.

Social engineering in schools restricts students in many of the
ways Huxley describes. Over-organization in such areas as courses,
schedules, truancy regulations, and classroom management lead to
the kind of problems Huxley notes in giving organizations precedence over persons. A student in a contemporary large school has
many of the same feelings of alienation that occur to factory workers. A modern school can be efficient enough now to control the
entire process from registration to instruction by computers.

Huxley raises serious questions about social science, social
policy, and social engineering. The problems are educational in the
sense that the schools produce those who would be social scientists, social engineers, and policy makers. They also produce consumers of social ideas. If an excellent job is done in producing
engineers without producing critical consumers, the schools will
have made a striking contribution toward the Brave New World
Huxley warns against.

The shortest and broadest road to the nightmare of Brave New
World leads, as I have pointed out, through over-population and the
accelerating increase of human numbers—twenty-eight hundred millions today, fifty-five hundred millions by the turn of the century, with
most of humanity facing the choice between anarchy and totalitarian

control. But the increasing pressure of numbers upon available resources is not the only force propelling us in the direction of totalitarianism. This blind biological enemy of freedom is allied with immensely powerful forces generated by the very advances in technology of which we are most proud. Justifiably proud, it may be added; for these advances are the fruits of genius and persistent hard work, of logic, imagination and self-denial—in a word, of moral and intellectual virtues for which one can feel nothing but admiration. But the Nature of Things is such that nobody in this world ever gets anything for nothing. These amazing and admirable advances have had to be paid for. Indeed, like last year's washing machine, they are still being paid for—and each installment is higher than the last. Many historians, many sociologists and psychologists have written at length, and with a deep concern, about the price that Western man has had to pay and will go on paying for technological progress. They point out, for example, that democracy can hardly be expected to flourish in societies where political and economic power is being progressively concentrated and centralized. But the progress of technology has led and is still leading to just such a concentration and centralization of power. As the machinery of mass production is made more efficient it tends to become more complex and more expensive—and so less available to the enterpriser of limited means. Moreover, mass production cannot work without mass distribution; but mass distribution raises problems which only the largest producers can satisfactorily solve. In a world of mass production and mass distribution the Little Man, with his inadequate stock of working capital, is at a grave disadvantage. In competition with the Big Man, he loses his money and finally his very existence as an independent producer; the Big Man has gobbled him up. As the Little Men disappear, more and more economic power comes to be wielded by fewer and fewer people. Under a dictatorship the Big Business, made possible by advancing technology and the consequent ruin of Little Business, is controlled by the State—that is to say, by a small group of party leaders and the soldiers, policemen and civil servants who carry out their orders. In a capitalist democracy, such as the United States, it is controlled by what Professor C. Wright Mills has called the Power Elite. This Power Elite directly employs several millions of the country's working force in its factories, offices and stores, controls many millions more by lending them the money to buy its products, and, through its ownership of the media of mass communication, influences the thoughts, the feelings and the actions of virtually everybody. To parody the words of Winston Churchill, never have so many been manipulated so much by so few. We are far indeed from Jefferson's ideal of a genuinely free society composed of a hierarchy of self-governing units—"the elementary republics of the wards, the county republics, the State republics and the Republic of the Union, forming a gradation of authorities."

We see, then, that modern technology has led to the concentration of economic and political power, and to the development of a society controlled (ruthlessly in the totalitarian states, politely and inconspicuously in the democracies) by Big Business and Big Government. But societies are composed of individuals and are good only insofar as they help individuals to realize their potentialities and to lead a happy and creative life. How have individuals been affected by the technological advances of recent years? Here is the answer to this question given by a philosopher-psychiatrist, Dr. Erich Fromm:

> Our contemporary Western society, in spite of its material, intellectual and political progress, is increasingly less conducive to mental health, and tends to undermine the inner security, happiness, reason and the capacity for love in the individual; it tends to turn him into an automaton who pays for his human failure with increasing mental sickness, and with despair hidden under a frantic drive for work and so-called pleasure.

Our "increasing mental sickness" may find expression in neurotic symptoms. These symptoms are conspicuous and extremely distressing. But "let us beware," says Dr. Fromm, "of defining mental hygiene as the prevention of symptoms. Symptoms as such are not our enemy, but our friend; where there are symptoms there is conflict, and conflict always indicates that the forces of life which strive for integration and happiness are still fighting." The really hopeless victims of mental illness are to be found among those who appear to be most normal. "Many of them are normal because they are so well adjusted to our mode of existence, because their human voice has been silenced so early in their lives, that they do not even struggle or suffer or develop symptoms as the neurotic does." They are normal not in what may be called the absolute sense of the word; they are normal only in relation to a profoundly abnormal society. Their perfect adjustment to that abnormal society is a measure of their mental sickness. These millions of abnormally normal people, living without fuss in a society to which, if they were fully human beings, they ought not to be adjusted, still cherish "the illusion of individuality," but in fact they have been to a great extent deindividualized. Their conformity is developing into something like uniformity. But "uniformity and freedom are incompatible. Uniformity and mental health are incompatible too. . . . Man is not made to be an automaton, and if he becomes one, the basis for mental health is destroyed."

In the course of evolution nature has gone to endless trouble to see that every individual is unlike every other individual. We reproduce our kind by bringing the father's genes into contact with the mother's. These hereditary factors may be combined in an almost infinite number of ways. Physically and mentally, each one of us is unique. Any culture which, in the interests of efficiency or in the name of some political or religious dogma, seeks to standardize the human individual, commits an outrage against man's biological nature.

Science may be defined as the reduction of multiplicity to unity. It seeks to explain the endlessly diverse phenomena of nature by ignoring the uniqueness of particular events, concentrating on what they have in common and finally abstracting some kind of "law," in terms of which they make sense and can be effectively dealt with. For examples, apples fall from the tree and the moon moves across the sky. People had been observing these facts from time immemorial. With Gertrude Stein they were convinced that an apple is an apple is an apple, whereas the moon is the moon is the moon. It remained for Isaac Newton to perceive what these very dissimilar phenomena had in common, and to formulate a theory of gravitation in terms of which certain aspects of the behavior of apples, of the heavenly bodies and indeed of everything else in the physical universe could be explained and dealt with in terms of a single system of ideas. In the same spirit the artist takes the innumerable diversities and uniquenesses of the outer world and his own imagination and gives them meaning within an orderly system of plastic, literary or musical patterns. The wish to impose order upon confusion, to bring harmony out of dissonance and unity out of multiplicity is a kind of intellectual instinct, a primary and fundamental urge of the mind. Within the realms of science, art and philosophy the workings of what I may call this "Will to Order" are mainly beneficent. True, the Will to Order has produced many premature syntheses based upon insufficient evidence, many absurd systems of metaphysics and theology, much pedantic mistaking of notions for realities, of symbols and abstractions for the data of immediate experience. But these errors, however regrettable, do not do much harm, at any rate directly—though it sometimes happens that a bad philosophical system may do harm indirectly, by being used as a justification for senseless and inhuman actions. It is in the social sphere, in the realm of politics and economics, that the Will to Order becomes really dangerous.

Here the theoretical reduction of unmanageable multiplicity to comprehensible unity becomes the practical reduction of human diversity to subhuman uniformity, of freedom to servitude. In politics the equivalent of a fully developed scientific theory or philosophical system is a totalitarian dictatorship. In economics, the equivalent of a beautifully composed work of art is the smoothly running factory in which the workers are perfectly adjusted to the machines. The Will to Order can make tyrants out of those who merely aspire to clear up a mess. The beauty of tidiness is used as a justification for despotism.

Organization is indispensable; for liberty arises and has meaning only within a self-regulating community of freely co-operating individuals. But, though indispensable, organization can also be fatal. Too much organization transforms men and women into automata, suffocates the creative spirit and abolishes the very possibility of freedom. As usual, the only safe course is in the middle, between the extremes of *laissez-faire* at one end of the scale and of total control at the other.

During the past century the successive advances in technology have been accompanied by corresponding advances in organization. Complicated machinery has had to be matched by complicated social arrangements, designed to work as smoothly and efficiently as the new instruments of production. In order to fit into these organizations, individuals have had to deindividualize themselves, have had to deny their native diversity and conform to a standard pattern, have had to do their best to become automata.

The dehumanizing effects of over-organization are reinforced by the dehumanizing effects of over-population. Industry, as it expands, draws an ever greater proportion of humanity's increasing numbers into large cities. But life in large cities is not conducive to mental health (the highest incidence of schizophrenia, we are told, occurs among the swarming inhabitants of industrial slums); nor does it foster the kind of responsible freedom within small self-governing groups, which is the first condition of a genuine democracy. City life is anonymous and, as it were, abstract. People are related to one another, not as total personalities, but as the embodiments of economic functions or, when they are not at work, as irresponsible seekers of entertainment. Subjected to this kind of life, individuals tend to feel lonely and insignificant. Their existence ceases to have any point or meaning.

Biologically speaking, man is a moderately gregarious, not a completely social animal—a creature more like a wolf, let us say, or an elephant, than like a bee or an ant. In their original form human societies bore no resemblance to the hive or the ant heap; they were merely packs. Civilization is, among other things, the process by which primitive packs are transformed into an analogue, crude and mechanical, of the social insects' organic communities. At the present time the pressures of over-population and technological change are accelerating this process. The termitary has come to seem a realizable and even, in some eyes, a desirable ideal. Needless to say, the ideal will never in fact be realized. A great gulf separates the social insect from the not too gregarious, big-brained mammal; and even though the mammal should do his best to imitate the insect, the gulf would remain. However hard they try, men cannot create a social organism, they can only create an organization. In the process of trying to create an organism they will merely create a totalitarian despotism.

Brave New World presents a fanciful and somewhat ribald picture of a society, in which the attempt to recreate human beings in the likeness of termites has been pushed almost to the limits of the possible. That we are being propelled in the direction of Brave New World is obvious. But no less obvious is the fact that we can, if we so desire, refuse to co-operate with the blind forces that are propelling us. For the moment, however, the wish to resist does not seem to be very strong or very widespread. As Mr. William Whyte has shown in his remarkable book, *The Organization Man*, a new Social Ethic is replacing our traditional ethical system—the system in which the individual is primary. The key words in this Social Ethic are "adjustment," "adaptation," "socially oriented behavior," "belongingness," "acquisition of social skills," "team work," "group living," "group loyalty," "group dynamics," "group thinking," "group creativity." Its basic assumption is that the social whole has greater worth and significance than its individual parts, that inborn biological differences should be sacrificed to cultural uniformity, that the rights of the collectivity take precedence over what the eighteenth century called the Rights of Man. According to the Social Ethic, Jesus was completely wrong in asserting that the Sabbath was made for man. On the contrary, man was made for the Sabbath, and must sacrifice his inherited idiosyncrasies and pretend to be the kind of standardized good mixer that organizers of group activity regard as ideal for their purposes. This ideal man is the man who displays "dynamic conformity" (delicious phrase!) and an intense loyalty to the group, an unflagging desire to subordinate himself, to belong. And the ideal man must have an ideal wife, highly gregarious, infinitely adaptable and not merely resigned to the fact that her husband's first loyalty is to the Corporation, but actively loyal on her own account. "He for God only," as Milton said of Adam and Eve, "she for God in him." And in one important respect the wife of the ideal organization man is a good deal worse off than our First Mother. She and Adam were permitted by the Lord to be completely uninhibited in the matter of "youthful dalliance."

> Nor turned, I ween,
> Adam from his fair spouse, nor Eve the rites
> Mysterious of connubial love refused.

Today, according to a writer in the *Harvard Business Review*, the wife of the man who is trying to live up to the ideal proposed by the Social Ethic, "must not demand too much of her husband's time and interest. Because of his single-minded concentration on his job, even his sexual activity must be relegated to a secondary place." The monk makes vows of poverty, obedience and chastity. The organization man is allowed to be rich, but promises obedience ("he accepts authority without resentment, he looks up to his superiors"—*Mussolini ha sempre ragione*) and he must be prepared, for the greater glory of the organization that employs him, to forswear even conjugal love.

It is worth remarking that, in *1984*, the members of the Party are compelled to conform to a sexual ethic of more than Puritan severity. In *Brave New World*, on the other hand, all are permitted to indulge their sexual impulses without let or hindrance. The society described in Orwell's fable is a society permanently at war, and the aim of its rulers is first, of course, to exercise power for its own delightful sake and, second, to keep their subjects in that state of constant tension which a state of constant war demands of those who wage it. By crusading against sexuality the bosses are able to maintain the required tension in their followers and at the same time can satisfy their lust for power in a most gratifying way. The society described in *Brave New World* is a world-state, in which war has been eliminated and where the first aim of the rulers is at all costs to keep their subjects from making trouble. This they achieve by (among other methods) legalizing a degree of sexual freedom (made possible by the abolition of the family) that practically guarantees the Brave New Worlders against any form of destructive (or creative) emotional tension. In *1984* the lust for power is satisfied by inflicting pain; in *Brave New World*, by inflicting a hardly less humiliating pleasure.

The current Social Ethic, it is obvious, is merely a justification after the fact of the less desirable consequences of over-organization. It represents a pathetic attempt to make a virtue of necessity, to extract a positive value from an unpleasant datum. It is a very unrealistic, and therefore very dangerous, system of morality. The social whole, whose value is assumed to be greater than that of its component parts, is not an organism in the sense that a hive or a termitary may be thought of as an organism. It is merely an organization, a piece of social machinery. There can be no value except in relation to life and awareness. An organization is neither conscious nor alive. Its value is instrumental and derivative. It is not good in itself; it is good only to the extent that it promotes the good of the individuals who are the parts of the collective whole. To give organizations precedence over persons is to subordinate ends to means. What happens when ends are subordinated to means was clearly demonstrated by Hitler and Stalin. Under their hideous rule personal ends were subordinated to organizational means by a mixture of violence and propaganda, systematic terror and the systematic manipulation of minds. In the more efficient dictatorships of tomorrow there will probably be much less violence than under Hitler and Stalin. The future dictator's subjects will be painlessly regimented by a corps of highly trained social engineers. "The challenge of social engineering in our time," writes an enthusiastic advocate of this new science, "is like the challenge of technical engineering fifty years ago. If the first half of the twentieth century was the era of the technical engineers, the second half may well be the era of the social engineers" —and the twenty-first century, I suppose, will be the era of World Controllers, the scientific caste system and Brave New World. To the question *quis custodiet custodes?*—Who will mount guard over our guardians, who will engineer the engineers?—the answer is a bland denial that they need any supervision. There seems to be a touching belief among certain Ph.D.'s in sociology that Ph.D.'s in sociology will never be corrupted by power. Like Sir Galahad's, their strength is as the strength of ten because their heart is pure—and their heart is pure because they are scientists and have taken six thousand hours of social studies.

Alas, higher education is not necessarily a guarantee of higher virtue, or higher political wisdom. And to these misgivings on ethical and psychological grounds must be added misgivings of a purely scientific character. Can we accept the theories on which the social engineers base their practice, and in terms of which they justify their manipulations of human beings? For example, Professor Elton Mayo tells us categorically that "man's desire to be continuously associated in work with his fellows is a strong, if not the strongest human characteristic." This, I would say, is manifestly untrue. Some people have the kind of desire described by Mayo; others do not. It is a matter of temperament and inherited constitution. Any social organization based upon the assumption that "man" (whoever "man" may be) desires to be continuously associated with his fellows would be, for many individual men and women, a bed of Procrustes. Only by being amputated or stretched upon the rack could they be adjusted to it.

Again, how romantically misleading are the lyrical accounts of the Middle Ages with which many contemporary theorists of social relations adorn their works! "Membership in a guild, manorial estate or village protected medieval man throughout his life and gave him peace and serenity." Protected him from what, we may ask. Certainly not from remorseless bullying at the hands of his superiors. And along with all that "peace and serenity" there was, throughout the Middle Ages, an enormous amount of chronic frustration, acute unhappiness and a passionate resentment against the rigid, hierarchical system that permitted no vertical movement up the social ladder and, for those who were bound to the land, very little horizontal movement in space. The impersonal forces of over-population and over-organization, and the social engineers who are trying to direct these forces, are pushing us in the direction of a new medieval system. This revival will be made more acceptable than the original by such Brave-New-Worldian amenities as infant conditioning, sleep-teaching and drug-induced euphoria; but, for the majority of men and women, it will still be a kind of servitude.

section FOUR

Radical School Ideas

"Democracy means government by the uneducated, while aristocracy means government by the badly educated."
—G. K. Chesterton

"I have never let schooling interfere with my education."
—Mark Twain

chapter 11

Directions for Change

The vogue for radical school reform seems to be increasing at the present time. The free school movement has been a by-product of the youthful counter-culture and civil rights movements. Young militants see the schools as a means for altering the destructive effects of a society hooked on war, racism, and elitistic competition at the expense of other meaningful forms of human existence. The free school movement, a desire for radical school reform, has taken on much of the overtones of the hip culture along with much of the sentimental and romantic rhetoric which accompanies it.

Conversations concerning the development of the free schools typically involve ideas about the abandoning of curriculum, the necessity for open classrooms, confrontation and dialogue with the students and the teacher as co-equals, elimination of the formal physical setting of the classroom, and the utilization of the community and the community-related facilities such as stores, factories, parks, and family life. The movement assumes that formal teacher training, educational requirements for students, and efficient school administration are not only unnecessary but are probably destructive to the basic and essential purpose of a good education. Part of the rhetoric which is common to this trend is an assumption that moral choices and moral imperatives as such have no place in this school, but that the school should be completely devoid of sanctions and taboos, of rules and rituals, and that the children's interests, motives, and humanistic concerns should not only determine the curriculum but the nature of the day, its length, its setting, and the overall purpose of the school process. In many ways this approach parallels the attempt of the rock culture in music, the hip scene in general, and the counter-culture in all its manifestations to provide an educational form, an avenue for children, which is directly antagonistic to the values and sanctions of the establishment. In this sense these new schools at all levels, whether the child care centers for preschool children or a free university envisioned by many university radicals, are providing for the first time a meaningful forum for children as well as adults who wish to engage in a humanistic dialogue divorced from the usual consumer orientation and competitive-destructive ethos which has dominated the traditional American public educational scene.

The problem inherent in most of this discussion about free schools is not that many of the ideas are not meaningful and highly exciting to those who have not heard them before, but rather that they approach the topic of the free school without considering the literature and theoretical materials which have long existed on free schools of this very type. The movement itself is quite hostile to critical analysis and rational inquiry. Unlike the hip culture in general, it is often actually antagonistic to careful intellectual inquiry and thoughtful discussion. In this sense, much of the free school movement is anti-intellectual and extremely shallow as a careful analysis of the needs and methods involved in the development of good educational practice.

Seldom in the discussions of the free school movement does one hear a clear analysis of the traditions of Pestalozzi, Montessori, and Freobel, because typically their ideas as well as the experiences of others like Bertrand Russell, A.S. Neil, and John Dewey have not been considered in a careful manner. It is assumed by many free school advocates that one simply needs to provide a romantic concern for children and ignore the scientific, humanistic, and behavioral literature which indicates that free schools could be established which would vastly improve the present day educational approach, but which would also be quite different from either the machine-like schools of the present technological society or the sentimental utopias of a future free-form society.

Freedom versus Authority in Education

Bertrand Russell

The following article by Bertrand Russell clearly presents the difficulties which are present in genuinely free and effective forms of education. He argues that neither the state nor the church nor the family is seriously interested in the process of open inquiry and the development of free and carefully informed opinion. They are rather motivated by other interpretations of the child's best interest. Generally, the attempt made by the state as well as the church is to control the thought process of the child for the purpose of subservience to a supposedly higher goal which has been established by the state or the church. The same is true for the family's goals in general, since the family places its own status or income above the actual needs of the child. In essence, Russell argues that if the child is allowed to follow his own inclinations and is surrounded by teachers who are not frightened by divergence and nonconforming opinions, the child will move toward intellectual and social development at a level corresponding with his abilities and needs. The Russell thesis is one with which many behaviorists would also concur, namely that if the child is allowed to move out toward an educational environment that provides several different alternative modes of activity and inquiry, the child will select those activities which reinforce his own developing interests and needs. The conditioning process which the state and the church and the family desire from the schools is inevitably destructive and counterproductive in terms of bringing out the more natural social and intellectual interests of the child. Whatever natural curiosity and human concern the child may have is usually destroyed by the arbitrary and shallow educational process which is characteristic of most traditional school systems. For the purpose inevitably is to produce the conforming and jingoistic citizen full of parochial beliefs without any real awareness or understanding of the complexity of human existence. This kind of person is far more

Reprinted by permission of the publisher, George Allen & Unwin Ltd. from Bertrand Russell, *Sceptical Essays*, copyright 1928.

easy to manipulate by the capitalist or socialist society and is also far more subject to the appeals of bigotry, war, and other forms of irrational human conflict. The kind of free education for which Russell argues is rarely possible within the public schools of the United States and probably is rarely found within any national culture because, by its very nature, the true educational process will be quite alienative to the exploitive and manipulatory ends of the state, the church, or the family. The questions that may be asked are the following: Is it possible for a modern-day society to maintain schools provided by public expense which essentially provide the groundwork for a rational analysis of the very existence of the state and for the deficits and failings of the society in which the child is educated? Can one expect that the school system will evoke the same financial support and also expect it will be free and able to provide a truly free and informed educational process? Or is it necessary and inevitable that public schools remain in the dismal wasteland of intellectual conformity and general subservience to the interest of the state? Finally, what kind of a school would be best suited to more fully develop the kind of human being whose evolving interests, both social and intellectual, are the concerns of the school itself rather than the external dictates of either the state, the church, or the family?

Freedom, in education as in other things, must be a matter of degree. Some freedoms cannot be tolerated. I met a lady once who maintained that no child should ever be forbidden to do anything, because a child ought to develop its nature from within. "How if its nature leads it to swallow pins?" I asked; but I regret to say the answer was mere vituperation. And yet every child, left to itself, will sooner or later swallow pins, or drink poison out of medicine bottles, or fall out of an upper window, or otherwise bring itself to a bad end. At a slightly later age, boys, when they have the opportunity, will go unwashed, overeat, smoke till they are sick, catch chills from sitting in wet feet, and so on—let alone the fact that they will amuse themselves by plaguing elderly gentlemen, who may not all have Elisha's powers of repartee. Therefore one who advocates freedom in education cannot mean that children should do exactly as they please all day long. An element of discipline and authority must exist; the question is as to the amount of it, and the way in which it is to be exercised.

Education may be viewed from many standpoints; that of the State, of the Church, of the schoolmaster, of the parents, or even (though this is usually forgotten) of the child itself. Each of these points of view is partial; each contributes something to the ideal of education, but also contributes elements that are bad. Let us examine them successively, and see what is to be said for and against them.

We will begin with the State, as the most powerful force in deciding what modern education is to be. The interest of the State in education is very recent. It did not exist in antiquity or the Middle Ages; until the Renaissance, education was only valued by the Church. The Renaissance brought an interest in advanced scholarship, leading to the foundation of such institutions as the Collège de France, intended to offset the ecclesiastical Sorbonne. The Reformation, in England and Germany, brought a desire on the part of the State to have some control over universities and grammar schools, to prevent them from remaining hotbeds of "Popery." But this interest soon evaporated. The State took no decisive or continuous part until the quite modern movement for universal compulsory education. Nevertheless the State, now, has more to say to scholastic institutions than have all the other factors combined.

The motives which led to universal compulsory education were various. Its strongest advocates were moved by the feeling that it is in itself desirable to be able to read and write, that an ignorant population is a disgrace to a civilized country, and that democracy is impossible without education. These motives were reinforced by others. It was soon seen that education gave commercial advantages, that it diminished juvenile crime, and that it gave opportunities for regimenting slum populations. Anti-clericals perceived in State education an opportunity of combating the influence of the Church; this motive weighed considerably in England and France. Nationalists, especially after the Franco-Prussian War, considered that universal education would increase the national strength. All these other reasons, however, were at first subsidiary. The main reason for adopting universal education was the feeling that illiteracy was disgraceful.

This institution, once firmly established, was found by the State to be capable of many uses. It makes young people more docile, both for good and evil. It improves manners and diminishes crime; it facilitates common action for public ends; it makes the community more responsive to direction from a center. Without it, democracy cannot exist except as an empty form. But democracy, as conceived by politicians, is a form of *government*, that is to say, it is a method of making people do what their leaders wish under the impression that they are doing what they themselves wish. Accordingly, State education has acquired a certain bias. It teaches the young (so far as it can) to respect existing institutions, to avoid all fundamental criticism of the powers that be, and to regard foreign nations with suspicion and contempt. It increases national solidarity at the expense both of internationalism and of individual development. The damage to individual development comes through the undue stress upon authority. Collective rather than individual emotions are encouraged, and disagreement with prevailing beliefs is severely repressed. Uniformity is desired because it is convenient to the administrator, regardless of the fact that it can only be secured by mental atrophy. So great are the resulting evils that it can be seriously questioned whether universal education has hitherto done good or harm on the balance.

The point of view of the Church as regards education is, in practice, not very different from that of the State. There is, however, one important divergence: the Church would prefer that the laity should not be educated at all, and only gives them instruction when the State insists. The State and the Church both wish to instill beliefs which are likely to be dispelled by free inquiry. But the State creed is easier to instill into a population which can read the newspaper, whereas the Church creed is easier to instill into a wholly illiterate population. State and Church are both hostile to thought, but the Church is also (though now surreptitiously) hostile to instruction. This will pass, and is passing, as the ecclesiastical authorities perfect the technique of giving instruction without stimulating mental activity —a technique in which, long ago, the Jesuits led the way.

The schoolmaster, in the modern world, is seldom allowed a point of view of his own. He is appointed by an education authority, and is "sacked" if he is found to be educating. Apart from this economic motive, the schoolmaster is exposed to temptations of which he is likely to be unconscious. He stands, even more directly than the State and the Church, for discipline, officially he knows what his pupils do not know. Without some element of discipline and authority, it is difficult to keep a class in order. It is easier to punish a boy for showing boredom than it is to be interesting. Moreover, even the best schoolmaster is likely to exaggerate his importance, and to deem it possible and desirable to mould his pupils into the sort of human beings that he thinks they ought to be. Lytton Strachey describes Dr. Arnold walking beside the Lake of Como and meditating on "moral evil." Moral evil, for him, was whatever he wished to change in his boys. The belief that there was a great deal of it in them justified him in the exercise of power, and in conceiving of himself as a ruler whose duty was even more to chasten than to love. This attitude—variously phrased in various ages—is natural to any schoolmaster who is zealous without being on the watch for the deceitful influence of self-importance. Nevertheless the teacher is far the best of the forces concerned in education, and it is primarily to him or her that we must look for progress.

Then, again, the schoolmaster wants the credit of his school. This makes him wish to have his boys distinguish themselves in athletic contests and scholarship examinations, which leads to care for a certain selection of superior boys to the exclusion of the others. For the rank and file, the result is bad. It is much better for a boy to play a game badly himself than to watch others playing it well. Mr. H. G. Wells, in his *Life of Sanderson of Oundle*, tells how this really great schoolmaster set his face against everything that left the faculties of the average boy unexercised and uncared for. When he became head master, he found that only certain selected boys were expected to sing in chapel; they were trained as a choir, and the rest listened. Sanderson insisted that all should sing, whether musical or not. In this he was rising above the bias which is natural to a schoolmaster who cares more for his credit than for his boys. Of course, if we all apportioned credit wisely there would be no conflict between these two motives: the school which did best by the boys would get the most credit. But in a busy world spectacular successes will always win credit out of proportion to their real importance, so that some conflict between the two motives is hardly avoidable.

I come now to the point of view of the parent. This differs according to the economic status of the parent: the average wage-earner has desires quite different from those of the average professional man. The average wage-earner wishes to get his children to school as soon as possible, so as to diminish bother at home; he also wishes to get them away as soon as possible, so as to profit by their earnings. When recently the British Government decided to cut down expenditure on education, it proposed that children should not go to school before the age of six, and should not be obliged to stay after the age of thirteen. The former proposal caused such a popular outcry that it had to be dropped: the indignation of worried mothers (recently enfranchised) was irresistible. The latter proposal, lowering the age for leaving school, was not unpopular. Parliamentary candidates advocating better education would get unanimous applause from those who came to meetings, but would find, in canvassing, that unpolitical wage-earners (who are the majority) want their children to be free to get paid work as soon as possible. The exceptions are mainly those who hope that their children may rise in the social scale through better education.

Professional men have quite a different outlook. Their own income depends upon the fact that they have had a better education than the average, and they wish to hand on this advantage to their children. For this object they are willing to make great sacrifices. But in our present competitive society, what will be desired by the average parent is not an education which is good in itself, but an education which is better than other people's. This may be facilitated by keeping down the general level, and therefore we cannot expect a professional man to be enthusiastic about facilities for higher education for the children of wage-earners. If everybody who desired it could get a medical education, however poor his parents might be, it is obvious that doctors would earn less than they do, both from increased competition and from the improved health of the community. The same thing applies to the law, the civil service, and so on. Thus the good things which the professional man desires for his own children he will not desire for the bulk of the population unless he has exceptional public spirit.

The fundamental defect of fathers, in our competitive society, is that they want their children to be a credit to them. This is rooted in instinct, and can only be cured by efforts directed to that end. The defect exists also, though to a lesser degree, in mothers. We all feel, instinctively, that our children's successes reflect glory upon ourselves, while their failures make us feel shame. Unfortunately, the successes which cause us to swell with pride are often of an undesirable kind. From the dawn of civilization till almost our own time—and still in China and Japan—parents have sacrificed their children's happiness in marriage by deciding whom they were to marry, choosing almost always the richest bride or bridegroom available. In the Western world (except partially in France) children have freed themselves from this slavery by rebellion, but parents' instincts have not changed. Neither happiness nor virtue, but worldly success, is what the average father desires for his children. He wants them to be such as he can boast of to his cronies, and this desire largely dominates his efforts for their education.

Authority, if it is to govern education, must rest upon one or several of the powers we have considered: the State, the Church, the schoolmaster, and the parent. We have seen that no one of them can be trusted to care adequately for the child's welfare, since each wishes the child to minister to some end which has nothing to do with its own well-being. The State wants the child to serve for national aggrandizement and the support of the existing form of government. The Church wants the child to serve for increasing the power of the priesthood. The schoolmaster, in a competitive world, too often regards his school as the State regards the nation, and wants the child to glorify the school. The parent wants the child to glorify the family. The child itself, as an end in itself, as a separate human being with a claim to whatever happiness and well-being may be possible, does not come into these various external purposes, except very partially. Unfortunately, the child lacks the experience required for the guidance of its own life, and is therefore a prey to the sinister interests that batten on its innocence. This is what makes the difficulty of education as a political problem. But let us first see what can be said from the child's own point of view.

It is obvious that most children, if they were left to themselves, would not learn to read or write, and would grow up less adapted than they might be to the circumstances of their lives. There must be educational institutions, and children must be to some extent under authority. But in view of the fact that no authority can be wholly trusted, we must aim at having as little authority as possible, and try to think out ways by which young people's natural desires and impulses can be utilized in education. This is far more possible than is often thought, for, after all, the desire to acquire knowledge is natural to most young people. The traditional pedagogue, possessing knowledge not worth imparting, and devoid of all skill in imparting it, imagined that young people have a native horror of instruction, but in this he was misled by failure to realize his own shortcomings. There is a charming tale of Tchekov's about a man who tried to teach a kitten to catch mice. When it wouldn't run after them, he beat it, with the result that even as an adult cat it cowered with terror in the presence of a mouse. "This is the man," Tchekov adds, "who taught me Latin." Now cats teach their kittens to catch mice, but they wait till the instinct has awakened. Then the kittens agree with their mammas that the knowledge is worth acquiring, so that discipline is not required.

The first two or three years of life have hitherto escaped the domination of the pedagogue, and all authorities are agreed that those are the years in which we learn most. Every child learns to talk by its own efforts. Anyone who has watched an infant knows that the efforts required are very considerable. The child listens intently, watches movements of the lips, practices sounds all day long, and concentrates with amazing ardor. Of course grown-up people encourage it by praise, but it does not occur to them to punish it on days when it learns no new word. All that they provide is opportunity and praise. It is doubtful whether more is required at any stage.

What is necessary is to make the child or young person feel that the knowledge is worth having. Sometimes this is difficult because in fact the knowledge is not worth having. It is also difficult when only a considerable amount of knowledge in any direction is useful, so that at first the pupil tends to be merely bored. In such cases, however, the difficulty is not insuperable. Take, for instance, the teaching of mathematics. Sanderson of Oundle found that almost all his boys were interested in machinery, and he provided them with opportunities for making quite elaborate machines. In the course of this practical work, they came upon the necessity for making calculations, and thus grew interested in mathematics as required for the success of a constructive enterprise on which they were keen. This method is expensive, and involves patient skill on the part of the teacher. But it goes along the lines of the pupil's instinct, and is therefore likely to involve less boredom with more intellectual effort. Effort is natural both to animals and men, but it must be effort for which there is an instinctive stimulus. A football match involves more effort than the treadmill, yet the one is a pleasure and the other a punishment. It is a mistake to suppose that mental effort can rarely be a pleasure; what is true is that certain conditions are required to make it pleasurable, and that, until lately, no attempt was made to create these conditions in education. The chief conditions are: first, a problem of which the solution is desired; secondly, a feeling of hopefulness as to the possibility of obtaining a solution. Consider the way David Copperfield was taught arithmetic:

> Even when the lessons are done, the worst is yet to happen, in the shape of an appalling sum. This is invented for me, and delivered to me orally by Mr. Murdstone, and begins, "If I go into a cheesemonger's shop, and buy five thousand double-Gloucester cheeses at fourpence-halfpenny each, present payment"—at which I see Miss Murdstone secretly overjoyed. I pore over these cheeses without any result or enlightenment until dinner-time; when, having made a mulatto of myself by getting the dirt of the slate into the pores of my skin, I have a slice of bread to help me out with the cheeses, and am considered in disgrace for the rest of the evening.

Obviously the poor boy could not be expected to take any interest in the cheeses, or to have any hope of doing the sum right. If he had wanted a box of a certain size, and had been told to save up his allowance until he could buy enough wood and nails, it would have stimulated his arithmetical powers amazingly.

There should be nothing hypothetical about the sums that a child is asked to do. I remember once reading a young boy's own account of his arithmetic lesson. The governess set the problem: If a horse is worth three times as much as a pony, and the pony is worth £22, what is the horse worth? "Had he been down?" asks the boy. "That makes no difference," says the governess. "Oh, but James (the groom) says it makes a great difference." The power of understanding hypothetical truth is one of the latest developments of logical faculty, and ought not to be expected in the very young. This, however, is a digression, from which we must return to our main theme.

I do not maintain that *all* children can have their intellectual interests aroused by suitable stimuli. Some have much less than average intelligence, and require special treatment. It is very undesirable to combine in one class children whose mental capacities are very different: the cleverer ones will be bored by having things explained that they clearly understand, and the stupider ones will be worried by having things taken for granted that they have not yet grasped. But subjects and methods should be adapted to the intelligence of the pupil. Macaulay was made to learn mathematics at Cambridge, but it is obvious from his letters that it was a sheer waste of time. I was made to learn Latin and Greek, but I resented it, being of the opinion that it was silly to learn a language that was no longer spoken. I believe that all the little good I got from years of classical studies I could have got in adult life in a month. After the bare minimum, account should be taken of tastes, and pupils should only be taught what they find interesting. This puts a strain upon teachers, who find it easier to be dull, especially if they are overworked. But the difficulties can be overcome by giving teachers shorter hours and instruction in the art of teaching, which is done at present in training teachers in elementary schools, but not teachers in universities or public schools.

Freedom in education has many aspects. There is first of all freedom to learn or not to learn. There is freedom as to what to learn. And in later education there is freedom of opinion. Freedom to learn or not to learn can only partially be conceded in childhood. It is necessary to make sure that all who are not imbecile learn to read and write. How far this can be done by the mere provision of opportunity, only experience can show. But even if opportunity alone suffices, children must have the opportunity thrust upon them. Most of them would rather play out of doors, where the necessary opportunities would be lacking. Later on, it might be left to the choice of young people whether, for instance, they should go to the university; some would wish to do so, others would not. This would make quite as good a principle of selection as any to be got from entrance examinations. Nobody who did not work should be allowed to stay at a university. The rich young men who now waste their time in college are demoralizing others and teaching themselves to be useless. If hard work were exacted as a condition of residence, universities would cease to be attractive to people with a distaste for intellectual pursuits.

Freedom as to what to learn ought to exist far more than at

present. I think it is necessary to group subjects by their natural affinities; there are grave disadvantages in the elective system, which leaves a young man free to choose wholly unconnected subjects. If I were organizing education in Utopia, with unlimited funds, I should give every child, at the age of about twelve, some instruction in classics, mathematics, and science. After two years, it ought to be evident where the child's aptitudes lay, and the child's own tastes would be a safe indication, provided there were no "soft options." Consequently I should allow every boy and girl who so desired to specialize from the age of fourteen. At first, the specialization should be very broad, growing gradually more defined as education advanced. The time when it was possible to be universally well informed is past. An industrious man may know something of history and literature, which requires a knowledge of classical and modern languages. Or he may know some parts of mathematics, or one or two sciences. But the ideal of an "all-around" education is out of date; it has been destroyed by the progress of knowledge.

Freedom of opinion, on the part of both teachers and pupils, is the most important of the various kinds of freedom, and the only one which requires no limitations whatever. In view of the fact that it does not exist, it is worth while to recapitulate the arguments in its favor.

The fundamental argument for freedom of opinion is the doubtfulness of all our beliefs. If we certainly knew the truth, there would be something to be said for teaching it. But in that case it could be taught without invoking authority, by means of its inherent reasonableness. It is not necessary to make a law that no one shall be allowed to teach arithmetic if he holds heretical opinions on the multiplication table, because here the truth is clear, and does not require to be enforced by penalties. When the State intervenes to ensure the teaching of some doctrine, it does so *because* there is no conclusive evidence in favor of that doctrine. The result is that the teaching is not truthful, even if it should happen to be true. In the State of New York, it was till lately illegal to teach that Communism is good; in Soviet Russia, it is illegal to teach that Communism is bad. No doubt one of these opinions is true and one false, but no one knows which. Either New York or Soviet Russia was teaching truth and proscribing falsehood, but neither was teaching truthfully, because each was representing a doubtful proposition as certain.

The difference between truth and truthfulness is important in this connection. Truth is for the gods; from our human point of view it is an ideal towards which we can approximate, but which we cannot hope to reach. Education should fit us for the nearest possible approach to truth, and to do this it must teach truthfulness. Truthfulness, as I mean it, is the habit of forming our opinions on the evidence, and holding them with that degree of conviction which the evidence warants. This degree will always fall short of complete certainty, and therefore we must be always ready to admit new evidence against previous beliefs. Moreover, when we act on a belief, we must, if possible, only take such action as will be useful even if our belief is more or less inaccurate; we should avoid actions which are disastrous unless our belief is *exactly* true. In science, an observer states his results along with the "probable error"; but who ever heard of a theologian or a politician stating the probable error in his dogmas, or even admitting that any error is conceivable? That is because in science, where we approach nearest to real knowledge, a man can safely rely on the strength of his case, whereas, where nothing is known, blatant assertion and hypnotism are the usual ways of causing others to share our beliefs. If the fundamentalists thought they had a good case against evolution, they would not make the teaching of it illegal.

The habit of teaching some one orthodoxy, political, religious, or moral, has all kinds of bad effects. To begin with, it excludes from the teaching profession men who combine honesty with intellectual vigor, who are just the men likely to have the best moral and mental effect upon their pupils. I will give three illustrations. First, as to politics: a teacher of economics in America is expected to teach such doctrines as will add to the wealth and power of the very rich; if he does not, he finds it advisable to go elsewhere, like Mr. Laski, formerly of Harvard, now one of the most valuable teachers in the London School of Economics. Second, as to religion: the immense majority of intellectually eminent men disbelieve the Christian religion, but they conceal the fact in public, because they are afraid of losing their incomes. Thus on the most important of all subjects most of the men whose opinions and arguments would be best worth having are condemned to silence. Third, as to morals: Practically all men are unchaste at some time of their lives; clearly those who conceal this fact are worse than those who do not, since they add the guilt of hypocrisy. But it is only to the hypocrites that teaching posts are open. So much for the effects of orthodoxy upon the choice and character of teachers.

I come now to the effect upon the pupils, which I will take under two heads, intellectual and moral. Intellectually, what is stimulating to a young man is a problem of obvious practical importance, as to which he finds that divergent opinions are held. A young man learning economics, for example, ought to hear lectures from individualists and socialists, protectionists and free-traders, inflationists and believers in the gold standard. He ought to be encouraged to read the best books of the various schools, as recommended by those who believe in them. This would teach him to weigh arguments and evidence, to know that no opinion is certainly right, and to judge men by their quality rather than by their consonance with preconceptions. History should be taught not only from the point of view of one's own country, but also from that of foreigners. If history were taught by Frenchmen in England, and by Englishmen in France, there would be no disagreements between the two countries, because each would understand the other's point of view. A young man should learn to think that all questions are open, and that an argument should be followed wherever it leads. The needs of practical life will destroy this attitude all too soon when he begins to earn his living; but until that time he should be encouraged to taste the joys of free speculation.

Morally, also, the teaching of an orthodoxy to the young is very harmful. There is not only the fact that it compels the abler teachers to be hypocrites, and therefore to set a bad moral example, but there is also, what is more important, the fact that it encourages intolerance and the bad forms of herd instinct. Edmund Gosse, in his *Father and Son*, relates how, when he was a boy, his father told him he was going to marry again. The boy saw there was something his father was ashamed of, so at last he asked, in accents of horror: "Father, is she a Pædo-Baptist?" And she was. Until that moment, he had believed all Pædo-Baptists to be wicked. So children in Catholic schools believe that Protestants are wicked, children in any school in an English-speaking country believe that atheists are wicked, children in France believe that Germans are wicked, and children in Germany believe that Frenchmen are wicked. When a school accepts as part of its task the teaching of an opinion which cannot be intellectually defended (as practically all schools do), it is compelled to give the impression that those who hold an opposite opinion are wicked, since otherwise it cannot generate the passion required for repelling the assaults of reason. Thus for the sake of orthodoxy the children are rendered uncharitable, intolerant, cruel, and bellicose. This is unavoidable so long as definite opinions are prescribed on politics, morals, and religion.

Finally, arising out of this moral damage to the individual, there is untold damage to society. Wars and persecutions are rife everywhere, and everywhere they are rendered possible by the teaching in the schools. Wellington used to say that the battle of Waterloo was won on the playing-fields of Eton. He might have said with more truth that the war against revolutionary France was instigated in the classrooms of Eton. In our democratic age, Eton has become unimportant; now, it is the ordinary elementary and secondary school that matters. In every country, by means of flag-waving, Empire Day, Fourth-of-July celebrations, Officers' Training Corps, etc., everything is done to give boys a taste for homicide, and girls a conviction that men given to homicide are the most worthy of respect. This whole system of moral degradation to which innocent boys and girls are exposed would become impossible if the authorities allowed freedom of opinion to teachers and pupils.

Regimentation is the source of the evil. Education authorities do not look on children, as religion is supposed to do, as human beings with souls to be saved. They look upon them as material for grandiose social schemes: future "hands" in factories or "bayonets" in war or what not. No man is fit to educate unless he feels each pupil an end in himself, with his own rights and his own personality, nor merely a piece in a jig-saw puzzle, or a soldier in a regiment, or a citizen in a State. Reverence for human personality is the beginning of wisdom, in every social question, but above all in education.

Education as Growth

John Dewey

John Dewey is unquestionably the most discussed (and cussed) of American philosophers. Although his ideas on education have never been widely implemented, he is blamed for every aberration of the young. Benjamin Spock is not even a close second. Dewey inhabits the same place in most people's minds as does Karl Marx—that region to which are consigned the little understood but obviously pestilential purveyors of ideas.

Reprinted by permission of Kappa Delta Pi, An Honor Society in Education. From *Experience and Education*, John Dewey, Collier Books Edition, 1963.

One of the most salient points which Dewey makes in the following selection is that educators have no philosophy of education. All they have is a collection of multi-purpose public relations clichés. The charge that educators fail to think systematically about what they do is echoed in other selections in this book.

Dewey's own philosophy of education assumes the desirability of exploiting experience for intellectual enrichment. One can think of Dewey as being an intellectual hedonist. Experience is to be aggressively sought and plumbed. To the extent that any experience inhibits the acquisition or exploitation of subsequent experiences, it is mis-educative. The purpose of school, then, is to assist students in extracting as much meaning as possible from their experiences and to give students experiences that will lead to continued intellectual growth.

Dewey's emphasis on personal growth will be heartily endorsed by many free-spirited youth. However, Dewey espouses growth as an end in itself, without specifying desirable directions which growth might take. Personal aggrandizement, even if of an intellectual sort, may not impress those youth who are socially conscious as being the most worthy of goals toward which one can aspire. Dewey did have a social morality, but his life attests to this more convincingly than do his writings on education.

In short, the point I am making is that rejection of the philosophy and practice of traditional education sets a new type of difficult educational problem for those who believe in the new type of education. We shall operate blindly and in confusion until we recognize this fact; until we thoroughly appreciate that departure from the old solves no problems. What is said in the following pages is, accordingly, intended to indicate some of the main problems with which the newer education is confronted and to suggest the main lines along which their solution is to be sought. I assume that amid all uncertainties there is one permanent frame of reference: namely, the organic connection between education and personal experience; or, that the new philosophy of education is committed to some kind of empirical and experimental philosophy. But experience and experiment are not self-explanatory ideas. Rather, their meaning is part of the problem to be explored. To know the meaning of empiricism we need to understand what experience is.

The belief that all genuine education comes about through experience does not mean that all experiences are genuinely or equally educative. Experience and education cannot be directly equated to each other. For some experiences are mis-educative. Any experience is mis-educative that has the effect of arresting or distorting the growth of further experience. An experience may be such as to engender callousness; it may produce lack of sensitivity and of responsiveness. Then the possibilities of having richer experience in the future are restricted. Again, a given experience may increase a person's automatic skill in a particular direction and yet tend to land him in a groove or rut; the effect again is to narrow the field of further experience. An experience may be immediately enjoyable and yet promote the formation of a slack and careless attitude; this attitude then operates to modify the quality of subsequent experiences so as to prevent a person from getting out of them what they have to give. Again, experiences may be so disconnected from one another that, while each is agreeable or even exciting in itself, they are not linked cumulatively to one another. Energy is then dissipated and a person becomes scatterbrained. Each experience may be lively, vivid, and "interesting," and yet their disconnectedness may artificially generate dispersive, disintegrated, centrifugal habits. The consequence of formation of such habits is inability to control future experiences. They are then taken, either by way of enjoyment or of discontent and revolt, just as they come. Under such circumstances, it is idle to talk of self-control.

Traditional education offers a plethora of examples of experiences of the kinds just mentioned. It is a great mistake to suppose, even tacitly, that the traditional schoolroom was not a place in which pupils had experiences. Yet this is tacitly assumed when progressive education as a plan of learning by experience is placed in sharp opposition to the old. The proper line of attack is that the experiences which were had, by pupils and teachers alike, were largely of a wrong kind. How many students, for example, were rendered callous to ideas, and how many lost the impetus to learn because of the way in which learning was experienced by them? How many acquired special skills by means of automatic drill so that their power of judgment and capacity to act intelligently in new situations was limited? How many came to associate the learning process with ennui and boredom? How many found what they did learn so foreign to the situations of life outside the school as to give them no power of control over the latter? How many came to associate books with dull drudgery, so that they were "conditioned" to all but flashy reading matter?

If I ask these questions, it is not for the sake of wholesale condemnation of the old education. It is for quite another purpose. It is to emphasize the fact, first, that young people in traditional schools do have experiences; and, secondly, that the trouble is not the absence of experiences, but their defective and wrong character—wrong and defective from the standpoint of connection with further experience.

The positive side of this point is even more important in connection with progressive education. It is not enough to insist upon the necessity of experience, nor even of activity in experience. Everything depends upon the *quality* of the experience which is had. The quality of any experience has two aspects. There is an immediate aspect of agreeableness or disagreeableness, and there is its influence upon later experiences. The first is obvious and easy to judge. The *effect* of an experience is not borne on its face. It sets a problem to the educator. It is his business to arrange for the kind of experiences which, while they do not repel the student, but rather engage his activities are, nevertheless, more than immediately enjoyable since they promote having desirable future experiences. Just as no man lives or dies to himself, so no experience lives and dies to itself. Wholly independent of desire or intent, every experience lives on in further experiences. Hence the central problem of an education based upon experience is to select the kind of present experiences that live fruitfully and creatively in subsequent experiences.

Later, I shall discuss in more detail the principle of the continuity of experience or what may be called the experiential continuum. Here I wish simply to emphasize the importance of this principle for the philosophy of educative experience. A philosophy of education, like any theory, has to be stated in words, in symbols. But so far as it is more than verbal it is a plan for conducting education. Like any plan, it must be framed with reference to what is to be done and how it is to be done. The more definitely and sincerely it is held that education is a development within, by, and for experience, the more important it is that there shall be clear conceptions of what experience is. Unless experience is so conceived that the result is a plan for deciding upon subject-matter, upon methods of instruction and discipline, and upon material equipment and social organization of the school, it is wholly in the air. It is reduced to a form of words which may be emotionally stirring but for which any other set of words might equally well be substituted unless they indicate operations to be initiated and executed. Just because traditional education was a matter of routine in which the plans and programs were handed down from the past, it does not follow that progressive education is a matter of planless improvisation.

The traditional school could get along without any consistently developed philosophy of education. About all it required in that line was a set of abstract words like culture, discipline, our great cultural heritage, etc., actual guidance being derived not from them but from custom and established routines. Just because progressive schools cannot rely upon established traditions and institutional habits, they must either proceed more or less haphazardly or be directed by ideas which, when they are made articulate and coherent, form a philosophy of education. Revolt against the kind of organization characteristic of the traditional school constitutes a demand for a kind of organization based upon ideas. I think that only slight acquaintance with the history of education is needed to prove that educational reformers and innovators alone have felt the need for a philosophy of education. Those who adhered to the established system needed merely a few fine-sounding words to justify existing practices. The real work was done by habits which were so fixed as to be institutional. The lesson for progressive education is that it requires in an urgent degree, a degree more pressing than was incumbent upon former innovators, a philosophy of education based upon a philosophy of experience.

I remarked incidentally that the philosophy in question is, to paraphrase the saying of Lincoln about democracy, one of education of, by, and for experience. No one of these words, *of*, *by*, or *for*, names anything which is self-evident. Each of them is a challenge to discover and put into operation a principle of order and organization which follows from understanding what educative experience signifies.

It is, accordingly, a much more difficult task to work out the kinds of materials, of methods, and of social relationships that are appropriate to the new education than is the case with traditional education. I think many of the difficulties experienced in the conduct of progressive schools and many of the criticisms leveled against them arise from this source. The difficulties are aggravated and the criticisms are increased when it is supposed that the new education is somehow easier than the old. This belief is, I imagine, more or less current. Perhaps it illustrates again the *Either-Or* philosophy, springing from the idea that about all which is required is *not* to do what is done in traditional schools.

I admit gladly that the new education is *simpler* in principle than the old. It is in harmony with principles of growth, while there is very much which is artificial in the old selection and arrangement of subjects and methods, and artificiality always leads to unnecessary complexity. But the easy and the simple are not identical. To discover what is really simple and to act upon the discovery is an exceedingly difficult task. After the artificial and complex is once institutionally established and ingrained in custom and routine, it is easier to walk in the paths that have been beaten than it is, after taking a new point of view, to work out what is practically involved in the new point of view. The old Ptolemaic astronomical system was more complicated with its cycles and epicycles than the Copernican system. But until organization of actual astronomical phenomena on the ground of the latter principle had been effected the easiest course was to follow the line of least resistance provided by the old intellectual habit. So we come back to the idea that a coherent *theory* of experience, affording positive direction to selection and organization of appropriate educational methods and materials, is required by the attempt to give new direction to the work of the schools. The process is a slow and arduous one. It is a matter of growth, and there are many obstacles which tend to obstruct growth and to deflect it into wrong lines.

I shall have something to say later about organization. All that is needed, perhaps, at this point is to say that we must escape from the tendency to think of organization in terms of the *kind* of organization, whether of content (or subject-matter), or of methods and social relations, that mark traditional education. I think that a good deal of the current opposition to the idea of organization is due to the fact that it is so hard to get away from the picture of the studies of the old school. The moment "organization" is mentioned imagination goes almost automatically to the kind of organization that is familiar, and in revolting against that we are led to shrink from the very idea of any organization. On the other hand, educational reactionaries, who are now gathering force, use the absence of adequate intellectual and moral organization in the newer type of school as proof not only of the need of organization, but to identify any and every kind of organization with that instituted before the rise of experimental science. Failure to develop a conception of organization upon the empirical and experimental basis gives reactionaries a too easy victory. But the fact that the empirical siences now offer the best type of intellectual organization which can be found in any field shows that there is no reason why we, who call ourselves empiricists, should be "pushovers" in the matter of order and organization.

Suffer, Little Children

Max Rafferty

Max Rafferty, the former superintendent of public instruction in California and right-wing candidate for the U.S. Senate, attacks the pragmatists for their life-adjustment approach to education. He does not think the curriculum should be a tedious compendium of mundane knowledge and skills but rather a collection of soul-stirring challenges to excellence. He feels that students have been deprived of great heroes with whom to identify and noble feats toward which to aspire.

Almost all the heroes named by Rafferty as worthy of inclusion in the curriculum are historical, fictional characters. Even Rafferty's prose style is redolent of his immersion in a romanticized past. Thus, it can be inferred that history and the literature of the past would figure heavily in a Rafferty-designed curriculum. Rafferty further implies that the sullied present is its own teacher, and the purpose of the schools is to give students the moral propulsion with which they can rise above the current miasma of mediocrity. In recent speeches Rafferty has indicated that the present is becoming increasingly distasteful to him, especially as it is reflected in the young.

Rafferty's despairing of idealism in the young must sound a strange note to those who think the youth of today are far more idealistic than their immediate predecessors. If young people *are* becoming more idealistic, can schools rightly claim some credit for this? Or would that be to stand reality on its head, since youthful activism is so often directed against the schools? And might it be that activism does not indicate idealism unless it reflects the biases of the observer?

It was the final agony for the great city. Despite the patient subtleties of Hannibal and the frenzied trumpetings of the great war elephants, Destiny and Carthage had at last come face to face. A hundred battles and a hundred thousand dead had led only to this: the Roman legions thundering at the gates, and Famine gripping Punic bellies in the seething ant hill that was the city. The fairest daughters of the oligarchy had long since pledged their lives to Ashtoreth and their lustrous locks to be shorn and braided and woven into bowstrings for the black Numidian archers who manned the crumbling walls. The fat and hook-nosed merchant princes had lumbered forth to bargain with the grim invader, to offer bribes of gold and slaves and Tyrian purple. They had remained to decorate the ubiquitous crosses which dotted the open plain about the dying city. Their piping screams mingled with the ribald taunts of their tormentors and with the whistling and thudding of the great siege engines.

The shape of Ate, that fiery-faced and typically Roman goddess of destruction, brooded visibly over the hovels and palaces of the doomed metropolis.

In the exact center of the city, a vast and sinister form reared itself against the African sky. Cast in gleaming bronze, it squatted on its haunches leering at the teeming hordes that sobbed and surged about its massive pedestal, spurred on to their desperate worship by the howling of their priests. On this, the last night of the city's life, Carthage swarmed and groveled at the feet of Moloch. Lit with the glow of myriad torches, the god seemed slowly to shine with some inner radiance, and, as the night grew older and cachinnations of the mob more frenzied, the slitted eyes of Moloch cast two beams of lurid crimson through the murk. Within the brazen belly of the god, his priests had kindled great fires which heated the huge idol to incandescence and caused the obscene features to shimmer fiendishly in the waves of heat.

An inclined runway led from the ground before the god to the door which now gaped open just below his navel. Up this ramp, driven by hippopotamus-hide whips in the hands of the foaming priests, stumbled and crept the children of Carthage. Babes in the arms of their older brothers and sisters, toddlers scarce able to lisp their mothers' names, wide-eyed little maids and sturdy boys, they went to the embrace of Moloch. They were garlanded with flowers, decked with jewels, and mad with fear. Below and gazing up at the shrinking victims genuflected their tearless elders, stabbing the night air with their shrieks to the god, imploring that the sacrifice be accepted and the destruction of the city averted.

One by one, sobbing and crying to their unhearing parents, the little ones were prodded and whipped to the edge of the runway, where they gazed down into Hell itself before they toppled pitifully into the molten bowels of the grinning god. The stench of burning flesh reached even to the nostrils of the besieging Romans, who paused, white-faced, beside their rams and catapults. Above the roar of maddened thousands, the red-hot countenance of Moloch glowed satiated, and promised victory upon the morrow.

The next day, the Romans sacked the city.

All the Carthaginians who had watched their children broil were tossed screaming from the city walls, entombed in flaming buildings, or spitted like geese upon the short swords of the legionaries. Moloch himself was thrown down, shattered into fragments, and spat upon.

Carthage was destroyed as no other city has ever been destroyed.

"Who shall offend one of these little ones," said a Greater than Moloch, "it were better for him that a millstone were hanged around his neck, and that he were drowned in the depths of the sea."

Never did a city so richly deserve its fate.

The great wheel of history has turned ponderously full-circle since the Punic Wars. A happier time for children dawned a century ago, and in that Golden Age a whole new pantheon of youthful gods and goddesses came down from Mount Olympus and made old Earth a magic place for boys and girls.

Wilfred of Ivanhoe rode stirrup to stirrup with Cœur de Lion, and the evil hold of Torquilstone burned eternal witness to the power of youth and goodness. Laughing and shouting in the same great company rode Arthur with his Table Round, forever splintering their lances in the cause of right, and leading forth the massed chivalry of France came Bayard, without fear and without reproach. A little to one side strode Christian, arms folded and eyes fixed steadfastly upon the Eternal City, but always with his good sword ready for the onset of Apollyon. Roistering and invincible swaggered Porthos, Athos and Aramis, with the young D'Artagnan, ever ready to draw those magic blades, the wonder of the world, for truth and glory and the Queen. The horn of Roland echoed through the pass at Roncesvalles, and somehow caught and mingled with the blast of Robin Hood, calling down the misty years upon his merry men of Sherwood.

Were not these fit gods for the children of mankind?

Apart and in a merry company leaped and played the Child Immortals. Hand in hand with long-haired Alice walked Christopher Robin, bright eyes alert for talking rabbits and greedy little bears.

Sturdy Jim Hawkins counted his pieces of eight and chaffed with Captain Flint, while young Tom Sawyer kept a wary lookout for the menace that was Injun Joe. A battered raft floated to immortality upon the broad bosom of the Father of Waters, and Huck became the apotheosis of all boys everywhere. Meg, Jo and Beth chattered gaily to Amy, and Dorothy skipped arm in arm with the Scarecrow down the yellow brick road.

When in any age have children had such shining exemplars?

It remained for our own generation to turn its back upon the heroes of the children and to mold a twentieth-century version of Moloch. His new name is Utilitarianism, and his priests are the pragmatists. Their ritual involves the endless repetition of the mystic words "adjustment to environment." Their goal is the destruction of all that cannot be statistically demonstrated, the immolation of fancy and fantasy and all that makes men different from the brutes. Even the nursery rhymes which have come down to us from time immemorial have been pronounced "reactionary" and "sordid." Hansel and Gretel have been dehydrated and neutralized to the status of Cincinnati children on a Sunday-school picnic, and Jack the Giant-Killer to a schoolboy swatting flies. Everything that was fearful and wonderful and glamorous has been leveled off to the lowest common denominator.

Ulysses and Penelope have been replaced by Dick and Jane in the textbooks of our schools. The quest for the Golden Fleece has been crowded out by the visit of Tom and Susan to the zoo. The deeds of the heroes before Troy are now passé, and the peregrinations of the local milkman as he wends his way through the stodgy streets and littered alleys of Blah City are deemed worthy of numberless pages in our primers. The sterile, stone-age culture of the Pueblo Indians looms large in our curriculum but the knightly Crusaders are ignored. Jackie pursues his insipid goal of a ride in the district garbage truck with good old crotchety Mr. Jones while the deathless ride of Paul Revere goes unwept, unhonored and unsung. It is interesting, and certainly significant, that modern education has deliberately debunked the hero to make room for the jerk. The lofty exception to the rank and file, whom all of us could envy and emulate, has been compelled to give way to the Great Mediocrity, the synthesis of all that is harmless and safe and banal among us.

Today, after two thousand years, again we worship Moloch. We sacrifice our children to him, and ululate his praises while all that is bright and promising in the generation which will follow us droops in the hot breath of the commonplace.

Moloch today is fashioned in the blasphemous image of Ourselves.

He is Daddy in the second-grade readers who comes mincing home with his eternal briefcase from his meaningless day in his antiseptic office just in time to pat Jip the dog and carry blonde little Laurie into the inevitable white bungalow on his stylishly padded shoulders.

He is Mommy in the third-grade books, always silk-stockinged and impeccable after a day spent over the electric range, with never a cross word on her carefully made-up lips and never an idea in her empty head.

He is Dick and Jane and Tom and Susan, and all the insufferable nonentities who clutter up the pages of our texts with their vapid ditherings about humdrum affairs which could never be of conceivable interest to anyone above the level of an idiot.

The crimson eyes of Moloch glare out at us from a thousand courses of study wherein pyramids are built in miniature but Egypt is ignored, igloos constructed but the vast panorama of the Northland forgotten, Kachina masks contrived but the place of the Indian in American history relegated to the realm of the unimportant. The voice of Moloch resounds throughout the land, averring in its oleaginous Teachers College accent that only the child's felt needs must be met, that memorization is a sin against the Holy Ghost, and that homework went out with the mustache cup. Haroun-al-Raschid, he whispers, is fascist, Tom Swift a rapacious capitalist, and Charlemagne a bloody old medievalist. The wars we fought were selfish wars; the people we died to free were pawns upon the chessboard of economic determinism; the precious documents that milestone our liberties were strait jackets fitted to the proletariat.

The children are being ushered along a facile runway, paved ever so smoothly with construction units and field trips, socializations and sharings, assemblies and group dynamics. The priests who prod them forward are hot-eyed, with telltale patches of saliva gathering in the corners of their mouths; they are devotees of the mediocre, which they worship under the sacred alias of Democratic Methods. They have been crammed to the craw with educationism, as long ago the zombie followers of the Old Man of the Mountain were stuffed with hashish. Their temples are the great universities which marble the land, stretching out their thousand campaniles to a Heaven of Demonstrable Utility and turning out swarms of neophytes each year to preach the gospel of Group Adaptation. Their secret crypts and inner sanctums are the graduate schools, which confer upon the masters of the cult certain cabalisms and charms in the guise of critiques and seminars, but which avoid any tinge of concern with literary or cultural refinements as a Moslem would a pork chop.

At the end of the runway lies, as it lay twenty centuries ago, a special kind of hell. We have improved somewhat upon the Carthaginians in the kind of fire which we provide and in the special types of fuel with which we stoke the flames. Just as our idol is no longer of massy bronze, so also is our conflagration one of the spirit rather than the flesh. But it burns deep.

It scorches genius.

It sears creative imagination to the bone.

It withers nonconformity.

All the pleasant flights of fancy which have brightened the horizons of our young for decades past—Peter Pan and Cinderella, Hercules and Thor—are grist for this monstrous, flaming mill. The slag and ashes are later shoveled into shape and substituted for the shimmering originals, ashes in the inane persons of Bill the Delivery Boy or Mr. Kindly, the Tugboat Operator.

Words that America has treasured as a rich legacy that have sounded like trumpet calls above the clash of arms and the fury of debate, are fading from the classrooms, and so from life itself. "Liberty and Union, now and forever, one and inseparable. . . ." "I only regret that I have but one life to give for my country. . . ." "Millions for defense, but not one cent for tribute. . . ." Search for these golden phrases in vain today in the textbooks of too many of our schools, in the hearts and minds of too many of our children. The golden words are gone, and in their place brain-numbing accounts of the nation's second-class mail service or units on the trucking industry and Highway 66. We must all, you see, grow up to be mailmen or truckers. We have no need of Websters, nor of Nathan Hales.

If education is not to hand down from generation to generation the priceless treasures of the ages, what indeed is it to do? How can it justify its own existence? Can it be that our great goal is to teach our sons and daughters to twitch in convulsive tremors of adjustment to the ever-shifting kaleidoscope of modern life? Can we justify the billions that we spend if the results are to be found largely in the areas of finger painting, folk dancing, and the writing of business letters? Is it possible that Rousseau and Pestalozzi, Plato and Barnard have come at last to this tragic conclusion of their dreams and hopes?

O my brothers in this game of blindman's buff with children's lives, let us strike off the blindfolds. Let us look long and earnestly at what we are doing.

We are teaching trivia.

Do not take my word. If you find the dose unpalatable, if you balk at the nauseous implications, try your pupils.

Watch the abler ones grow dull and apathetic, bored and lack-luster, as they yawn and watch the clock over the stupid adventures of Muk-Muk the Eskimo Boy or Little Pedro from Argentina. Then, suddenly, as though opening an enchanted window upon a radiant pageant, give them the story of the wrath of Achilles. Let them stand with Casabianca upon the burning deck. Trek with them in spirit to the Yukon, and with glorious Buck let them answer the call of the wild. Place them upon the shot-swept shrouds of the *Bonhomme Richard*, and let them thrill to those words flashing like a rapier out of our past, "I have not yet begun to fight." Kneel with them behind the cotton bales at New Orleans with Andy Jackson at their side as the redcoats begin to emerge from the mist of the Louisiana swamps and the sullen guns of Lafitte begin to pound.

Watch their faces.

See the eyes brighten and the spirits ruffle. See the color come, the backs straighten, the arms go up. They dream, they live, they glow.

This is teaching. This is what you trained to do. You have done what any teacher worth his salt would mortgage his future to achieve, and you have set the ardent, selfless joy of learning flaming in those eager faces.

Thus you may hurl the eternal lie into the teeth of those who decry the significance of subject matter, who sneer at history and poetry and mythology and all those magical creations of the human mind which have raised man to a place a little lower than the gods.

Let us lift our heads. Let us say to these diluters of curricula, these emasculators of texts, these mutilators of our past, "We have had enough of you. The world is weary of you. The stage is ready for new actors. With your jargon of behaviorism and Gestalt and topological vectors and maturation levels, you have muddied the clear waters of childhood long enough. You have told us to teach the whole child, but you have made it impossible to teach him anything worth learning. Litte by little you have picked the meat from the bones of Education and replaced it with Pablum. You have done your best to produce a race of barely literate savages."

These things we can say, and we can follow words with deeds.

What say you, brothers?

Shall we continue to shovel the children into the maw of Moloch?

Children of the Apocalypse

Peter Marin

Peter Marin has been a fellow at the Center for the Study of Democratic Institutions and director of Pacific High School. He is coauthor with Allan Cohen of *Understanding Drug Use*. Marin sees the freedom of the young as bearing with it a terrifying rootlessness and isolation. The school, which occupies so much of the time of youth, intensifies this sense of desolation by its fraudulent interpersonal relationships. The school is not a community but a collection of roles which repress authenticity and human contact. The creation of an honest and loving milieu is most likely to come about through individual decisions to assume responsibility for others. (This revolution-by-personal-witness was prophesied by Charles Reich in his bestselling book *The Greening of America*.)

Marin has concluded from his observations of the young that excessive freedom can be oppressive. People need the psychological warmth of culture and community. They need a supportive environment from which they can venture out into an uncertain world and to which they can harken in periods of anxiety. Looked at from another angle, people need a sense of significance, something which elicits commitment. Marin recommends that the starting point from which the young can regain this be other people.

The tenor and the title of Marin's article convey his great alarm. However, the picture he paints is impressionistic and based upon his personal involvement with schools and youth. How accurately his images reflect the reader's experience is for the reader to determine. In particular, has Marin captured the reality of the schools? Does education, as it is practiced in the schools familiar to the reader, consist of a congeries of hypocritical encounters among all who participate?

To oppose Fascism, we need neither heavy armaments nor bureaucratic apparatuses. What we need above all is a different way of looking at life and human beings. My dear friends, without this different way of looking at life and human beings, we shall ourselves become Fascists.
—Silone

I am not really interested in "education" as a subject. What moves me more are the problems of the young. At best, questions about education should be treated topically: as a way of living with the present, of *making do*. But there is something beyond that too, a way of looking at men and women, a visionary expectation, that keeps us seeking the most human ways of making do. But the most human ways of making do these days have little to do with our rhetoric about the public schools, and we forget in the midst of it what we really owe the young.

But knowing what we owe them means knowing what is going on, and it is hard to get a fix on that. Whatever happens is shrouded in folds of propaganda and rhetoric, abstraction and fantasy. *Revolution, Repression, The Age of Aquarius, The Counter-Culture, Law and Order, The Great Society, The Death of Reason, The Psychedelic Revolution.* . . . It goes on and on—a vast illusion comprised of banners and winking neon meanings that fog the frantic soup in which we swim: the mixture of innocent yearning and savagery, despair and exhilaration, the grasping for paradise lost, paradise *now*, the reaching for a sanity that becomes, in frustration, a new kind of madness.

If this is not the kingdom of apocalypse, it is at least an apocalyptic condition of the soul. We want the most simple human decencies, but in our anguish we are driven to extremes to find them. We reach blindly for whatever offers solace. We yearn more than ever for some kind of human touch and seem steadily less able to provide it. We drift in our own confusion, chattering about the "future": at once more free and more corrupt, more liberated and bound, than any others on the face of the earth.

In the midst of it, adrift, the young more than ever seem beautiful but maimed, trying against all odds to salvage something from the mess. With daring and luck many seem to survive, and some few thrive, but too many others—more than we imagine—already seem destined to spend their lives wrestling with something very close to psychosis. Despite all our talk we have not adequately gauged their suffering. Theirs is a condition of the soul that marks the dead end of the beginnings of America—a dreadful anomy in which one loses all access to others and the self: a liberation that is simultaneously the most voluptuous kind of freedom and an awful form of terror.

Merely to touch in that condition, or to see one another, or to speak honestly is to reach across an immense distance. One struggles with the remnants of a world-view so pervasive, so perverse, that everyone must doubt whether it is possible to see anything clearly, say it honestly, or enter it innocently. The tag ends of two dozen different transplanted foreign cultures have begun to die within us, have already died, and the young have been released into what is perhaps the first true "American" reality—one marked, above all, by the absence of any coherent culture.

The problem is not merely that the "system" is brutal and corrupt, nor that the war has revealed how savage and cynical a people we are. It is, put simply, that "social reality" seems to have vanished altogether. One finds among the young a profound and befuddled sense of loss—as if they had been traumatized and betrayed by an entire world. What is release and space for some is for the others a constant sense of separation and vertigo—a void in which the self can float or soar but in which one can also drift unmoored and fall; and when one falls, it is forever, for there is nothing underneath, no culture, no net of meaning, nobody else.

That is, of course, what we have talked about for a century: the empty existential universe of self-creation. It is a condition of the soul, an absolute loss and yearning for the world. One can become anything—but nothing makes much sense. Adults have managed to evade it, have hesitated on its edges, have clung to one another and to institutions, to beliefs in "the system," to law and order. But now none of that coheres, and the young seem unprotected by it all, and what we have evaded and even celebrated in *metaphor* has become, for a whole generation, a kind of daily emotional life.

The paradox, of course, is that the dissolution of culture has set us free to create almost anything—but it also deprived us of the abilities to do it. Strength, wholeness, and sanity seem to be functions of *relation*, and relation, I think, is a function of culture, part of its intricate web of approved connection and experience, a network of persons and moments that simultaneously offer us release and bind us to the lives of others. One "belongs" to and in culture in a way that goes beyond mere politics or participation, for belonging is both simpler and more complex than that: an immersion in the substance of community and tradition, which is itself a net beneath us, a kind of element in which men seem to float, protected.

That is, I suppose, what the young have lost. Every personal truth or experience puts them at odds with the "official" version of

Children of the Apocalypse

things. There is no connection at all between inner truth and what they are expected to be; every gesture demanded and rewarded is a kind of absolute lie, a denial of their confusion and need. The "drifting free" is the sense of distance; it is distance—not a "generation" gap, but the huge gulf between the truth of one's own pain and possibilities and the world's empty forms. Nothing supports or acknowledges them, and they are trapped in that gulf, making the best of things, making everything up as they go along. But that is the most basic and awful task of all, for it is so lonely, so dangerous, so easily distracted and subverted, so easily swayed. The further along one gets the more alone one is, the more fragile and worried, the deeper into the dark. It is there, of course, that one may need help from adults, but adults have no talent for that at all; we do not admit to being in the dark—how, then, can we be of any use?

If all this is so, what sense can one make of the public schools? They are stiff, unyielding, microcosmic versions of a world that has already disappeared. They are, after all, the state's schools, they do the state's work, and their purpose is the preservation of things as they were. Their means are the isolation of ego and deflection of energy. Their main structural function is to produce in the young a self-delusive "independence"—a system of false consciousness and need that actually renders them dependent on institutions and the state. Their corrosive role-playing and demand systems are so extensive, so profound, that nothing really human shows through—and when it does, it appears only as frustration, exhaustion, and anger.

That, of course, is the real outrage of the schools: their systematic corruption of the relations among persons. Where they should be comrades, allies, equals, and even lovers, the public schools make them "teacher" and "student"—replaceable units in a mechanical ritual that passes on, in the name of education, an "emotional plague"; a kind of ego and personality that has been so weakened, so often denied the experience of community or solitude, that we no longer understand quite what these things are or how to achieve them.

Whatever one's hopes or loves, each teacher is engaged daily in that same conspiracy to maim the young. But I am talking here about more than the surface stupidities of attendance requirements, grades, or curriculum. Those can be changed and updated. But what seems truly untouchable is what lies behind and beneath them: the basic irredeemable assumptions about what is necessary, human, or good; the treatment of the person, time, choice, energy, work, community, and pleasure. It is a world-view so monolithic and murderous that it becomes a part of us even while we protest against it.

I remember returning one fall to a state college in California after a summer in the Mexican mountains. I had been with my friends, writing, walking, making love—all with a sense of freedom and quietude. That first day back I felt as I always did on campus, like a sly, still undiscovered spy. After all, what was it all to me? I walked into my first class and began my usual pitch: They would grade themselves, read what they wanted or not at all, come to class or stay home. It was all theirs to choose—their learning, their time, their space. But they were perplexed by that. Was it some kind of trick? They began to question me, and finally one of them asked, exasperated: "But what can we do if we don't know what you *want*?"

It was a minimal satori. I could not speak. What ran through my mind was not only the absolute absurdity of the question but the lunacy of our whole charade: the roles we played, the place we met, the state's mazelike building, the state's gigantesque campus, and, beyond all that, what we mean by "schooling," how we had been possessed by it. I knew that whatever I answered would be senseless and oppressive, for no matter how I disclaimed my role, whatever I said would restore it. So I stood there instead in silence, aware that what I had taken lightly to be mad was indeed mad, and that one could never, while there, break through those roles into anything real.

Well, almost never. The most human acts I have ever found in our colleges and high schools are the ones most discouraged, the surreptitious sexuality between teachers and students. Although they were almost always cramped and totally exploitive, they were at least some kind of private touch. I used to imagine that one fine afternoon the doors of all the offices would open wide with a trumpet blast, and teachers and students would emerge to dance hand in hand in total golden nakedness on the campus lawns in a paroxysm of truth. In a sense, what I imagined then is close to what sometimes happens more realistically in the student strikes and demonstrations. One finds in the participants a sense of exhilaration and release, a regained potency and a genuine transformation of feeling: the erotic camaraderie of liberation. There is an immense and immediate relief at the cessation of pretense. It is one's role, as well as the rules, which is transgressed, and one somehow becomes stronger, more real—and suddenly at home.

But that doesn't happen often, and usually only in the colleges, and the young are left elsewhere and almost always to suffer in silence the most destructive effect of the schools—not their external rules and structure, but the ways in which we internalize them and falsify ourselves in order to live with them. The state creeps in and gradually occupies us; we act and think within its forms; we see through its eyes and it speaks through our mouths—and how, in that situation, can the young learn to be alive or free?

We try. We open the classroom a bit and loosen the bonds. Students use a teacher's first name, or roam the small room, or go ungraded, or choose their own texts. It is all very nice; better, of course, than nothing at all. But what has it got to do with the needs of the young? We try again. We devise new models, new programs, new plans. We innovate and renovate, and beneath it all our schemes always contain the same vacancies, the same smells of death, as the schools. One speaks to planners, designers, teachers, and administrators; one hears about schedules and modules and curricular innovation—new systems. It is always "materials" and "technique," the chronic American technological vice, the cure that murders as it saves. It is all so smug, so progressively right—and yet so useless, so far off the track. One knows there is something else altogether: a way of feeling, access to the soul, a way of speaking and embracing, that lies at the heart of all yearning or wisdom or real revolution. It is that, precisely, that has been left out. It is something the planners cannot remember: the living tissue of community. Without it, of course, we shrivel and die, but who can speak convincingly about that to those who have never felt it?

I remember talking to one planner about what one wants from others.

"Respect," he said. "And their utmost effort."

"But all I want," I said, "is love and a sense of humor."

His eyes lit up. "I see," he said. "You mean positive feedback."

Positive feedback. So we debauch our own sweet nature. I don't want positive feedback, nor do the young. What they need is so much more important and profound—not "skills" but qualities of the soul; daring, warmth, wit, imagination, honesty, loyalty, grace, and resilience. But one cannot be taught those things; they cannot be programed into a machine. They seem to be learned, instead, in activity and communion—in the *adventurous presence of other real persons*.

But there is no room in the schools for that. There is no real hope of making room there. Those who want to aid the young must find some other way to do it. Yes, I know, that is where most of the young still are. I can hear the murmurs protesting that only the demented, delinquent, or rich can go elsewhere. But that is just the point. Now it is time to cut loose from the myth. We must realize once and for all that, given the real inner condition of the young, the state's schools are no place to try to help them.

But if that is the case, my friends ask, what *do* you do? I have no easy answers. There are cultural conditions for which there are no solutions, turnings of the soul so profound and complex that no system can absorb or contain them. How would one have "solved" the Reformation? Or first-century Rome? One makes accommodations and adjustments, one dreams about the future and makes plans to save us all, but in spite of all that, because of it, what seems more important are the private independent acts that become more necessary every day: the ways we find as *private persons* to restore to one another the strengths we should have now—whether to make the kind of revolution we need or to survive the repression that seems likely.

What I am talking about here is a kind of psychic survival: our ability to live decently beyond institutional limits and provide for our comrades enough help to sustain them. What saves us as men and women is always a kind of witness: the quality of our own acts and lives. This is the knowledge, of course, that institutions bribe us to forget, the need and talent for what Kropotkin called "mutual aid"— the private asumption of responsibility for others.

I remember talking one evening with a student who was arguing the need for burning things down. Her face was a stiff, resisting mask of anger and grief.

"But what else," she said, "can I do?"

I wasn't sure. "Try to get to the bottom of things. Try to see clearly what we need."

"But when I see clearly," she said, "I freak out."

"That's why we need friends," I said.

"But I have no friends."

And she began to cry. That is it precisely. How does one really survive it? There is nothing for such pain save to embrace it, to heal it with warmth, with one's own two hands. One comes to believe that what each of us needs is an absolute kind of lover—not for the raw sex, but for what is sometimes beneath and intrinsic to it: a devoted open presence to perceive, acknowledge, and embrace what we are.

That is the legitimacy which comes neither from the ballot nor the gun, a potency, resilience, and courage that one can learn only by feeling at home in the world. But how can the young feel that? There are few such lovers, and the other old ways are gone. Once upon a time one had a lived relation to culture, or place, or the absolute. But God has vanished and the culture is tattered and savage and "place" has become the raw, empty suburb or the ghetto.

What else is left? Not much. Only others: those adrift in the same dark, one's brothers and sisters, comrades and lovers—the broken isolate bits of a movable kingdom, an invisible "community" that shares, inside, a particular fate. It is only in their eyes and arms, in their presence and affection, that one becomes real, is given back, and discovers the extent of one's being.

What we are talking about here are really acts of love, the gestures by which one shares with others the true dimension and depth of the world. Those gestures are a form of revelation, for they restore to others a sense of what is shared. But one can only make them when one feels free, when the space we inhabit is our own, an open environment, a "field" in which we can begin to see clearly, act freely—and be real.

I know that this is shaky ground. How can one explain what one means by real? It is experiential and subjective: a quality and condition of some kind of deeply inhabited moment. We talk about ecstasy and ego-death and peak experience, but those seem equally imperfect ways of describing the experience of *being in the world.* One *is.* That is all. Our chronic sense of isolation dissolves; there is a correspondence, an identity, between inner and outer, world and world. It is a making whole; it knits together the self at the same time that the self is felt to be a part, the heart, of what surrounds it.

What it is, always, is a reclamation of our proper place in the world—and those who want to help the young must realize that it cannot happen in the schools. Perhaps, after all, it doesn't really matter whether we transgress their limits by leaving them or while staying within them, so long as we learn to ignore them wherever we are. Can one do that while still in the state's schools? I don't think so. But perhaps some teachers want to try—and why not? Perhaps it *is* worth the effort and anguish—as long as one always remembers that one's primary obligation is not to the system, not the state, but to the young—and not as a teacher, but as an equal and ally. That obligation—like a doctor's or lawyer's—is absolute, more important than our own comfort or job, and it can be satisfied only when one is willing to refuse, point-blank, to do anything that really damages the young—no matter who programs or asks for it. One must be willing to suspend the rules, refuse one's role, reject the system—and live instead with the young—wherever you find them—as the persons we really are. If that is impossible in the schools, then one must be willing to leave the schools and take the young, too—into the street, into one's own home—wherever we can live sensibly together.

Perhaps what schools need are "escape committees" of resistance devoted, like the draft resistance, to discovering alternatives for the young. We have plenty of working models, places such as the First Street School in New York or Berkeley's Other Ways; the "free schools" scattered on either coast; community day-care centers and ghetto storefront schools; female liberation groups; communes of all kinds; free clinics; therapeutic centers like Synanon; experimental colleges; the hard-edged courage of the Panthers and Young Lords.

All of these function in different ways as an education in liberation: the attempts of people to move past institutions and do for themselves what the state does not.

Not everyone can do it, of course. It is a scary idea. Our heads are heavy with a fear of "dropping out." The institutional propaganda convinces too many of us that there is one world here and another there, and that there is some kind of illegitimate limbo where our actions dissolve in the air. But *there* is simple private life, the life of the street, the free relations between persons, and it is only there, these days, that one can be free or real enough to serve the young. But if it is dangerous out there, it is also incredibly lovely at times, full of learning, full of freedom, and only those who have lived or traveled with the young in those open fields know just how exhilarating, if exhausting, it is.

But what about the future? When I talk with my friends these days the sugarplum visions dance in their heads, and they tell me about their systems and salvations, or the dawning age of Aquarius and the new consciousness. Well, I want to believe it. But these days there is also the cop at the door with his gun, and the new mechanical men, and also something in me, the old Adam, the old father, whispering *not yet, not yet.* I remember a man I knew in New York who ate nothing but bologna and cheese sandwiches, and when he broke his jaw and had to sip through a straw he dumped bologna and cheese and bread in his blender, added milk, and had his usual sandwich.

Which is to say, the future changes, but we may not. Whatever there is on the other side of this confusion will be, at best, not so different from what we already have now, on occasion, in our best moments. No new senses, no third sexes, no cosmic orgasms, no karmic rebirths. No, if we are daring and lucky, what will be "revolutionary" will simply be that more of us, all of us, will have more of a chance for a decent human life—good comrades and lovers, a few touches of ecstasy, some solitude and space, a sense of self-determination.

I once asked a student what she would do if she awoke in paradise.

"Walk around," she said. "Get something to eat."

I don't have any other answer. We will do what we do now—but we will do it better. We will sit talking with friends around a table, do some decent work, hold one another guiltlessly in our arms, touch a bit more softly, more knowingly. We will understand a bit more and dance a bit more and breathe a bit more and even think a little more—and all, perhaps, a bit more intelligently, more bravely.

That isn't much, but it is also almost everything, and what we are forced to do now is learn how to do all that for ourselves. There is no one to show us how—no program, no system. One can only have such lives by trying to live them, and that is what the young are trying to do these days, all on their own, whether we help them or not. The few real teachers I know, those really serving the young, are simply those who try to live such lives in their company, as freely and humanly as they can. The rest of "education" is almost always rhetoric and nonsense.

chapter 12

Strategies for Change

In important respects, radicalism and education are mutually antagonistic. Radicalism is directed toward change, but that sector of the status quo which is most resistant to change is often said to be the schools. Educational structures have such staying power that they long outlast the status quo in which they were formed and frequently become anachronistic. Unfortunately, as some of these structures decline in appropriateness, they ascend in sanctity. School districts, school system boundaries, and local school financing are cases in point.

Not only does education have persistent structures, it itself is defined as being preservative in purpose. The goal is to socialize the younger generation, i.e., to sell the culture to the kids. Even where this goal is not pursued obsessively, there are still consciousness-constricting curricula and stultifying regimens to serve as guarantors of the status quo.

This situation is fraught with irony in view of one of the most publicly-touted goals of education—the development of the ability to think critically. The cultural analysis implicit in this kind of thinking is itself a radical act and can lead to radical alterations in society. Alas, the goal exists mostly as rhetoric rather than as a polestar that guides practice. Students are not presented with radical perspectives from which to critique their culture, including the subculture of the school, nor are they seriously confronted with utopian schemes from which to conceive an alternative culture.

The keen sense of *déja vu* which many parents experience during visitors' days at the local school is silent testimony to the immutability of formal education. The fact that the local school may not even be in the same geographical region as the school the parents attended evinces the truly glacial dimensions of education.

To propose large-scale reforms for so intractable an operation must surely seem like vanity and a chasing after wind. But we have entered into a time of acute cultural malaise which increases the prospects for change. Indeed, a talent for the apocalyptic vision and the drastic recommendation is in demand these days. Educational radicalism, at least in print, has enjoyed a boom market. However, it does not appear that those who control the levers of power have taken this literature seriously. Or perhaps the system is so complexly self-sustaining that it is no longer meaningful to talk as though a relative handful of people are in charge. Unified mass disaffection may be necessary to wreak changes advocated by the radicals, at which time the radical perspective will have become the conventional wisdom.

The purpose of education is at least an implicit concern in all the radical statements. Many right-wing radicals view education as essentially intellectual in purpose. They feel that systematic intellectual training has been sacrificed to a maudlin preoccupation with social adjustment and interpersonal relations. As a result, the schools do several things badly rather than one thing well. Others of the right wing perceive a glaring discrepancy between the intellectual purpose of education and the controlling force behind most schools. They insist that a public education is a contradiction in terms. No school beholden to as powerful and repressive an institution as government can enjoy genuine intellectual freedom.

For some on the left, school is perceived as an insidious political and economic contrivance for fitting people to the system. Others do not think the public school is inherently bad, but they do consider it to be outrageously monopolistic in its present form. Compulsory attendance, the single neighborhood school, and even the uniformity among schools do not offer much choice. Students who find their official option to be intolerable and flee it, physically or mentally, are turned over to correctional or psychiatric agencies, clearly indicating where society thinks the fault lies. Some writers focus on designing alternatives to this monolith, others on creating the mechanisms which will facilitate the establishment of the alternatives.

School Daze

Medford Evans

This article appeared in a journal of opinion which is published and
edited by Robert Welch, who is also the founder and leader of the
John Birch Society. The author of the article is an associate editor
of the journal. He has a doctorate from Yale and was once an administrative officer on the U.S. Atomic Energy Project. The books
which he has written are *Secret War for the A-Bomb*, *The Usurpers*,
and *The Assassination of Joe McCarthy*.

Evans avers that, in any school it operates, the government
will not permit challenges to itself and has the power to prevent
such challenges. Therefore, public education is never free in the
intellectual sense. Furthermore, all true education has a religious
element, so that government-run schools are in violation of the principle of church-state separation. (On this point, Evans is in sharp
disagreement with a fellow right-winger, Billy James Hargis, who
argues in an earlier article in this book that it is legally permissible
for government-run schools to have a religious orientation.) Evans
concludes that the government's responsibility for education should
be limited to guaranteeing the autonomy of private schools.

Evans does not discuss the impact his proposal for insuring
intellectual freedom would have on equality of educational opportunity. If education is conducted solely through private schools, it
could guarantee that the poor would be even less well educated than
they are now, and the cycle of intergenerational poverty would be
even more thoroughly institutionalized. Either Evans has ideas for
precluding these eventualities, or he is prepared to risk such disastrous consequences because he is convinced that the alternative—
the continuation of government-run schools—is worse. The reader
will have to draw his own conclusions about the latter possibility,
and part of his data can consist of the examples which Evans gives
of ways that the government tramples intellectual freedom in the
schools it operates.

Reprinted by permission of the publisher from *American Opinion*, March
1970, pp. 48–61.

The natural relationship between government and education is shown in the case of Socrates and the city of Athens. He was the greatest teacher of the most cultivated capital of classical antiquity, and the Athenians killed him. I need scarcely remind you of how the Roman government in Jerusalem put to death the Master Teacher of all time. Government is by its nature hostile to education, for government (a necessary evil) is repressive, whereas education (an inherent good) is liberating.

The one great and tragic fallacy in traditional American thought is the popular presumption that a free government depends upon a system of governmentally operated schools. It is true that without free schools free government cannot succeed, but the terms need to be examined carefully.

A government is "free" when the individual citizens have the maximum freedom of choice in all things—religion, occupation, leisure, etc.—consistent with that protection against crime and foreign invasion for which governments are established in the first place. The "etc." in the parenthetical list above includes nothing more obviously than education. A school is "free" when its teachers can offer such instruction as they feel themselves qualified to give, and students can choose such courses as they feel themselves qualified to take.

The foregoing adaptation of the law of the free market applies most exactly at the university level, where "academic freedom"—a term corrupted by use, but perfectly valid in its proper sense—is most clearly of the essence of the institution. Since a university has as its purpose the preservation and enlargement of knowledge, and is as it were the cerebrum of the body politic, it would be rendered useless for this proper purpose if it were subjected, in matters relating to knowledge, to the decisions of any other institution. The office of the State in matters of education is to protect the university and the persons therein. It is the province of the church to bless and pray for all—and, while it is of utmost importance to note that universities never flourished until they were founded with the blessing of the church beginning in the Middle Ages, it must be remembered that it is the function of the university itself to define and cultivate the highest arts and sciences of which mankind may be capable.

The lower schools exist, both historically and logically, to prepare for entrance into the universities—or for some other designated specific purpose, usually vocational training, or perhaps avocational training—such as academies of karate or the dance. Despite the popularity, however, of the concept of vocational training, the large school enrollments of modern times all rest upon aspirations which may be economic or social in tone, but which lead inevitably to the selection by the majority of a curriculum generally known as "college preparatory." This because no one in a free society wants to have precluded the possibility of going to college (and thus, *in theory*, of pursuing the "higher learning") even if he has little or no practical interest in actually going.

Vocational schools are seldom if ever so large as unspecialized schools; for one reason because few people want to commit themselves or their children to a specialty too early, while everybody wants as much as possible of the kind of general culture associated with real or fancied lives of civilized leisure.

The choice of an educational curriculum, which at the university level is ideally made by the student himself, is at the primary level necessarily made by the parent. *Academic freedom for young children means freedom for their parents to decide what kind of schooling they shall have.* It also means freedom for schoolmasters to offer any kind of schooling which they believe parents will patronize.

Both parents and schoolmasters will make their decisions largely on the basis of what they understand are the requirements of the colleges and universities to which it is presumed the majority of children may very well want to go. Thus it appears that the universities, though they need not (and as a rule do not and will not) have operational authority over the lower schools, have what an organizational expert might call a functional or staff authority. And these universities, as we observed at the outset, are necessarily free of coercion by outside bodies, notably by the State.

Universities and lower schools *must* be independent of State control!

History and philosophy combine to demonstrate fully that governments tend inevitably to be cruel and corrupt, that government is indeed a "necessary evil." True education involves learning both parts of that grammatical junction. Yet what government can look with equanimity upon schools operated by itself which teach that government is an evil, whether necessary or not?

Parents who love their children and want them to be adequately warned of the danger of tyranny from which no actual government is ever totally exempt will not want to send their children to government schools. Caesar will not teach anyone to be skeptical of Caesar.

The Master said it was lawful to pay tribute to Caesar—in Caesar's own coin. It is to God, however, that we are to render the things which are God's. And surely nothing is more clearly from God than wisdom, wherever it is found. It cannot be bought with dollars or forced with bayonets. The proverb, "There is no royal road to learning," applies equally to the constitutional republic. No form of government can legislate knowledge—and this applies to the most legitimately delegated sovereign power every bit as fully as to the most tyrannical king.

The only difference is that the legitimate government will be quicker to recognize and admit the limitations of its jurisdiction. Duly elected legislatures have done foolish things, but it took King Canute to try to dictate to the tide. What Americans need to remember is that even if Canute's command to the tide to stop had been properly ratified as a Constitutional amendment it would have been just as foolish. Some things are beyond the province of government, and among those things are discovery of, and instruction in, the laws of nature.

Yet experience shows that no government, having as it does the power to tax and the power to punish, including the death penalty if necessary, can refrain, when controversy reaches a certain point, from attempting to legislate or adjudicate and enforce its own concept of *truth*. The most comprehensive example is that of the Soviet Union, where Stalin's reign of teror was used to establish Lysenko's theory of biology. But that is only one illustration of education in Russia. Bereday, Brickman, and Read, in *The Changing Soviet School* (Houghton Mifflin, 1960), write:

> *The Soviet system is a methodical plan for the education of all citizens. It stems from the confidence, which can be traced back through Marx and Rousseau to Francis Bacon, that man, by the use of reason, can provide by legislation for all present and future social emergencies. Not only do the Communists believe that their Party should have the power to legislate for social change; they also claim that it has the wisdom to determine what that change should be.*

This, properly, horrifies thoughtful Americans. Yet it is not essentially different from what the federal courts are attempting to do in the public schools of the United States today. What is different in America from the totalitarian approach to education in Russia is that, so far, we still have in this country the right to operate private schools. How long we shall continue to have that right is problematic, considering that no less important an educator than James Bryant Conant, former president of the supposedly *private* Harvard University, is on record in favor of government-operated schools. Which seems puzzling until you reflect that Harvard intends to operate the government.[1]

[1] Real academic freedom, however, is incompatible with government operation even at the second level of authority. More soberly speaking, insofar as it is true that Harvard promotes operation of the lower schools by a gov-

A basic reason why schools should not be operated by the government (at any level), at least in the United States, is that no such operation can fail to violate the American principle of the separation of church and State. The State, not being concerned with ultimate truth, but with such practical tasks as national defense and local law enforcement, can be (and should be) separated from religious dogma. Any education, however, which is complete enough to be worthy of the name, cannot be so separated.

To illustrate: education cannot avoid consideration of history. History cannot be taught without consideration of Jesus of Nazareth. How do you explain to a child why we call this "1970" without referring to the birth of Jesus? Then, how do you refer to one Who was so important that the calendar hinges on His birth without telling the child something about Him? How do you tell about Him without telling that He said He was the Son of God? With an already sophisticated audience you can slide over that, but in your elementary school there is no avoiding the question, however phrased: *Well, was He or not?*

There seem to be only three possible answers : (1) Yes, (2) No, (3) I don't know. Any one of the three commits you to a religious position—Christian, anti-Christian, or agnostic. Note that agnosticism is a philosophical position on a religious question—in other words, it *is* a theological position—and not simple ignorance.

No educational system can pretend to simple ignorance regarding Christ. Such ignorance would disqualify the educators more completely than simple ignorance regarding Shakespeare or Socrates or Napoleon. To be sure, there are immense areas of ignorance concerning them all—Napoleon, Shakespeare, Jesus, Socrates, to name them in reverse chronological order—but there is more knowledge, more evidence, concerning them all than any one scholar is able totally to digest. Any educated person has an attitude toward each of those figures. But any possible attitude toward *Jesus* is a religious attitude, and no one can (or should) avoid communicating his own attitude toward Jesus to those whom he is assigned to instruct in history.

A similar thing could obviously be said of Buddha or Mohammed. I could no more avoid revealing to a history class that I do believe the claims of Jesus, and do not believe those of Mohammed,

---

ernment which in turn is controlled by Harvard (and this is perilously near the truth), it means that Harvard has changed in its own nature from a university to a conspiracy. Harvard's motto, VERITAS, truth, should be changed to POTESTAS, power.

than a professor at Cairo could avoid revealing the opposite, or a professor at Yeshiva or (perhaps) Harvard could avoid revealing that he did not believe the claims of either Jesus or Mohammed.

I do not think that the government should compel people to be Christians. Salvation is free and not to be imposed by taxes and the power of the sword. But if, being a Christian, I do not want Christianity imposed by governmental power, it should be obvious that I would object even more to having Mohammedanism so imposed, and do object to having agnosticism-verging-toward-atheism so imposed. Which is what is happening now, and all that possibly can happen when a nonreligious government operates an educational system which is inextricably involved with religious questions. (I have mentioned only the most obvious of such questions: there are many others.)

But what shall we do? We do not have an established religion. Under the Constitution we cannot have one nationally, and we no longer have one in any of the states. (Though the Constitution permits one in the states, the Supreme Court does not: and, to be fair, none of the states seem any longer to want one.) Since there is no legal way for state or national government to prescribe what religion shall be taught in the schools, but the schools will inevitably teach some kind of religion (perhaps only the more powerfully if in disguised form), what shall we do?

The answer is simple enough. We have freedom of religion, we need *freedom of schools*—genuine academic freedom. And it is no more possible to have freedom of education under government operation than it is to have freedom of religion. Education cannot be separated from religion, but both can be separated from government, and neither will flourish properly unless they both are so separated. The American adventure is one of the glorious chapters of history (and one of our finest slogans has been separation of church and State), but we have not been perfect, and possibly the most fundamental mistake we have made has been to cement ever more closely during recent years the union of school and State. The Supreme Court, with its enormous capacity for error, has removed prayer from the schools. What it should have done, in a self-denying judgment, is to remove itself from the schools.

Itself and the rest of government too. The decision could have been based on the First Amendment, which provides, as you recall, that "Congress shall make no law respecting an establishment of religion [*by the way, it says* respecting *an establishment of religion, which would mean that Congress cannot Constitutionally prevent a state from establishing religion any more than it can compel it—but*

let that pass], or prohibiting the free exercise thereof [*the Court,
however, prohibits the free exercise thereof*]; or abridging the freedom of speech or of the press; or of the right of the people peaceably
to assemble and to petition the Government for a redress of grievances."

If the Court could read English, the foregoing would mean that
the federal government could not legislate concerning the conduct of
an educational program, certainly not concerning the operation of a
formal school system. First, because such a program is inevitably
religious in character, or essentially affected with religion, and religion is "off limits" to the federal government (though not to state
governments, except as a matter of prudence). Second, because the
guaranteed freedom of religion, speech, the press, and assembly
cover every aspect of school operation, except discipline, which in the
case of mature students is covered by property and contract rights,
and in the case of minor children by delegation of disciplinary authority from the parents to the teacher.

These rights and freedoms, which are explicit in the Constitution except for parental authority (which is an inherent right, *more*
basic than the Constitution), are destroyed by federal intervention in
the schools, and endangered (because of the overwhelming force
involved) by *any* kind of governmental intervention.

The Burger Court has gone further than any other agency in
America in usurping parental responsibility and authority by denying
"freedom of choice." Reread the passage from *The Changing Soviet
School* quoted above, with minor substitutions in the wording, as
follows: "Not only do the [*Justices*] believe that [*the Court*] should
have the power to legislate for social change; they also claim that it
has the wisdom to determine what that change should be." Heretofore
obvious political intervention into the operation of educational institutions has been quickly branded by accrediting agencies (which are,
and should be, private) as a violation of academic freedom. Yet there
has never before been such massive political intervention, such flagrant violation of academic freedom, as that by the federal government under the leadership of the Warren and Burger courts.

The supreme irony is that this intrusion of State power into
the scholastic realm has on the one hand been most intensely urged
by Liberal "anti-fascists," while on the other hand the only close
historical parallel to the current revolution in America's public schools
is found in the record of Hitler's Germany. Opposed as the German
and American educational experiments are in specifics, they are at
one in being based on (1) an arbitrary definition by government of
the national ideals, and (2) a theory of race. In each case academic

theory and practice are subjected to iron control by the regime. Americans traditionally do not believe that this is good for the regime, and nobody seriously believes that it is good for the academy.

In cases before the federal courts contesting the application of *Brown v. Topeka* (*e.g.,* in *Stell* and *Evers*) the rulings have so far invariably been to the effect that evidence and argument concerning academic standards and achievement are irrelevant. The job of the schools, under the administration of the federal judiciary and the staff supervision of the Department of Health, Education and Welfare, is not to teach individuals but to revolutionize society. It should occasion no surprise that in the nation's capital, Washington, D.C., and the nation's metropolis, New York, N.Y., teaching has declined as the revolution has advanced.

What needs to be emphasized in this connection is that the revolution in question is not one by the people against the government, but by the government against the people. Which is another way of saying that federal control of state-operated schools has turned out to be, along with alienation of the armed services, the decisive factor in the establishment of a dictatorial regime—above the Constitution, because it "interprets" the Constitution; independent of the market, because it has the arbitrary power of taxation, the dole, and confiscation; secure from foreign attack, because it has already united itself with similar regimes abroad; and, immune to criticism, because it controls the media of mass communication and the educational system.

But far though this revolution has "progressed," it is not yet fully accomplished and need never be. So simple a thing as patronage of private schools by parents who want their children to be free can interrupt the momentum of the revolution, preserve us a nation, and make possible a renascence of sound learning—which can never be under the stultifying, rigidifying pressure of the Leviathan State.

There are three sound motives for undertaking the labor of operating a school: (1) love of money, (2) love of man, specifically of children and young people, (3) love of learning itself. I posit that all are subsumed under the love of God—which is obviously the case with the last two, neither of which is liable to excess.

The love of money, in contrast, is dangerous in the extreme, being "the root of all [*kinds of*] evil," but—if not inordinate and if properly reined—a most useful incentive. It is more appropriately the incentive of those who run vocational or elementary and secondary schools than of the governing bodies of colleges and universities, where it is all too readily transformed into an outwardly decorous but inwardly ravaging lust for power. Which seems to be what is wrong with the Ivy League. And is certainly what is wrong with the vast State monopolies called the public schools, or state institutions of higher learning.

The antidote for the evils of avarice and ambition in the academic profession, as in the rest of the economic world, is free competition. Let the State not only refrain from operating schools itself, but let it in its capacity as guardian of the public safety serve (for it cannot and will not simply ignore education) as a watchdog to prevent educational monopolies in restraint of intellectual trade in the free marketplace of ideas. Then let academic entrepreneurs find some risk capital and go into the school business. If they market a good product they will make an honest profit. The product will be judged by the success of their alumni. This is not a new idea, but has heretofore been the secret of the prosperity of the most famous universities and preparatory schools in the country, as well as of less prestigious but honorably useful business and correspondence schools.

It will and should be quickly observed that there is, however, a bit more to it than that. The religious, the charitable, motive is still the dominant one in sound education. (There isn't enough money in the world to get a man to grade freshman themes merely for pay.) Universities came into existence in the Middle Ages as a product of Christianity. Even Harvard was founded with a religious purpose. When universities lose this purpose (and they lose it when they are integrated with the government) they inevitably, if they do not die first, degenerate into conspiracies for the seizure of power. Church organizations can, of course, do the same thing. This is a chance inherent in history.

If, however, the university, or the educational system at lower levels, be a creature of the State, then there is no *chance* involved: power is the business of the State, and no other State institution in this country quite equals the university as an instrument of power. Where is the state legislature that can control the state university? The church would be the rival of, or superior to both if the church were established as part of government. We have avoided that. State education is just as bad. The academic scene at, say, the University of California in Berkeley, or at San Francisco State across the bay, was described by Shakespeare's Ulysses in *Troilus And Cressida*:

> *Then everything includes itself in power.*
> *Power into will, will into appetite.*
> *And appetite, an universal wolf.*
> *So doubly seconded with will and power,*
> *Must make perforce an universal prey,*
> *And last eat up himself.*

The most neglected motive for operating an institution of learning is simply the love of learning. This, too, is religious in character (it is confusion of religion and science which occasions the too frequent hostility between them). After all, nothing is more clearly of God than light and truth, and the search for their source is the search of God. Those who are genuinely absorbed in this search do not despise the State—indeed they are grateful to it, for the exercise of limited power is necessary, and the fact that it is exercised by non-academic persons is precisely what frees the academically committed to pursue their search.

Sound learning cannot continue at any level without academic freedom. Academic freedom is impossible in a State-operated educational system. No country—not revolutionary France, not Soviet Russia, not the bureaucratized United States—has ever succeeded or can ever succeed in a program of massive, centrally controlled education.

There are three prerequisites (if you will excuse the academic term) to the educational health of a nation: (1) a religious impulse to pursue learning with God-given talents devoted to His glory, (2) a free economy in which professors and pedagogues may earn their living through employment of their skills in the service of individuals or institutions, (3) exclusion of government—particularly, in the United States, of the national government—from interference with academic freedom, either by intervention in the operation of private schools or by ruinous competition through operation of monopolistic, tax-supported systems.

Dr. George Charles Roche III, in his excellent new book *Education In America*, writes:

> *Education in America has become a reflection of the insistence that education be a function of government, cost free to participating students, fully financed at taxpayer expense. What originated as local schooling, supported by taxation in the immediate community (and therefore somewhat responsive to local and parental wishes) has inexorably moved toward bureaucratic bigness—the fate of all publicly funded projects. . . .*
>
> *. . . The only lasting solution is to remove education from the hands of government, restoring responsibility to the student and the parent. . . . Religion thrives after more than a century of separation of church from state. Is there any compelling reason why voluntary support of education should not be given a similar opportunity?*
>
> *Educational reform must begin with parents as individuals, with the recognition that better upbringing for their children lies in their hands, not in the hands of the state.*

The world does not go just according to blueprint—whether radical or conservative—and heretofore an America founded on love of liberty has been able to survive a national mania for tax-supported schools. But the governmental and educational developments of the past quarter-century indicate that the people of this country must soon choose between, on the one hand, limited government and private schools; or, on the other, what we have come to call public schools and totalitarian government.

The Alternative to Schooling

Ivan Illich

Ivan Illich first came to public notice as a controversial religious figure. As a Catholic priest, he was an outspoken advocate of the interests of island and mainland Puerto Ricans and a critic of the American church's cultural obtuseness in its relations with Puerto Ricans. When later he became director of the church-sponsored Center for Intercultural Documentation in Cuernavaca, Mexico, his group therapy sessions resulted in several defections from the priesthood, which did not ingratiate Illich with the Vatican. He became increasingly infuriated with America's cultural imperialism and began developing justifications for violent revolution. Subsequent altercations with the Holy See ensued, and Illich's relationship with that agency has become quite murky. He continues as director of the Center for Intercultural Documentation, which is no longer church-affiliated.

From his conviction that schools are really political and economic agencies engaged in personality manipulation—a conviction shared by Eldridge Cleaver—Illich has devised a scheme for deschooling society. In place of schools will be four networks of educational resources from which people can obtain the education they want as they want it. The networks will be built around learning materials, learning companions, skill instructors, and educational counselors and leaders. The counselors will be available to advise people on the most promising educational options for themselves and their children. Citizens will contribute to the networks as well as extract from them. One of the plan's recommendations is that the acquisition of further learning be made contingent upon sharing the learning which one already has. Thus, a large portion of the population would act as teachers at different points in their own educational careers.

The Illich proposal has a solid libertarian base. The kind and quantity of education one receives would be a personal decision. The proposal also outlines a mechanism by which people can continue their education throughout their lives with relative ease. In addition, the proposal is intended to equalize educational opportunity by equalizing access to educational resources. An idea of how utopian the proposal is can be had by trying to imagine who might lobby for it.

For generations we have tried to make the world a better place by providing more and more schooling, but so far the endeavor has failed. What we have learned instead is that forcing all children to climb an open-ended education ladder cannot enhance equality but must favor the individual who starts out earlier, healthier, or better prepared; that enforced instruction deadens for most people the will for independent learning; and that knowledge treated as a commodity, delivered in packages, and accepted as private property once it is acquired, must always be scarce.

In response, critics of the educational system are now proposing strong and unorthodox remedies that range from the voucher plan, which would enable each person to buy the education of his choice on an open market, to shifting the responsibility for education from the school to the media and to apprenticeship on the job. Some individuals foresee that the school will have to be disestablished just as the church was disestablished all over the world during the last two centuries. Other reformers propose to replace the universal school with various new systems that would, they claim, better prepare everybody for life in modern society. These proposals for new educational institutions fall into three broad categories: the reformation of the classroom within the school system; the dispersal of free schools throughout society; and the transformation of all society into one huge classroom. But these three approaches—the reformed classroom, the free school, and the worldwide classroom—represent three stages in a proposed escalation of education in which each step threatens more subtle and more pervasive social control than the one it replaces.

I believe that the disestablishment of the school has become inevitable and that this end of an illusion should fill us with hope. But I also believe that the end of the "age of schooling" could usher in the epoch of the global schoolhouse that would be distinguishable only in name from a global madhouse or global prison in which education, correction, and adjustment become synonymous. I therefore believe that the breakdown of the school forces us to look beyond its imminent demise and to face fundamental alternatives in education. Either we can work for fearsome and potent new educational devices that teach about a world which progressively becomes more opaque and forbidding for man, or we can set the conditions for a new era in which technology would be used to make society more simple and transparent, so that all men can once again know the facts and use the tools that shape their lives. In short, we can disestablish schools or we can deschool culture.

In order to see clearly the alternatives we face, we must first distinguish education from schooling, which means separating the humanistic intent of the teacher from the impact of the invariant structure of the school. This hidden structure constitutes a course of instruction that stays forever beyond the control of the teacher or of his school board. It conveys indelibly the message that only through schooling can an individual prepare himself for adulthood in society, that what is not taught in school is of little value, and that what is learned outside of school is not worth knowing. I call it the hidden curriculum of schooling, because it constitutes the unalterable framework of the system, within which all changes in the curriculum are made.

The hidden curriculum is always the same regardless of school or place. It requires all children of a certain age to assemble in groups of about thirty, under the authority of a certified teacher, for some 500 to 1,000 or more hours each year. It doesn't matter whether the curriculum is designed to teach the principles of fascism, liberalism, Catholicism, or socialism; or whether the purpose of the school is to produce Soviet or United States citizens, mechanics, or doctors. It makes no difference whether the teacher is authoritarian or permissive, whether he imposes his own creed or teaches students to think for themselves. What is important is that students learn that education is valuable when it is acquired in the school through a graded process of consumption; that the degree of success the individual will enjoy in society depends on the amount of learning he consumes; and that learning *about* the world is more valuable than learning *from* the world.

It must be clearly understood that the hidden curriculum translates learning from an activity into a commodity—for which the school monopolizes the market. In all countries knowledge is regarded as the first necessity for survival, but also as a form of currency more liquid than rubles or dollars. We have become accustomed, through Karl Marx's writings, to speak about the alienation of the worker from his work in a class society. We must now recognize the estrangement of man from his learning when it becomes the product of a service profession and he becomes the consumer.

The more learning an individual consumes, the more "knowledge stock" he acquires. The hidden curriculum therefore defines a new class structure for society within which the large consumers of knowledge—those who have acquired large quantities of knowledge stock—enjoy special privileges, high income, and access to the more powerful tools of production. This kind of knowledge-capitalism has been accepted in all industrialized societies and establishes a rationale for the distribution of jobs and income. (This point is especially important in the light of the lack of correspondence between schooling and occupational competence established in studies such as Ivar Berg's *Education and Jobs: The Great Training Robbery*.)

The endeavor to put all men through successive stages of enlightenment is rooted deeply in alchemy, the Great Art of the waning Middle Ages. John Amos Comenius, a Moravian bishop, self-styled Pansophist, and pedagogue, is rightly considered one of the founders of the modern schools. He was among the first to propose seven or twelve grades of compulsory learning. In his *Magna Didactica*, he described schools as devices to "teach everybody everything" and outlined a blueprint for the assembly-line production of knowledge, which according to his method would make education cheaper and better and make growth into full humanity possible for all. But Comenius was not only an early efficiency expert, he was an alchemist who adopted the technical language of his craft to describe the art of rearing children. The alchemist sought to refine base elements by leading their distilled spirits through twelve stages of successive enlightenment, so that for their own and all the world's benefit they might be transmuted into gold. Of course, alchemists failed no matter how often they tried, but each time their "science" yielded new reasons for their failure, and they tried again.

Pedagogy opened a new chapter in the history of Ars Magna. Education became the search for an alchemic process that would bring forth a new type of man, who would fit into an environment created by scientific magic. But, no matter how much each generation spent on its schools, it always turned out that the majority of people were unfit for enlightenment by this process and had to be discarded as unprepared for life in a man-made world.

Educational reformers who accept the idea that schools have failed fall into three groups. The most respectable are certainly the great masters of alchemy who promise better schools. The most seductive are popular magicians, who promise to make every kitchen into an alchemic lab. The most sinister are the new Masons of the Universe, who want to transform the entire world into one huge temple of learning. Notable among today's masters of alchemy are certain research directors employed or sponsored by the large foundations who believe that schools, if they could somehow be improved, could also become economically more feasible than those that are now in trouble, and simultaneously could sell a larger package of services. Those who are concerned primarily with the curriculum claim that it is outdated or irrelevant. So the curriculum is filled with new packaged courses on African Culture, North American Imperialism, Women's Lib, Pollution, or the Consumer Society. Passive learning is wrong—it is indeed—so we graciously allow students to decide what and how they want to be taught. Schools are prison houses. Therefore, principals are authorized to approve teach-outs, moving the school desks to a roped-off Harlem street. Sensitivity training becomes fashionable. So, we import group therapy into the classroom. School, which was supposed to teach everybody everything, now becomes all things to all children.

Other critics emphasize that schools make inefficient use of modern science. Some would administer drugs to make it easier for the instructor to change the child's behavior. Others would transform school into a stadium for educational gaming. Still others would electrify the classroom. If they are simplistic disciples of McLuhan, they replace blackboards and textbooks with multimedia happenings; if they follow Skinner, they claim to be able to modify behavior more efficiently than old-fashioned classroom practitioners can.

Most of these changes have, of course, some good effects. The experimental schools have fewer truants. Parents do have a greater feeling of participation in a decentralized district. Pupils, assigned by their teacher to an apprenticeship, do often turn out more competent than those who stay in the classroom. Some children do improve their knowledge of Spanish in the language lab because they prefer playing with the knobs of a tape recorder to conversations with their Puerto Rican peers. Yet all these improvements operate within predictably narrow limits, since they leave the hidden curriculum of school intact.

Some reformers would like to shake loose from the hidden curriculum, but they rarely succeed. Free schools that lead to further free schools produce a mirage of freedom, even though the chain of attendance is frequently interrupted by long stretches of loafing. Attendance through seduction inculcates the need for educational treatment more persuasively than the reluctant attendance enforced by a truant officer. Permissive teachers in a padded classroom can easily render their pupils impotent to survive once they leave.

Learning in these schools often remains nothing more than the acquisition of socially valued skills defined, in this instance, by the consensus of a commune rather than by the decree of a school board. New presbyter is but old priest writ large.

Free schools, to be truly free, must meet two conditions: First, they must be run in a way to prevent the reintroduction of the hidden curriculum of graded attendance and certified students studying at the feet of certified teachers. And, more importantly, they must provide a framework in which all participants—staff and pupils—can free themselves from the hidden foundations of a schooled society. The first condition is frequently incorporated in the stated aims of a free school. The second condition is only rarely recognized, and is difficult to state as the goal of a free school.

It is useful to distinguish between the hidden curriculum, which I have described, and the occult foundations of schooling. The hidden curriculum is a ritual that can be considered the official initiation into modern society, institutionally established through the school. It is the purpose of this ritual to hide from its participants the contradictions between the myth of an egalitarian society and the class-conscious reality it certifies. Once they are recognized as such, rituals lose their power, and this is what is now beginning to happen to schooling. But there are certain fundamental assumptions about growing up— the occult foundations—which now find their expression in the ceremonial of schooling, and which could easily be reinforced by what free schools do.

Among these assumptions is what Peter Schrag calls the "immigration syndrome," which impels us to treat all people as if they were newcomers who must go through a naturalization process. Only certified consumers of knowledge are admitted to citizenship. Men are not born equal, but are made equal through gestation by Alma Mater.

The rhetoric of all schools states that they form a man for the future, but they do not release him for his task before he has developed a high level of tolerance to the ways of his elders: education *for* life rather than *in* everyday life. Few free schools can avoid doing precisely this. Nevertheless they are among the most important centers from which a new life-style radiates, not because of the effect their graduates will have but, rather, because elders who choose to bring up their children without the benefit of properly ordained teachers frequently belong to a radical minority and because their preoccupation with the rearing of their children sustains them in their new style.

The most dangerous category of educational reformer is one who argues that knowledge can be produced and sold much more effectively on an open market than on one controlled by school. These people argue that most skills can be easily acquired from skill-models if the learner is truly interested in their acquisition; that individual entitlements can provide a more equal purchasing power for education. They demand a careful separation of the process by which knowledge is acquired from the process by which it is measured and certified. These seem to me obvious statements. But it would be a fallacy to believe that the establishment of a free market for knowledge would constitute a radical alternative in education.

The establishment of a free market would indeed abolish what I have previously called the hidden curriculum of present schooling—its age-specific attendance at a graded curriculum. Equally, a free market would at first give the appearance of counteracting what I have called the occult foundations of a schooled society: the "immigration syndrome," the institutional monopoly of teaching, and the ritual of linear initiation. But at the same time a free market in education would provide the alchemist with innumerable hidden hands to fit each man into the multiple, tight little niches a more complex technocracy can provide.

Many decades of reliance on schooling has turned knowledge into a commodity, a marketable staple of a special kind. Knowledge is now regarded simultaneously as a first necessity and also as society's most precious currency. (The transformation of knowledge into a commodity is reflected in a corresponding transformation of language. Words that formerly functioned as verbs are becoming nouns that designate possessions. Until recently dwelling and learning and even healing designated activities. They are now usually conceived as commodities or services to be delivered. We talk about the manufacture of housing or the delivery of medical care. Men are no longer regarded fit to house or heal themselves. In such a society people come to believe that professional services are more valuable than personal care. Instead of learning how to nurse grandmother, the teen-ager learns to picket the hospital that does not admit her.) This attitude could easily survive the disestablishment of school, just as affiliation with a church remained a condition for office long after the adoption of the First Amendment. It is even more evident that test batteries measuring complex knowledge-packages could easily survive the disestablishment of school—and with this would go the compulsion to obligate everybody to acquire a minimum package in the knowledge stock. The scientific measurement of each man's worth and the alchemic dream of each man's "educability to his full humanity" would finally coincide. Under the appearance of a "free" market, the global village would turn into an environmental womb where pedagogic therapists control the complex navel by which each man is nourished.

At present schools limit the teacher's competence to the classroom. They prevent him from claiming man's whole life as his domain. The demise of school will remove this restriction and give a semblance of legitimacy to the life-long pedagogical invasion of everybody's privacy. It will open the way for a scramble for "knowledge" on a free market, which would lead us toward the paradox of a vulgar, albeit seemingly egalitarian, meritocracy. Unless the concept of knowledge is transformed, the disestablishment of school will lead to a wedding between a growing meritocratic system that separates learning from certification and a society committed to provide therapy for each man until he is ripe for the gilded age.

For those who subscribe to the technocratic ethos, whatever is technically possible must be made available at least to a few whether they want it or not. Neither the privation nor the frustration of the majority counts. If cobalt treatment is possible, then the city of Tegucigalpa needs one apparatus in each of its two major hospitals, at a cost that would free an important part of the population of Honduras from parasites. If supersonic speeds are possible, then it must speed the travel of some. If the flight to Mars can be conceived, then a rationale must be found to make it appear a necessity. In the technocratic ethos poverty is modernized: Not only are old alternatives closed off by new monopolies, but the lack of necessities is also compounded by a growing spread between those services that are technologically feasible and those that are in fact available to the majority.

A teacher turns "educator" when he adopts this technocratic ethos. He then acts as if education were a technological enterprise designed to make man fit into whatever environment the "progress" of science creates. He seems blind to the evidence that constant obsolescence of all commodities comes at a high price: the mounting cost of training people to know about them. He seems to forget that the rising cost of tools is purchased at a high price in education: They decrease the labor intensity of the economy, make learning on the job impossible or, at best, a privilege for a few. All over the world the cost of educating men for society rises faster than the productivity of the entire economy, and fewer people have a sense of intelligent participation in the commonweal.

A revolution against those forms of privilege and power, which are based on claims to professional knowledge, must start with a transformation of consciousness about the nature of learning. This means, above all, a shift of responsibility for teaching and learning. Knowledge can be defined as a commodity only as long as it is viewed as the result of institutional enterprise or as the fulfillment of institutional objectives. Only when a man recovers the sense of personal responsibility for what he learns and teaches can this spell be broken and the alienation of learning from living be overcome.

The recovery of the power to learn or to teach means that the teacher who takes the risk of interfering in somebody else's private affairs also assumes responsibility for the results. Similarly, the student who exposes himself to the influence of a teacher must take responsibility for his own education. For such purposes educational institutions—if they are at all needed—ideally take the form of facility centers where one can get a roof of the right size over his head, access to a piano or a kiln, and to records, books, or slides. Schools, TV stations, theaters, and the like are designed primarily for use by professionals. Deschooling society means above all the denial of professional status for the second-oldest profession, namely teaching. The certification of teachers now constitutes an undue restriction of the right to free speech: the corporate structure and professional pretensions of journalism an undue restriction on the right to free press. Compulsory attendance rules interfere with free assembly. The deschooling of society is nothing less than a cultural mutation by which a people recovers the effective use of its Constitutional freedoms: learning and teaching by men who know that they are born free rather than treated to freedom. Most people learn most of the time when they do whatever they enjoy; most people are curious and want to give meaning to whatever they come in contact with; and most people are capable of personal intimate intercourse with others unless they are stupefied by inhuman work or turned off by schooling.

The fact that people in rich countries do not learn much on their own constitutes no proof to the contrary. Rather it is a consequence of life in an environment from which, paradoxically, they cannot learn much, precisely because it is so highly programed. They are constantly frustrated by the structure of contemporary society in which the facts on which decisions can be made have become elusive. They live in an environment in which tools that can be used for creative purposes have become luxuries, an environment in which channels of communication serve a few to talk to many.

A modern myth would make us believe that the sense of impotence with which most men live today is a consequence of technology that cannot but create huge systems. But it is not technology that makes systems huge, tools immensely powerful, channels of communication one-directional. Quite the contrary: Properly controlled, technology could provide each man with the ability to understand his environment better, to shape it powerfully with his own hands, and to permit him full intercommunication to a degree never before possible. Such an alternative use of technology constitutes the central alternative in education.

If a person is to grow up he needs, first of all, access to things, to places and to processes, to events and to records. He needs to see, to touch, to tinker with, to grasp whatever there is in a meaningful setting. This access is now largely denied. When knowledge became a commodity, it acquired the protections of private property, and thus a principle designed to guard personal intimacy became a rationale for declaring facts off limits for people without the proper credentials. In schools teachers keep knowledge to themselves unless it fits into the day's program. The media inform, but exclude those things they regard as unfit to print. Information is locked into special languages, and specialized teachers live off its retranslation. Patents are protected by corporations, secrets are guarded by bureaucracies, and the power to keep others out of private preserves—be they cockpits, law offices, junkyards, or clinics—is jealously guarded by professions, institutions, and nations. Neither the political nor the professional structure of our societies, East and West, could withstand the elimination of the power to keep entire classes of people from facts that could serve them. The access to facts that I advocate goes far beyond truth in labeling. Access must be built into reality, while all we ask from advertising is a guarantee that it does not mislead. Access to reality constitutes a fundamental alternative in education to a system that only purports to teach *about* it.

Abolishing the right to corporate secrecy—even when professional opinion holds that this secrecy serves the common good—is, as shall presently appear, a much more radical political goal than the traditional demand for public ownership or control of the tools of production. The socialization of tools without the effective socialization of know-how in their use tends to put the knowledge-capitalist into the position formerly held by the financier. The technocrat's only claim to power is the stock he holds in some class of scarce and secret knowledge, and the best means to protect its value is a large and capital-intensive organization that renders access to know-how formidable and forbidding.

It does not take much time for the interested learner to acquire almost any skill that he wants to use. We tend to forget this in a society where professional teachers monopolize entrance into all fields, and thereby stamp teaching by uncertified individuals as quackery. There are few mechanical skills used in industry or research that are as demanding, complex, and dangerous as driving cars, a skill that most people quickly acquire from a peer. Not all people are suited for advanced logic, yet those who are make rapid progress if they are challenged to play mathematical games at an early age. One out of twenty kids in Cuernavaca can beat me at Wiff 'n' Proof after a couple of weeks' training. In four months all but a small percentage of motivated adults at our CIDOC center learn Spanish well enough to conduct academic business in the new language.

A first step toward opening up access to skills would be to provide various incentives for skilled individuals to share their knowledge. Inevitably, this would run counter to the interest of guilds and professions and unions. Yet, multiple apprenticeship is attractive: It provides everybody with an opportunity to learn something about almost anything. There is no reason why a person should not combine the ability to drive a car, repair telephones and toilets, act as a midwife, and function as an architectural draftsman. Special-interest groups and their disciplined consumers would, of course, claim that the public needs the protection of a professional guarantee. But this argument is now steadily being challenged by consumer protection associations. We have to take much more seriously the objection that economists raise to the radical socialization of skills: that "progress" will be impeded if knowledge—patents, skills, and all the rest—is democratized. Their argument can be faced only if we demonstrate to them the growth rate of futile diseconomies generated by any existing educational system.

Access to people willing to share their skills is no guarantee of learning. Such access is restricted not only by the monopoly of educational programs over learning and of unions over licensing but also by a technology of scarcity. The skills that count today are know-how in the use of highly specialized tools that were designed to be scarce. These tools produce goods or render services that everybody wants but only a few can enjoy, and which only a limited number of people know how to use. Only a few privileged individuals out of the total number of people who have a given disease ever benefit from the results of sophisticated medical technology, and even fewer doctors develop the skill to use it.

The same results of medical research have, however, also been employed to create a basic medical tool kit that permits Army and Navy medics, with only a few months of training, to obtain results, under battlefield conditions, that would have been beyond the expectations of full-fledged doctors during World War II. On an even simpler level any peasant girl could learn how to diagnose and treat most infections if medical scientists prepared dosages and instructions specifically for a given geographic area.

All these examples illustrate the fact that educational considerations alone suffice to demand a radical reduction of the professional structure that now impedes the mutual relationship between the scientist and the majority of people who want access to science. If this demand were heeded, all men could learn to use yesterday's tools, rendered more effective and durable by modern science, to create tomorrow's world.

Unfortunately, precisely the contrary trend prevails at present. I know a coastal area in South America where most people support themselves by fishing from small boats. The outboard motor is certainly the tool that has changed most dramatically the lives of these coastal fishermen. But in the area I have surveyed, half of all outboard motors that were purchased between 1945 and 1950 are still kept running by constant tinkering, while half the motors purchased in 1965 no longer run because they were not built to be repaired. Technological progress provides the majority of people with gadgets they cannot afford and deprives them of the simpler tools they need.

Metals, plastics, and ferro cement used in building have greatly improved since the 1940s and ought to provide more people the opportunity to create their own homes. But while in the United States, in 1948, more than 30 percent of all one-family homes were owner-built, by the end of the 1960s the percentage of those who acted as their own contractors had dropped to less than 20 percent.

The lowering of the skill level through so-called economic development becomes even more visible in Latin America. Here most people still build their own homes from floor to roof. Often they use mud, in the form of adobe, and thatchwork of unsurpassed utility in the moist, hot, and windy climate. In other places they make their dwellings out of cardboard, oil-drums, and other industrial refuse. Instead of providing people with simple tools and highly standardized, durable, and easily repaired components, all governments have gone in for the mass production of low-cost buildings. It is clear that not one single country can afford to provide satisfactory modern dwelling units for the majority of its people. Yet, everywhere this policy makes it progressively more difficult for the majority to acquire the knowledge and skills they need to build better houses for themselves.

Educational considerations permit us to formulate a second fundamental characteristic that any post-industrial society must possess: a basic tool kit that by its very nature counteracts technocratic control. For educational reasons we must work toward a society in which scientific knowledge is incorporated in tools and components that can be used meaningfully in units small enough to be within the reach of all. Only such tools can socialize access to skills. Only such tools favor temporary associations among those who want to use them for a specific occasion. Only such tools allow specific goals to emerge in the process of their use, as any tinkerer knows. Only the combination of guaranteed access to facts and of limited power in most tools renders it possible to envisage a subsistence economy capable of incorporating the fruits of modern science.

The development of such a scientific subsistence economy is unquestionably to the advantage of the overwhelming majority of all people in poor countries. It is also the only alternative to progressive pollution, exploitation, and opaqueness in rich countries. But, as we have seen, the dethroning of the GNP cannot be achieved without simultaneously subverting GNE (Gross National Education—usually conceived as manpower capitalization). An egalitarian economy cannot exist in a society in which the right to produce is conferred by schools.

The feasibility of a modern subsistence economy does not depend on new scientific inventions. It depends primarily on the ability of a society to agree on fundamental, self-chosen anti-bureaucratic and anti-technocratic restraints.

These restraints can take many forms, but they will not work unless they touch the basic dimensions of life. (The decision of Congress against development of the supersonic transport plane is one of the most encouraging steps in the right direction.) The substance of these voluntary social restraints would be very simple matters that can be fully understood and judged by any prudent man. The issues at stake in the SST controversy provide a good example. All such restraints would be chosen to promote stable and equal enjoyment of scientific know-how. The French say that it takes a thousand years to educate a peasant to deal with a cow. It would not take two generations to help all people in Latin America or Africa to use and repair outboard motors, simple cars, pumps, medicine kits, and ferro cement machines if their design does not change every few years. And since a joyful life is one of constant meaningful intercourse with others in a meaningful environment, equal enjoyment does translate into equal education.

At present a consensus on austerity is difficult to imagine. The reason usually given for the impotence of the majority is stated in terms of political or economic class. What is not usually understood is that the new class structure of a schooled society is even more powerfully controlled by vested interests. No doubt an imperialist and capitalist organization of society provides the social structure within which a minority can have disproportionate influence over the effective opinion of the majority. But in a technocratic society the power of a minority of knowledge capitalists can prevent the formation of true public opinion through control of scientific know-how and the media of communication. Constitutional guarantees of free speech, free press, and free assembly were meant to ensure government by the people. Modern electronics, photo-offset presses, time-sharing computers, and telephones have in principle provided the hardware that could give an entirely new meaning to these freedoms. Unfortunately, these things are used in modern media to increase the power of knowledge-bankers to funnel their program-packages through international chains to more people, instead of being used to increase true networks that provide equal opportunity for encounter among the members of the majority.

Deschooling the culture and social structure requires the use of technology to make participatory politics possible. Only on the basis of a majority coalition can limits to secrecy and growing power be determined without dictatorship. We need a new environment in which growing up can be classless, or we will get a brave new world in which Big Brother educates us all.

The Universal Trap

Paul Goodman

Paul Goodman, one of America's best known anarchists and a
prolific author of social criticism, has been a longtime opponent
of the educational establishment. As the title of one of his most
acclaimed books indicates, Goodman thinks American education
causes students to grow up absurd.

Goodman's major objection to the schools is that they are
artificial and prevent students from developing and testing their
talents through encounters with real occupational worlds. Students
cannot make adequately informed career choices until they have
experimented with occupational alternatives. It is patently stupid
to invest a great deal of time, money, and effort in earning credentials for a job one really does not care to perform.

In the following article, Goodman rejects the commonly held
superstitions that formal schooling is good for everyone and can
be made palatable to everyone. He doubts that attending school is
the best way for most youths to spend their time. The relationship
between schooling and career exists not because schooling guarantees necessary job skills but because it develops submissive attitudes. Goodman recommends that educational conferences be
devoted to conceiving alternatives to schooling and suggests some
of his own.

I

A conference of experts on school drop-outs will discuss the background of poverty, cultural deprivation, race prejudice, family and
emotional troubles, neighborhood uprooting, urban mobility. It will
explore ingenious expedients to counteract these conditions, though it
will not much look to remedying them—that is not its business. And
it will suggest propaganda—e.g., no school, no job—to get the youngsters back in school. It is axiomatic that they ought to be in school.

Reprinted by permission of the publisher from Paul Goodman, *The
Urban School Crisis—An Anthology of Essays*, New York: League for Industrial Democracy and United Federation of Teachers, 1966.

After a year, it proves necessary to call another conference to cope with the alarming fact that more than 75% of the drop-outs who have been cajoled into returning, have dropped out again. They persist in failing; they still are not sufficiently motivated. What curricular changes must there be? How can the teachers learn the life-style of the underprivileged?

Curiously muffled in these conferences is the question that puts the burden of proof the other way: What are they drop-outs from? Is the schooling really good for them, or much good for anybody? Since, for many, there are such difficulties with the present arrangements, might not some better arrangements be invented? Or bluntly, since schooling undertakes to be compulsory, must it not continually review its claim to be useful? Is it the only means of education? Isn't it unlikely that *any* single type of social institution could fit almost every youngster up to age 16 and beyond? (It is predicted that by 1970, 50% will go to college.)

But conferences on drop-outs are summoned by school professionals, so perhaps we cannot hope that such elementary questions will be raised. Yet neither are they raised by laymen. There is a mass superstition, underwritten by additional billions every year, that adolescents must continue going to school. The middle-class *know* that no professional competence—i.e., status and salary—can be attained without many diplomas; and poor people have allowed themselves to be convinced that the primary remedy for their increasing deprivation is to agitate for better schooling. Nevertheless, I doubt that, *at present or with any reforms that are conceivable under present school administration*, going to school is the best use for the time of life of the majority of youth.

II

Education is a natural community function and occurs inevitably, since the young grow up on the old, toward their activities, and into (or against) their institutions; and the old foster, teach, train, exploit, and abuse the young. Even neglect of the young, except physical neglect, has an educational effect—not the worst possible.

Formal schooling is a reasonable auxiliary of the inevitable process, whenever an activity is best learned by singling it out for special attention with a special person to teach it. Yet it by no means follows that the complicated artifact of a school system has much to do with education, and certainly not with good education.

Let us bear in mind the way in which a big school system might have nothing to do with education at all. The New York system turns over $700 millions annually, not including capital improvements. There are 750 schools, with perhaps 15 annually being replaced at an extra cost of $2 to $5 millions each. There are 40,000 paid employees. This is a vast vested interest, and it is very probable that—like much of our economy and almost all of our political structure, of which the public schools are a part—it goes on for its own sake, keeping more than a million people busy, wasting wealth, and pre-empting time and space in which something else could be going on. It is a gigantic market for textbook manufacturers, building contractors, and graduate-schools of Education.

The fundamental design of such a system is ancient, yet it has not been altered although the present operation is altogether different in scale from what it was, and therefore it must have a different meaning. For example, in 1900, 6% of the 17-year-olds graduated from high school, and less than ½% went to college; whereas in 1963, 65% graduated from high school and 35% went on to something called college. Likewise, there is a vast difference between schooling intermitted in life on a farm or in a city with plenty of small jobs, and schooling that is a child's only "serious" occupation and often his only adult contact. Thus, a perhaps outmoded institution has become almost the only allowable way of growing up. And with this pre-empting, there is an increasing intensification of the one narrow experience, e.g., in the shaping of the curriculum and testing according to the increasing requirements of graduate schools far off in time and place. Just as our American society as a whole is more and more tightly organized, so its school system is more and more regimented as part of that organization.

In the organizational plan the schools play a non-educational and an educational role. The non-educational role is very important. In the tender grades, the schools are a baby-sitting service during a period of collapse of the old-type family and during a time of extreme urbanization and urban mobility. In the junior and senior high school grades, they are an arm of the police, providing cops and concentration camps paid for in the budget under the heading "Board of Education." The educational role is, by and large, to provide—at public and parents' expense—apprentice-training for corporations, government, and the teaching profession itself, and also to train the young, as New York's Commissioner of Education has said (in the Worley case), "to handle constructively their problems of adjustment to authority."

The public schools of America have indeed been a powerful, and beneficent, force for the democratizing of a great mixed population. But we must be careful to keep reassessing them when, with changing conditions, they become a universal trap and democracy begins to look like regimentation.

III

Let me spend a page on the history of the compulsory nature of the school systems. In 1961, in *The Child, the Parent, and the State*, James Conant mentions a possible incompatibility between "individual development" and "national needs"; this, to my mind, is a watershed in American philosophy of education and puts us back to the ideology of Imperial Germany, or on a par with contemporary Russia.

When Jefferson and Madison conceived of compulsory schooling, such an incompatibility would have been unthinkable. They were in the climate of the Enlightenment, were strongly influenced by Congregational (town-meeting) ideas, and were of course makers of a revolution. To them, "citizen" meant society-*maker*, not one "participating in" or "adjusted to" society. It is clear that they regarded themselves and their friends as citizens existentially, so to speak; to make society was their breath of life. But obviously such conceptions are worlds removed from, and diametrically opposed to, our present political reality, where the ground rules and often the score are pre-determined.

For Jefferson, people had to be taught in order to multiply the sources of citizenly initiative and to be vigilant for freedom. Everybody had to become literate and study history, in order to make constitutional innovations and be fired to defend free institutions, which was presumably the moral that history taught. And those of good parts were to study a technological natural philosophy, in order to make inventions and produce useful goods for the new country. By contrast, what are the citizenly reasons for which we compel everybody to be literate, etc.? To keep the economy expanding, to understand the mass-communications, to choose between indistinguishable Democrats and Republicans. Planning and decision-making are lodged in top managers; rarely, and at most, the electorate serves as a pressure-group. There is a new emphasis on teaching science but the vast majority will never use this knowledge and will forget it; they are consumers.

Another great impulse for compulsory education came from the new industrialism and urbanism during the three or four decades after the Civil War, a time also of maximum immigration. Here the curricular demands were more mundane: in the grades, literacy and arithmetic; in the colleges, professional skills to man the expanding economy. But again, no one would have spoken of an incompatibility between "individual development" and "national needs," for it was considered to be an open society, abounding in opportunity. Topically, the novels of Horatio Alger, Jr., treat schooling as morally excellent as well as essential for getting ahead; and there is no doubt that the immigrants saw education-for-success as also a human value for their children. Further, the school-system was not a trap. The 94% who in 1900 did not finish high school had other life opportunities, including making a lot of money and rising in politics. But again, by and large this is not our present situation. There is plenty of social mobility, opportunity to rise—except precisely for the ethnic minorities who are our main concern as drop-outs—but the statuses and channels are increasingly stratified, rigidified, cut and dried. Most enterprise is parceled out by feudal corporations, or by the state; and these determine the requirements. Ambition with average talent meets these rules or fails; those without relevant talent, or with unfortunate backgrounds, cannot even survive in decent poverty. The requirements of survival are importantly academic, attainable only in schools and universities; but such schooling is ceasing to have an initiating or moral meaning.

We do not have an open economy; even when jobs are not scarce, the corporations and state dictate the possibilities of enterprise. General Electric swoops down on the high schools, or IBM on the colleges, and skims off the youth who have been pre-trained for them at public or private expense. (Private college tuition runs upward of $6000, and this is estimated as a third or less of the actual cost for "education and educational administration.") Even a department store requires a diploma for its salespeople, not so much because of the skills they have learned as that it guarantees the right character: punctual and with a smooth record. And more generally, since our powers-that-be have opted for an expanding economy with a galloping standard of living, and since the powers of the world are in an arms and space race, there *is* a national need for many graduates specifically trained. Thus, even for those selected, the purpose is irrelevant to citizenly initiative, the progress of an open society, or personal happiness, and the others have spent time and effort in order to be progressively weeded out. Some drop out.

IV

It is said that our schools are geared to "middle-class values," but this is a false and misleading use of terms. The schools less and less represent *any* human values, but simply adjustment to a mechanical system.

Because of the increasing failure of the schools with the poor urban mass, there has developed a line of criticism—e.g., Oscar Lewis, Patricia Sexton, Frank Riessman, and even Edgar Friedenberg— asserting that there is a "culture of poverty" which the "middle-class" schools do not fit, but which has its own virtues of spontaneity, sociality, animality. The implication is that the "middle class," for all its virtues, is obsessional, prejudiced, prudish.

Pedagogically, this insight is indispensable. A teacher must try to reach each child in terms of what he brings, his background, his habits, the language he understands. But if taken to be more than technical, it is a disastrous conception. The philosophic aim of education must be to get each one out of his isolated class and into the one humanity. Prudence and responsibility are not middle class virtues but human virtues; and spontaneity and sexuality are not powers of the simple but of human health. One has the impression that our social-psychologists are looking not to a human community but to a future in which the obsessionals will take care of the impulsives!

In fact, some of the most important strengths that have historically belonged to the middle class are flouted by the schools: independence, initiative, scrupulous honesty, earnestness, utility, respect for thorough scholarship. Rather than bourgeois, our schools have become petty-bourgeois, bureaucratic, time-serving, gradgrind-practical, timid, and *nouveau riche* climbing. In the upper grades and colleges, they often exude a cynicism that belongs to rotten aristocrats.

Naturally, however, the youth of the poor and of the middle class respond differently to the petty-bourgeois atmosphere. For many poor children, school is orderly and has food, compared to chaotic and hungry homes, and it might even be interesting compared to total deprivation of toys and books. Besides, the wish to improve a child's lot, which on the part of a middle class parent might be frantic status-seeking and pressuring, on the part of a poor parent is a loving aspiration. There is here a gloomy irony. The school that for a poor Negro child might be a great joy and opportunity is likely to be dreadful; whereas the middle class child might be better off *not* in the "good" suburban school he has.

Other poor youth, herded into a situation that does not fit their disposition, for which they are unprepared by their background, and which does not interest them, simply develop a reactive stupidity very different from their behavior on the street or ball field. They fall behind, play truant, and as soon as possible drop out. If the school situation is immediately useless and damaging to them, their response must be said to be life-preservative.

The reasonable social policy would be not to have these youth in school, certainly not in high school, but to educate them otherwise and provide opportunity for a decent future in some other way. How? In my opinion, the wise thing would be to have our conferences on *this* issue, and omit the idea of drop-out altogether. But the brute fact is that our society isn't really interested; the concern for the drop-outs is mainly because they are a nuisance and a threat and can't be socialized by the existing machinery.

Numerically far more important than these overt drop-outs at 16, however, are the children who conform to schooling between the ages of 6 to 16 or 20, but who drop out internally and day-dream, their days wasted, their liberty caged and scheduled. And there are many such in the middle class, from backgrounds with plenty of food and some books and art, where the youth is seduced by the prospect of money and status but even more where he is terrified to jeopardize the only pattern of life he knows.

It is in the schools and from the mass media, rather than at home or from their friends, that the mass of our citizens in all classes learn that life is inevitably routine, depersonalized, venally graded; that it is best to toe the mark and shut up; that there is no place for spontaneity, open sexuality, free spirit. Trained in the schools, they go on to the same quality of jobs, culture, politics. This *is* education, mis-education, socializing to the national norms and regimenting to the national "needs."

John Dewey used to hope, naively, that the schools could be a community somewhat better than society and serve as a lever for social change. In fact, our schools reflect our society closely, except that they *emphasize* many of its worst features, as well as having the characteristic defects of academic institutions of all times and places.

V

Can it be denied that in some respects the drop-outs make a wiser choice than many who go to school, not to get real goods but to get money? Their choice of the "immediate"—their notorious "inability to tolerate delay"—is not altogether impulsive and neurotic. The bother is that in our present culture, which puts its entire emphasis on the consumption of expensive commodities, they are so nagged by inferiority, exclusion, and despair of the future that they cannot enjoy their leisure with a good conscience. Because they know little, they are deprived of many profound simple satisfactions and they never know what to do with themselves. Being afraid of exposing themselves to awkwardness and ridicule, they just hang around. And our urban social arrangements—e.g., high rent—have made it impossible for anybody to be decently poor on a "low" standard. One is either in the rat-race or has dropped out of society altogether.

As a loyal academic, I must make a further observation. Mainly to provide Ph.D.'s, there is at present an overwhelming pressure to gear the "better" elementary schools to the graduate-universities. This is the great current reform, genre of Rickover. But what if the top of the ladder is corrupt and corrupts the lower grades? On visits to 70 colleges everywhere in the country, I have been appalled at how rarely the subjects are studied in a right academic spirit, for their truth and beauty and as part of humane international culture. The students are given, and seek, a narrow expertise, "mastery," aimed at licenses and salary. They are indoctrinated with a national thought-lessness that is not even chauvinistic. Administrators sacrifice the community of scholars to aggrandizement and extramurally sponsored research.

Conversely, there is almost never conveyed the sense in which learning is truly practical, to enlighten experience, give courage to initiate and change, reform the state, deepen personal and social peace. On the contrary, the entire educational system itself creates professional cynicism or the resigned conviction that Nothing Can Be Done. If this is the University, how can we hope for aspiring scholar-ship in the elementary schools? On the contrary, everything will be grades and conforming, getting ahead not in the subject of interest but up the ladder. Students "do" Bronx Science in order to "make" M.I.T. and they "do" M.I.T. in order to "make" Westinghouse; some of them have "done" Westinghouse in order to "make" jail.

VI

What then? The compulsory system has become a universal trap, and it is no good. Very many of the youth, both poor and mid-dle class, might be better off if the system simply did not exist, even if they then had no formal schooling at all. (I am extremely curious for a philosophic study of Prince Edward County in Virginia, where for some years schooling did not exist for Negro children.)

But what would become of these children? For very many, both poor and middle class, their homes are worse than the schools, and the city streets are worse in another way. Our urban and suburban environments are precisely not cities or communities where adults naturally attend to the young and educate to a viable life. Also, per-haps especially in the case of the overt drop-outs, the state of their body and soul is such that we must give them refuge and remedy, whether it be called school, settlement house, youth worker, or work camp.

There are thinkable alternatives. Here are half a dozen directly relevant to the subject we have been discussing, the system as compulsory trap. In principle, when a law begins to do more harm than good, the best policy is to alleviate it or try doing without it.

i. Have "no school at all" for a few classes. These children should be selected from tolerable, though not necessarily cultured, homes. They should be neighbors and numerous enough to be a society for one another and so that they do not feel merely "different." Will they learn the rudiments anyway? This experiment cannot do the children any academic harm, since there is good evidence that normal children will make up the first seven years school-work with four to seven months of good teaching.

ii. Dispense with the school building for a few classes; provide teachers and use the city itself as the school—its streets, cafeterias, stores, movies, museums, parks, and factories. Where feasible, it certainly makes more sense to teach using the real subject-matter than to bring an abstraction of the subject-matter into the school-building as "curriculum." Such a class should probably not exceed 10 children for one pedagogue. The idea—it is the model of Athenian education—is not dissimilar to youth gang work, but not applied to delinquents and not playing to the gang ideology.

iii. Along the same lines, but both outside and inside the school building, use appropriate *unlicensed* adults of the community—the druggist, the storekeeper, the mechanic—as the proper educators of the young into the grown-up world. By this means we can try to overcome the separation of the young from the grown-up world so characteristic in modern urban life, and to diminish the omnivorous authority of the professional school-people. Certainly it would be a useful and animating experience for the adults. (There is the beginning of such a volunteer program in the New York and some other systems.)

iv. Make class attendance not compulsory, in the manner of A. S. Neill's Summerhill. If the teachers are good, absence would tend to be eliminated; if they are bad, let them know it. The compulsory law is useful to get the children away from the parents, but it must not result in trapping the children. A fine modification of this suggestion is the rule used by Frank Brown in Florida: he permits the children to be absent for a week or a month to engage in any worthwhile enterprise or visit any new environment.

v. Decentralize an urban school (or do not build a new big building) into small units, 20 to 50, in available store-fronts or clubhouses. These tiny schools equipped with record-player and pin-ball machine, could combine play, socializing, discussion, and formal teaching. For special events, the small units can be brought together into a common auditorium or gymnasium, so as to give the sense of the greater community. Correspondingly, I think it would be worthwhile to give the Little Red Schoolhouse a spin under modern urban conditions, and see how it works out: that is, to combine all the ages in a little room for 25 to 30, rather than to grade by age.

vi. Use a pro rata part of the school money to send children to economically marginal farms for a couple of months of the year, perhaps 6 children from mixed backgrounds to a farmer. The only requirement is that the farmer feed them and not beat them; best, of course, if they take part in the farm-work. This will give the farmer cash, as part of the generally desirable program to redress the urban-rural ratio to something nearer to 70% to 30%. (At present, less than 8% of families are rural.) Conceivably, some of the urban children will take to the other way of life, and we might generate a new kind of rural culture.

I frequently suggest these and similar proposals at teachers colleges, and I am looked at with an eerie look—do I really mean to *diminish* the state-aid grant for each student-day? But mostly the objection is that such proposals entail intolerable administrative difficulties.

Above all, we must apply these or any other proposals to particular individuals and small groups, without the obligation of uniformity. There is a case for uniform standards of achievement, lodged in the Regents, but they *cannot* be reached by uniform techniques. The claim that standardization of procedure is more efficient, less costly, or alone administratively practical, is often false. Particular inventiveness requires thought, but thought does not cost money.

Education Vouchers

Christopher Jencks

Christopher Jencks, a contributing editor of *New Republic*, is on the faculty of the Harvard Graduate School of Education. He is co-author with David Riesman of *The Academic Revolution*. Jencks discusses the voucher plan which he developed at the Center for the Study of Public Policy in conjunction with the Office of Economic Opportunity. The plan calls for publicly-funded vouchers with which parents can pay for the kind of education they want their children to have. This is seen as a means of breaking down the educational homogeneity within regions and facilitating genuine educational choice. The plan includes safeguards against such obvious pitfalls as hucksterism and discriminatory school admission policies. However, the funding agency which will oversee the plan is not envisioned as a certifier of teachers or an accreditor of programs. This would compromise the diversity which the plan is intended to encourage.

An aspect of the voucher plan which is not stressed in the Jencks' article or in the general publicity is the plan's implications for teachers. Informal talks with teachers elicit a healthy skepticism about the plan's feasibility but also an anxiety about its personal consequences. The plan is seen as a definite threat to the job security now enjoyed by tenured teachers. At least one state teachers' convention has already gone on record as opposing the plan. It does not appear that many teachers welcome the plan as an opportunity to get more job *satisfaction,* even if less job security. The educational variety which the plan encourages can meet the needs and desires of teachers as well as students and parents.

Jencks is currently trying to arrange a three-year tryout of the voucher plan. He cannot do so without the extensive cooperation of education officials, at the state and local level, of some state in the union. At this writing, the necessary cooperation has yet to be obtained.

OEO announced in May that it hopes to fund an experiment which would provide parents with vouchers to cover the cost of educating their children at the school of their choice. This news has provoked considerable liberal opposition, including charges that the experiment is unconstitutional, that it is part of a Nixon plot to perpetuate segregation, and that it would "destroy the public school system." What, then, does OEO really have in mind?

If state and local cooperation is forthcoming, the first step will be the establishment of an Educational Voucher Agency (EVA) in some community. This EVA will resemble a traditional board of education in that it will be locally controlled and will receive federal, state, and local funds for financing the education of all local children. But it will differ from a traditional board in that it will not operate any schools of its own. That responsibility will remain with existing school boards, both public and private. The EVA will simply issue vouchers to all parents of elementary school children in its area. The parents will take these vouchers to a school in which they want to enroll their child. This may either be an existing public school, a new school opened by the public school board to attract families who would otherwise withdraw their children from the public system, an existing private school, or a new private school opened especially to cater to children with vouchers. If the school meets the basic eligibility requirements laid down by the EVA, it will be able to convert its vouchers into cash, which will cover both its operating expenses and the amortization of capital costs. Such a system would enable anyone starting a school to get public subsidies, so long as he followed the basic rules laid down by the EVA and could persuade enough parents to enroll their children in his school. It would also give low-income parents the same choice about where they sent their children that upper-income parents now have. This would include all the public and private schools participating in the system.

The effect of these changes on the quality of education would depend on how effectively the EVA regulated the newly created marketplace, and especially on the rules it laid down for determining which schools could cash vouchers and which schools could not. Since the EVA would presumably be controlled by the same political forces that now dominate local school boards, some prophets anticipate that it would soon develop a regulatory system as complex and detailed as that now governing the public schools. If this happened, both publicly and privately managed voucher schools would soon be entangled in the usual bureaucratic and political jungle, in which everything is either required or forbidden. They would probably end up indistinguishable from existing public schools. Nothing would have changed, either for better or for worse.

This vision may, however, be unnecessarily gloomy. Today's public school has a captive clientele. As a result, it in turn becomes the captive of a political process designed to protect the interests of its clientele. The state, the local board, and the school administration establish regulations to ensure that no school will do anything to offend anyone of political consequence. By trying to please everyone, however, the schools often end up pleasing no one. The voucher system seeks to free schools from these managerial constraints by eliminating their monopolistic privileges. Under a voucher system, parents who do not like what a school is doing can simply send their children elsewhere. Schools which attract no applicants go out of business. But those which survive have a much greater claim to run their own affairs in their own way.

Most opponents of the voucher system worry more about the possibility that the EVA would establish too few regulations than about the possibility that it would establish too many. They particularly fear the development of a system in which schools would compete with one another in terms of social and/or academic exclusiveness, much as colleges now do. Left to their own devices, many schools would restrict admission to the brightest and most easily educated youngsters, leaving the more difficult children to somebody else. Many would also try to increase their operating budgets by charging supplemental tuition. This would have the not-always-accidental effect of limiting the number of low-income children in the more expensive schools.

An unregulated system of this kind would have all the drawbacks of other unregulated markets. It would produce even more racial and economic segregation than the existing neighborhood school system. It would also widen the expenditure gap between rich and poor children, giving the children of the middle-classes an even larger share of the nation's educational resources than they now get, while reducing the relative share going to the children of the poor.

Fortunately, OEO has shown no signs of funding a completely unregulated voucher system. Rather, OEO is contemplating an experiment in which extremely stringent controls are placed on participating schools' admissions policies, and also on their tuition charges. At the same time, it is hoping for an experiment which places minimal restraint on schools' staffing practices and programs.

In order to cash vouchers, a school would have to offer every applicant a roughly equal chance of admission. To ensure this, the school would have to declare each spring how many children it could take the following year. Parents would apply to schools each spring, and unless a school had more applicants than places, it would have to take everyone who had applied. If there were more applicants than places, the school would have to fill at least half its places by a lottery among applicants. It would also have to show that it had accepted at least as high a proportion of minority group students as had applied. Thus no school would be able to cream off the most easily educated children or dump all the problem children elsewhere.

The redemption value of a middle- or upper-income family's voucher would approximate what the local public schools are currently spending on upper-income children. Vouchers for children from low-income families would have a somewhat higher redemption value. This reflects the fact that schools with high concentrations of low-income children also tend to have more than their share of educational problems. It should also help discourage schools from trying to attract exclusively middle-class applicants. Participating schools would have to accept every child's voucher as full payment for his education, regardless of its value. Otherwise, parents who could afford to supplement their children's vouchers would inevitably have a better chance of getting their children into high cost schools than parents who could not supplement the voucher.

These regulations would not result in as much racial or economic integration as massive compulsory busing. But that is hardly a likely alternative. The real alternative is the continuation of the neighborhood school, whose racial and economic composition inevitably and deliberately reflects the racial and economic exclusiveness of the private housing market. Under a voucher system, no child could be excluded from any participating school simply because his family was not rich enough or white enough to buy a house near the school. Furthermore, the EVA would pay transportation costs, so that every family would have genuinely equal access to every participating school. Most families, both black and white, would doubtless continue to prefer schools near their homes. But at least no family would be legally or financially required to choose such a school if they thought it was educationally inadequate. Those black parents who wanted their children to attend integrated schools would be in an excellent position to ensure that they did so.

If all goes according to plan, the OEO experiment would be far more permissive with regard to schools' staffing and curricular policies than with regard to admissions. Schools would have to conform to existing state and local regulations governing private schools, but these are relatively lenient in most states. Experience suggests that while such leniency results in some abuses, the results over the long run seem to be better than the results of detailed legal and administrative regulations of the kind that shape the public schools. While these regulations often seem rational on their face (as in the case of teacher certification requirements), they generally create more problems than they solve. Teaching and learning are subtle processes, and they seem to resist all attempts at improvement by formal regulation. Rule books are seldom subtle enough to prevent the bad things that can happen in schools, and are seldom flexible enough to allow the best things.

So instead of telling schools whom to hire, what to teach, or how to teach it, the EVA will confine itself to collecting and disseminating information about what each school is doing. Every family will be given extensive information about every participating school. This should ensure that families are aware of all the choices open to them. It should also help discourage misleading advertising, or at least partially offset the effects of such advertising.

One common objection to a voucher system of this kind is that many parents are too ignorant to make intelligent choices among schools. Giving parents a choice will, according to this argument, simply set in motion an educational equivalent of Gresham's Law, in which hucksterism and mediocre schooling drive out high quality institutions. This argument seems especially plausible to those who envisage the entry of large numbers of profit-oriented firms into the educational marketplace. The argument is not, however, supported by much evidence. Existing private schools are sometimes mere diploma mills, but on the average their claims about themselves seem no more misleading, and the quality of the services they offer no lower, than in the public schools. And while some private schools are run for little but profit, this is the exception rather than the rule. There is no obvious reason to suppose that vouchers would change all this.

A second common objection to vouchers is that they would "destroy the public schools." Again, this seems farfetched. If you look at the educational choices made by wealthy parents who can already afford whatever schooling they want for their children, you find that many still prefer their local public schools if these are at all adequate. Furthermore, most of those who now leave the public system do so in order to attend high-cost, exclusive private schools. While some parents would doubtless continue to patronize such schools, they would receive no subsidy under the proposed OEO system.

Nonetheless, if you are willing to call every school "public" that is ultimately responsible to a public board of education, then there is little doubt that a voucher system would result in some shrinkage of the "public" sector and some growth of the "private" sector.

If, on the other hand, you confine the label "public" to schools which are really equally open to everyone within commuting distance, you discover that the so-called public sector includes relatively few public schools. Instead, racially exclusive suburbs and economically exclusive neighborhoods serve to ration access to good "public" schools in precisely the same way that admissions committees and tuition charges ration access to good "private" schools. If you begin to look at the distinction between public and private schooling in these terms, emphasizing accessibility rather than control, you are likely to conclude that a voucher system, far from destroying the public sector, would greatly expand it, since it would force large number of schools, public and private, to open their doors to outsiders.

A third objection to vouchers is that they would be available to children attending Catholic schools. This is not, of course, a necessary feature of a voucher system. An EVA could perfectly easily restrict participation to non-sectarian schools. Indeed, some state constitutions clearly require that this be done. The federal Constitution may also require such a restriction, but neither the language of the First Amendment nor the legal precedents is clear on this issue. The First Amendment's prohibition against an "establishment of religion" can be construed as barring payments to church schools, but the "free exercise of religion" clause can also be construed as requiring the state to treat church schools in precisely the same way as other private schools. The Supreme Court has never ruled on a case of this type (e.g., GI Bill payments to Catholic colleges or Medicare payments to Catholic hospitals). Until it does, the issue ought to be resolved on policy grounds. And since the available evidence indicates that Catholic schools have served their children no worse than public schools, and perhaps slightly better, there seems no compelling reason to deny them the same financial support as other schools.

The most common and most worrisome objection to a voucher system, in my view, is that its results depend on the EVA's willingness to regulate the marketplace vigorously. If vouchers were used on a large scale, state and local regulatory efforts might be uneven or even nonexistent. The regulations designed to prevent racial and economic segregation seem especially likely to get watered down at the state and local level, or else to remain unenforced. This argument applies, however, to *any* educational reform, and it also applies to the existing system. If you assume any given EVA will be controlled by overt or covert segregationists, you must also assume that this will be true of the local board of education. A board of education that wants to keep racist parents happy hardly needs vouchers to do so. It only needs to maintain the neighborhood school system. White parents who want their children to attend white schools will then find it quite simple to move to a white neighborhood where their children will be suitably segregated. Except perhaps in the South, neither the federal government, the state government, nor the judiciary is likely to prevent this traditional practice.

If, on the other hand, you assume a board which is anxious to eliminate segregation, either for legal, financial, or political reasons, you must also assume that the EVA would be subject to the same pressures. And if an EVA is anxious to eliminate segregation, it will have no difficulty devising regulations to achieve this end. Furthermore, the legal precedents to date suggest that the federal courts will be more stringent in applying the Fourteenth Amendment to voucher systems than to neighborhood school systems. The courts have repeatedly thrown out voucher systems designed to maintain segregation, whereas they have shown no such general willingness to ban the neighborhood school. Outside the South, then, those who believe in integration may actually have an easier time achieving this goal than they will with the existing public school system.

chapter 13

Tactics of Change

This chapter is concerned with more immediate, less elaborate steps that can be taken to effect change in education. To some readers this might suggest an inherently non-radical position—a willingness to work within the system, modest melioration, mere liberalism. It is true that radical tactics are not always employed in the service of radical strategies or theories. They may be used to realign the practices of an institution with its purposes. That is, they can be used to redeem an institution as well as replace it. Thus, small acts may not be anti-system, but they can still constitute radical departures from established practice. The early draft-card burnings, while an easy physical action to take, significantly dramatized and spurred anti-war sentiment because they were a radical psychological and moral leap and because they bore a high risk. However, the burnings did not signal a rejection of the American system. The Saul Alinsky tactics of dumping dead rats from the slums on the steps of city hall or having blacks picket the suburban homes of slum-lords are also radical in their deviation from conventional means of petitioning. Likewise, the placing of a large notice in the *New York Times* by the staff of a Harlem school, imploring help in reversing the wretched physical deterioration of the school building, was certainly a radical circumvention of the normal channels for grievance redress in the New York City school system. (It got results.)

In each of the foregoing instances, radical tactics were resorted to because normal tactics had proven unproductive. The radical tactics were the outcries of desperate people against unresponding or unsatisfactorily responding power terminals. While there have been successes in the use of such tactics—and successes for society at large —two unfortunate results have occurred. In some instances the system developed counter-tactics for preventing or deflecting the radical tactics, and this brought on an escalatory situation of moves and counter-moves to the point where anti-personnel bombs were being home manufactured for use against the police. In other circumstances the success of radical tactics bred an impatience with anything that was less than radical. Only radicalism was serious; everything else was a game. It hardly needs saying that this attitude has been augmented by systemic resistance to change, the schools being a clear case of such resistance.

Among the radical tacticians of education are those who argue for a downward assumption of power. Rather than constantly seek permission from impassible and hyper-cautious administrators, teachers are exhorted to go ahead on their own best instincts and judgments and leave the administration to make its blustering accommodation to *fait accompli*. Specific techniques by which teachers can radically alter the atmosphere of a school are sometimes provided. One of these techniques is abrupt role change, to create a disorientation that will enhance perception. Changes in teacher education are also proposed to give prospective teachers practice at being the kinds of people they say they want to develop.

Some tacticians do not view an increase in teacher power as an improvement. They are too distressed by the power to abuse students which teachers already exercise with such abandon. If anyone should be empowered, it is the students. They are the ones who need to get up on their hind legs and assert their human prerogatives. No one else in the educational structure can be expected to put a stop to student debasement, since everyone else reaps psychological gratification from it. In addition to the contemptuous treatment to which they are subjected, many students are also made to feel worthless by the unrealistic career goals which are imposed on them. To survive, students must develop a severe skepticism toward what it is the schools tell them about themselves and what the schools tell them is important. Students may even find it necessary to quit the official schools and devise their own more congenial alternatives.

Still other tacticians promote parent power. Community control is the path they would take to better schools. The panacea of democracy—all power to the people—is where it is at for these tacticians.

The Continuum

Anthony Barton

This article by Anthony Barton was published in the radical Canadian education journal *This Magazine is about Schools*. For those who have no previous acquaintance with the journal and wish a condensed one, there is an anthology of the better pieces which have appeared in the magazine, entitled, strangely enough, *This Book is about Schools*.

Barton contends that since schools have a variety of students, they should make provision for a diversity of learning and living styles. Students who thrive in a structured and orderly situation should have it; those who fare best amidst disorganization should be able to wallow in this. These would be the two poles of a school's environmental continuum. Barton supplies a checklist with which the reader can gauge how balanced is the continuum of a given school. He also suggests a host of ways by which any imbalance can be corrected.

Barton desires a diversity similar to that which is a goal of Christopher Jencks' voucher plan. The difference is that Barton hopes to create it *within* existing schools rather than among schools, many of which would be new. This may, at first blush, make Barton look like the more realistic of the two men. He is not asking for a new system but simply some modifications in the present one. The question is whether the schools, as they now exist, can really accommodate the modifications proposed by Barton. Can Barton's full environmental spectrum be housed in a single school? Could students be allowed to flit about the spectrum as the mood strikes them? If so, could the same prerogative be accorded to teachers? Could a single administration be charged with coordinating all of this, and would it be necessary to have an administration that was representative of the various living and learning styles in the school? Barton may only have intended his

This article first appeared in *This Magazine is about Schools*, Vol. 4, Issue 1. Address is 56 Esplanade St. E., Rm. 401, Toronto, Canada. Reprinted by permission.

article as a goad to the injection of a little more diversity, but
carried to its logical (and radical) conclusion, it may have as
many difficulties to overcome as the voucher plan.

When a friend of mine began teaching last autumn, the Principal gave
him a whistle and told him to carry it all times and to blow it whenever a child stepped out of line in the corridor. In another Ontario
school, an art teacher unlocked her immaculate art room and
explained that the desks were in rows to keep the janitor happy. In a
teacher training college in the States, some of the girls in their final
year were bewildered when asked to crawl on their nylon knees to
join a class of nine-year-olds working on the floor. In a public school
in Port Perry, I watched small boys being despatched in groups of
four to urinate into four urinals, and it transpired that the teacher
had been allotted a "lavatory time" upon her arrival at the school.
For thirty years she had been sending children to urinate at
11:17 a.m. These are examples of structure working against the interests of children in our schools. It is important to realize that the adults
responsible are unaware of what they are doing. The Principal thinks
that whistles are a good way to keep order. (TO KEEP WHAT?)
The art teacher protests regularly. (WHY?) The nylon girls want to
get out and teach. (WHOM?) The despatcher of urinators considers
compulsory lavatory a necessary part of public school life. (DON'T
MAKE A MESS ON THE FLOOR.) It is time that they learnt to
be *spreaders*. Imagine a superbly confident animal creeping through
the rain forest, in tune with its environment, ears pricked and every
sense alert.

Spread Out, Men

If you are a teacher who knows how to spread, this implies
that you are aware of the nature of the school in which you work and
of the part which you play in keeping the fabric of the school taut.
You know how far you and your class can go this year without tear-
ing the fabric, you are planning to go that far, and nothing short of
an earthquake is going to stop you. It's like riding a horse; confidence
is a part of it. If you do not think of yourself as a built-in spreader,
that is to say as a part of the very structure of the learning community, then you may find it hard to act on your own initiative. When
an idea strikes you, you will talk it over with your colleagues in the
staff room, or ask someone for permission to do it . . . in other words,
you will mess about and create obstacles rather than go ahead and

implement the idea on your own. An example of this is the Visit to the Indians.

Put Up Your Hands, I've Got You Covered

Not long ago, in an Ontario school, a young man teaching a social studies course discovered that members of his class had never met or talked with Indians, although there was a Reserve within easy driving distance. He went to the Principal and asked if he might take the students to the Indians. The Principal paced up and down for a while muttering about precedents and politics, but eventually said yes, it might be arranged. The students received the news with excitement and began to speculate about Indians of their own age. How did they date? Where did they go on Saturday nights? What were their homes like? Then the teacher was called back to the Principal's office. The visit was to take place in three weeks' time, a bus had been ordered for the entire class, and the Indian Band had been notified. The class was to prepare a list of twenty questions about Indian life, and this list was to be submitted for the approval of Mrs. Grumbacher, a member of staff with many years' experience, who had agreed to accompany the expedition to help keep order and to prevent the occurrence of anything politically inexpedient. Possibly the young man might have cancelled the project at this moment, but he decided that any kind of visit would be better than none, and made polite noises of concurrence. Three weeks later the students trooped out of a bright yellow bus onto a stage where they were seated in rows looking down on an audience of Indians. Appointed members of the class rose to their feet one by one to read aloud the prepared questions, from which Mrs. Grumbacher had removed diligently all references to sex, colour and creed. The Principal had sent the questions to the Indians in advance to make quite sure that all went smoothly, so an Indian spokesman rose in reply to each question and read a prepared answer. After that, the students were shepherded back into the bus, and that was the Visit to the Indians.

Don't Blame the Authorities, It's Too Easy

The teacher was to blame. If at the beginning he had stopped to estimate how small was the spread of the school in which he was working, and how small was the spread of the Principal's mind, he would have asked nobody's permission to do anything. Probably he would have motored a handful of interested students to the Reserve and given them a chance to make friends there. Maybe a few young Indians would have returned the visit, sitting in on classes and discussing this and that. Then, after the event, the teacher might have mentioned the matter to the Principal, if only to keep the poor man abreast of the good things happening in his school.

FACE THE CONTINUUM

The question arises: How does one estimate the spread of a school? Sometimes it is useful to make a list of what the institution has, and what it has not. Think of a school which you know well and see how many items on the following list apply to it. Find a pencil and draw a smiling face beside each item   ☺
which exists in the school.

The Continuum Check List (50 items)

○ A notice on the wall prohibiting something.
○ A system of bells or speakers with which it is possible to interrupt the work of many people simultaneously.
○ A classroom with a chalkboard, set of chairs with built-in book racks, and a tidy floor.
○ A bulletin board with a timetable pinned to it.
○ A set of thirty or more identical books or a row of thirty or more private lockers too small to fit a guitar.
○ A computer terminal dispensing programmed instruction.
○ A system whereby meals are prepared by those other than students and staff.
○ An understanding that the school is run by the staff, who respect the wishes of the students.
○ A room which students enter only with the permission of a member of staff.
○ A library in which as many books as possible are numbered and catalogued.
○ A locked storeroom from which an appointed member of the staff dispenses stationery or other materials.
○ A janitor who sweeps the corridors regularly.
○ A cold wall which is hard to touch and is painted a pastel shade.
○ An asphalt playground.
○ A daily assembly.
○ Organized competitive games.

○ A telephone which students use only with the permission of a member of staff.

○ Large television sets used by whole classes to watch educational TV.

○ A stage with lighting, flats and curtains.

○ A carpeted resource centre or library with audio-visual equipment in carrels with headphones for students to use quietly.

○ A swimming pool.

○ Supervised visits to places outside the school by large numbers of students.

○ A room which members of the staff use only with the permission of a student.

○ A garden or grounds with mown lawns and trim paths.

○ Still and movie cameras which students are told how to use.

○ A precision instrument, such as a telescope or a machine tool, which students use under supervision.

○ Still and movie cameras which students use without instruction.

○ A resource centre or library in which students are free to use projectors and record players and to make a noise and a mess.

○ A copying machine free for the use of students and staff.

○ A hobbies room open to all and equipped with benches, power tools and materials.

○ A flexible area with an overhead grid carrying power and communications, which is used for informal drama, movie-making, discussions and dances.

○ A number of mobile chairs, tables, cameras, spotlamps, mirrors and "hospital" screens.

○ An open storeroom from which people take what they need when they need it.

○ A warm wall painted a bold colour, into which your fingers sink.

○ Unsupervised visits to places outside the school by small numbers of students.

○ A large surface (such as the walls and ceiling of an auditorium) on which people paint murals and slogans.

○ Unrestricted use of a telephone, or unrestricted use of all the audio-visual equipment in the school.

○ An informal cooking area where students fry eggs and brew cocoa when they feel like it.

○ An understanding that decisions affecting the community are made by students and staff together.

○ A room serving no particular purpose.
○ A school vehicle which students drive.
○ A bin filled with free learning materials.
○ A pile of junk, or a room which is *never* tidy.
○ Spontaneous non-competitive games.
○ Trees which are climbed.
○ Space in which people run.
○ Water with which people play.
○ Mud in which people roll.
○ Long grass in which people lie.
○ Sky.

Consider the *number* of items that you checked. The more the better. If you checked less than half of the items, your school must lack facilities which are essential to the well-being of its inmates. Consider the *spread*. Are the items which you checked spread all over the place? They should be. If your checks are clustered thickly in one part of the continuum and spread thinly in another, then there is work to be done in the thin area. The missing faces are neglected children. After all, a school is a mixture of many different kinds of students and teachers. If it fails to spread itself evenly right across the continuum, it will surely harm some of its people, if only by ignoring them. Drawing faces on a continuum list is a quick way to discover some of the things that are missing. It can help you to decide which way to spread your budget and which gaps to fill in first. For example, I know of a school near Erie with a beautiful library filled with beautiful children's books on beautiful shelves, beautifully catalogued by a beautiful librarian. The place is so beautiful that the majority of the children avoid it like the plague. The smiling faces are clustered at the structured end of the continuum and none of the messy kids in the school are given a chance to express themselves. If I were teaching there, I think that I might have to use my plan for messing up libraries.

(A) Use own money to buy hundreds of old books and magazines, records, slides, filmstrips and postcards.
(B) Borrow an educational research paper weighing about 2 lbs. With the paper tucked under your arm, approach the librarian. Your class is experimenting for one month with a system of unstructured learning which involves the library. Can you count upon the librarian's assistance for the duration of the project? Consult your algebraic notes and murmur experiment, system, project. The librarian will agree to help.

(C) Fill a dignified plastic bin with your books and magazines and discuss with the librarian the best position for it in the library. Explain that the material in the bin is deliberately unlabelled and uncatalogued. Say the experiment requires that children be given the freedom to rummage in the bin and to take away whatever catches their fancy, without signing for anything.

(D) A week later, return with an undignified bin twice the size, with the words FREE! TAKE WHAT YOU WANT! written all over it. Add the records, slides, postcards and filmstrips. From this point on, the children are your best ambassadors. No librarian can fail to note the pleasure which such a bin of materials provides. Learning occurs like lightning. Suddenly, the library is full of interested students.

(E) Towards the end of the month, make sure that it is the librarian who suggests that the experiment continue indefinitely. Begin to mutter about assistance from library funds.

(F) Within a year, all going well, the librarian will have come to realize that about 30% of the children in a school learn best from material which has not been organized, and that in order to cater to those children ONE THIRD OF THE LIBRARY BUDGET has to be ear-marked for books and records which are *never* catalogued, *never* labelled and which the children are allowed to *take away* and *never return*. A good library spreads itself across the continuum.

But there is more to a school than the library. A Principal who diagnoses a surfeit of structure in his establishment may have to rally his staff, students and parents to carry out a crash programme. Here is a ten point plan for loosening up.

How To Soften Your Hard School

1. Use the corridors. Sell the steel lockers for scrap and use the money to buy cushions. Scatter the cushions around the corridors and let the students lie around on the floor. Have the floor cleaned very seldom but leave brooms about.

2. Take all the AV equipment out of the storeroom and put it in the corridors. Let the students use it when they feel the need for it. Let them break projectors, tape-recorders and viewers. Let them take machines home, steal tapes.

3. Hire a xerox machine and put it in the corridor. Place no restrictions whatever upon its use. Find a kid willing to keep it running. Put a thermofax copier in the corridor too. With a mountain of paper and acetate.

4. Open up the library. Take the doors off their hinges. Roll up the carpet and sell it. Let the students cut up the books with scissors.

Provide scissors, paste, paper. With the money provided by the sale of the carpet, buy:

a. *A bucket full of magazines.*
b. *A bucket full of comics.*
c. *A bucket full of newspapers.*
d. *Several incomprehensible thick medical tomes.*
e. *A number of books in Chinese, Japanese, Sanskirt and other languages.*
f. *A barrow-load of old books.*
g. *Photographs, maps, geological maps, plans, blueprints, research papers.*
h. *A bin of scrap film, clear leader, and old prints of movies.*
i. *A pile of large reproductions of great works of art, new and old.*
j. *Masses of records of all kinds.*
k. *A stack of mail-order catalogues, models kits, calendars, and so on.*
l. *Circular stands full of cheap paperbacks by journalists, hack novelists.*

Let the children destroy and re-fashion material. Be farsighted. Allow a child to learn by breaking, if you judge that the learning is worth more than the thing broken. Very often it is.

5. Announce that the school will be open all around the clock all year. Rip out any steel grills designed to slide across corridors. Unbar windows. Abandon all official paperwork, or give it to some student who would like to do it for you. Join in, start doing your own research in the library, on a pet topic, or build a model aeroplane. HAVE A BONFIRE of all personal files. I.Q. scores, examination results, attendance records and the like.

6. Build a rough annex onto the school—with a corrugated iron roof, a wood stove, naked plumbing and bare, dangling light-bulbs. Supply paints and brushes for home-made murals. Forbid the janitor to enter the annex at any time.

7. Sell those big, heavy television sets—and buy little Japanese ones for small groups and individuals. Get a VTR and let the kids record commercials, static, programs, anything. If you can afford it ($1400) buy a back-pack camera and recorder for instant TV.

8. Invite the world in. Lure real artists, engineers, labourers, nurses, scientists, technicians, typists into the school to work with the students. Many parents are qualified experts . . . put them to work inside the school.

9. Let the students out into the world. Let them travel as individuals or in very small groups to investigate insurance buildings, crawl down sewers, and watch courtrooms, washrooms, construction projects. Let them fly to Alaska, telephone long, long distance to talk

to Professors in California. PUT TELEPHONES IN THE CLASS-ROOMS.

10. *Invite Ford Foundation and others to visit. Show them your extraordinary school and ask for money, lots of money. And ask for computer terminals, teaching machines and other gimmicks. Keep asking.*

If you are frightened to attempt such sweeping changes, try quietly rearranging existing facilities. The technological wonders of our North American society are founded upon the concept of repetition, a concept which envelops us in clocks, apartment blocks and newspapers. Repetition is not the only way to work wonders, and in certain areas of the school you may change the whole atmosphere if you *search out repetition and break it up.* If there is a room furnished with tubular chairs and another furnished with wooden chairs, mix them. If there are desks arranged in rows, heap them in the corner. If anything is screwed to the floor, unscrew it. Unplug the electric clocks. In the words of Professor Northcote Parkinson, "Where there is a magnificent marble wall, gash a hole in it."

Let me hasten to add that this advice applies only to those who become aware that their schools are too structured. Many free schools need the reverse treatment; all their smiling faces are crammed into the unorganized end of the continuum. For free school people, here is a ten-point plan for tightening up.

How To Harden Your Soft School

1. *Establish a system for supplying the school with materials. On several occasions I have walked into a free school and been bitterly disappointed by the lack of materials. No school dedicated to making a decent mess should open its doors before it has obtained two truck loads, say 5 tons, of begged, borrowed and stolen information in the shape of string, glue, magnets, records, magazines, books, paints, test-tubes, chemicals, transistors, advertisements, felt pens, catalogues, newspapers, fossils, rocks, microscopes, herbs, wire, acetate, slide-rules, typewriters, tapes, film stock, stuffed owls, old pieces of machinery, cloth, thread, animals, bones, fishing flies, photographs, paintings, slides and films. Treat information like water from a tap.*

2. *Put your finances upon a sound footing.*

3. *Organize a few books. Wade into the sea of information, clear a few shelves, and arrange thirty reference books in alphabetical order. Stick numbers on their spines, stamp them NOT TO BE REMOVED and chain them to the shelf. While you are in the mood, padlock a few doors and windows.*

4. *Make a hard room. Set aside at least one room to represent the organized side of life. If you can afford it, build a laboratory with identical stools, gas taps, electrical outlets and small sinks for washing retorts. Have a ten-week course in the laboratory for which interested students have to sign in advance and attend at regular times. If you have no science teacher, immediately appoint a meticulous chemist.*

5. *Stop choosing new students—to fit the community. The next person whom you choose should be unlike anyone else you've ever had before.*

6. *Establish a school uniform. Hair must reach the shoulders. All clothes must be so outrageously comfortable that they appear to be a uniform worn by abnormal children and their teachers. Mom pops a piece of TV chicken into her mouth and shudders. If there were no electric bells, detentions and examinations, our kids might look like that.*

7. *Build a barn—and write the Seven Commandments on the wall. Animal farm is an excellent alternative to public education, if all you want to do is set up an alternative.*

8. *Enjoy a hard ritual every morning. Knit a flag and sing a song.*

9. *Rule and divide. Post rules for using the telephone, create a shortage of paper, and generally gum up communications. Watch people develop stiff backs, stiff collars and stiff upper lips.*

10. *Divide and rule. To really harden the school, create a lavatory for children only, a staff room for adults only, and a sewing room for girls only. Have tense discussions about Sex and the Generation Gap.*

At a McLuhan seminar last winter, the bosses of several radio stations described the audiences at which they aimed: the acid rock teenagers, the cultured intellectuals and so on. One man said that he ran a strictly M.O.R. station: pop classics and Hollywood musical songs. Let us beware of middle-of-the-road education. Let us try to put more diversity into both the free schools and the public schools. It is not easy to understand what diversity means. Admit to yourself that your school should have a full range of teachers (nervous, calm, irascible, busy and slothful) and you may have to admit also that your school has no slothful teacher. A School Board has to have courage to hire a slothful teacher deliberately. But if you don't, in no time at all Departments of Applied Diversity and white-coated Continuum Specialists will spring up to do it for you. Badly.

Teaching as a Subversive Activity

Neil Postman and Charles Weingartner

Postman and Weingartner are professors of education at New York University and Queens College, respectively. In this selection from their well-received book of the same title, they present 16 ways by which teachers can acquire a fresh perception of the educational process. They deny that these proposals are any more bizarre than what now goes on in school. The proposals are reminiscent of Thorstein Veblen's "trained incapacity" and Robert Merton's "bureaucratic mentality" and even the old saw about not being able to see the forest for the trees. What they amount to is the accusation that teachers are so damn busy doing their job that they forget the purpose of the job. Means have been transposed into ends, and everybody scurries about efficiently ineffective. The proposals are designed to jar from their unthinking state those charged with teaching others how to think.

An obvious intent of the Postman-Weingartner recommendations is to yank away the props on which teachers lean. Long-established and unquestioned habits will be denied the conditions that make them possible. Teachers will be re-introduced to the uncertainty and confusion and fumbling and anxiety of the young. No longer will certitude and rectitude be the identifying traits of homo pedagogus. All that teachers will have left is their wits—their ability to find meaning and purpose. In a most profound way, they will no longer even be teachers, only learners. Perhaps then they will be able to carry out their essential mission—to help students develop strategies for survival in a changing world.

Thus, the Postman-Weingartner approach is really future-oriented. In this respect, it reminds one of Theodore Brameld's query as to why schools always have a well-staffed department of history but no department of the future. Schools typically are so concerned with transmitting this or that heritage that they

Reprinted by permission of the publisher. From *Teaching as a Subversive Activity*, by Neil Postman and Charles Weingartner, New York: The Dial Press, 1969.

overlook the future into which we are all rushing or being pushed, depending on one's sense of control over his own destiny. It is Postman and Weingartner's purpose to help teachers increase students' control over that destiny.

We want to make several bizarre proposals that are designed to change the perceptions of teachers now functioning in the schools. We know from the available research that sometimes perceptions can be changed if the point of view of the perceiver is shifted. Perception change has even been known to occur when a different point of view has been *forced* on a perceiver. That is, when the perceiver is put into an environment that makes it difficult, if not impossible, for him to function with his old assumptions. In these circumstances change does not happen automatically, or often, but it does happen enough times to warrant an effort. And so we will now put before you a list of proposals that attempt to change radically the nature of the existing school environment. Most of them will strike you as thoroughly impractical but only because you will have forgotten for the moment that the present system is among the most impractical imaginable, if the facilitation of learning is your aim. There is yet another reaction you might have to our proposals. You might concede that they are "impractical" and yet feel that each one contains an idea or two that might be translated into "practical" form. If you do, we will be delighted. But as for us, none of our proposals seems impractical or bizarre. They seem, in fact, quite conservative, given the enormity of the problem they are intended to resolve. As you read them, imagine that you are a member of a board of education, or a principal, or supervisor, or some such person who might have the wish and power to lay the groundwork for a new education.

1. *Declare a five-year moratorium on the use of all textbooks.*

Since with two or three exceptions all texts are not only boring but based on the assumption that knowledge exists prior to, independent of, and altogether outside of the learner, they are either worthless or harmful. If it is impossible to function without textbooks, provide every student with a notebook filled with blank pages, and have him compose his own text.

2. *Have "English" teachers "teach" Math, Math teachers English, Social Studies teachers Science, Science teachers Art, and so on.*

One of the largest obstacles to the establishment of a sound learning environment is the desire of teachers to get something they think they know into the heads of people who don't know it. An English teacher teaching Math would hardly be in a position to fulfill this desire. Even more important, he would be forced to perceive the "subject" as a learner, not a teacher. If this suggestion is too impractical, try numbers 3 and 4.

3. Transfer all the elementary-school teachers to high school and vice versa.

4. Require every teacher who thinks he knows his "subject" well to write a book on it.

In this way, he will be relieved of the necessity of inflicting his knowledge on other people, particularly his students.

5. Dissolve all "subjects," "courses," and especially "course requirements."

This proposal, all by itself, would wreck every existing educational bureaucracy. The result would be to deprive teachers of the excuses presently given for their failures and to free them to concentrate on their learners.

6. Limit each teacher to three declarative sentences per class, and 15 interrogatives.

Every sentence above the limit would be subject to a 25-cent fine. The students can do the counting and the collecting.

7. Prohibit teachers from asking any questions they already know the answers to.

This proposal would not only force teachers to perceive learning from the learner's perspective, it would help them to learn how to ask questions that produce knowledge.

8. Declare a moratorium on all tests and grades.

This would remove from the hands of teachers their major weapons of coercion and would eliminate two of the major obstacles to their students' learning anything significant.

9. Require all teachers to undergo some form of psychotherapy as part of their in-service training.

This need not be psychoanalysis; some form of group therapy or psychological counseling will do. Its purpose: to give teachers an opportunity to gain insight into themselves, particularly into the reasons they are teachers.

10. Classify teachers according to their ability and make the lists public.

There would be a "smart" group (the Bluebirds), an "average" group (the Robins), and a "dumb" group (the Sandpipers). The lists would be published each year in the community paper. The I.Q. and reading scores of teachers would also be published, as well as the list of those who are "advantaged" and "disadvantaged" by virtue of what they know in relation to what their students know.

11. Require all teachers to take a test prepared by students on what the students know.

Only if a teacher passes this test should he be permitted to "teach." This test could be used for "grouping" the teachers as in number 10 above.

12. *Make every class an elective and withhold a teacher's monthly check if his students do not show any interest in going to next month's classes.*

This proposal would simply put the teacher on a par with other professionals, e.g., doctors, dentists, lawyers, etc. No one forces you to go to a particular doctor unless you are a "clinic case." In that instance, you must take what you are given. Our present system makes a "clinic case" of every student. Bureaucrats decide who shall govern your education. In this proposal, we are restoring the American philosophy: no clients, no money; lots of clients, lots of money.

13. *Require every teacher to take a one-year leave of absence every fourth year to work in some "field" other than education.*

Such an experience can be taken as evidence, albeit shaky, that the teacher has been in contact with reality at some point in his life. Recommended occupations: bartender, cab driver, garment worker, waiter. One of the common sources of difficulty with teachers can be found in the fact that most of them simply move from one side of the desk (as students) to the other side (as "teachers") and they have not had much contact with the way things are outside of school rooms.

14. *Require each teacher to provide some sort of evidence that he or she has had a loving relationship with at least one other human being.*

If the teacher can get someone to say, "I love her (or him)," she should be retained. If she can get two people to say it, she should get a raise. Spouses need not be excluded from testifying.

15. *Require that all the graffiti accumulated in the school toilets be reproduced on large paper and be hung in the school halls.*

Graffiti that concern teachers and administrators should be chiseled into the stone at the front entrance of the school.

16. *There should be a general prohibition against the use of the following words and phrases:*—teach, syllabus, covering ground, I.Q., makeup, test, disadvantaged, gifted, accelerated, enhancement, course, grade, score, human nature, dumb, college material, and administrative necessity.

. . . We want to say a further word about the seriousness of the foregoing proposals. Consider, for example, proposals 14 and 15, which some people might regard as facetious, if not flippant. Proposal 14 would require a teacher to present evidence of his having had a loving relationship with another person. Silly, isn't it? What kinds of evidence must teachers presently offer to qualify for their jobs? A list of "courses." Which of these requirements strikes you as more bizarre? From the student's point of view, which requirement would seem more practical? Bear in mind that it is a very difficult thing for one person to learn anything significant from another. Bear in mind, too, that it is probably not possible for such learning to occur unless there is something resembling a loving relationship between "teacher" and learner. Then ask yourself if you can think of anything sillier than asking an applicant for a teaching job if he has taken a course in Victorian literature?

Proposal 15 concerns making the school's graffiti public in the manner in which various slogans and mottos now adorn school halls and facades. . . . It is astonishing that so many people do not recognize the extent to which hypocrisy and drivel poison the whole atmosphere of school. And where will you find more concentrated hypocrisy and drivel than on the walls of classrooms, and in the halls, and on the facades of school buildings? To replace these with intimately felt observations would be neither tasteless nor eccentric. Unless, of course, your sense of propriety includes attempting to deceive the young.

Finally, we want to say that, in spite of our belief that it is unreasonable to expect the current crop of teachers to change sufficiently to permit an educational revolution to occur, it is sometimes surprising to discover how wrong we can be. There are teachers—some of whom have been at it for ten or 15 years—who know how desperately change is needed, and who are more than willing to be agents of such change. Such people cannot be dismissed, and, in fact, we spend a considerable amount of our time trying to locate them and lend them support. But the teachers of the future must bring this revolution off or it will not happen.

Organizing Parents To Beat the System

Ellen Lurie

Ellen Lurie was a member of the New York City People's Board of Education, which was formed by a group of parents who were walked out on by the official Board of Education. Before that,

From *How To Change the Schools*, by Ellen Lurie. Copyright © 1970 by Ellen Lurie. Reprinted by permission of Random House, Inc.

Mrs. Lurie had served for five years on Local Board 6, from which she resigned in protest against the powerlessness of parents against the board. Since 1967, Ellen Lurie has been training director for United Bronx Parents and a strong fighter for local control in education.

Community control of the schools has come to be a ringing shibboleth in most minority-group neighborhoods. The statistics on academic performance have convinced many minority-group members that the job of educating cannot safely be entrusted to professional educators alone. Converting community control from slogan to reality is the rub, however. The following selection consists of Ellen Lurie's very practical suggestions for effecting this conversion. The selection also leads one to question the degree of community control in the suburbs, where such control is usually presumed to prevail.

Community control raises perplexing issues of democracy versus rationality. If, as Max Weber contended, the rational bureaucracy is one in which authority and expertise exist in direct proportion to each other, is it rational to have nonprofessionals running the schools? On the other hand, is professional control democratic? How should a balance between rationality and democracy be struck? Or is this a false dichotomy in the matter of education? Looking at the dilemma from the perspective of recent headlines, one has to draw a line between parent power and teacher power, both of which are ideas whose time has obviously arrived.

Choose Specific Tangible Issues Which Are Important to Parents.

Don't be abstract, vague or intellectual. Select nitty-gritty demands—the more specific the better.

Go after several things at once, including a number of easily won issues. Parents will be encouraged by their success and will then gain the strength and self-confidence to tackle the more difficult problems.

Get things which parents want right now. If there are also some long-range demands (e.g., a new school), be sure you are also fighting for some immediate help at the same time (e.g., repair of the broken toilets at once).

Parents Must Develop Their Own List of Grievances and Demands.

No outside group, no matter how dedicated or concerned, can do this job. Don't let anyone tell you what you should be demanding.

One of the main reasons parent campaigns fail is that they are not really "parent" campaigns at all. The principal or some teachers have manipulated some parents into fighting for a particular program, and this sort of ruse soon falls apart.

Different groups of parents want different things. For example, in one elementary school, the parents of the children who come by bus may want to improve the lunch facilities and the transportation schedule; the Spanish-speaking parents may want to increase the number of bilingual teachers; the parents of the children in the top class may want French taught in the third grade. All of these demands are legitimate. All of the various groups should be encouraged to meet by themselves and prepare their own list of grievances and demands.

Parents must then come together and decide *priorities*. Which issues are the most important for all parents? Which are the most important for the different types of parents? Be careful that you don't concentrate only on those issues which the most powerful members of the parent association want. Be sure that you *hear* what all the various parents are saying. Be sure you include a wide cross-section of grievances and demands on your final list. (The UFT goes into bargaining sessions with more than six hundred different demands from all the various teacher chapters.)

Your Parent Group Must Be Representative, but Even More Important, it Must Include, in Large Numbers, Those Parents Who Have the Most Serious Grievances.

Many parent groups fail because they are not truly representative. Usually parent associations are heavily weighted to include mainly those parents who are satisfied with the school and trust the administration. Those parents will have an extremely narrow list of grievances. In a sense they are the "company union." It is crucial that parents do not argue with each other over the validity of a particular grievance. For example, if some parents believe that some teachers are bigoted, this is a very real issue to them. Just because other parents do not share this grievance is no reason to eliminate it. All parents want qualified, unprejudiced teachers. This is a good and legitimate demand.

Many parent groups fail because some of their members feel obliged to defend the school system from all criticism. Parents should defend and protect their children and other parents; it is up to the school employees to defend the system. If the parent association has become a "company union" you may want to set up your own parent group, or you may want to challenge the parent association to run a new election. However, a split of this sort is potentially dangerous and might weaken your group. If you can pull all the parents into a common group first, try to do so. But, priority should go to those parents whose children are suffering the most in the school. Parents whose children are doing all right simply will not fight as hard, nor will they risk very much. If keeping the parents united means losing the support of your angriest parents, forget it. It would be better to split.

Do Your Own Research—Gather Facts Carefully To Support Your Demands.

Fact-finding is a good organizing tool. As parents try to gather more information about their problems, they can get angrier and angrier with the system.

However, they can also get worn-out. The most important fact for you is the way the parents and students feel about your school. Document your stories and grievances, and be sure to *protect* the *anonymity* of everyone concerned.

When fact-finding, go directly to the source if you can. For example, if you want to find out about Title I regulations, go to Washington to find out how things *can* be done; don't go to board headquarters in Brooklyn, because all you will learn there is why things cannot be done your way.

Use various resources to help you gather data. Church groups, community agencies and colleges that wish to support you can be really helpful in securing the information you need. Just be sure that they only want to help you, and don't intend to take you over.

Don't believe things you read or things you are told, if your eyes tell you differently. Often the Board of Education will show parents some facts on paper which will testify that all the children are reading or that the school is not overcrowded. Our own eyes tell us that they are lying. We see that the kids can't read and we see how crowded the school is. Believe what you see, not what they tell you. And make them come and see what you see.

Publicize Your Grievances and Demands and Broaden Your Support.

Many parent groups take their grievances to the officials too soon. Once you develop your list of demands, you must first be sure that most of the parents agree with you. Hold meetings, distribute flyers, encourage other parents to add to the list and provide additional documentation for those grievances they support. Get some community groups to support your demands—early in the game before you run into any trouble. And remember, "support" means just that. You are not inviting them to veto your demands or modify them. You are asking their support and sponsorship. Invite community leaders to come into your school and see for themselves why you need what you are asking for. But don't let them try to supervise you, censor you, or manipulate you. You can appreciate their advice, but remember, a parent campaign must be run by parents. If your demands are good ones, undoubtedly there will be some teachers in your school who will be willing to support you.

Decide Whom You will See To Discuss Your Grievances.

Before you start running around from one agency to another, plan your campaign. If your demands are relatively simple, perhaps you only have to see your *principal*. But most likely you will need to go at least one step beyond him. Always bring your demands to your principal first, however. See which ones he will support; try to get him to do something about at least one or two of the grievances— these will be your first victories, and you should thank him and publicize them. But if he disagrees with you, that should *not* stop you if your grievances are valid.

Force your local school board to deal with your complete list of grievances. Make them help you avoid the buck-passing game. If you have fifteen different demands, for example, you could easily be sent to see fifteen different officials. One way to deal with this runaround is to force your local school board to handle everything; they should invite all the various officials who have power to one meeting with you so that you and your fellow parents are not worn out running from one to another.

Get your local board or the chancellor of schools or the mayor to tell you in *writing* who has the final authority to determine each of the problems on your list. There is no point in wasting time seeing a lot of people with no decision-making power.

Once You Get a Meeting To Present Your Grievances, Be Sure To:

√ take a good-sized group representing a cross-section of parents. Do not limit your group to only two or three members; this will antagonize too many parents. The UFT negotiating team consists of twelve or more members.

√ find out how long your meeting will last. If you prepare a half-hour presentation, but the meeting is scheduled to last only a half hour, you will have let them off the hook because there won't be enough time to force them to answer you.

√ find out in advance whom the board plans to have attend the meeting. If they are inviting many "experts," bring along your own experts. If they are inviting other parent groups, find out in advance and decide if you still want to go under those conditions. Or perhaps you will want to caucus with those other parent groups in advance.

√ doublecheck on the morning of your meeting to make sure the person you think you are seeing will really be there. Decide in advance whether or not you will keep the appointment if he keeps you waiting or if he delegates you to an assistant.

√ make sure you do not take up the entire meeting with your presentation. You must force them to respond to you.

√ have one member of your group take minutes. But insist that the school official put all promises into *writing*. You might want to stay there while he dictates the "agreement" to his secretary, or else you may be surprised that the letter you receive later in no way resembles the agreement you thought you had.

√ if the school official tells you he must "study" the matter further, give him a time limit within which he must render a decision or meet with you again. Schedule a follow-up appointment then and there.

Some Things To Do To Avoid Their Buck-passing.

√ *Play one agency against another.* If you are on good terms with the borough president, make him bring all the different officials together to meet with you. If they don't come, he will be angry at their arrogance and support you.

√ *Go over the head of the official who is stalling you.* When you waste time with an underling, unless you are getting some information you need, you are really being stalled. If an official will not see you, go over his head. For example, if the School Lunch Division won't see you, go to the Department of Agriculture, which partially subsidizes them. If the head of School Construction stalls you, pressure the mayor or city council, which supplies school construction funds.

√ *If the "proper channels" are clogged, use some improper ones.* If an official will not give you an appointment in his office, go picket his home or his church, until he agrees to meet with you.

√ *Disrupt their routine business-as-usual operation until they stop stalling you.* If you are given the run-around, learn to recognize it and get angry. Sit in, picket, do whatever you can to force them to meet and deal with you; don't make it easy for them to ignore you.

√ *Turn the tables and do some buck-passing yourself.* If a principal asks you to help him get an additional secretary for the school, tell him you can't because the "community" is disappointed that he didn't help solve their problems. Or if your group is demonstrating and you receive a phone call from a downtown politician asking you to call off your demonstration, tell him, "It is out of my hands; I have no control over that group, because they are so angry."

√ *Every time you are stalled, expose it to the rest of the parents.* If you have an appointment, role-play in advance what might happen, so the parents will recognize the brush-off. Then come back and write up a flyer and tell the rest of the neighborhood all about it. Or when you go through proper channels, and get nowhere, expose it; put your story into a flyer and tell everyone. If you keep your fellow parents informed every step of the way, they will be with you if and when you are forced into using more "extreme" tactics.

Never, Never, Never Attack Other Parents or Parent Groups.

√ Don't let the Board of Education divide and conquer you.

√ If you walk into a meeting where other parents have been invited to argue with you, ask to meet with them without any professionals present, or else leave. Take on those parents in private; don't fall into the system's trap by fighting among each other, and letting the school officials off the hook.

√ Even when you agree to disagree with the other parents, you can fight the system for what you want without fighting the parents.

√ Never take away something from another parent group. Always demand that you get as much as they got; but don't be trapped into fighting another group to give up something for your sake. There is enough to go around for everyone, but the school system likes to make us fight among each other for the crumbs while it controls the real pie.

Keep Your Neighbors Informed and Keep Broadening Your Local Base of Support.

√ Don't get so wrapped up in meetings "downtown" that you lose contact with your fellow parents and neighbors.

√ During any negotiation, keep local demonstrations, rallies and picket lines going. Distribute flyers telling everyone what is happening.

√ Don't depend on citywide media to tell your story. If you take lots of parents to all the meetings, they will see what is going on and they will spread the word.

√ Never stop inviting other local organizations to join with you.

Go to churches, political clubs, antipoverty agencies and everyone else to tell them about your campaign and invite their sponsorship. This will prevent the Board of Education from calling you extremists or other unfavorable names. Get the most legitimate groups in your community to lend their support. If you are campaigning for things parents really want, this should not be too difficult.

Don't Worry Too Much about City-wide Support.

√ Local issues are best won locally. And parents can wear themselves out by going to many meetings in other parts of the city.

√ It would be wonderful if we had a citywide movement of parents. But don't try to push this artificially too soon. Fight for the things you need in your own community and the rest will follow.

√ On the other hand, when opportunities arise to tell your story to the rest of the city, use them. For example, at various dedication ceremonies for new schools or parks, there is usually a television crew. Use those ceremonies for demonstrations about your grievances, and you may get some city-wide attention. Use special public hearings and meetings in the same way.

√ If citywide groups want to support you, invite them to come to your area and see what is going on. Don't keep leaving your own community to go to meetings; this will only weaken you.

√ Force decision-makers to come into your community for meetings and hearings.

Keep Your Sense of Humor and Find Ways To Deflate and Ridicule the Officials.

The struggle is hard and long. If you get too intense or uptight, you will be worn out long before you can win. There is humor in the most critical situations. Learn to seek it out, for it will keep you going.

Beware of Advisory Committees, Dialogues, Consultations, etc.

You are interested in setting up a pattern of negotiation between two equal groups: parents and school officials. You should not walk into a situation where you are asked to give advice which they can easily ignore.

√ *Pick your own leadership.* This is really one of the basic problems facing parent groups. If you don't like the procedures which are in effect for selecting parent leadership, force a change. (For example, in District 5, parents in several schools have won the point that they will not have to pay dues in order to vote for parent leaders or to vote on other crucial issues.) Unless parents work out a way to choose their own leadership (without manipulation by principals, teachers or community groups) we will be faced by splinter groups and "appointed" parent groups that have been hand-picked by the school administration.

Learn to Escalate Your Fight if You Reach a Bottleneck.

√ Timing and pacing are crucial. Don't start off by threatening a boycott. That should be the last possible tactic and threat.

√ But if you are blocked from getting what you want, start refusing to participate in anything. For example, they need parents to help write Title I proposals. If you are angry about a custodian and they won't discuss this with you, refuse to sit in on Title I discussions.

√ Parents have a great deal of *negative power*. By refusing to do certain things, they can be very strong.

√ Don't split up over tactics. If one group of parents wants to circulate a petition and another wants to do something more radical, let them both do their thing.

√ Remember that the issue you are fighting will determine your tactics. If you want something fairly conventional (i.e., more reading teachers) you can use one set of tactics, but if you are after something which is less "acceptable" (i.e., you want to interview your own staff), then you will need to formulate a different set of tactics.

√ Parents who have connections and contacts high up in the system will choose one type of tactics when escalating their fight. Parents who are more powerless will have to do some less "respectable," more sensational things to get attention. Choose those techniques that are available to your group.

√ Persevere. Whatever you do, don't give up. You may win a few fights this year and a few more next year, but if there is a particular issue you can't win the first time around, go back to it. Don't let the board tell you, "It can't be done." The UFT has learned that things that "could not be done" five years ago, can be done today. Parents too must learn to stick with their demands until they win.

The Great Refusal Begins

William K. Stevens

The following report from the *New York Times* is a somewhat dramatic note on which to end this book, but the incident with which it deals is by no means unique. What the students in Milwaukee have done is but one manifestation of the mushrooming free school movement. This movement is luxuriating in the climate of disaffection which surrounds the public schools.

The responses of university professors in the Milwaukee area and college admissions officers around the country show that the free school movement has sparked enthusiasm in some very auspicious quarters. A traditional excuse which traditional teachers have used for remaining traditional is that they have no right to compromise their students' chances of being admitted to college. Now it turns out that they may, in fact, be enhancing their students' chances by breaking the lock-step of tradition.

In time it may not be necessary for students to leave the public school system to get the kind of education they want. If a sufficient and strategically located number of free schools exist, the power of their examples may be too contagious for the public schools to resist. The increasingly politicized students of the public schools might begin to insist that they be allowed to enjoy the attractive alternatives offered by the free schools. Thus, the Milwaukee situation may be a reliable herald of the education of tomorrow.

Bill Ahlhauser, Belinda Behne, Jim Boulet and 32 other Milwaukee teen-agers—among them some of the brightest and most successful students in the city's most highly regarded public and private schools —believe that much of their high school experience has been a waste of time.

So these three and their companions, 15 to 19 years old, have dropped out of their old schools and formed the Milwaukee Independent School, in which each student chooses what he wants to study, how he wants to study it and where. The school is getting under way this week.

A Growing Revolt

The attempt has inspired no great enthusiasm in public administrators charged with enforcing the state's compulsory attendance law. For the time being, they are considering the students as absent from school. Ultimately, the matter may become a legal test case.

M.I.S., as the school is commonly called, is in the avant garde of educational reform, the latest in a series of attempts in various parts of the country to establish alternatives to conventional schools, both public and private, but particularly state-operated ones, that have a virtual monopoly power over most students.

It is a peaceful manifestation of a growing revolt against secondary education as it is practiced in the United States.

"Too many things are done in school only for the school's purposes and not the students'," says Bill Ahlhauser, who maintained a 95 average when he attended Marquette High, a prestigious Jesuit parochial school.

"There is an extreme lack of respect for students in many schools. Students' initiative and creativity are impeded and inhibited. It [school] is terribly dull, and the kids are pitted against each other for grades and rank in class."

"Kids are pumped through the system like products, never learning to think at all," says Miss Behne, a slim, animated 17-year-old who until a few weeks ago made A's and B's at John Marshall High School, which is generally regarded as one of Milwaukee's best.

The Basic Premises

Jim Boulet, 18, describes a typical class at Riverside High School, where he was a senior last semester, this way:

"Here was this nice sterile little cubicle, and you'd turn your mind off when you went inside. When you got out you'd turn it back on. What went on [in the classroom] had nothing to do with the world, and they called this learning."

The new school is based on these premises: that all students have serious personal interests; that these interests should be the starting point for education; that they should be developed and enriched by firsthand contact with human life, and that the function of reading, writing and formal academic inquiry is to facilitate this process.

Learning, the students say, never stops. It goes on outside school. Consequently, they will spend only a few hours a week in the somewhat dilapidated white frame building that they have rented to serve as library, discussion hall and home base.

They have spent most of the last 10 days painting and plastering the inside of the building. And today they got down to the business of planning their programs of study.

Typically, a student will study a given subject under a qualified volunteer from the community—a Shakespearean scholar at one city college, a biochemist at another, an artist, an electronics engineer from a private concern, for example. About 90 such volunteer teachers have agreed to take part.

In addition, some students will learn by holding part-time jobs, others by living for brief periods in specialized settings. Jim Boulet, for example, wants to study religion. So he plans to live in a monastery, then with a rabbi, then with a minister.

Communication Stressed

All the students are to undertake individual projects tied to their own interests, some of them consisting of conventional research and some dealing with community matters, such as planning a recreation center.

There will be a special emphasis on the development of basic communications skills, such as analytical reading, invective writing and coherent speech.

The students are being aided in working out their programs by Paul H. Krueger, who left his post as a professor of education at the University of Wisconsin's Milwaukee campus to become full-time coordinator of the school, and two students from his former department.

Mr. Krueger's salary is being paid by community donations. So far, $4,500 has been raised. About $40,000 is needed. Although the school is tuition-free, some parents have made contributions.

This experiment in educational self-determination is closely allied to the development of student-operated "free universities" and experimental colleges in recent years.

Such schools have been set up, for example, in Syracuse, Rochester and Cortland, N. Y.; Palo Alto, Calif., and Washington. More recently, parents of elementary-school children in New York and Washington have taken their children out of conventional schools and organized their own classes.

The new school here has been greeted by parents of its students with a mixture of enthusiasm and foreboding. Some sympathize with their children's concerns but worry about the risks involved. Others are out-and-out converts.

One public school administrator, Theodore J. Kuemmerlein, who is assistant superintendent for pupil personnel, feels this way:

"Anytime your top students leave school, it concerns you. It makes you wonder what we're not offering to meet their needs."

Mr. Kuemmerlein, who is charged with enforcing the compulsory school attendance law in Milwaukee, has ruled that unless and until the new school is declared a bona fide school under state law, its students are to be considered absent. Just who has the authority to make the bona fide declaration seems unclear, he said.

This raises a fundamental question: Who should determine what education is?

The students take the position that they themselves should. Mr. Kuemmerlein said that the City Attorney was considering the matter, and that it could eventually go to court.

The students believe that what goes on in their former schools, for the most part, is not education. According to them, negative features of conventional schooling include emphasis on pleasing and out-guessing the teacher, rather than on discovering, exploring and thinking; an almost total divorcement of school work from reality as perceived by students and an over-reliance on grades.

These views are closely aligned with those of high school students in other parts of the country.

Premium on Conformity

In a much-noted critique delivered to the Mongtomery County, Md., school board a year ago, students charged that their system— generally regarded as one of the best in the nation—was based on fear of bad grades and on an insistence on blind obedience. They also said that the schools placed a premium on conformity.

Timothy A. Simone, an 18-year-old graduate of Germantown High School here talked with the Maryland students two summers ago. A year later he became the prime organizer of the new school here. He was joined by Bill Ahlhauser as co-coordinator, and they set about bringing the school into existence.

They wrote to colleges all over the country to inquire about how enrollment in the school here would affect chances of a student's admission. Many, including Harvard University, replied that it would have no adverse effect. One, Fordham University, said that it would enhance a student's chances.

Some of the students plan to take standardized college entrance examinations when the time comes, and most are confident they will have no trouble with them because they can be "crammed" for.

When the word got around in Milwaukee that the new school was about to start, 80 students applied for the 35 places available. The 35 were chosen by lot. They turned out to to be the sons and daughters of white, middle-class families, although two blacks had applied.

Many of the students know with some certainty what studies they are going to pursue. But for others, Mr. Krueger says, there may be initial problems in getting used to a nonrigid, nonauthoritarian arrangement.

But although the risks seem high and success is unassured there appears to be little chance that many of the students will go back to conventional schools.

Bibliographic Essay

We have attempted to provide the reader a direct acquaintance with radical literature which is playing a significant role in changes in the overall society and the school system within that society. While these readings may be helpful as an entry point into radical ideas of our time, they are merely a beginning and not a thorough sampling of all extremes of the radical social-political dialogue. It would, in fact, be impossible to adequately sample all views in any one volume. In the same sense, the following bibliographic essay is provided to suggest materials the editors feel can augment the readings. It, too, must be selective because of the sheer amount of available sources and our limited space. The essay represents our judgment of stimulating, scholarly and/or representative radical literature.

THE SOCIAL-POLITICAL DIALOGUE

Within the context of the established social and economic system of the United States one may view far-left and far-right positions as alternative radical solutions to problems characteristic of contemporary American society. Among these problems are racism, violence, poverty, crime, colonialism, war, counter-culture, drugs, corruption, urban decay, pollution, social welfare, public education, and the quality of daily life. Most of the current alternatives to these issues may be traced to more basic ideas regarding the relation of man to social system. Today's radical attacks on American policies, practices, and institutions are the descendants of radical ideas of the past. There are, of course, variations and nuances which contribute a unique flavor and vitality to the radicalism of any age, but relatively little is entirely original in present day divergent views on the nature of man and society. This is not an argument to simply read history and discount the late-twentieth-century radicals. Rather, it proposes that radical alternatives to current problems be seen in their broader context of intellectual and activist traditions.

There has been a long history of radical political activity, both left and right, throughout American society. Communism, socialism, fascism, anarchism, and forms of monarchism have long-term roots in American history. Ideas outside of traditional, republican, capitalistic theory have come from historically radical traditions but now seem routinely taken for granted. These include social security, agricultural subsidies, unemployment insurance, CIA and FBI, food and drug laws, medicare, welfare, and free public education. Further, the struggle between those who would limit the social and economic opportunities of the masses and those who would enlarge and equalize opportunities is very old, and radical solutions toward either goal have been advanced throughout time.

The Social-Democratic View

Traditional socialists believe that through education and gradual enlightenment, the masses will choose a socialist blueprint for America in a peaceful democratic manner. *Dissent* magazine represents this point of view as a "journal devoted to radical ideas and the values of socialism and democracy." Many other journals including *Ramparts*, *New Republic*, *The Nation*, *The Progressive*, *Liberation*, and others represented in the readings, have been critical of American policies within the social-democratic tradition. *The New York Review of Books* is in this same political style, but is better known for its exaggerated literary brutality. *I. F. Stone's Bi-Weekly Newsletter* is very aggressive and smugly polemical but is widely read by the white-collar liberal and establishment academics.

Some of the books in this socialist tradition include Michael Harrington's *Toward a Democratic Left* and Irving Howe's *Beyond the New Left* and *Essential Works of Socialism*. These provide a rationale for socialism in America. A collection of *Ramparts'* articles titled *Eco-Catastrophe*, David McReynolds' *We Have Been Invaded by the 21st Century*, and Bernard K. Johnpoll's *Pacifist's Progress: Norman Thomas and the Decline of American Socialism* are books in this same vein. Publications of the League for Industrial Democracy, a socialist organization, are important reading in this area.

Revolutionists on the Left

Many groups and individuals of the left wing believe that America's problems cannot be meaningfully changed by the traditional socialist gradualism. They argue for revolutionary strategies including disruption, power showings, and potential violence. Their basic attacks are on the capitalistic system which is viewed as a rapacious beast that thrives on the subjugation and economic exploitation of the masses. Among the magazines which represent this view are *The Monthly Review, Antithesis, Political Affairs, American Dialog,* and *The Militant. Vocations for Social Change,* a publication of the radical left, contains articles on education as a means for change. *Despite Everything* and *Black and Red* are also radical left publications of current vintage.

Major writers of the communist ideology have continued to provide intellectual support for far-left groups. Karl Marx's *Capital* presents a thoughtful analysis of the capitalistic system. The *Manifesto of the Communist Party* by Marx and Engels is a short, popularized version of Marx's ideas and offers a revolutionary credo for those desiring a radical alternative to capitalism. The *Collected Works* of V. I. Lenin are useful because they present the strategies and arguments utilized in the successful campaign to revolutionize Tsarist Russia. Georgii V. Plekhanov's *Materialist's Conception of History* would be a reasonable initiation to the extensive writings on defense of Marxism applied to Russian society. Eaton's *Political Economy* is a well-written and simplified introduction to Marx's economic theory, and Meszaros' *Marx's Theory of Alienation* shows the continuity between early Marx writings and his later work on economic determinism.

Many current writers reflect a Marxist viewpoint while fleshing out a theoretical framework against contemporary social problems. Paul A. Baran and Paul M. Sweezy exemplify this in their book *Monopoly Capital.* Herbert Aptheker's works, such as *The Nature of Democracy* and *Freedom and Revolution,* share this position in the discussion of freedom and democracy as based historically in bourgeois concepts.

On imperialism and colonialism, there are several important sources. The *Selected Articles and Speeches* of Ho Chi Minh present his attitudes toward the Vietnam war, the communists, the Catholics in Vietnam, land reform, and intellectuals. A collection of articles by important figures in this area may be found in William J. Pomeroy's *Guerilla Warfare and Marxism. Reminiscences of the Cuban Revolutionary War* by Che Guevara provides a step by step account of the war and a handbook on guerilla warfare. *Regis Debray and the Latin American Revolution,* edited by Leo Huberman and Paul Sweezy, describes Debray's concept of the development of uninterrupted guerilla force as a successful revolutionary process. Debray's own *Revolution in the Revolution* is a good first-hand statement. Wilfred Burchett's *Vietnam Will Win* explains the North Vietnamese point of view and is introduced by the writings of David Dellinger, a leader in American anti-war activities. *White Niggers of America* by Pierre Vallieres is a revolutionary document produced in prison as an autobiography of a Canadian active in the Quebec Liberation Front.

Kwame Nkrumah, active as head of state in Ghana and revolutionary writer within the Marxist framework, has several books including *Dark Days in Ghana, Class Struggle in Africa,* and *The Old Colonialism, the Last Stage of Imperialism.* W. A. Williams in *The Roots of the Modern American Empire* analyzes the American farmer as a large factor in enlarging America's overseas "empire" to provide expanding markets. Tarik Ali, a leader in the revolutionary socialist movement in England, has edited *New Revolutionaries–Left Opposition* in which several authors argue that the ideas of revolutionary socialism have "been suppressed and distorted, both in capitalistic countries and by most of the traditional communist regimes."

MILITANT LITERATURE

There has been proliferation of publications on race relations emphasizing militancy. Black writers have led this literature, but other groups have been evolving. *Custer Died for Your Sins* by Vine Deloria, excerpted in the readings, exemplifies this for American Indians. Dee Brown's *Bury My Heart at Wounded Knee* presents a scholarly and thoroughly readable history of the mistreatment of Indians. The journals *El Grito* and *Con Safos* contain articles on the struggles of Spanish surnamed, and *El Malcriado* treats the farm workers organizing under the AFL-CIO. *Challenge* is a periodical published by the Progressive Labor Party and is geared to Puerto Ricans and blacks. Black writings in this area abound. A brief selection of these would include Frantz Fanon's *A Dying Colonialism, The Wretched of the Earth,* and *Black Skin, White Mask. Seize the Time* by Bobby Seale is the story of the Black Panther Party which publishes the newspaper *The Black Panther.* The W. E. B. Du Bois Clubs publish *Insurgent.* Eldridge Cleaver's *Soul on Ice* and George Jackson's *Soledad Brother* are books which show the growth of militancy during prison confinement. *The Last Years of Malcolm X* by George Breitman and *Malcolm X's Autobiography* present the development of an important militant leader. *Black America and the World Revolution* by Claude Lightfoot represents another black militant view. *The Radical Study Guide,* published by the Africa Research Group, provides a handy reference bibliography of radical writing on militant strategies for social change.

YOUTH MOVEMENT WRITING

The world-wide youth movement is in basic opposition to the materialistic and technocratic aspects of modern life. The new left and portions of the new right which emphasize libertarianism, share many of the goals and values of this youth revolution. The movement represents an alienation from and revulsion against traditional beliefs of "the American Way of Life." They see the American dream more as a nightmare with political empire, establishment hypocrisy and deceit, and easy co-optation of their affluent and liberal parents. Corruption and duplicity in government and the apparent refusal of the system to examine the depth of decay and pathology have encouraged the growth of the movement. Movement literature cannot be presented as a coherent whole, for it is diffuse and contains many divergent strains from anarchy to communalism, violence to pacifism, super-realism to mystical romanticism, and self-denial to hedonism.

A book by Paul Jacobs and Saul Landau *The New Radicals* is a good beginning point for seeing wholistic aspects of the movement. *The Making of a Counter Culture* by Theodore Roszak, excerpted in the readings, is a relatively dispassionate analysis of youthful oppoisiton to the technocratic society. Charles Reich's *The Greening of America* is an exceedingly popular treatment of American problems as caught in consciousness levels. Magazines reflecting youth movement ideas include *Consumption, Beau Cocoa, Caterpillar, Leviathan, December, East Village Other, Chinook*, and *The Green Revolution*. There are a vast number of underground papers, broadsheets, one-time published journals and literary magazines that treat the movement in one or another dimension. *The Small Press Review* is a good source for excerpts, reprints, and addresses of many of these.

Political backgrounds for new left thinking include C. Wright Mills' *Power, Politics and People* and *The Power Elite*. Jacques Ellul's *Technological Society*, which deals with the human costs involved in our destructive and alienating social system, is another important work here. *Alienation and Freedom* by Robert Blauner studies factory life in an intensive manner. R. D. Laing has become a leading author for some areas of the youth movement through such works as *The Politics of Experience, Self and Others*, and *Knots*, a collection of short dialogues in free verse format.

The writings of Herbert Marcuse and Norman O. Brown are especially important in the movement's attempt to achieve a nonrepressive civilization less involved with work, guilt, and personal oppression. Marcuse's *One Dimensional Man, Eros and Civilization*, and *Negations* are good starting points. His complete essay "Repressive Tolerance," found in Robert Wolff, Barrington Moore and Herbert Marcuse, *A Critique of Pure Tolerance*, is also worthy of reading. Brown's *Life Against Death* and *Love's Body* are significant in understanding the new mysticism and hedonism.

What may be termed the new radical morality has many sources, but good entry points are: Norman Mailer's *The White Negro*, Gary Snyder's *Earth Household*, Jack Kerouac's *On the Road* and *Dharma Bums*, Allen Ginsberg's *Howl* and *Sunflower Sutra*, Lawrence Ferlinghetti's *Coney Island* and *Mexican Night*, Alan Watts' *Way of Zen* and *Psychotherapy: East and West*, and D. T. Suzuki's *Zen Buddhism* as edited by W. Barrett. To understand the role of street theater in the movement and the politics of joy, read *Revolution for the Hell of It* by Abbie Hoffman, Jerry Rubin's *Do It!, Paradise Now* by Julian Beck, and see excursions by the New York Bread and Puppet Theater and the San Francisco Mime Troupe. Writings on the drug scene in its earlier period are Aldous Huxley's *Doors of Perception* and Alan Watts' *The Joyous Cosmology: Adventures in the Chemistry of Consciousness.* Timothy Leary's contributions, including *High Priest* and the *Politics of Ecstasy,* have earned him notoriety in this area. He is also an editor of *Psychedelic Review,* a journal dealing with drug experience.

An interesting collection of underground newspaper articles may be seen in *The Hippie Papers,* edited by Jerry Hopkins. John Birmingham's editing of high-school underground papers is contained in *Our Time is Now.* Additional journals which cover aspects of the movement are *The Partisan,* sponsored by Youth Against War and Fascism, *New Left Notes* and *CAW!,* which are SDS publications.

DIVERGENT VIEWS ON THE RIGHT

As with the radical left, there is no single group or ideology which dominates the radical right. There are, however, some areas of agreement and general concern. Among these tend to be strong nationalism and super-partriotism, high regard for individual liberties, and an emphasis on religious support for social actions. As a part of the nationalism values in right-wing thought, anti-communism has become a rallying point because of communism's presumed threat to individual liberty and to the capitalistic economic system. The radical right also has long-term roots in American and European history. Its intellectual traditions go back through Edmund Burke, the Puritan writers, John C. Calhoun, Irving Babbitt, Alexander Hamilton, and John Adams. These writers expressed a conservative philosophy regarding the nature and propensities of man and society that serves to buttress the arguments made by many contemporary right-wing authors. Throughout much of the literature of the right is a form of elitism; sometimes presented in economic terms as rule by the wealthy; sometimes offered in aristocratic terms by birthright; and sometimes given in racial superiority terms. There is also a reverence for tradition, law, and the established powers.

The radical right aggressively rejects the populist, liberal social legislation as an encroachment on state's and individual's rights. It often expresses views that are closer to those of European royalists than to middle-range conservatism and liberalism in America. Several movements among right-wing activists to demonstrate their positions and attain social action have considerable notoriety. Among these are the Coughlinites, the Minutemen, the McCarthyites, and the Birchers. William Buckley, editor of *National Review,* and L. Brent Bozell present a defense of Senator Joseph McCarthy's tactics during the 1950s in *McCarthy and His Enemies.* John Roy Carlson discusses Father Charles Coughlin in his *Under Cover: My Four Years in the*

Nazi Underworld of America. David Bennett's *Demagogues in the Depression* examines the radical Union Party movement in America by dealing with Father Coughlin, Gerald L. K. Smith, Dr. Francis Townsend, and Reverend William Lemke. McCarthy's own *Major Speeches and Debates of Senator Joe McCarthy Delivered in the United States Senate, 1950–51*, published by the Government Printing Office, contains the basic positions of the right regarding communism and its internal and external threat to the United States. Strong patriotism, tied often to fundamentalist religion and racial separation, is the basis for many publications of the right. Magazines and newspapers in this area include *The Pilgrim Torch, The Stormtrooper* (American Nazi Party), *National Renaissance Bulletin, White Power,* and *The Citizen* (Citizens Council of America). This thread of patriotism and religion permeates the anti-communist writings found in newsletters and magazines like the *Dan Smoot Report, Life Line, Manion Forum, The Liberty Bell, The Cross and the Flag,* and the *Christian Anti-Communist Crusade Newsletter.* The Minutemen's publication is titled *On Target.*

Among the curently read books of the right is Dan Smoot's *The Invisible Government,* which examines the Council of Foreign Relations for liberal and left-wing thinking. Gary Allen in *The Bankers* explains how funds for international communist conspiracy are provided and the resulting threat to American society. *The Death of a Nation* and *None Dare Call It Treason* by John A. Stormer discuss the spiritual and political demise of America at the hands of left-wing and liberal interests. John T. Flynn presents an analysis of American problems resulting from *The Roosevelt Myth.* Flynn's book *While You Slept* examines the mistakes made by the United States in its relations with Asia.

Ayn Rand, a well-known and respected writer and philosopher for the right wing, has published several books and established a formal point of view known as Objectivism. The journal *The Objectivist* is published under her editorship, and another journal *Invictus* is a west coast objectivist publication. Among Rand's better known books are *Capitalism, the Unknown Ideal, Atlas Shrugged, The Fountainhead,* and *The Virtue of Selfishness.*

Reed Benson and Robert Lee explain *What's Wrong with the United Nations* in their pamphlet indicating that the U.N. is dominated by left-wing interests. Dr. Fred Schwartz, organizer of the Christian Anti-Communist Crusade and a well-known speaker for ultra-conservative causes, details the communist threat in *You Can Trust the Communists.* E. Merrill Root, regular contributor to *American Opinion* and an academic scholar, has been particularly concerned with education as a tool of leftists. His works include *Brainwashing in the High Schools* and *Collectivism on Campus.* Max Eastman, formerly a Marxist, has written *Reflections on the Failure of Socialism,* and Friedrick Hayek's *The Road to Serfdom* is a carefully written account of the inherent problems in the socialist argument.

The basic work of the John Birch Society is *The Blue Book of the John Birch Society* which presents the organization's rationale and operating structure. They also publish a *Bulletin* for members. Robert Welch, founder of the society, has published many letters and pamphlets including *The Life of John Birch* and *The Patriot*. He is also editor of *American Opinion*. *Peace Symbols* is an *American Opinion* reprint stressing the relation between the peace movement and anti-religious activities.

A number of publications which stress the moral, philosophic, or economic thinking of the right include *The Naked Capitalist* by Cleon Skousen, *The Fearful Master* by G. Edward Griffin, *Economics in One Easy Lesson* by Henry Hazlitt, *What is a Communist* by Lubor Zink, *Ill Fares the Land* by Dan P. Van Gorder, *The Law and Cliches of Socialism* by Frederic Bastiat, and the several works of Russell Kirk including *A Program for Conservatives* and *Road to Revolution*.

Among the more recent conservative and right-wing books of interest are Barry Goldwater's *Conscience of a Conservative* and John Lukacs' *The Passing of the Modern Age*. *Frankly Speaking* is a collection of ideas by Spiro T. Agnew, and William F. Buckley's anthology, *Did You Ever See a Dream Walking—America's Conservative Thought in the Twentieth Century*, is a good set of readings.

The New Guard, the periodical of the Young Americans for Freedom, is a current source for ideas of youth on the right. The same is true for the magazine *The New Right*, published by the National Youth Alliance. *Human Events*, published in Washington, D.C., generally favors limited constitutional government and increased individual freedom. *Liberty Letter*, the official paper of the Liberty Lobby, has had the highest paid circulation of any periodical of the right wing. Other contemporary periodicals on the right include *Wire Magazine*, *The Independent American*, and *New Individualist Review*.

Sources in Education

Although many of the previously noted publications carry articles and comments on education, there is a body of literature which specifically examines defects, proposals, and alternatives for education in unusual and radical ways. To gain an understanding of the revolution developing in educational thought, there are a number of important works. Paul Goodman is noteworthy in this regard. His *Growing Up Absurd* and *Compulsory Miseducation* are striking examples of brilliant social criticism directed at education. Edgar Z. Friedenberg's many writings, including *The Vanishing Adolescent*, *Coming of Age in America*, and *The Dignity of Youth and Other Atavisms*, are excellent in style, readability, and provocation.

Books which convey the problems of contemporary education in personal writings about experiences and proposals include John Holt's *How Children Fail* and *How Children Learn*, Herbert Kohl's

36 Children, Jonathan Kozol's Death at an Early Age, James Herndon's The Way It Spozed to Be, and Nat Hentoff's Our Children Are Dying. An excellent autobiographical account of teaching Maori children and discoveries about alternatives for schooling is Sylvia Ashton-Warner's Teacher. The Lives of Children by George Dennison explains an inner-city educational experiment conducted in New York. Other praiseworthy accounts of inner-city teaching are to be found in Gloria Channon's Homework, Jim Haskins' Diary of a Harlem Schoolteacher, Esther Rothman's The Angel Inside Went Sour, and, of course, Bel Kaufman's Up the Down Staircase. A good autobiographical account of suburban teaching is James Herndon's How to Survive in Your Native Land. Obviously, A. S. Neill's contributions to radical educational practice, as described in Summerhill: A Radical Approach to Child Rearing, should not be overlooked. Practical suggestions for the creation of alternative schools are contained in Rasberry Exercises by Salli Rasberry and Robert Greenway.

Additional suggestions for schools are found in Holt's The Underachieving School and Kohl's Teaching the Unteachable and The Open Classroom. Large district school reform ideas developed in England and translatable to America can be found in Lady Plowden, et. al., Children and Their Primary Schools. Radical School Reform, edited by Ronald and Beatrice Gross, contains a collection of articles by many authors cited in this bibliographic essay. This Book is about Schools, edited by Satu Repo, is another good collection, and Charles Silberman's Crisis in the Classroom is a thorough critique of American education.

There are relatively few radical periodicals in education, considering the large number of journals in the field. The best periodical to date is This Magazine is about Schools. Other publications include The New School of Education Journal, The Summerhill Society Bulletin, The New Schools Exchange Newsletter, and No More Teachers, Dirty Looks.

Organizations that support radical school ideas have been developing. Among these are the New Schools Exchange, 2840 Hidden Valley Lane, Santa Barbara, California; the Teacher Drop-Out Center, University of Massachusetts, Amherst, Massachusetts; and the Society for Educational Reconstruction, 558 South Willard Street, Burlington, Vermont.

PERIODICAL INDICES AND BIBLIOGRAPHIES

A flood of newspaper and magazine literature from radical sources has been an American tradition since pre-revolutionary times. Many of these periodicals publish one or two issues and decease; most have limited circulations and are seldom seen on library shelves even in good universities; and many are underground, virtually secret organs of exotic groups. It would be impossible to accurately catalogue all of these publications, but there are some sources of information which provide bibliographies, summaries, and reprints of sizable amounts of this radical literature. U.S. Directory Service, P.O. Box 1832, Kansas City, Missouri, offers the *Guide to the American Left*, *Guide to the American Right*, and the *Wilcox Report* as comprehensive bibliographies of periodicals with addresses. These guides include over 8,000 entries. *Schism*, 1109 West Vine Street, Mount Vernon, Ohio, is a journal which reprints excerpts from right- and left-wing publications. A similar reprint publication which samples right and left writing and comments on them is *Left/Right Digest*, published by the American Jewish Committee, 10 Commerce Court, Newark, New Jersey. Walter Goldwater's annotated bibliography, *Radical Periodicals in America, 1890–1950*, is a fine source for earlier works and was the basis for initiation of a radical journal reprint series now available through Greenwood Reprint Corporation of Westport, Connecticut. Greenwood has republished over 400 volumes of radical periodicals. Hammond Book Services, Box 108, Upham, North Dakota, has an annotated bibliography of left-wing books. *From Radical Left to Extreme Right*, edited by Robert H. Muller, is an annotated bibliography with comments from radical periodical editors. It is available from Campus Publishers, 711 North University Avenue, Ann Arbor, Michigan. Information regarding small magazines and underground newspapers that contain political, economic, educational, artistic, and literary comments may be obtained in the *Directory of Little Magazines*, the *Small Press Review*, and the *Directory of Small Press Editors*, from DUSTBOOKS, 5218 Scottwood Road, Paradise, California. *Radical's Digest*, 516 Fifth Avenue, New York, provides excerpts from radical periodicals. Over 90 pamphlets on subjects from politics to education are available from the Radical Education Project, Box 561-A, Detroit, Michigan.

Addresses for Periodicals Cited

American Dialog, 32 Union Square, Room 804, New York City 10003
American Opinion, 395 Concord Avenue, Belmont, Massachusetts 02178
Antithesis, P.O. Box 773, San Francisco, California 94101
Beau Cocoa, P.O. Box 409, New York City 10035
Black and Red, P.O. Box 973, Kalamazoo, Michigan 49005
The Black Panther, Box 2967, Custom House, San Francisco, California 94126
Bulletin of the John Birch Society, 395 Concord Avenue, Belmont, Massachusetts 02178
CAW!, Box 332, Cooper Station, New York City 10003
Caterpillar, 36 Greene Street, New York City, 10003
Challenge, GPO Box 808, Brooklyn, New York 10001
Chinook, 1452 Pennsylvania, Suite 21, Denver, Colorado 80203
Christian Anti-Communist Crusade Newsletter, P.O. Box 890, 124 East First Street, Long Beach, California 90801
The Citizen, 315–25 Plaza Building, Jackson, Mississippi 39201

Con Safos, P.O. Box 31085, Los Angeles, California 90031
Consumption, 4208 Eighth Street, N.E., Seattle, Washington 98105
The Cross and the Flag, P.O. Box 27895, Los Angeles, California 90027
Dan Smoot Report, Box 9538, Dallas, Texas 75214
December, P.O. Box 274, Western Springs, Illinois 60558
Despite Everything, 1937½ Russell Street, Berkeley, California 94703
Dissent, 509 Fifth Avenue, New York City 10017
East Village Other, 20 East 12th Street, New York City 10003
El Grito, P.O. Box 9275, Berkeley, California 94709
El Malcriado, P.O. Box 130, Delano, California 93215
The Green Revolution, Route 1, Box 129, Freeland, Maryland 21053
Human Events, 410 First Street, S.E., Washington, D.C. 20003
I. F. Stone's Bi-Weekly Newsletter, 4420 29th Street, N.W., Washington, D.C. 20008
Insurgent, 954 McAllister Street, San Francisco, California 94115
Invictus, 5151 State College Drive, Los Angeles, California 90032
Leviathan, 330 Grove Street, San Francisco, California 94102
Liberation, 339 Lafayette Street, New York City 10012
The Liberty Bell, P.O. Box 2333, El Cajon, California 92021
Liberty Letter, 300 Independence Avenue, S.E., Washington, D.C. 20003
Life Line, 4330 North Central Expressway, Dallas, Texas 75206
Manion Forum, St. Joseph Bank Building, South Bend, Indiana 46601
The Militant, 873 Broadway, New York City 10003
The Monthly Review, 116 West 14th Street, New York City 10011
The Nation, 333 Avenue of the Americas, New York City 10014
National Renaissance Bulletin, Box 10, New York City 10024
National Review, 150 East 35th Street, New York City 10016
The New Guard, 1221 Massachusetts Avenue, N.W., Suite A, Washington, D.C. 20005
New Individualist Review, Ida Noyes Hall, University of Chicago, Chicago, Illinois 60637
New Left Notes, 1103 East 63rd Street, Chicago, Illinois 60637
New Republic, 1244 19th Street, N.W., Washington, D.C. 20036
The New Right, 813 DuPont Circle Building, Washington, D.C. 20036
The New School of Education Journal, 4304 Tolman Hall, University of California, Berkeley, California 94720
The New Schools Exchange Newsletter, 2840 Hidden Valley Lane, Santa Barbara, California 93103
The New York Review of Books, 250 West 57th Street, New York City 10019
No More Teachers, Dirty Looks, 1445 Stockton Avenue, San Francisco, California 94133
The Objectivist, 120 East 39th Street, New York City 10016
On Target, P.O. Box 172, Independence, Missouri
Other Scenes, 204 West 10th Street, New York City 10014
The Partisan, 58 West 25th Street, New York City 10010
The Pilgrim Torch, P.O. Box 257, Englewood, Colorado 80110
Political Affairs, 23 West 26th Street, New York City 10010
The Progressive, 408 West Gorham, Madison, Wisconsin 53703
Psychedelic Review, 290 Seventh Street, San Francisco, California 94103
Ramparts, 301 Broadway, San Francisco, California 94133
The Stormtrooper, Box 22071, Dallas, Texas 75222
The Summerhill Society Bulletin, 339 Lafayette Street, New York City 10012

This Magazine is about Schools, 56 Esplanade St. East, Suite 301, Toronto 215, Ontario, Canada

Vocations for Social Change, Canyon, California 94516

The Warpath, United Native Americans, Inc., P.O. Box 26149, San Francisco, California 94126

White Power, Box 5505, Arlington, Virginia 22205

Wire Magazine, 549 Masten Avenue, Buffalo, New York 14209

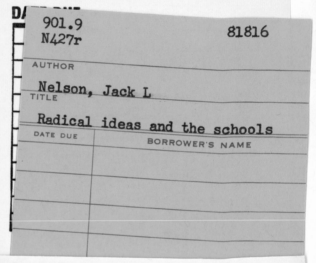